INFORMATION TECHNOLOGY

Textbook for Class IX
(As per CBSE Syllabus Code 402)

Komalpreet Kaur
Yogesh Kumar

www.bpbonline.com

FIRST EDITION 2021
REPRINT 2023

ISBN: 978-93-91392-43-7

Distributors:

BPB PUBLICATIONS
20, Ansari Road, Darya Ganj
New Delhi-110002
Ph: 23254990/23254991

DECCAN AGENCIES
4-3-329, Bank Street,
Hyderabad-500195
Ph: 24756967/24756400

MICRO MEDIA
Shop No. 5, Mahendra Chambers,
150 DN Rd. Next to Capital Cinema,
V.T. (C.S.T.) Station, MUMBAI-400 001
Ph: 22078296/22078297

BPB BOOK CENTRE
376 Old Lajpat Rai Market,
Delhi-110006
Ph: 23861747

To View Complete BPB Publications Catalogue Scan the QR Code:

Published by Manish Jain for BPB Publications, 20 Ansari Road, Darya Ganj, New Delhi-110002 and Printed by him at Repro India Ltd, Mumbai

www.bpbonline.com

Dedicated to

My Parents

About the Author(s)

- **Komalpreet Kaur** has good experience in writing research documents of Computer and Electronics. She has done her Masters in Technology in Electronics and Communication and have 3 + years of experience in Research and IT field. She is also pursuing her Ph.D. from Punjabi University, Patiala. Her research areas include Artificial Intelligence, Machine Learning, Natural Language Processing, Wireless Sensor Network, IoT and Communication.
- **Dr. Yogesh Kumar** is working as Associate Professor Department of Computer Engineering, Indus University Ahmedabad Gujarat. He has done his Ph.D. CSE from Punjabi University, Patiala. Prior to this, he has done his M.Tech CSE from Punjabi university, Patiala. He is having total 14 years of experience including teaching and research. His research areas include Artificial Intelligence, Computer Vision, Machine Learning and Data Science.

Acknowledgements

There are a few people I want to thank for the continued and ongoing support they have given me during the writing of this book. First and foremost, I would like to thank my parents for putting up with me while I was spending many weekends and evenings on writing—I could have never completed this book without their support.

This book wouldn't have happened if I hadn't had the support from some of the key vendors and partners in the EUC space. My gratitude goes to the team at BPB Publications for providing valuable insights into some of the new features.

— KomalPreet Kaur

Preface

Book is as per the latest curriculum under NSQF Scheme, and helps students to:

- ✓ Familiarize with the effective and written communication skills
- ✓ Identifying the principle components of computers
- ✓ Understand Self-management skills along with ability of self-analysis in context of entrepreneurial skills
- ✓ Know the importance of green skills and challenges of environment protection
- ✓ Work safely on computer
- ✓ Get basic knowledge about the sector and the democratic data entry operator jobs suitable for this sector
- ✓ Know about Microsoft Word, Excel and PowerPoint window with various formatting parts associated with it

Book is divided into two parts, Part-A is related to Employability Skills and Part-B contains Vocational Skills. The first part starts with Communication skills, Self-Management kills and effective oral and written communication skills help learner to interact with people and customers in their daily lives. It also demonstrates the self-management skills. Afterward, the Information and communication technology skills help to identify the principle components of a computer system along with the demonstration of the basic skills of using computer. The Entrepreneurial Skills gives an ability to provide self-analysis in context of entrepreneurial skills and abilities and knowledge of the importance of green skills in meeting the challenges of suitable development and environment protection is demonstrated in Green Skills chapter of this book. The other part of the book is linked with the Introduction of IT-ITeS industry, Data Entry and keyboarding skills that helps in working on computer safely, starting a computer along with opening and using the related software. This also covers the procedure to exit from the software, shut down the computer and other basic things. It also helps reader in using computer for data entry process by following the rules and guidelines for data entry to increase the speed and accuracy of undertaking the data entry. The other chapters introduce the Microsoft Office with readers that to demonstrate the usage of Microsoft Word, Making Spreadsheet on Excel as well as making presentation on PowerPoint along with doing different formatting work to make it more efficient that helps them in identifying as well as controlling the hazards in the workplace that pose a danger or threat to their safety or health.

Downloading the code bundle and coloured images:

Please follow the link to download the
Code Bundle and the *Coloured Images* of the book:

https://rebrand.ly/3b11a9

Errata

We take immense pride in our work at BPB Publications and follow best practices to ensure the accuracy of our content to provide with an indulging reading experience to our subscribers. Our readers are our mirrors, and we use their inputs to reflect and improve upon human errors, if any, that may have occurred during the publishing processes involved. To let us maintain the quality and help us reach out to any readers who might be having difficulties due to any unforeseen errors, please write to us at:

errata@bpbonline.com

Your support, suggestions and feedbacks are highly appreciated by the BPB Publications' Family.

BPB is searching for authors like you

If you're interested in becoming an author for BPB, please visit **www.bpbonline.com** and apply today. We have worked with thousands of developers and tech professionals, just like you, to help them share their insight with the global tech community. You can make a general application, apply for a specific hot topic that we are recruiting an author for, or submit your own idea.

The code bundle for the book is also hosted on GitHub at **https://github.com/bpbpublications/INFORMATION-TECHNOLOGY**. In case there's an update to the code, it will be updated on the existing GitHub repository.

We also have other code bundles from our rich catalog of books and videos available at **https://github.com/bpbpublications**. Check them out!

PIRACY

If you come across any illegal copies of our works in any form on the internet, we would be grateful if you would provide us with the location address or website name. Please contact us at **business@bpbonline.com** with a link to the material.

If you are interested in becoming an author

If there is a topic that you have expertise in, and you are interested in either writing or contributing to a book, please visit **www.bpbonline.com**.

REVIEWS

Please leave a review. Once you have read and used this book, why not leave a review on the site that you purchased it from? Potential readers can then see and use your unbiased opinion to make purchase decisions, we at BPB can understand what you think about our products, and our authors can see your feedback on their book. Thank you!

For more information about BPB, please visit **www.bpbonline.com**.

Table of Contents

SECTION – A

SECTION – B

SECTION-A

1 Communication Skills

Learning Outcomes

After this chapter, you will have the knowledge of:

- Communication process.
- Importance and characteristics of communication.
- Various elements in communication cycle.
- Various methods of communication and factors affecting perspective communication.
- Helps in writing paragraph: By getting knowledge of basic writing skills such as a phrase, sentence and speech, articles.

INTRODUCTION

Communication is the process of sharing information between two or more people. The art of communication involves the art of communicating that involves the ability to listen, understand and give the right message to another person. It is a must for speaking and writing in a proper way. While working in IT-field, all these communication aspects play an important role as it helps them in understanding the needs of the client. One should be able to write and speak in any situation properly.

The word communication is derived from the Latin word *communis* that means to impart, to share, to participate or to make common. Communication has become a basic need for interacting with each others. A resolution comes in the field of communication by the invention of computer technology and satellite through which one can communicate throughout the world.

SESSION 1: CYCLE OF COMMUNICATION

Communication is a process of sharing information between two or multiple persons. There is a number of ways to communicate like written, visually, vocally, and non-verbally. Communication involves both transmission and understanding it. There is a need of sender and receiver where the sender sends the message and in response, get feedback from the receiver as given in below figure 1.1 Communication process.

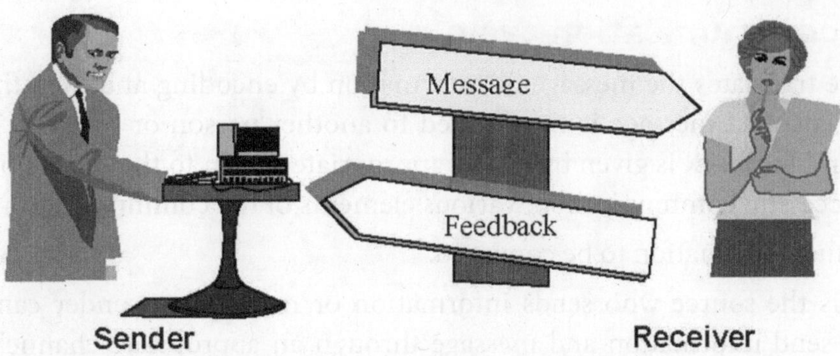

Figure 1.1: Communication process

When the sent messages are successfully delivered to the receiver and understood by them, then communication is said to be effective communication.

Characteristics of communication

Characteristics of communication are given below:

- Continuous process: Process of communication is not static; it is a continuous and dynamic process. The nature, situation and contents of the communication keep changing.
- Social activity: Communication is a social activity in which all people of society are involved in sharing feelings, information, and emotions. Social activity is a process of sharing meaning and relates it to one another by people.
- Mutual understanding: For communication and to understand it, there must understand between sender and receiver.
- Two-way process: Communication is a two-way process in which there is need of both sender and receiver either single or multiple, and they must respond to each other to have effective communication. In the case of one-way communication sender send a message without any expectation of feedback.
- Lead to reaction or response: Communication leads to some response or reaction from the receiver side according to the information sent by the sender. As to have successful communication, there is a need for quick and right response or reaction from the sender side after understanding it.

Importance of communication skills

In every field of life, either in professional, personal, social and more - an important role is played by communication skills. Communications not only include verbal communication, but it also includes everything's like posture, visual aspects, body language that appeals to the listener.

Communication is necessary when you want to apply on a job then at the time of interview good communication skills work in impressing the boss for selecting him/her for the applied job. Even to get success, there is a need for communication skills that forms the base for a cooperative relationship with other people like vendors, employees, customers, suppliers, and more. Effective communication encourages active participation in cohesive teamwork and group discussion that help in building a relationship with others.

The importance of communication skills is ability to listen, speak, question, and write with clarity get increased by progress in the career of people to have a successful professional and personal life. The main agenda behind having positive communication is treating people in the same way as you want to be treated by others.

Elements of a communication cycle

The sender or source translates the message or information by encoding and then through a medium of communication, an encoded message is transmitted to another person or receiver. Then at the receiver side, it is decoded, and feedback is given by taking appropriate action to the sender by understanding the message. To have successful communication, various elements of the communication cycle are:

- Message: The actual information to be conveyed.
- Sender: Sender is the source who sends information or message. A sender can be a single person or a group who send information and message through an appropriate channel as shown in below figure 1.2.

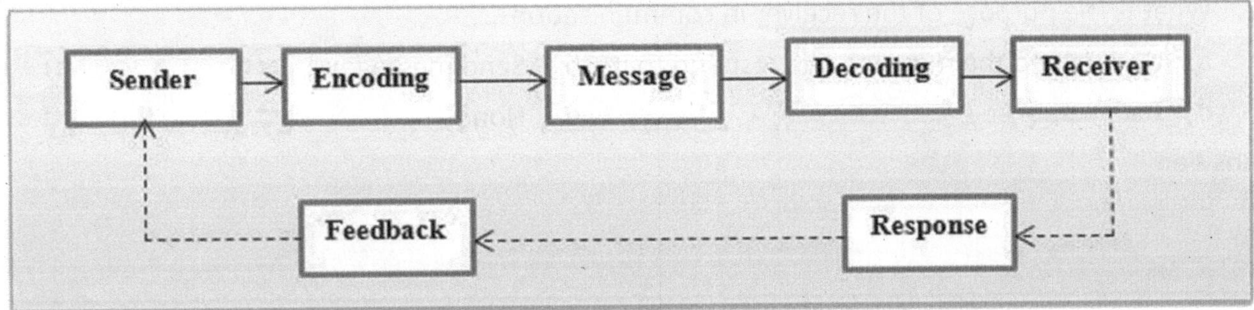

Figure 1.2: Communication cycle

- Encoding: Encoding or converting data or information into the coded language that is not understood by any other person. It can be encoded by selecting specific alphabet, words or symbols that are clear to both sender and receiver. Various encoding schemes available are hamming code, ASCII codes, and more.
- Receiver: Receiver is the person or group who will receive the sent information or message by sender and understand it by decoding. A miss-communication may take place if the receiver interprets the wrong message.
- Communication channel: An appropriate channel or medium is selected by the sender to send a message. The communication channel can be faxed, electronic mail, letters, face-to-face, telephone calls, and more.
- Decoding: The encoded information is decoded at the receiver side to understand the sent message or information. The messages should be decoded according to the pattern used by the receiver while encoding it that helps in having correct information. For example, if a message is encoded using the hamming code, then it should be decoded using the same coding scheme.
- Feedback: Feedback is the response given to sender information. To complete the communication cycle, a feedback should be a response by the receiver. The communication cycle will break down when feedback is missing.

Summary

- Communication is a process of sharing information between two or multiple persons.
- There is number of ways to communicate like written, visually, vocally, and non-verbally.
- When the sent messages are successfully delivered to the receiver and understood by them, then communication is said to be effective communication.
- In every field of life, either in professional, personal, social and more- an important role is played by communication skills.
- Main elements of the communication cycle are sender, encoding, message, decoding, receiver, communication channel, and feedback.

Self-Assessment

MULTIPLE CHOICE QUESTIONS.

1. The communication word is derived from the Latin word communis that means:

   a. To share b. impart c. both a and b d. None

2. What is the purpose of the receiver in communication?

   a. Understand the message and respond to it b. Send message

   c. Take response d. None

Answer

1. c 2. a

QUESTIONS

1. What is communication?
2. What are the characteristics of communication?
3. Give various elements of the communication cycle.

PROJECT WORK

Make a chart of the communication cycle

SESSION 2: METHODS OF COMMUNICATION

Communication is the process of exchanging information, data, and ideas among various people throughout the world. There are various methods for expressing the message, and these methods are selected by considering various factors. These factors can be a type of receiver, like whether they are painter, graphic designers, sculptors, artist and other factors are the availability of time, length of the message, the expenditure involved, the urgency of the message, and emotional level between both sender and receiver.

Methods of communication

As mentioned above, different methods of communication are used by people according to their needs and other various factors. Broadly they are classified into the following three types:

- Verbal communication
- Non-verbal communication
- Visual communication

Verbal communication

In this type of communication, a message is delivered using words as it is the most powerful and accurate tools in expressing and sharing ideas. While communicating a mutually understanding language like Hindu, Chinese, English, Punjabi, Spanish, and many more language is used. Verbal communication can be done orally or by writing.

Figure 1.3: Verbal communication

The two primary forms of verbal communication are:

- **Oral communication:** Oral communication is the way of expressing ideas and information through spoken words and considered as a more natural form of communication as compared to written form due to immediate clarification and feedback is involved in it. In order to make the whole process powerful, there is the involvement of both sender and receiver who listen and respond accordingly.

  The effectiveness of oral communication depends on:

  o Pace that is, how fast or slow person is speaking.

- o Clarity in pronunciation (speaking correct and clear words).
- o Pitch or volume (how loud or soft is the voice of sender and receiver).
- o Fluency (how fluent or ease and accuracy you are speaking).
- o Length of communication (the message should be concise and short as interest is loose by the listener when message become long), and more.

Figure 1.4: Oral communication

The following are the advantages:

- o Prompt feedback is provided by it.
- o Cost-efficient.
- o Help in interpersonal and building relationships.
- o It is preferred in confidential or private matters.

The following are the disadvantages:

- o No legal validity.
- o Sometimes a message is not understandable due to different accents and pace of voice.
- o It can lead to miscommunication due to the involvement of emotions.
- o Not suitable for exchange of lengthy messages.

✦ Written **communication**: In this form, written messages are used to convey a message and is considered as a most formal way. While using written communication, people should have to choose words carefully, and its placement should be in order.

The examples of written communication are:

o Letters	o Emails	o Notices
o Memorandums	o Resumes	o Reports, and many more.

Some standard medium of written communication as messengers and SMS are WhatsApp, social media, emails, and many more. The message should be complete, concise and meaningful to have effective written communication.

Figure 1.5: Written communication

The following are the advantages:

- o Written content has legal validity.
- o It helps the user to draft a comprehensive message.
- o In case of lengthy messages, it is considered a suitable mode.

The following are the disadvantages:

- o The postage cost is involved in it.
- o For message, drafting needs a long time.
- o It has delays issues in decision making due to feedback.

According to Albert Mehrabian, a more impact is given by non-verbal communication (93%) as compared to verbal communication which counts (7%).

Non-verbal communication

In this communication, method information is exchanged using all other things except word. As it includes gestures, postures, eye contact, facial expressions, fingers, and various other body and oral communication is supported in it. In the absence of verbal communication, feelings and thoughts are convey using non-verbal signs.

The various elements involved in non-verbal communication are:

- Facial expression: Even before the hearing we first see on person face that is the most noticeable aspect of non-verbal communication,
- Gestures: In the absence of words, a gesture that include pointing fingers, waving, and more like body and hand movement are involved in it.
- Voice: The other person than the speaker read its voice and listen to words through which they judge whether the speaker is in anger, confidence, affection, and sarcasm.
- Body language: User communicates various messages through body language that includes eye movements, postures, hand gestures, facial expressions, and more.
- Eye gaze: This includes movement of eyes like staring, looking and blinking that helps in determining whether a person is honest or not.
- Physical contact, dress, and appearance are other factors of non-verbal communication.

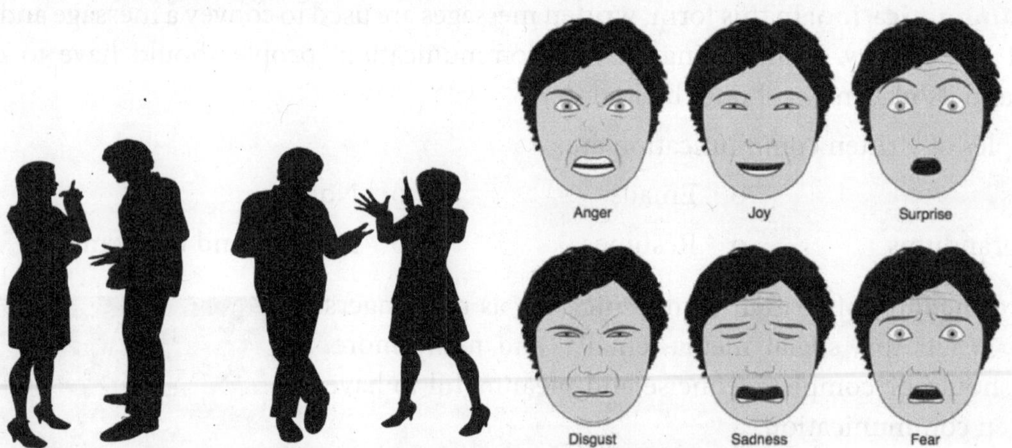

Figure 1.6: Non-verbal communication

The following are the advantages:

- It complements verbal communication.
- It helps handicapped people.

The following are the disadvantages:

- Not easy to recognize non-verbal messages that can result in miss-communication.
- Necessary explanation and long conversation are not possible.

Visual communication

A sense of sight used in any verbal and non-verbal communication is visual communication. Any method that relies on pictures, illusions, and graphics for sharing messages comes under graphic or visual communication. These are used to put a lasting and penetrative impact on receivers mind through:

- PowerPoint presentation
- Charts
- Graphs
- Maps
- White and blackboards
- Paper handouts
- Models, and many more

Creative minds create visual images using textures, colors, shapes that communicate messages along with emotions, experiences, concepts, textures and lifestyles. This is a commonly used method of communication in the education field.

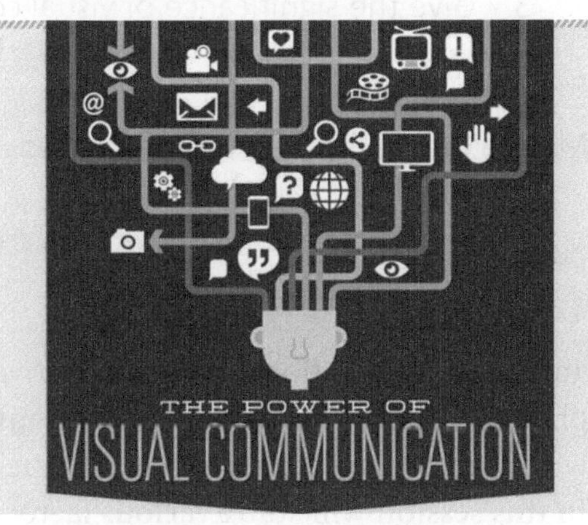

Figure 1.7: Visual communication

The following are the advantages:

1. Oral communication becomes more meaningful by addition of models, diagrams and graphs visual aids.
2. Communication becomes more interesting.
3. Complex data becomes easy to understand.

The following are the disadvantages:

1. Aids used in it are costly.
2. Sometimes information becomes complex.
3. Take a large time to communicate.

Summary

- Communication is the way the process of exchanging information, data, and ideas among various people throughout the world.
- Methods of communication are broadly classified into verbal communication, non-verbal communication, and visual communication.
- In Verbal communication, a message is delivered using words as it is the most powerful and accurate tools in expressing and sharing ideas.
- In non-verbal communication, information is exchanged using all other things except word.
- Any method that relies on pictures, illusions, and graphics for sharing messages comes under graphic or visual communication.

Self-Assessment

MULTIPLE CHOICE QUESTIONS.

1. In verbal communication message is delivered using:

   a. Spoken or written message b. Message that uses words of any language

   c. both a and b d. None

2. Which of the following is not an example of written communication?

   a. Emails b. Reports c. body language d. Letters

Answer

1. c   2. c

QUESTIONS

1. Name three methods of communication.
2. Differentiate oral and written communication.
3. Give the significance of visual communication.

PROJECT WORK

Make a presentation on common body language errors that must be avoided while communicating.

SESSION 3: FACTORS AFFECTING PERSPECTIVES IN COMMUNICATION

Take communication after perspective in offered by every discipline that helps in understanding the phenomenon of humans such as communities, societies, organizations, and groups. How the economy works and make decisions about perspectives and resources can be predicted from an economic perspective. In this session will study various factors affecting perspectives in communication, and more.

Perspective in communication

Perspective is the point of view of an individual through which one understands every communication and event happening around us. Everyone has different ways of seeing everything due to which everyone has different perspectives. How messages are transmitted, influenced the individual, and collective behaviour and how those messages are sustained, create and change communities and culture by exploring medium, patterns and content of messages comes under communication perspective.

Every people interpret and convey messages through the filters of their motives, beliefs, knowledge, and understanding. On the basis of these filters, a perspective is made by people and reflects in the way they see the world and every situation. Communication perspective helps in understanding the most persistent issues related to culture, political, and social faced by our nation and world.

Factors affecting perspective in communication

The important factors affecting the perspective in communication are:

- Visual perspective: It is a mental block that comes from your own visual perception of something. It is actually a tendency by which people will only focus on parts of a scenario that is most disposed to notice. While sending, receiving, interpreting and analyzing a message communication gets affected according to the way one perceives any event or subject. There can be a barrier in communication if visual perceptions of two people are not similar. As most of the visual perceptions are judgment like:
  - o Mental ability
  - o Qualification
  - o Financial status of the person

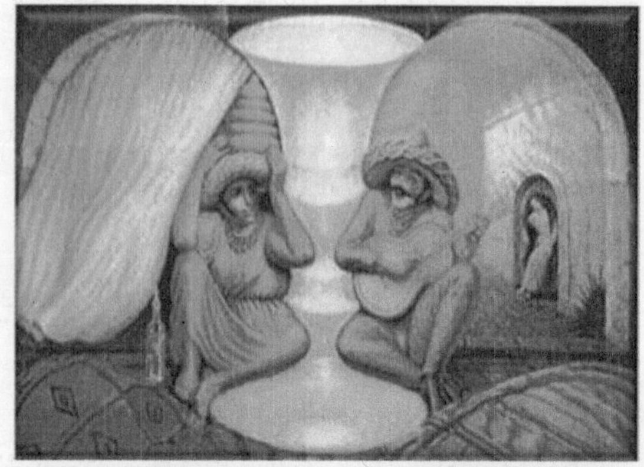

Figure 1.8: Visual perspective

In this picture, some will see one old woman and men in the picture, on the other hand, some will see two men sitting, and one is playing the guitar. Firstly what you will see depends on your visual perception.

- Language: Even in the interpretation of words, perception plays an important role in any communication process. The requirement is sender and receiver should be able to understand each other language. According to the way, one interprets a word, and there can be a different meaning of it.

  A problem can come in language perception if two people from a different background as one know only Hindi language and others know only English than a communication failure will take place.

Figure 1.9: Language perspective

- Past experience: Sometimes, we predict what will happen next according to the past perception we have about the same situation. As the past experience about meeting someone will shape your attitude towards situation, place or people. Past experience of two people can or cannot be the same, and then according to that, they will have their own attitude and approach of doing the same thing.

  For example, you went for an interview and got rejected due to your confidence level, but your fellows or friends have motivated you then you will perform well when you next time go for an interview. On the other hand, if nobody has motivated you after your bad experience of the first interview, then you will feel nervous while giving your next interview.

Figure 1.10: Past experience perspective

Note: **Throughout our lives, we face both negative and positive experience but don't let it affect the way you respond with other people.**

- Prejudices: Prejudices are prejudgment that is not based on experience, logic, or any fact. If sender or receiver have prejudices in their mind that it can result in communication failure. It is a negative attitude that is due to personal preferences and culture and when one at according to their prejudices then it results in discrimination and in these cases decisions or judgment about someone is taken without finding the necessary information about that person.

Figure 1.11: Prejudices

- Feelings: In communication, an important role is played by our mind emotional or feelings state. As people will react to same situation in different ways when they are sad and happy. How someone is feeling at a particular time will depend on the way they reach on a particular situation and the way they interact with people around them. The other perspective is how you feel about the person you are communicating.

For example, if you are sad due to something happening at your workplace then you will react rudely with your kids when they irritate you on the other hand you will treat them well when you got appreciation at your workplace.

- Environment: If communication takes place in smelly, noisy, dark, over-crowded then communication process gets affected. No one behaves in the same way in every environment.

  For example, the teacher feels irritated when communicating with one student and other are making noise and the communication take place in a darkroom will be less effective as sender and receiver will not able to do eye contact with them.

- Attitude: It is the mindset of one individual in taking a decision or responding to the same situation.

  For example: According to some people the below-given bottle of Coca-Cola is half-filled, on the other hand, others will say it is half empty. Who will have what opinion about it is depends on attitude or perception of oneself in that situation?

Figure 1.12: Example of attitude as a perspective

Summary

- Perspective is the point of view of an individual through which one understands every communication and event happening around us.
- Factors affecting the perspective in communication are visual perspective, language, past experience, prejudices, feelings, belief, environment, attitude, and more.
- There can be a problem in language perception if two people from a different background as one know only Hindi language and others know only English than a communication failure will take place.
- Past experience of two people can or cannot be the same, and then according to that, they will have their own attitude and approach of doing the same thing.
- Prejudices are prejudgment that is not based on experience, logic or any fact. If sender or receiver have prejudices in their mind that it can result in communication failure.
- If communication takes place in smelly, noisy, dark, over-crowded, then communication process gets affected.
- Attitude is the mind-set of one individual in taking a decision or responding to the same situation.

Self-Assessment

MULTIPLE CHOICE QUESTIONS.

1. Which of the following is not a factor affecting perspective in communication?

   a. Feelings　　b. Prejudice　　c. Attitude　　d. Love

2. Perspective is an individual's

   a. Point of view　　b. Activity　　c. Body language　　d. None

Answer

1. d   2. a

QUESTIONS

1. What do you mean by perspective in communication?
2. Name 5 factors affecting perspective on the communication.
3. Briefly explain prejudices.

PROJECT WORK

Do a group discussion on various factors that affects the perspective in communication by giving examples for each.

SESSION 4: KNOWLEDGE OF BASIC WRITING SKILLS

In order to express ourselves, sentences are written that should be correct; otherwise, its meaning gets changed. The sentence makes includes correct choices of words, their organization into the right sequence of a sentence. Sentence is a group of words communicating the right message and phrase are a group of words that not make any sense.

The seven elements of communication are used to improve professional communication skills and increase the chances of having a correct message that delivers the right meaning.

These 7C's are:

- Clear (message should be clear, not confusing)
- Correct (No spelling and grammatical errors)
- Complete (Message should include all required information)
- Concrete (Supported with figures and facts)
- Concise (Message should be short and to the point)
- Consideration (Receivers opinion, mindset, knowledge, the background should be considered by sender)
- Courteous (Should consider the viewpoints and feelings of the receiver)

Writing Skills

In order to have an effective written communication, both sender and receiver should be able to share their message without any confusion, grammatical errors easily. Any laps at with sender or receiver side lead to miss communication. Use of correct grammar, selection of right words and easy sentence structure making are important aspects of writing skills.

Avoid using too technical, difficult words as it will be difficult for a receiver to understand it if he/she belongs from a non-technical background. Try to using sentences for expressing messages instead of or words.

Phrase

Words are used to express our ideas and thoughts while communicating with each other. A sentence is a group of words that make complete sense.

For example, I am going, behind the table, and more.

These group of words are not known as a sentence as they are not making complete sense and known as phrases. The phrase is a group of words that gives only hint about the message sender want to communicate. It doesn't have an object and a subject.

For example:

- **Phrase:** I am sitting
- **Sentence:** I am sitting on the table

If finite verbs or objects is added in the phrase then it becomes a sentence. For example: early in the morning, difficult task, hard work, and more.

These all are phrases, and in a sentence, it will be: I daily wake up early in the morning, it is a difficult task to do, and we all must have to do hard work.

Noun, verb, adjective, adverbial, and prepositional are five types of phrases.

- Noun phrase act like a noun in a sentence. Example: The yellow house is for sale. Where, the yellow house is a noun phrase.
- Verb phrase is a group of helping and main verbs within a sentence. Example: She was walking quickly to the mall. Where was walking is a verb.
- Adjective phrase is built around an adjective and consist of articles and adjectives. Example: The woman on board is my aunty, Dolli. Where on the boat is an adjective
- Adverbial phrase is built around adverb by adding words before or after it. Example: I will sit in silence. Where in silence is an adverbial phrase.
- Prepositional phrase always begins with a preposition followed by a noun. Example: The store at the corner sells patties. Where at the corner is a prepositional phrase.

Sentence

As mentioned in the last section, a group of words that make complete sense is called a sentence. It must consist of predicate and subject.

Examples:

- **Not a sentence:** Understand too much is there
- **Sentence:** There is too much to understand

The first one is not a sentence as it doesn't make any sense, and the second one is considered a sentence.

There are mainly four kinds of sentences as given below:

- Asserted or declarative sentence: The sentence that reports events, describe things and state facts. It is a simple sentence that indicates, declares or asserts, which gives positive or negative meaning.

  Example: This is my favourite movie
  My husband loves eating cake in the morning
- Interrogative sentence: These sentences are used to make enquiries and asking for information. At the end question mark is used and it starts with words like Why, What, When, How, and many more.

  Example: What do you mean by sentence?
  How often do you use the Internet?
- Imperative sentence: These are the sentences that express an order, advice, request, suggestion, direction, etc. It ends with a full stop or explanation sign.

Example: Never speak to me like this again.
Do not argue!

- Exclamatory sentence: These sentences express wonder, surprise, happiness, sorrow, sympathy or gratitude like strong and sudden feelings. It can form by either selecting how, what like words or oh, ah, hurrah, alas, oops like interjections.

  Example: I can't believe how fast that train was moving.
  Bravo! Well done!

Subject and predicate are two parts of every complete sentence. Where the subject is a word or group of words that convey the name of things or persons about whom we are speaking. On the other hand, the predicate is a part of a sentence that contains verbs and state something about the subject. Some of the examples to understand these two parts of the sentence are:

- Simran runs: In this Simran is a subject
- Simran and his dog Stella run on a beach: In this Simran and his dog Stella is a subject (multiple subjects)
- She is nice: She is a subject
- Samar is a good boy: Here Samar is subject and is a good boy is a predicate
- She was hit by a ball: Here hit by a ball is a predicate
- Stand up! : Stand up is a predicate

While writing the sentence keep is short, limit sentence contents, arrange sentence in proper sequence, and economize on words and design sentence that emphasize the topics.

Parts of speech

According to the functions in a sentence, it is classified into eight types are given below:

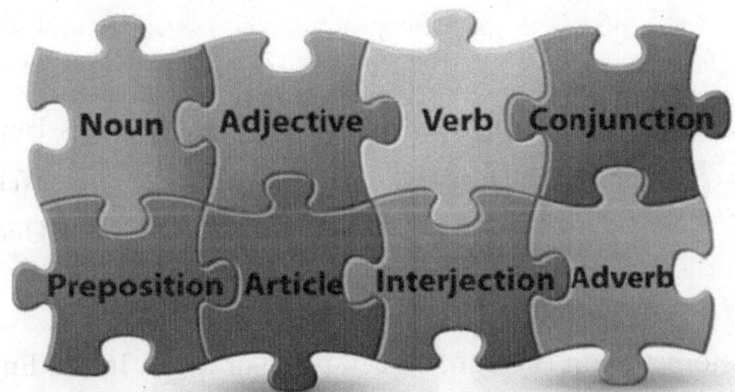

Figure 1.13: Parts of Speech

Part of speech	Function of word	Example words	Example sentences
Noun	It refers to the words used to name person, animals. Things, ideas, places, events.	Komal, Cat, Table, Music, Patiala, cocktail	Her name is Komal. Cutes can be extremely innocent. We live in Patiala.

Part of speech	Function of word	Example words	Example sentences
Pronoun	It is used in replacement of noun	She, I, He, We, you, some, their, ours	We are number one. My dog name is Stella.
Adjective	Used to describe noun or pronoun. It specifies quality, size and number	Some, like, sing, must have, work, cold, happy	I have two soft toys. She is feeling Cold.
Verb	It shows a state or action	Speaking, been, go, must, can, lived	As usual, the Simran missed their train. They are always prepared in an emergency. India is a country.
Adverb	Describe a verb, adjectives or another adverb	Very slowly, too, well, later, really, soon	She came yesterday. Komal dance well. The child is very talented.
Preposition	It refers to the word that specifies a location and shows the relation of a noun, noun phrase, a sentence with another word	Above, below, after, but, yet, from, with, throughout, under	Sam is hiding under the bed. The dog is under the chair
Conjunction	Joins words, clauses, phrases, sentences together,	And, but, while, because, if	This colour is very beautiful and soothing. I like garlic bread, but I don't like pasta.
Interjection	Used to convey strong emotion and usually put an exclamatory sign in the end	Hey! Wow! Ouch! Hi!	Hey! I said enough. Well! I don't know. Ouch! It hurts

Articles and its use

An article is a word used before a noun (person, object, place or idea). In the English language, there is a definite and indefinite article. 'A' and 'an' are Indefinite articles 'the' is a definite article. 'A' is used before the words starting with constants, and 'an' is used before words starting with vowels (A, E, I, O, U). It is mainly used to refer to a noun or group of nouns.

Indefinite articles

As mentioned above, indefinite articles are 'A' and 'An'. These articles are used before **Singular Countable Nouns (SCN)** that indicates a noun is not referring to any particular thing or person. Various rules for using indefinite articles are:

'A' and 'An' is used before the singular countable noun when it is mentioned for the first time.

- *Example:* I saw a good film yesterday

An orange
'A' can be used before Mr./Miss/Mrs. and first name or surname

- *Example:* A certain Miss Komal called me to ask about her medicine
'A' is used before a singular countable noun or adjective beginning with a constant sound
- *Example:* A beautiful flower
She ate a banana
'A' is used to express quantity or numbers
- *Example:* A dozen
I felt a bit depressed
'A' and 'An' is used after the words like rather, many, quite, such in certain structures
- *Example:* Many a friend of mine are not coming to school
'An' and 'a' perform the same function, but 'an' is used before vowels sound singular countable noun.
- *Example:* She wants to eat an orange
She works as an Engineer

While applying article focus on sound rather than words as sometimes it gives the sound of another word while pronouncing it.

Definite articles

'The' is a definite article used with a plural uncountable noun and singular countable noun. It mainly used in specifying thing, place, and person.

'The' is used to indicate a noun that is definite or has been previously specified in the context.

- *Example:* I like the clothes you gave me
'The' is used to indicate a unique noun
- *Example:* I Bhakra River is near to me
'The' is used to designate a natural phenomenon
- *Example:* The wind is blowing so hard
'The' is used to refer to a time period
- *Example:* I was very active in the past
'The' is used to indicate all the members of a family
- *Example:* I invited my friends for dinner

Make sure you don't use 'The' before a proper noun, colors, meals, names of materials, plural nouns, names of games used in general sense.

Paragraph writing

Paragraph is a number of related sentences focused on an idea. It forms a part of a larger piece of writing, such as a composition. The communication of idea inefficient and clear way is the basic aim of a paragraph that mainly discusses one aspect of the topic or subject.

Before writing the paragraph writer should be clear about the topic and what contents have to add in it. If there is no definite idea about the topic then there will be a lack of unity, clarity and focus.

According to the complexity or simplicity of the main idea, a paragraph-length may vary.

Note: **Paragraph should not be very short that idea is explained inadequately and it should not be too long that it covers not intended data.**

Before writing, paragraphs think about it and consider all relevant issues or ideas about it. While writing, it considers only relevant data related to the topic to make it short and fruitful. Some of the essential sections of the paragraph are:

- Paragraph topic: The first and foremost important thing before writing a paragraph is its subject or topic.
- Introduction: Start the paragraph with one or two sentence introduction about a topic that will be featured incomplete paragraph. It is also known as the topic sentence.
- Explanation: To clarify more about topic, give information about topic sentence in 7-8 sentences.
- Conclusion: In this section summarizes the whole sentences written about the topic.
- Proofread: It is the last and most important step to avoid mistakes and delivering a good paragraph. This writer should check the paragraph for grammatical mistakes and sentence making.

Regardless of the information contained in a paragraph, there are some rules or characteristics. Some of them are:

- Unity: Give paragraph unity, or it should concern with a single focus.
- Length: Keep them short and concise length of paragraph by avoiding unnecessary details.
- Introduction/Topic sentence: Make use of topic sentences.
- Coherence: It makes the paragraph easily understandable to a reader as in this each sentence will be related to the topic.
- Conclusion: Add a conclusion in the end that conclude about all the sentences written in the paragraph.

Use transition words or phrases like but, because, in fact, may more.

Summary

- To express ourselves, sentences are written that should be correct; otherwise, its meaning gets changed.
- The seven elements of communication are used to improve professional communication skills and increases the chances of having the correct message that delivers the right meaning.
- 7 C's of communication is clear, correct, complete, concrete, concise, consideration, and courteous.
- To have effective written communication, both sender and receiver should be able to and share their message without any confusion, grammatical errors easily. Any laps at with sender or receiver side lead to miss communication.
- Words are used to express our ideas and thoughts while communicating with each other.
- A sentence is a group of words that make complete sense.
- The phrase is a group of words that gives only hint about the message sender want to communicate.
- There is four kinds of sentences are asserted, interrogative, imperative and exclamatory.
- Subject and predicate are two parts of every complete sentence.
- Eight parts of speech are noun, adjective, verb, conjunction, preposition, article, interjection and adverb.
- An article is a word used before a noun (person, object, place or idea). In the English language, there is a definite and indefinite article. 'A' and 'an' are Indefinite articles 'the' is a definite article.

- Paragraph is a number of related sentences focused on an idea. It forms a part of a larger piece of writing, such as a composition.

Self-Assessment

MULTIPLE CHOICE QUESTIONS.

1. Which of the following is not the 7C's or elements of communication?

   a. Clear b. Complete c. Concentrate d. Concise

2. ________ article is used before words starting with vowels.

   a. A b. An c. The d. definite article

3. Which of the following is not a type of phrase?

   a. Noun b. Adjective c. Adverbial d. Pronoun

Answer

1. c 2. b 3. d

QUESTIONS

1. What is the phrase? Name a different kind of phrases?
2. Describe four types of sentences with an example of each.
3. Write a short note of effective paragraph writing.
4. What do you mean by article, its usage? Give their types with one example.

PROJECT WORK

Develop a paragraph on any of your favourite topics considering all essential sections of paragraphs.

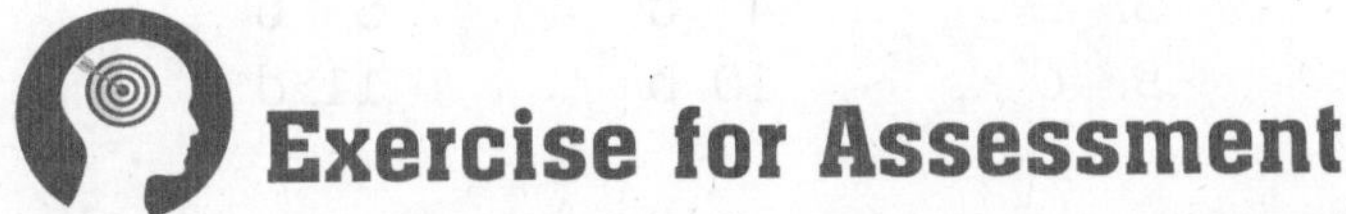

Exercise for Assessment

MULTIPLE CHOICE QUESTIONS.

1. Which of the following is not a characteristic of Communication?

   a. Continuous process b. Two-way process

   c. Mutual understanding d. One-way process

2. Verbal communication involves:

   a. Any message that uses words of different languages

   b. A written message

   c. A Spoken message

   d. Both b and c

3. Sender sends a message and in response gets __________ from receiver?

   a. Nothing b. Result c. Feedback d. All

4. __________ is the process of converting coded information into original form.
   a. Communication b. Encoding c. Feedback d. Decoding
5. One way communication is __________ due to absence of receiver response.
   a. Difficult b. Steady and slow c. Fast d. Effective
6. In verbal communication message is delivered using:
   a. Spoken or written message b. Message that uses words of any language
   c. Both a and b d. None
7. Which of the following is not a primary form of verbal communication?
   a. Oral communication b. Written communication
   c. Body language d. None
8. Which of the following is not an example of written communication?
   a. Emails b. Reports c. Body language d. Letters
9. Which of the following is the negative attitude, especially when it is related to hatred for some people?
   a. Feelings b. Attitude c. Prejudices d. Language
10. Group of words that make complete sense are
    a. Phrase b. Sentence c. Both a and b d. None
11. Which of the following is not a type of phrase?
    a. Noun b. Adjective c. Adverbial d. Pronoun
12. Which of the following is not a type of speech?
    a. Noun b. Pronoun c. Adverb d. Adjective

Answer

1. d	2. d	3. c	4. d	5. b	6. c
7. c	8. c	9. c	10. b	11. d	12. b

VERY SHORT QUESTIONS

1. What is communication?
2. Define encoding and decoding?
3. Name the methods of communication.
4. What is the significance of visual communication?
5. Give any two disadvantage of written communication.
6. Name the part of the sentence.
7. Define communication prospective.

SHORT QUESTIONS

1. What are the various characteristics of communication?
2. Define effective communication.
3. What do you understand by barriers to effective communication?

4. Define non-verbal communication. List the main elements of non-verbal communication.
5. What is visual communication? Give its any two advantages and disadvantages.
6. Enlist the factors affecting the perspective of communication.
7. How prejudices can affect the perception of communication.
8. Differentiate phrase and sentence with example.

LONG QUESTIONS

1. State the importance of effective communication?
2. Briefly explain the various elements of the communication cycle.
3. Write a short note on various methods of communication.
4. Define verbal communication? Give two primary forms of verbal communication.
5. What is perspective in communication? Explain any four factors affecting the perspective of communication.
6. Give various parts of speech?
7. Explain the meaning of phrases with example.
8. Write a short note on paragraph writing.

APPLICATION-BASED QUESTIONS

1. When you want to take permission from your parents for going out with your friends, do you have analyzed their response when they are in a good and bad mood? How it effects their response to your permission to go out with your friends.
2. Write any one instance where your prospective has influenced your behaviour towards your school best friend.
3. Komal is preparing for a declamation contest; help her in preparing a list of all the elements of non-verbal communication that she should have to consider while giving her speech.
4. Simran is a new principal of your school, and he wants to share his idea with his teaching staff. Compare the advantages and disadvantages of both oral and written communication and suggest him which form of communication is more effective.
5. Jass has to write a paragraph for a debate held in school, tell him all the essential sections of a paragraph that helps him in preparing a good paragraph.

PROJECT WORK

1. Roleplay with your friend on the communication process related to barriers of the communication process.
2. Roleplay in class to give an introduction of yourself that includes your name, class, school name, hobbies, qualities, and aim in life.
3. Do a group discussion of various characteristics of communication and what are the barriers affecting it.
4. Make a presentation on common body language errors that must be avoided while communicating.
5. Try all three methods of communication in your class for communicating and conveying a message to your friends. Then make a chart on various pros and cons of each method.

6. Do group discussion on how a communication cycle is disrupted by Non-verbal communication.
7. Play dumb Charades by following its rules to observe the non-verbal method of communication.

TEACHER NOTES

1. Make a group discussion in class on the best method for communication out of verbal, non-verbal and visual communication.
2. Arrange a paragraph writing competition in class and give feedback to students according to the paragraph written by them.

2 Self-Management Skills

Learning Outcomes

After this chapter, you will have the knowledge of:

- Self-management
- Importance of self-management
- Self-management skill
- What is self-confidence
- Factors influencing self-confidence
- Factors building self-confidence
- SWOT analysis

INTRODUCTION

Self-management refers to self-regulation or self-control; it is the ability to regulate one's thoughts, emotions, and behavior effectively in various situations. Self-management is about organizing your time, regulating actions, and more, to achieve predetermined goals. Having strong self-management skills helps a student do different activities effectively by cooperating with others in school, focusing on their tasks, managing time, and performing better in studies. It helps in facing any situation with confidence either related to school, college, home, or office in day to day life.

Take the example of your class teacher. She manages her home along with her work of teaching students, and many more. To do all these tasks effectively, she plans and delegates the responsibilities and then organizes the resources like time, money, etc. Then according to the priorities she allocates the resources. In this entire task, nobody directs her to set and achieve the goals; she self-manages it all by herself.

Therefore, self-management skills help in both personal and professional life. Self-management skills include:

- Self-awareness
- Self-control
- Self-confidence
- Problem solving
- Self-motivation
- Positive thinking
- Managing our emotions
- Anger
- Openness to learning new ideas and team work

SESSION 1: IMPORTANCE OF SELF-MANAGEMENT

Self-management is a key to manage everything around us. It makes you more organized, instills discipline, helps in achieving goals, helps in completing all work on time and effectively, enhances self-confidence, develops problem solving skills, and more.

All these are achieved by learning the following:

- Time management
- Settings goals and priorities
- Accepting people from different cultures
- Managing your emotions, mood, anger, team working ability, etc.

Self-management skills

The three key skills of self-management are:

- **Initiative:** It is the ability to work without always getting instructions for what needs to be done. This requires people to believe on their own capabilities even in difficult situations. It means using your mind and driving yourself to achieve your goals. Self believe is must in initiative as then only you will be able to go out of your way to solve problems without the need to be instructed by others.

  How to grow your Initiative skills:

  - Always look for various ways to simplify tasks.
  - Help your team members and colleagues when they need it.
  - Keep yourself organized and stay on top of activities.
  - Keep you plans and ambitions clear.

- **Organization:** You can plan your time, energy and resources effectively when you are organized in work and life. Being organized will help you save your energy and time and help in completing tasks effectively and get more productive results. The most important thing you should know is what should be done first and what can be done later. This is called prioritization of tasks.

  This includes preparation and availability of things when needed and must follow:

  - Defining and identification of specific tasks.
  - Breaking down goals into smaller and fruitful tasks: To achieve a bigger task or goal, you need to divide it into smaller parts and define your targets using SMART strategy.
  - Managing time so that right amount of time is given to right activity and assigning specific time slots to activities as per their importance. It includes:
    - Planning (learn to plan each day, week, month and year to control workload).
    - Fix time slots (before setting time slot, estimate the time required for completion of specific tasks).
    - Prioritize and schedule (Accommodate the planned tasks according to their priority or importance).
    - Spend right time on right activity (This includes setting time to complete the task).

In SMART strategy, S stands for specific, M stands for Measurable (like divide your tasks whose completion gives measurable outcome), A stands for Achievable (that means set a task that can be achieved), R stands for Realistic, and T stands for Time bound.

- **Accountability:** Both accountability and responsibility are similar but have different meaning. As one can share responsibility but accountability is specific to oneself. In case of responsibility one can blame other for any wrong actions but in accountability only you will be responsible and have to answer for your actions. If you say to yourself that you are accountable then it means you take ownership of responsibilities that come to your way.

  Some of the characteristics of accountability are:

  - **Avoid procrastination:** Procrastination means avoiding the important tasks that need to be completed. This includes choosing an easy task rather than doing the important difficult task. This must be avoided.

- o **Adopting problem** solving attitude is required in every area of work. Sometimes people have to face difficult situations even after planning or prioritizing everything. In these cases, a problem solving attitude helps in achieving goals on time.
- o **Managing your own emotions:** As emotions prevent us from working towards best and constructive solutions.
- o **Coping with distress:** There can be situations of injuries, accidents, illness, and death in a family that may impact your physical and emotional well-being. In those situations, surround yourself with people who can provide you the required practical and emotional support.

Importance of self-management

Self-management is important in every field of life as it teaches to be productively and efficiently achieve our goals. It also helps in managing time and completing tasks with less effort, managing stress, and prioritizing our tasks.

Figure 2.1: Self-management

Self-management also helps you with the following:

- ✦ **Organized:** With self-management, one gets the skills of organizing and allocating their time and resources while planning a task.
- ✦ **Teaches discipline:** When one makes an organized schedule and commits to follow it, they don't get distracted by unimportant tasks. They know that unimportant activities will result in delay or failing to achieve the target.
- ✦ **Attain goals:** If you have organized all the tasks and allocated the right amount of time for everything, then it helps you attain the goal on time.
- ✦ **Self-confidence enhancement:** If you set goals and achieve them then it will give you self-confidence in achieving more challenging tasks. It also gives you courage to take initiatives when any opportunity comes.
- ✦ **Respects from others:** If you are doing well and achieving good results, then you will get appreciated or respect by people surrounding you either in school, officer or at home.

Summary

- ⊙ Self-management refers to self-regulation or self-control; it is the ability to regulate one's thoughts, emotions, behavior effectively in various situations.
- ⊙ Self-management makes you more organized, instills discipline, helps in achieving goals, helps in completing all work on time and effectively, enhances self-confidence, helps you gain problem solving skills, and more.
- ⊙ To achieve a bigger task or goal, you need to divide it into smaller parts and define your targets using SMART strategy.
- ⊙ Accountability is specific to one's self.
- ⊙ Responsibility can be shared and you can blame others for any wrong action.
- ⊙ Self-management is important in every field of life as it teaches to be productively and efficiently achieve our goals.

Self-Assessment

MULTIPLE CHOICE QUESTIONS.

1. Which of the following shows the ability to participate as a team member?

   a. Interpersonal skills b. Communication skills

   c. Entrepreneur skills d. None

2. Self-management skills do not involve:

   a. Initiative b. Organization c. Management d. Accountability

Answer

1. b 2. c

QUESTIONS

1. What do you mean by self-management? How is it different from management?
2. What do you mean by Organization skills of self-management? Explain the SMART strategy used in it.
3. What does self-management help you with?

PROJECT WORK

Have a group discussion on importance of self-management.

SESSION 2: BUILDING SELF-CONFIDENCE

Self-confidence is a sense of trusting one's own abilities. If you are a hardworking, talented and intelligent person but have lack of confidence and don't take initiatives then other people will be unable to recognize your talent. With changes in practice and attitude, self-confidence can be developed. If you have self-confidence then you will start believing in your capabilities; you'll be willing to take risks and ready to accept any challenges.

Factors influencing self-confidence

There are various factors influencing self-confidence:

Social factors	Cultural factors	Physical factors
Society that consists of school, friends, family and neighborhood plays an important role in building and shaping our self-confidence. A long lasting impact is left on our outlook and attitude towards ourselves. How one perceives their self, gets affected by evaluation from teachers, friends, schoolmates, parents, etc.	Culture or characteristics of a community, society or group is reflected in its beliefs and practices. It includes culture behavior and development and children growing up in different cultures receive specific inputs from their environment.	In development of self-confidence in people an important role is played by healthy mind, healthy physique and good appearance. Person's self-confidence gets affected by the way they appear, in every culture. Behavior, body language and way of speaking reflect the level of confidence.

Factors building self-confidence

Building self-confidence is the process that takes efforts and commitment and it requires having a positive attitude about yourself. The below given factors and techniques help in having self-confidence and sustaining it for a long time:

- **Self-efficiency:** It is the belief in your own ability in dealing with various challenges and events. One can happily or easily tackle difficult situations by having confidence. Be assertive and have faith in your beliefs.
- **Positive thinking:** It is nothing but focusing on the positives even in the time of adversity. Positive thinking is referred to as your tendency to emphasize the positive aspects on other hand negative thinking is about emphasizing on less optimistic aspects of situation.
- **Self-esteem:** Self-esteem is a general feeling about your own self. People with low self-esteem are more affected by others' opinions about them. On other hand people with high self-esteem have positive feelings about themselves.
- **Locus of control:** It is the degree of perceiving the control over external or internal situation and is a belief that you are being controlled by internal locus or external locus.
- **Self-monitoring:** It is the extent to which you base your behavior on cues from other people and situations. Someone with high self-monitoring pays attention to what behavior is appropriate in certain situations like being hygienic, staying clean, spending time with positive people and having high ethical standards.
- **SWOT:** The SWOT stands for Strength, Weakness, Opportunity, and Threat and it is a useful technique for understanding opportunities and challenges. This analysis helps in recognizing one's abilities and talents along with choosing opportunities utilizing their core strengths. This is used for outlining the suitable goals and applies organizing skills on it.
- **Experience:** Always take the first step in every situation to gain experience and then keep practicing on it. Your self-confidence will increase with success in each situation and give you the ability to handle failures and overcome obstacles.

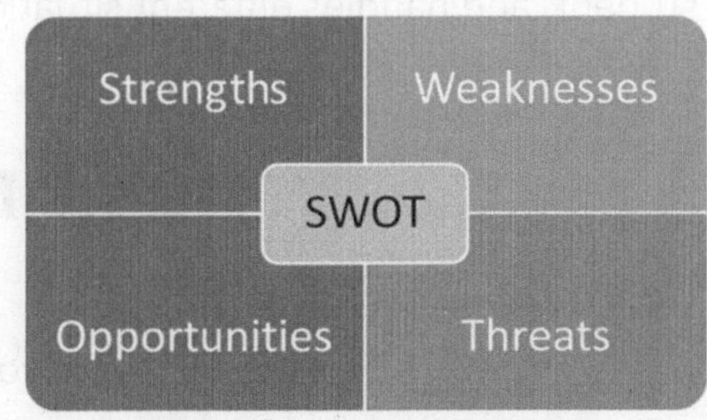

Figure 2.2: SWOT analysis

Summary

- Self-confidence is a sense of trusting one's own abilities and self.
- Social, cultural, and physical factors influence self-confidence.
- Building self-confidence is the process that takes efforts and commitment and it requires having a positive attitude about one's self.
- Self-efficiency, positive thinking, self-esteem, locus of control, self-management, experience, etc. are factors that build self-confidence.
- SWOT stands for Strength, Weakness, Opportunity, and Threat and it is a useful technique for understanding opportunities and challenges.

Self-Assessment

MULTIPLE CHOICE QUESTIONS.

1. Which of the following is not a factor influencing self-confidence:

   a. Social factors　b. Personal factors　c. Cultural factors　d. Physical factors

2. People with self-confidence have a___________ outlook:

   a. Negative　b. Arrogant　c. Outward　d. Positive

Answer

1. b　2. d

QUESTIONS

1. Name the three factors influencing self-confidence.
2. Explain SWOT technique for improving self-confidence.
3. Give any five factors for building self-confidence.
4. What do you mean by self-esteem?

PROJECT WORK

Observe the head girl of your school and write points on how she helps others, solves problems of every student, and handles different situations.

Exercise for Assessment

MULTIPLE CHOICE QUESTIONS.

1. __________ is the ability to work without always getting instructions from others.

   a. Self-confidence　b. Organization　c. Initiative　d. Accountability

2. R in SMART strategy stands for __________?

   a. Real　b. Rate　c. Realistic　d. Required

3. Self-management skills do not involve:

   a. Initiative　b. Organization　c. Management　d. Accountability

4. __________ is your ability to participate as a team member.

   a. Rational Abilities b. Personal qualities c. Interpersonal skill d. Communication skill

5. In SWOT, O stands for ____________

   a. Operation b. Organization c. Opportunity d. Openly

6. People with low self-esteem are more affected by:

   a. Personal matters b. Others thinking about them

   c. Work load d. None

7. People with self-confidence have a___________ outlook:

   a. Negative b. Arrogant c. Outward d. Positive

8. Which of the following refers to a belief about your own ability to deal with events and challenges?

   a. Self-esteem b. Self confidence c. Self-monitoring d. Self-efficacy

Answer

1. c 2. c 3. c 4. c 5. c 6. b 7. d 8. d

VERY SHORT QUESTIONS

1. What is self-management?
2. Write down the full form of SMART strategy.
3. Give two characteristics of accountability.
4. Name the three factors influencing self-confidence.
5. What do you mean by self-esteem?
6. How positive thinking helps in achieving the self-confidence.

SHORT QUESTIONS

1. What do you mean by self-management? Explain in brief.
2. Explain SMART strategy.
3. How being organized is one of the importance of self-management?
4. Differentiate accountability and responsibility.
5. Define self-confidence
6. Explain SWOT technique for improving self-confidence.

LONG QUESTIONS

1. What are the three key skills of self-management?
2. What is the importance of self-management? Explain five points of importance of self-management.
3. What do you mean by organization skills of self-management? Explain the SMART strategy used in it.
4. Give in detail any five factors for building self-confidence.
5. Write a short note on various factors influencing the self-confidence.

APPLICATION BASED QUESTIONS

1. You are organizing an annual function in your school, ese SWOT analysis to find out your strengths and weaknesses and work on your weaknesses to make your annual function perfect.
2. Arrange a press conference in your class and take interview of your topper, how he/she works or manages to get the highest score in the class.
3. Jaspreet focuses on playing and he is always unable to finish his homework. Give him a few suggestions for managing his time effectively and completing his homework on time and also get time for playing.

PROJECT WORKS

1. Find out your strengths and weaknesses using the SWOT technique. According to it, make a list to participate in various activities held in sports competitions conducted in your school. Then make one more list in which you need to mention potential difficulties you have faced in sporting activities.
2. Inculcate positive thoughts by repeating it to yourself for one month and observe how it has affects you.
3. List out your strengths and weaknesses, make a 2 week plan using the SMART strategy to work on your weaknesses and track your progress and then repeat it for next week.

TEACHER NOTES

1. Tell your students to use the SMART strategy for preparation and availability of things.
2. Give practical example of social, cultural, and physical factors influencing the self-confidence of students.

3 Information and Communication Technology Skills – I

Learning Outcomes

After this chapter, you will have the knowledge of:

- Information and communication technology
- Tools of ICT
- Role of ICT in personal life, e-commerce, learning and teaching, e-banking, entertainment, arts, social media, and communication
- Use of ICT in the workplace
- Computer system
- Basic components of computer system
- Brief about internal and external memory
- Various peripheral devices
- Start and shutdown the computer
- Software and its types
- Functioning of the operating system, types of operating system
- The disk operating system, steps to open dos, features, advantages, and disadvantages of DOS
- LINUX, its features
- EDUBUNTU, its features, and components
- Uses of the Internet
- Common terms used in Internet
- Email application, how to create Gmail account, signing out from a Gmail account, compose an email message, receiving and reply to emails
- Introduction to social media like Twitter, Facebook, YouTube, and WhatsApp
- Digital India with its objectives

INTRODUCTION

Information and Communication Technology (ICT) that includes a set of technological resources and tools used for communication, creation, storing, managing, and disseminating information. ICT includes the Internet, computers, telephony, and broadcasting technologies that take knowledge about how the computer works and how different computers communicate with each other. In digital technology, the information is translated into a binary format where each bit represents two distinct amplitudes, on the other hand, information is translated into varying amplitude electric pulses in case of analog technology.

SESSION 1: ROLE OF ICT

Everyday technology is used by people at their workplace and home. The resources and information can be access everywhere and anytime by ICT tools like:

- Computers
- Smartphones
- Internet
- E-mail and social network
- Watching TV shows, and more

For example: To find a job, you may have to search the Internet for job openings, create a resume on a computer, use email to send the resume, send messages through your phone to communicate and appear for telephonic interview and get your offer letter through email.

ICT skills enable us to connect with our friends and family, run our business, and communicate. Due to this, there is a need to acquire ICT skills by every person and build them to stay updated with the latest applications and software.

Information and Communication Technology (ICT)

Our daily life gets revolutionized with development in technology that has the emergence of a new global economy. Any information can be searched with one click. UNESCO defines informatics as the science dealing with implications of realization, use, design, and maintenance of information processing systems that include:

- Software
- Hardware
- Human aspects
- Organizational
- Commercial
- Industrial
- Political
- Government

Due to this, ICT will stay and prospects in the future. The computerization of work is getting more and more prevalent in every walk of life. There is not a single public official in which the computer is not used.

Tools of ICT

The ICT tools are any tool that facilitates storage, dissemination, management, and creation of information and communication. It includes television, radio-like traditional technologies along with computers, satellite systems, networks, and mobile phones like modern technologies. The video conferencing, teleconferencing, and social networking, like various applications and services associated with these technologies, come under ICT.

Brief of some of the ICT tools are:

- **Radio:** It is the oldest machines come under ICT tool that is used to work as a cricket transmission device, music listening, new device, and more. It is also used in today's era, like in cars; it comes as built-in part so that one can listen to the news, cricket commentary, Songs, and some of the fun done by RJs.
- **Mobile:** Earlier time, it was used for calls, but nowadays, it is loaded with various applications to complete tasks in few times. Like Paytm wallet and Google pay for money transfer, WhatsApp for messaging, Games, and many more can be downloaded in it.
- **TV:** TV comes in India in the 1980s that is a part of every middle class or richer household in India. It is used for watching movies, listening to news, see news channels, learning calculation tricks, and many more. The main motive of TV is for entertainment, and now it comes with HD viewing and a bigger and better one.
- **Email:** Email stands for electronic mail that reduces the load on the postal system. Nowadays Outlook by Microsoft, Yahoo mail, Hotmail, Rediff mail, and Gmail are major carriers of email messages. Various people are still using it even by the increase in hacking, phishing, cracking, spam.

Role of ICT

The quality of living has been improved by the invention of ICT by giving easy access to information and various services and products. It has changed the way of living, working, communicating with each other, and more. It make changes in both personal and business life.

ICT in personal Life

Various technologies and services can be access by ICT, and some of these are given below:

Figure 3.1: ICT in personal life

- **Information access:** One can access information related to health, social aspects, education, finance, current affairs, houses, and more, that helps in improving and enriching their lives.
- **E-commerce:** In this, one can buy or sell products online through the Internet after comparing them online and selecting the best one as per our requirements. It will save time and money as one can get the product at home. It also offers a range of products are:
  - o Toys
  - o Railway booking
  - o Flight booking
  - o Hotel booking
  - o Home products
  - o Electronics, and more.

Figure 3.2: ICT in e-commerce

- **Learning and teaching:** The quality of education gets enhanced with ICT by the provision of various learning tools to students, parents, and teachers. The Microsoft, G Suit, YouTube, Scribed, Java-tpoint, code.org, Kindle books, and more are available for students and teachers.
- **E-banking:** It enables the transaction anytime, anywhere, through the Internet. Nowadays, every traditional service provided by local banks are directly available online, which results in saving time, efforts, money. By e-banking, one can transfer money to any account, can check their account details, can make online payments for services and products, keep track of stock markets and withdraw money at any time through any ATM.

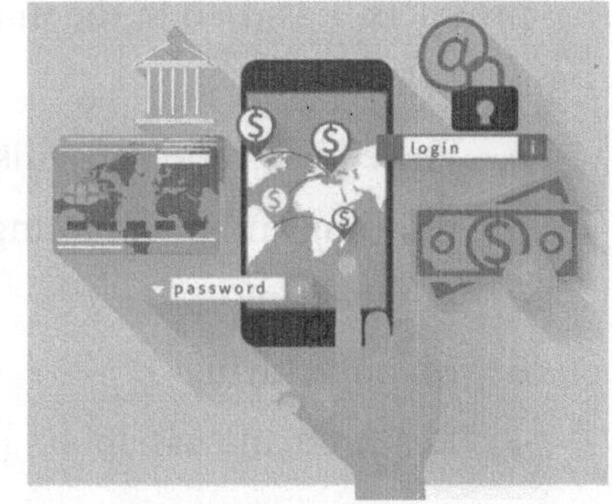

Figure 3.3: ICT in e-banking

- **Entertainment:** The entire entertainment industry has been revolutionized with ICT that provide a variety of activities like computer games. Watching movies, programs on TV, Live TV, Amazon prime video, Netflix, and many more, that provides entertainment contents through the Internet.

Figure 3.4: ICT in entertainment

- **Arts:** Artists have also been encouraged to explore their creativity through photography, painting, drawing, videography, designing like digital tools. It also enables the training and presentation of performing arts like drama, dance, and music.

- **Social media and communication:** Today, one can't imagine their life without mobile phones, social media networks, Facebook, Twitter, Snapchat, and WhatsApp. It helps people to stay connected with their friends and family living far away or near to them, enable accessing information regarding current issues and the use of Internet-based services.

Figure 3.5: ICT in social media and communication

- **Personal healthcare:** The Fitbit, I watch, and many more gadgets wearable gadgets help in monitoring heart rate and provide information on other physical fitness. One can search and learn about diseases according to their symptoms and can read precautions that can be taken to cure it.

Another area of personal life where ICT is used are social and political causes, connectivity to civic facilities, personal assistance, and other facilities.

ICT in the workplace

- **Industries:** Various industries are using robots and artificial intelligence in manufacturing their products. It is used in the mining industry for:
  - o Prospecting
  - o Power generation and distribution in power plants
  - o Building and maintaining networks in telecommunication and design
  - o Engineering
  - o Manufacturing
  - o Research and assembling, along with fault diagnosis and safety tests
- **E-governance:** The tax collection, licenses, exchange of information with citizens, and other government departments like document processing, providing government services can become possible by e-governance and digital India. Through government apps and websites, one can interact directly with the government through a platform provided by ICT.

  For digital empowerment, various apps are launched by the government; some of them are:
  - o BHIM stands for Bharat Interface for Money
  - o GST Rate Finder
  - o MyGov
  - o UMANG
  - o Swachh Bharat Abhiyaan App

Figure 3.6: ICT in e-governance

- **Medical services:** For manufacturing and cutting edge research in the pharmaceutical sector, and ICT is used that also helps in the management of the hospital, administration, doctors, nurses to diagnose, treat, and monitor patients. The advanced machine used for diagnosis and treatment of various diseases is developed by engineers using ICT.
- **Sports:** In the field of sports, various facilities like athletes training, recording speeds of players, selling of tickets, updating scoreboards are provided by ICT.

- **Education and training:** In developing content and conducting classroom training through expert lectures, videos, websites, apps, TV channels can be used for creating and transmitting educational content and providing online training to students effectively by ICT. Currently, various online training educational programs are available, and IGNOU is one of the universities that offer it.

Figure 3.7: ICT in education and training

- **Scientific research:** Reduction of speed, distance, and cost, real-time record of observation, analysis, and collaboration, large computations are some of the fields of scientific research where ICT is used.

Summary

- ICT stands for Information and Communication Technology that includes a set of technological resources and tools used for communication, creation, storing, managing, and disseminating information.
- UNESCO defines informatics as the science dealing with implications of realization, use, design, and maintenance of information processing systems that include software, hardware, human aspects, organizational, commercial, industrial, political, and government.
- Radio, mobile, TV, email are some of the tools of ICT.
- Email stands for electronic mail that reduces the load on the postal system. Nowadays Outlook by Microsoft, Yahoo mail, Hotmail, Rediff mail, and Gmail are major carriers of email messages.
- ICT is used in both personal and business life.
- E-banking enables the transaction anytime, anywhere, through the Internet.

Self-Assessment

MULTIPLE CHOICE QUESTIONS.

1. Which of the following is not a tool of ICT?

   a. Radio b. Mobile c. Email d. Software

2. Which of the following helps the user to stay connected with their friends and family?

   a. Talk b. WhatsApp c. Art d. All

Answer

1. d 2. b

FILL IN THE BLANKS

1. Through ____________ one can buy or sell products online through the Internet after comparing them online and selecting the best one as per our requirements.

2. Transactions can be done anytime, anywhere through the Internet by ________.
3. The taxes collection, licenses, exchange of information with citizens and other government departments can become possible by ______ and __________.
4. BHIM app was launched for digital empowerment, here BHIM stands for __________.

Answer

1. E-commerce 2. E-banking 3. E-Governance, Digital India
4. Bharat Interface for Money

TRUE FALSE

1. Information and communication technology is the full form of ICT (T/F)
2. A lot of postal system in India is being borne now by the Email systems (T/F)
3. ICT is used in Medical services, Sports, Education, and training, Research, etc. (T/F)

Answer

1. False 2. True 3. True

QUESTIONS

1. What do you mean by ICT?
2. What is E-banking? How it has ease the life of human beings.
3. What is the role of ICT in education and training?
4. Describe the radio and mobile as ICT tools.

PROJECT WORK

Prepare a presentation on the importance of various tools of ICT.

SESSION 2: VARIOUS COMPONENTS OF A COMPUTER AND ITS PERIPHERAL DEVICES

Computer is one of the biggest innovations of humankind that is influencing every sphere of life. It is being used in:

- Business
- Defense
- Healthcare
- Entertainment
- Education
- Personal use and more

From the time it was invented to now, there are lots of changes taken place in it like earlier it was unable to do some simple calculations, but now it is capable of performing complex operations and handling multiple tasks. And earlier its size was very big, but now it is reduced too much extend with improvement in quality.

Computer system

Computer stands for Common oriented machines particularly used for trade and education research. Number of instructions being executed by the computer to perform a variety of tasks. Computer is derived from word compute that means to calculate. Due to computer speed, storage capacity, accuracy, and versatility through it user can perform multiple tasks of various fields like:

- Designing
- Accounting
- Editing
- Typing documentation
- Railways and airlines booking
- News broadcasting and more

Along with these various advantages, it has some limitations as it cannot think it's own, it is brainless.

Basic components of computer system

A combination of hardware and software, makes the computer system. All touchable and physical components come under hardware, and instructions given to the computer to perform a particular task comes under software.

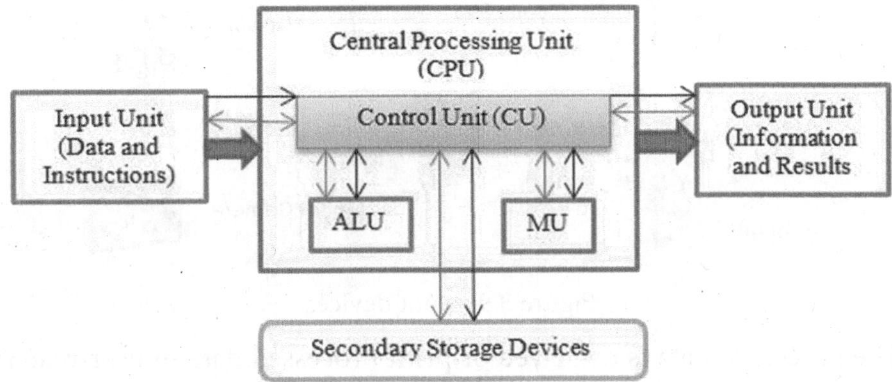

Figure 3.8: Components of computer

Hardware

All physical components of the computer system come under the hardware that includes input devices, output devices, storage devices, and processing devices. Some of the examples of hardware are monitor, keyboard, mouse, printers, CPU, and more.

The motherboard is a very important part of the computer as a number of important and critical components like memory, CPU, and connectors are assembled on the **Printed circuit board (PCB)**. It is made up of rigid plastic sheets, and on this sheet thin layer of aluminum and copper is printed that is known as traces. The computer performance can be enhanced by plugged in video cards, networks like expansion cards on it.

Software

To control the internet operation of computer, a set of programs software is used that instruct computer to do specific tasks. System and application are two types of software. On the computer's most important software is an **operating system (OS)** as to run any application or programs; there is a needfor OS in every general-purpose computer.

It understands input from the keyboard and sends output on the screen. It keeps track of directions and files on storage devices and controls all the peripheral devices connectedto it. Some of the popular operating systems are Windows, Linux, Android, Unix, and more. And there can be a graphic or text-based user interface of OS.

Nowadays, most of the operating systems have Graphical User Interface (GUI) that displays picture and images and enable the user to interact with a computer.

- **Input unit:** Input unit is the process of entering and collecting the data into the computer. All the incoming instructions and data are converted into a pattern of binary codes, which is understood by computers. After that,these binary codes being processed by a processor of the computer system.

Examples of Input devices are:

- o Keyboard
- o Mouse
- o Scanner
- o Joystick
- o Microphone
- o OCR
- o Light pen and more

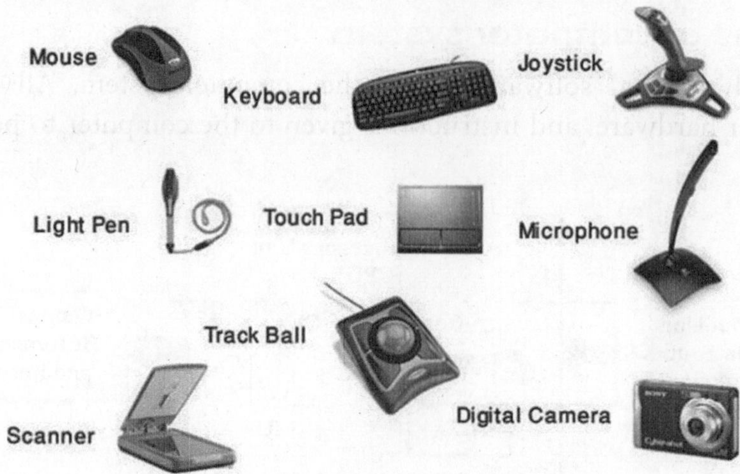

Figure 3.9: Input devices

✦ **Output unit:** The processed data is displayed or print processed data in user-readable form using the output unit. There are a number of output devices attachedto the computer. The output can be in the form of softcopy, hardcopy, or sound file. Some of the common output devices are monitor, printer, webcam, headphones, speaker, and many more.

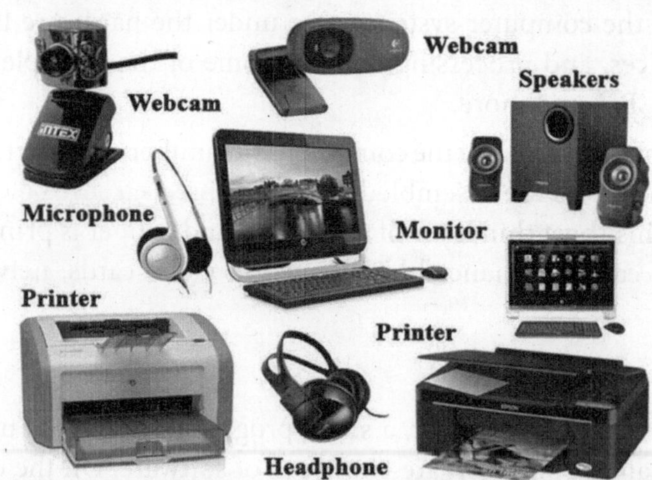

Figure 3.10: Output devices

✦ **CPU:** CPU stands for Central processing unit or processors that are considered as the brain of the computer. Processing is the action taken place to perform logical and arithmetic operations on the data to convert it into results. Another name given to CPU is microprocessor due to its small size that is a type of integrated circuit built on a tiny piece of silicon. A number of operations are performed by transistors in microprocessors that store and manipulate data.

Megahertz (MHz) is the unit to measure the speed of the microprocessor.

CPU consists of Arithmetic and Logical Unit (ALU), a Memory unit (MU), and Control Unit (CU):

- o ALU: ALU stands for the arithmetic logic unit that is used to perform all arithmetic and logical operations on the operands. Addition, subtraction, multiplication, and division are arithmetic operations. Greater than equal to, less than equal to, greater than, less than, not equal to are logic operations.
- o Control unit: The control unit controls the operation of every unit of the computer system and transfer of instructions or data in various units. Control units give a signal to components of a computer to execute any instructions.
- o Memory unit: It is the principle storage of computer that stores both instructions and data. These instructions and data can be stored permanently in the memory unit so that it can be retrieved when required. Other parts of the computer are linked with memory units so that data can be accessed or send to other connected parts.

Internal and external are two categories of computer memory:

- o Internal memory: The default memory of a computer is known as internal memory, main memory, or primary memory. In primary memory, programs or instructions are stored temporarily. It is fast in speed; that's why it is known as immediate access storage but has a very little capacity of storage.

  Random-access memory (RAM) and Read-only memory (ROM) are two internal memories that hold the data temporarily. RAM is volatile in nature as it lost data when the power supply is switched off. On the other hand, ROM is non-volatile, and data and instructions saved in ROM are not lost by switching off the power supply.

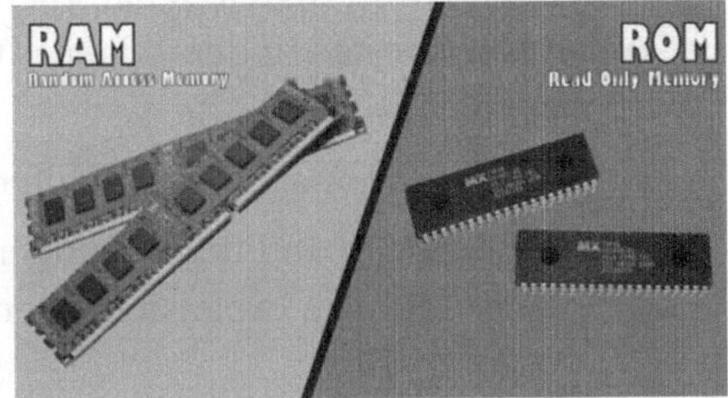

Figure 3.11: Internal memory

- o External memory: It is also known as secondary or auxiliary memory and used due to expensive, temporary, and less storage capacity of internal memory. So that when required, the data can be transferred to external memory from internal memory. It orders to make data permanent; it is used in a secondary storage device that makes it accessible for a long time. The disadvantage of external memory is its low speed.

  Example: CD/DVD, hard disks, pen drive, and more.

Figure 3.12: External memory

Peripheral devices

The input unit, output unit, and storage units are three major units of computer systems that are used for performing primary functions. To perform other functionality, one can connect some external or internal devices to computer systems that is known as peripheral devices.

These are attached to the computer system when there is a need for to perform special functions like video recording, image capturing and connecting to the Internet, and more. These all hardware peripheral devices are attached to computer system and controlled by it but are not coming under main components of computer systems like:

- Memory
- CPU
- Power supply
- Motherboard
- Hard disk
- RAM, and more.

The peripheral devices can be easily attached and removed from the computer system, just like a mouse, keyboard, printer, and scanners that can be easily attached and removed from the system.

The peripheral device can be categorized into two types:

- Internal
- External

Internal peripheral devices

These are part of a computer system and work as internal components. Some of the commonly used internal peripheral devices are:

- **Modem:** Modem stands for modulator/demodulator that is a hardware that allows devices to connect with the Internet. It converts or modulates the analog signal from telephone cable to digital signal before transferring data to the computer system as it understands only digital signal. Then at the computer end, it is converted or demodulates the digital signal into an analog signal.

DID YOU KNOW? The unit of modem speed, in bits per second (bps).

Further, they are classified into internal and external modem:

  - o In the case of an internal modem, there is a circuit board plugged into an expansion slot of the motherboard inside the computer.
  - o On the other hand, there is one small box connected to the telephone line or CPU, and it is kept outside the computer. Either USB or serial port is used to connect it and can be used with more than one computer.

Figure 3.13: Internal and external modem

- **Bluetooth adopter:** By the use of short-wavelength radio waves multiple devices can be connected through Bluetooth. It is able to connect only Bluetooth enabled devices with each other like car stereo and mobile phone, various laptops or computers, etc. The external Bluetooth can be used by embedding Bluetooth adapter in the form of a USB or small dongle.

Figure 3.12: Bluetooth adopter

- **Network Interface Card (NIC):** It is used to connect the computer with the local area network (LAN) and comes in the form of cards that fits in the computer motherboard expansion slot. There is a need for atleast one NIC in every computer that is a part of the network, and most of them are designed for a specific type of protocol, media, and network.

Figure 3.13: Network Inter Card (NIC)

The data flow between network and computer can be control by the network card, and its data rate is measured in Megabits per second (Mbps).

- **Wireless adaptor for Wi-Fi:** Wi-Fi stands for wireless fidelity that allows the computer to connect with the Internet or wirelessly communicate with each other. There is a need for wireless or Wi-Fi adaptor to connect wirelessly, and to enable a Wi-Fi, it is plugged into **peripheral component interconnect (PCI)** slot present inside the computer. Earlier it is generally connected through the USB port, but now most of the systems come with built-in Wi-Fi connectivity.

Figure 3.14: Wireless adaptor

External peripheral devices

Some of the external peripheral devices are:

- **Memory card reader:** Memory card reader enables the read and writing to a memory card and mostly used to transfer data to a computer or other storing devices. The main function of a card is to quickly transfer files to an SD card and taking backup of the most important files. In some memory card reader, there is only one single slot while other has multiple slots for different media and cards. It may be integrated into a computer, printer, and more.

Figure 3.15: Wireless adaptor

- **Smartphones:** Smartphone is a multipurpose computing device that can connect the computer to the internet through Hotspot feature and also enable the exchange of information with the computer. The various advanced features of smartphones are:
    - o Stronger hardware capabilities
    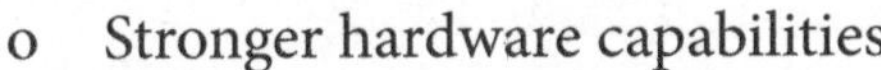
    - o Touch screen display
    - o Multimedia functionality
    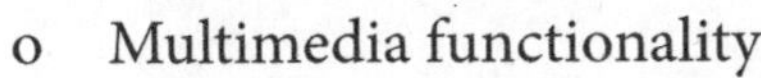
    - o Advanced operating systems
    - o Big size screen and more.

Figure 3.16: Smartphone

- **Digital camera:** This is a hardware device used to capture recording, still pictures, storing videos with sound in the digital formats. The digital or 0's and 1's format is the only format computer understands, and these are tiny dots pixels stored in digital cameras. It enables to display of images on the computer after clicking it, and whenever required, these images can be stored, deleted from the digital camera memory card.

Figure 3.17: Digital camera

- **Smartwatches:** It acts as a support device for smartphones that is synchronized with it using Bluetooth that unable to:
    - o Receive calls
    - o Making calls
    - o Sending messages
    - o Receiving messages
    - o Capturing images and more

  A media playback can be managed by increasing or decreasing voice from your watch. Some of the new generation smartwatch support:
    - o Calculators
    - o Digital maps
    - o Personal organizers
    - o Digital maps

Figure 3.18: Smart watch

GPS navigation, message notifications, calendar synchronization, can be done using smartwatches by accessing the internet.

Summary

- Computer is one of the biggest innovations of humankind that is influencing every sphere of life.
- Computer stands for Common oriented machines particularly used for trade and education research. Number of instructions is executed by a computer to perform a variety of tasks.
- Combination of Hardware and Software make the computer system
- CPU stands for Central processing unit or processors that is considered as the brain of the computer.
- CPU consists of ALU, MU, and CU.
- To do some specific functionality, external or internal devices can be connected to a computer system that is known as peripheral devices.
- The peripheral devices can be easily attached and removed from the computer system, just like a mouse, keyboard, printer, and scanners.

Self-Assessment

MULTIPLE CHOICE QUESTIONS.

1. Which of the following is a Volatile memory?

   a. ROM b. Internal c. External d. RAM

2. ___________ is not an internal peripheral device.

   a. Modem b. Wi-Fi adaptor c. NIC d. Memory card reader

Answer

1. d 2. c 3. c 4. d

FILL IN THE BLANKS

1. ____________ is the brain of computer.
2. ______________ is a multipurpose computing device that can connect computer to the internet through Hotspot feature and enable the exchange of information with a computer.
3. Modem stands for ___________
4. ____________ act as a support device for smartphones.
5. Digital camera is a hardware device used to capture recording, still pictures, storing videos with sound in _____________.

Answer

1. CPU 2. Smartphones 3. Modulator/Demodulator
4. Smart Watches 5. Digital format

TRUE FALSE

1. ROM is a non-volatile memory (T/F)
2. Speed of CPU is measured in Megahertz (MHz) (T/F)

3. CD/DVD, hard disk, pen drive, and RAM are example of External memory (T/F)
4. Modem speed is measured in Bits per second (bps) (T/F)

Answer

1. True 2. True 3. False 4. True

ANSWER THE FOLLOWING QUESTIONS

1. What do you mean by computer? Name various basic components of computer system.
2. Briefly explain the various basic components of computer system.
3. Gives components of CPU and their functioning.
4. Name five each input and output device.
5. What do you mean by peripheral? How peripheral help in doing various tasks.
6. Differentiate internal and external memory.

PROJECT WORK

Make a presentation on various peripheral devices and do a group discussion on it with your friends.

SESSION 3: BASIC OPERATIONS OF A COMPUTER

Computer system is consists of hardware and software; both are interdependent on each other. As computer will not work properly if any of the two is not working. This session helps to learn about various operations of computers like starting it, software and its types, commonly used operating systems and shut down the computer.

Starting computer

To start a computer: Switch on the main power supply | Switches on the UPS and monitor.

- By starting it, the booting process begins that check all the hardware and software installed in the computer is working properly and load all the needed files.
- The next step is a booting process that checks the functionality of all the connected hardware that includes primary and secondary storage devices.
- Once the computer passes the booting process next step is checking of **complementary metal-oxide-semiconductor** (CMOS) chip that stores the settings like password, date, and time of **basic input-output system (BIOS).**
- The BIOS includes instructions for loading basic computer hardware, and its main motive is to boot up an operating system on the computer.
- The operating system is loaded on the RAM after completion of all the steps of BIOS, then to define user configurations, a pre-configuration start-up routine is executed by OS.

Then with your username and password, you can log in to the computer system, and the operating system desktop will appear if you have entered the correct credentials. In some systems, you will not find the option of entering a username and password if you have not set it.

Shut down a computer

To shut down the computer simply click on Start button present on Desktop | Click on **Shut down** option This will fade away the desktop, and the computer will gradually shut down.

Software and its types

In general, sense software is a set of instructions or programs instructing a computer to do specific tasks, or it is a generic term used to describe programs of the computer. It tells the hardware to do possible tasks and enhances the capability of the hardware and directs computer for performing various operations.

Computer software is a programming code (either machine-level or code written for an operating system) that is executed on a computer processor.

The two types of software are:

- System software
- Application software

System software

It is collections of single or multiple programs that manage or control the overall performance and operation of a computer system. It is an interface between computer and user that is used for reading data from input devices, transmissions of information from input to output devices, and it also checks the order of working internal and external peripheral devices. It also converts instructions and data into 0's and 1's form that is understood by computer.

The four categories of system software are:

- Operating system
- Language processors
- Device drivers
- Utility software

These four are interrelated to each other.

Operating system: When you switch on the computer, OS is the first program that is a load on the computer. It is an interface between hardware and software of a computer that manages the overall functionality of the computer and its resources. It also monitors and controls the execution of other applications and programs by performing sending output to monitor, recognizing input from the keyboard, and controlling peripheral devices.

Examples: Windows, Macintosh (Mac), DOS, and Unix.

Objectives:

- The main objective of an operating system is to provide an interface between user and computer.
- Blocking unauthorized access to the system by securing the system.
- Managing and sharing of computer system hardware and software resources.
- Communicate with each user and application to get the status of any errors and operations.

Components of OS: To performing and achieving the objectives, shell and kernel are two main components of the operating system:

- Shell is an interface and outermost layer of OS that handle the interaction with users. It quick the process of taking input, then interprets it for OS and handles the output come from it.

- Kernel is an interface and core component of OS that handles the interaction between data processing and applications done at the hardware level. It is the first program that runs on an operating system when it is loaded into the memory and remains there until OS is not shut down.

The main functioning of the kernel is to:

- Manage input or output
- Manage memory
- Process management for execution of application and control system calls

The following are the functioning of OS:

- **Management of processor:** Various jobs are allocated to a processor to manage its working, and functions received enough time by every instructions by every instruction.
- **Management of memory:** The sharing of internal memory with various applications is managed by OS. It also ensures that memory allocated to one application is not used by others.
- **Management of file:** The storing, copying, deleting, and creation of files are handled by OS. It also maintains the integrity of stored data in these files.
- **Management of device:** OS also controls the working of all input and output devices by performing tasks according to the received requests from these devices and then communicates it back to requesting processes.
- **Security:** The confidentiality and integrity of the user's data are ensure by various techniques provided by the operating system. It provides username and password to protect the system from unauthorized access, activates firewalls that protect the system against instruction, and displays messages related to the vulnerability of the system.
- **Detection of errors:** OS checks system for any external threat or malicious software activity. It also checks hardware for any type of damage, and various alerts are displayed by OS so that users can take appropriate action to protect their system.

Types of OS

This section will study various types of the operating system. By evaluation the operating system, computers have taken a massive step towards high and excellent performance.

- **Batch OS:** The batch OS users cant directly interacts with the computer. In this type of OS, every user prepares their own job on a punch card like an offline device and submits it to the computer operator.
- **Time-sharing or multi-tasking OS:** The Multi-tasking OS enables users located at different shell or terminal to use a single computer system at the same time. The OS that is able to perform multiple tasks or processes using a single CPU or processor, then it is known as Multi-tasking OS.
- **Real-Time OS (RTOS):** RTOS is designed to handle real-life scenarios problems and has very short respond time to inputs; it can prioritize the processes and able to work independently. It is used in space software systems, military software systems, and booking air tickets.
- **Single user OS:** In this type of OS, and only a single user can access the resources at a particular time. Microsoft Windows 3.1, Microsoft DOS, and Microsoft 95 are some of the common single-user OS.
- **Multi-user OS:** It allows us to use more than one user to use the same computer at the same time. Unix, Linux, Microsoft window 2000, and many more are some of the multi-user OS. Windows 2000 was the first version of windows that allow creating multiple user accounts on a single machine.

- **Distributed OS:** It runs on computers located at different geographical areas interconnected through networks. It uses these number of processors located in different machines to provide a very fast computation to the users. The linked machines are allowed to access software, data, and process the tasks over a geographical network.
- **Multi-threading OS:** This type of OS allows us to run different parts of the program and application simultaneously. The execution response of some processes can get delayed due to the feature of multithreading.

Disk Operating System

Disk Operating System (DOS) is a type of system software that runs from a hard disk drive. This also refers to the specific family of DOS, which is known as a Microsoft disk operating system (MS-DOS). An operating system is anything that controls and commands the hardware of the computer and its peripheral device's control over the program and its functionality. DOS can support:

- Multiple networking
- Text editing functions
- Multiple directories
- Enhanced management of memory
- Disk compression and fragmentation

It is not easy to use for beginners due to its command-line utility, and it does not support multitasking as only one program can be run at a time. This OS is known as a disk operating system because it runs through hard disk. The IBM PC DOS was a rebranded version after that Apple, Apple Pro, Atari, Commodore, and TRSDOS are other companies that have manufactured it.

The following are the steps to open DOS:

- Click on **Start** | **All Programs** | Select **DOS** or command prompt
- Choose **Start** | Type Dos in search programs and files box | Click on the command prompt.

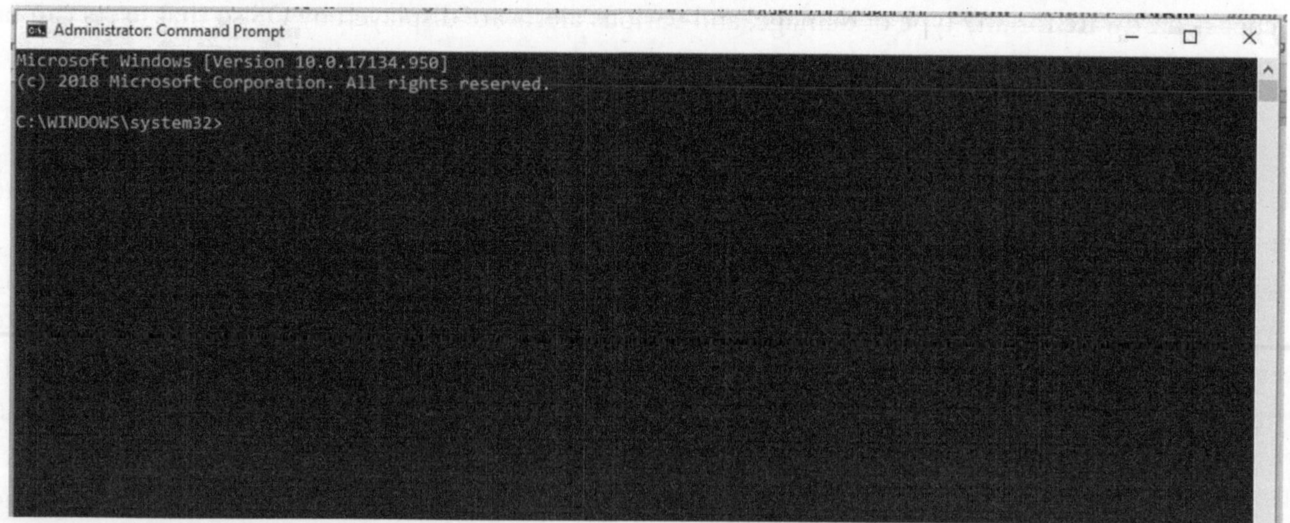

Figure 3.19: DOS prompt

The following are the features of DOS:

- The mouse cannot be used to operate it, Input in it is through basic system commands. It is a free OS.
- It uses a text-based interface and requires text and codes to operate.
- It does not support a graphical interface.
- It is a single-user operating system.

- It is a character-based interface system. It provides a command-line interface that allows users to type commands on DOS Prompt.
- It supports independent device input and output processes, or in another word, it can be said that it has the ability to function on a wide variety of devices regardless of the used software and hardware.
- It is programmed in assembly language that converts commands to binary language. Its speed is very high as compared to other operating systems.
- It provides an advanced error recovery feature as the user can attempt recovery on the occurrence of any failure rather than rebooting the OS.
- It is very helpful in making file management, for example, creating, editing, deleting files, and more.

The following are the advantages of DOS:

- We have direct access to the BIOS and its underlying hardware.
- Due to its size, it will boot much faster than any windows version; thus, it will run in a smaller system.
- It is very lightweight, so it does not have the overhead of the multitasking operating system.
- It is good for making workarounds for managing/administering an MS system, and for combining programs.

The following are the disadvantages of DOS:

- No multi-tasking supported by the OS.
- Difficulty in memory access when addressing more than 640 MB of RAM.
- Interrupt levels for hardware needs to be managed by our self.
- Automatic IRQ ordering is not supported by the OS.

LINUX

Linux OS is an open and free source that was developed by Linus Torvalds in 1991 at AT & T's Bell Laboratories. The main function of Linux OS is to manage the system resources or hardware and can act as an interface between user and computer system just like other OS. It was designed by considering UNIX compatibility; that's why its functioning is similar to UNIX. From the last 2 decades, it has become very popular due to its various features, as given in the below section.

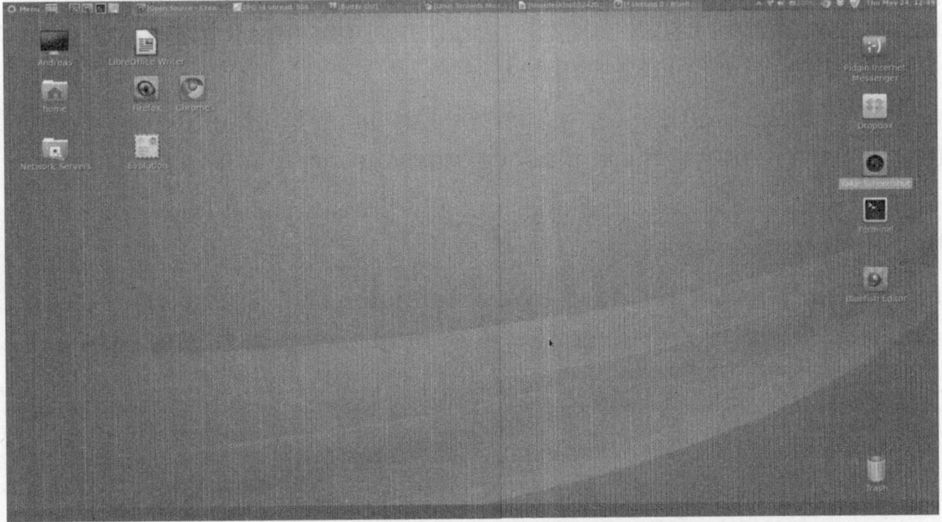

Figure 3.20: Linux desktop

The following are the Features of Linux:

- **Portable:** Portability means software can works on different types of the hardwares in the same way. Linux kernel and application programs support their installation on any kind of hardware platform.
- **Open source:** Linux source code is freely available, and it is a community based development project. Multiple teams work in collaboration to enhance the capability of the Linux operating system, and it is continuously evolving.
- **Multi-user:** Linux is a multiuser system that means multiple users can access system resources like memory/ ram/ application programs at the same time.
- **Multiprogramming:** Linux is a multiprogramming system that means multiple applications can run at the same time.
- **Hierarchical file system:** Linux provides a standard file structure in which system files/ user files are arranged.
- **Shell:** Linux provides a special interpreter program which can be used to execute commands of the operating system. It can be used to do various types of operations, call application programs and more.
- **Security:** Linux provides user security using authentication features like password protection/ controlled access to specific files/ encryption of data.
- **Live CD/USB:** Almost all Linux distros provide live CD/USB so that users can run/try it without installing it.
- **Application support:** It has its own software repository from where users can download and install many applications.

EDUBUNTU

It has a Graphical User Interface (GUI) that is known as Unity that allows users to interact with the computer system using graphical icons. It allows accessing your data on the web or your computer in a faster way. Earlier its name was Ubuntu Education Edition as it is built on the Ubuntu base. It is one of the best available free software that is designed for homes and computers.

The following are the features of Edubuntu:

- It is compatible with the existing operating systems on the computer machines and happily coexists with them and can share files with these operating systems.
- Due to the lack of specialized IT staff, educational institutions find it better to use Edubuntu because it enjoys Unix-like security from malware and viruses.
- A single server can manage multiple computer systems using Edubuntu, making it easily manageable. Edubuntu often helps in reducing the amount of time you spend administrating your computers.
- Edubuntu is free of cost, and therefore it does not add pressure on budgets of educational institutions while providing all the technologies.
- The main feature is the support provided by communities and experts can be contacted directly via mailing lists and IRC channels, including the Edubuntu developers themselves.

The following are the components of Edubuntu:

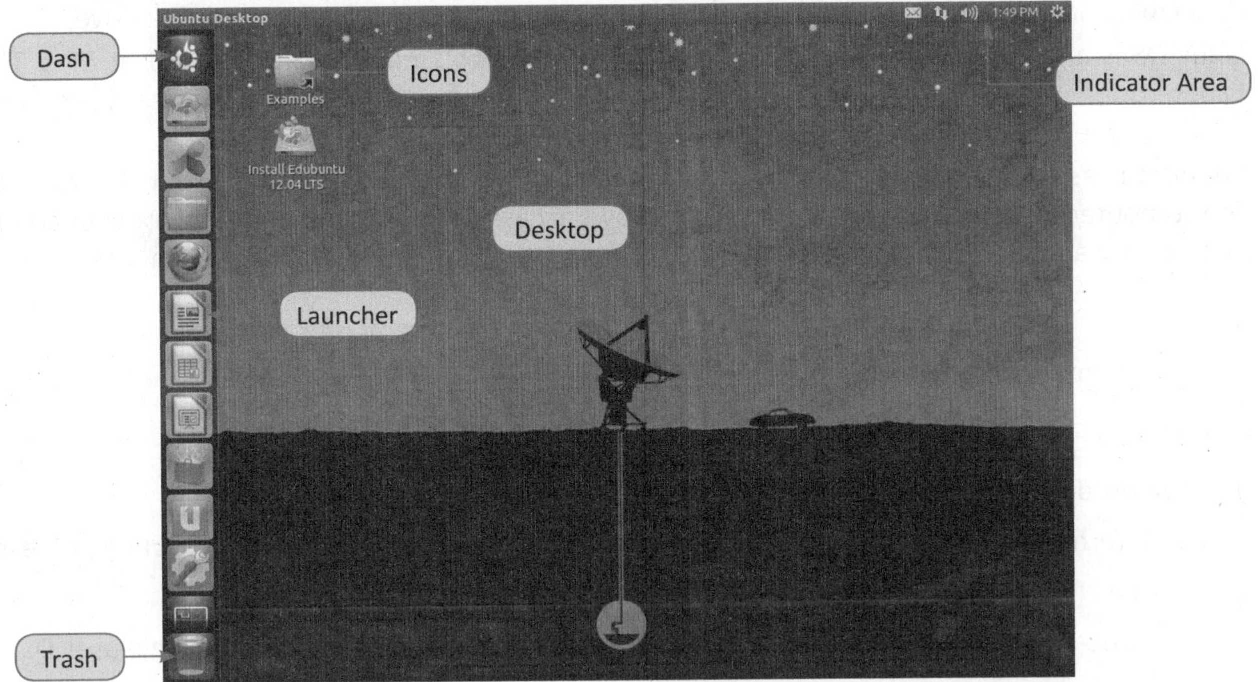

Figure 3.21: Edubuntu desktop

- **Desktop:** Desktop is the first thing that appears on turning on the computer. It has two bars, one on the left and the other on top. A desktop wallpaper is the image at the background of a desktop. Icons are small labeled symbols and pictures present on the desktop that are used to open some documents or programs.
- **Indicator area:** There is an Indicator area on the right side of the Menu bar that shows a calendar, clock, speaker volume, and more.
- **Launcher:** It is present on the left side of the desktop where the user adds their commonly used programs to access it easily. It also shows currently running application icons. All deleted files are stored in the trash..
- **The Dash:** It is present on top of the Launcher bar with the Edubuntu logo on it. A window will open towards the right side by clicking on the Dash icon that consists of the search bar at the top and icons of recently used applications, downloaded items, and files at the bottom.

Summary

- Computer system is consists of hardware and software; both are interdependent on each other.
- To start a computer, switch on the main power supply then switches on the UPS and monitor.
- The operating system is loaded on the RAM after completion of all the steps of BIOS, then to define user configurations, a pre-configuration start-up routine is executed by OS.
- To shut down the computer simply click on Start button present on **Desktop** | Click on **Shut down** option
- In general, sense software is a set of instructions or programs instructing a computer to do specific tasks, or it is a generic term used to describe programs of the computer.
- System software and application software are two types of software.
- Operating systems, language processors, device drivers, and utility software are four categories of system software.

- Shell and kernel are two components of OS.
- **Disk Operating System (DOS)** is a type of system software that runs from a hard disk drive.
- Linux OS is an open and free source that was developed by Linus Torvalds in 1991 at AT & T's Bell Laboratories. The main function of Linux OS is to manage the system resources or hardware and can act as an interface between user and computer system just like other OS.
- Edubuntu has a **Graphical User Interface (GUI)** that is known as Unity that allows users to interact with the computer system using graphical icons. It allows accessing your data on the web or your computer in a faster way.

Self-Assessment

MULTIPLE CHOICE QUESTIONS.

1. Password, Date, Time settings of BIOS are stored in ____________.
   a. Internal memory b. CMOS chip c. External memory d. Booting process
2. Through ________ OS one can perform multiple tasks using a single CPU
   a. Time-sharing OS b. Batch OS c. Multi-user OS d. Single user OS

Answer

1. B 2. C 3. A 4. C

FILL IN THE BLANKS

1. ____________ process checks the functionality of all the connected hardware that includes primary and secondary storage devices.
2. CMOS stands for ______________.
3. _________ support multiple networking, text editing functions, multiple directories, enhanced management of memory, disk compression and fragmentation.
4. Linux OS was developed by ________ in 1991 at AT and T's Bell Lab.
5. _________ is present on the left side of Edubuntu desktop where the user adds their commonly used programs to access it easily.

Answer

1. Booting process
2. Complementary metal-oxide semiconductor
3. DOS
4. Linus Torvalds
5. Launcher

TRUE FALSE

1. Shell is an interface and outermost layer of OS that handle the interaction with users. (T/F)
2. DOS uses a text-based interface and requires text and codes to operate (T/F)
3. DOS support multi-tasking (T/F)
4. Edubuntu allows users to interact with the computer system using graphical icons. (T/F)

Answer

1. True 2. True 3. False 4. True

ANSWER THE FOLLOWING QUESTIONS:

1. Write down the steps to start a computer.
2. What are operating systems and its objectives?
3. Name types of the operating system. Briefly describe any 3.
4. What is the full form of DOS? Give a brief description about it along with steps to open it.
5. When and who has developed the Linux. Give various features of Linux.

PRACTICAL WORK

Make a presentation on various types of the operating system.

SESSION 4: INTERNET AND ITS APPLICATIONS

Around the world, the internet is considered as a huge network of computers through which one can get any information stored on a web page on the World Wide Web. It is one of the largest databases available to us permanently and has become an important part of life. This all can be done by simply connecting your system to the Internet.

The tasks like shopping, banking, and communication can be done online, which were done through personal interaction. Through it in a few minutes, a message can be sent across the globe, anything can be bought online, and any transaction or information regarding transactions and balance can be check by sitting at home only.

Uses of internet

The Internet has been the most useful technology of modern times that help us in our daily lives, development of personal and professional lives.

- The Internet is used for communication.
- Gathering information by users for educational purposes.
- It is used by business professionals or doctors to filter the necessary information for their use.
- It is used in maintaining contacts with friends and relatives or with clients
- It is used for online shopping.
- It is used for Entertainment purposes by playing videos on YouTube, or watching serials on Netflix, and more.
- Internet in Office spaces allows having conferences and meetings over the Internet.
- It is used for online booking tickets of hotel, movies, trains, plane, and bus.
- Used for social networking as one can share their interests, stories, and knowledge with their friends and family around the world through Twitter, Facebook, and more.

Common terms used in internet

- ✦ **Internet browser:** Internet browser, Internet application software, and Web browser is an important software for connecting to the Internet. It is an interface between the World Wide Web and user that can be GUI based like:

- o Google Chrome
- o Internet Explorer
- o Opera
- o Mozilla Firefox
- o Lynx

The address or URL is type on the address bar of web page | press Go or Press Enter key; this will take you to type address site.

Every webpage has their unique URL. The web browser has facilities like:

- o Password management
- o Bookmarks and downloads
- o Spell checking
- o Tabbed browser
- o HTML access keys
- o Pop-up blocking
- o Search engine toolbars like functions

This software is specifically designed to convert HTML and XML computer code into human-readable documents:

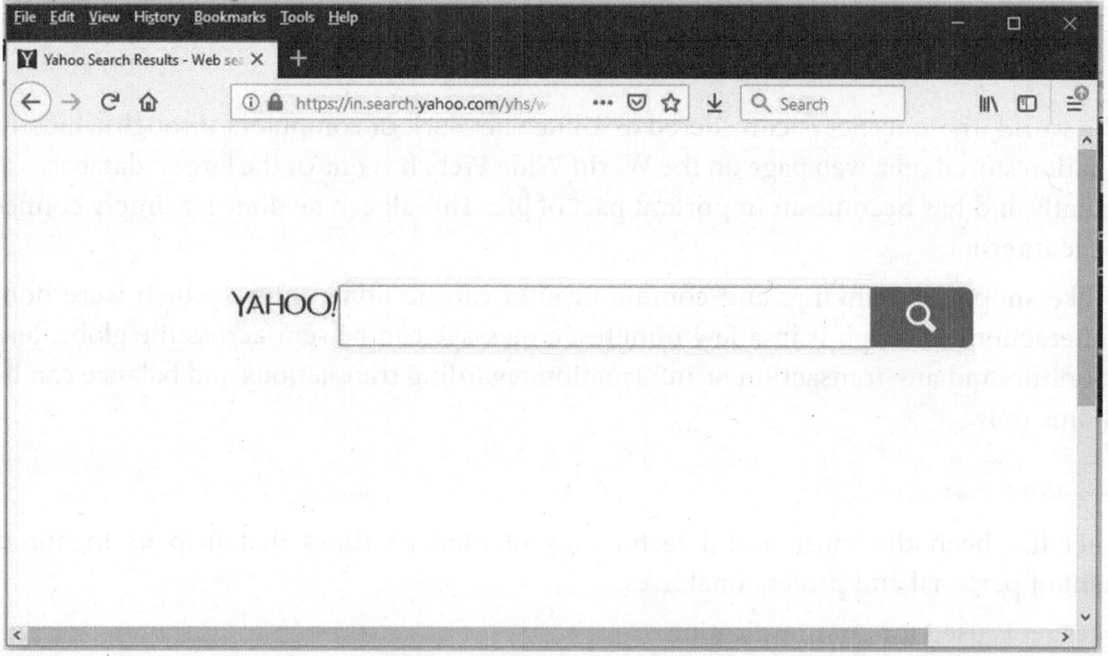

Figure 3.22: Internet browser

- **Webpages and websites:** Webpage is a digital page that contains:
  - o Hyperlinks
  - o Audios
  - o Tables
  - o Text
  - o Images and more

  The **Extensible Markup Language (XML)**, **Hypertext Markup Language (HTML)** and **Hypertext Pre-processor (PHP)**, and more markup languages are used to write webpages.

  Every web page has its unique web address that is known as **Universal Resource Locator (URL)**. A webpage is what you have seen in your browser when you are on the internet. On the other hand, websites are the parent web page or a name given to the collection of web pages by which the collection is known. Some commonly used websites are www.yahoo.com, www.rediff.com, www.google.com, and more.

- **Web portal:** It is a specially designed website that serves as a single point of access for information that can also be considered as a personalized or categorized content library. It helps in search navigation, information integration, notification, and personalization. It also provides features like collaboration, task management, application integration, and business intelligence.

Example of a web portal or portal is Internet portal of employees of the organization; educational institute provides separate portals for teachers, students, administration.

Email application

Email stands for Electronic mail that is the most popular internet application used to send or receive messages between various users. Earlier letters were sent to each other, and to have letters in hand, people have to wait for days. But now, with the invention of email, one can send and receive messages in a few seconds if the Internet is present. One can also send attachments like songs, images, videos, compressed files, documents, and more.

- **Email account:** Email account is an electronic mailbox on a network where a user sends emails or messages. As mentioned above user must have a register email address to send messages, and the user uses these account name and password to send messages and mention the email address of the user to who he/she wants to send a mail.
- **Email address:** The email address of the user is a must to use the services the email services that are a unique name to identify accounts on a network. There is a needfor email address of both the sender and receiver to send and receive emails. Both the postal address and email address are the same, and the recipient's email address is entered in the header part while sending email so that the computer sends it to the correct person.
- Email address is not case sensitive that means address can be written either in small or capital letters and doesn't contain any spaces between their names.
- User name and domain or host computer name are two parts of the email address separated by @ symbol. Where user name is the name of a personal account and domain name is the location of persons account separated with (at the rate) or @ symbol.
- The domain name is followed by domain extension that indicates the type of organization. For example, .com stands for a commercial organization.

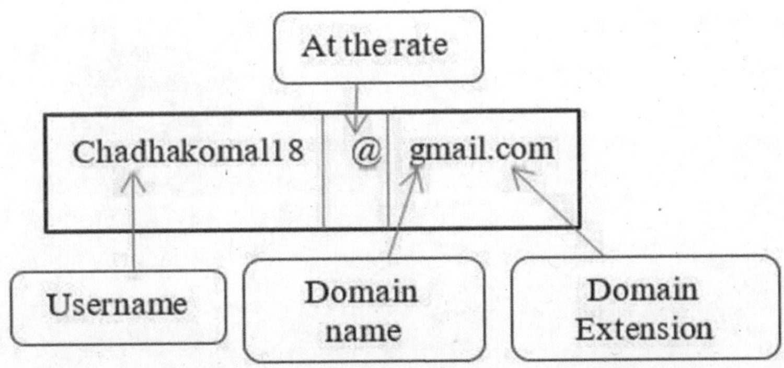

Figure 3.23: Elements of Electronic Mail

Example of email address: Chadhakomal18@gmail.com

Creating a Gmail account

First will start with creating an email account in Gmail, and in this case there is a need of the system, internet connection, and any web browser. The steps to create a Gmail account are:

1. Open web browser by double click on it
2. Type www.gmail.com in the address bar given on the top of Google Chrome browser window:

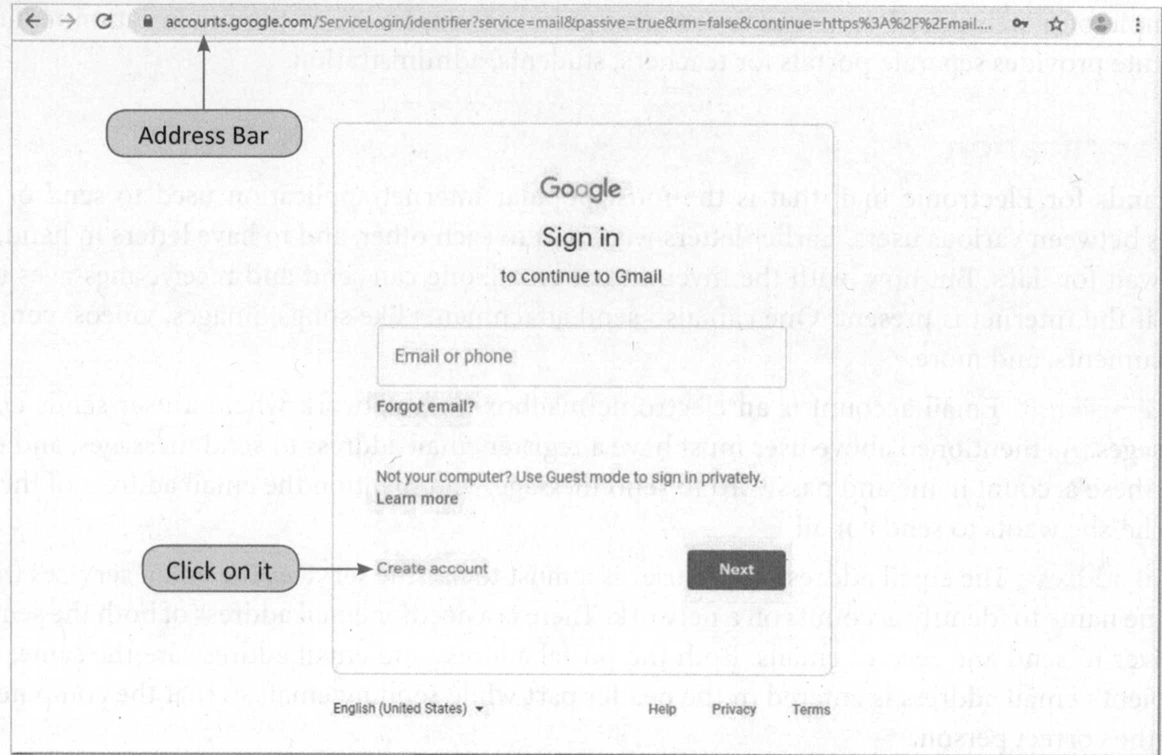

Figure 3.24: Sign up page of Gmail

3. Click on **Create account**. A registration form will appear on the screen:

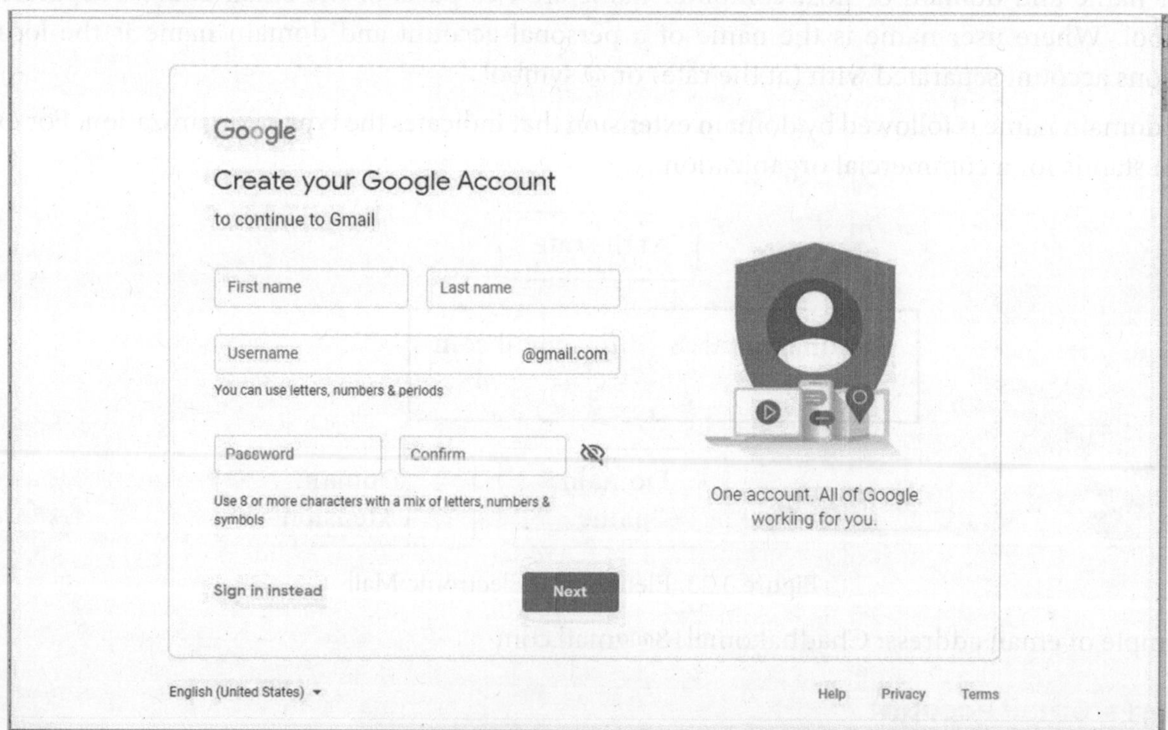

Figure 3.25: Registration form of Gmail

4. Fill First name and last name in the blank field.
5. Type username that you can recall. If the error comes of an existing username, then change it.
6. Type password that contains alphabets, numbers, special keys, and more.

7. Click on **Next** button given in the bottom:

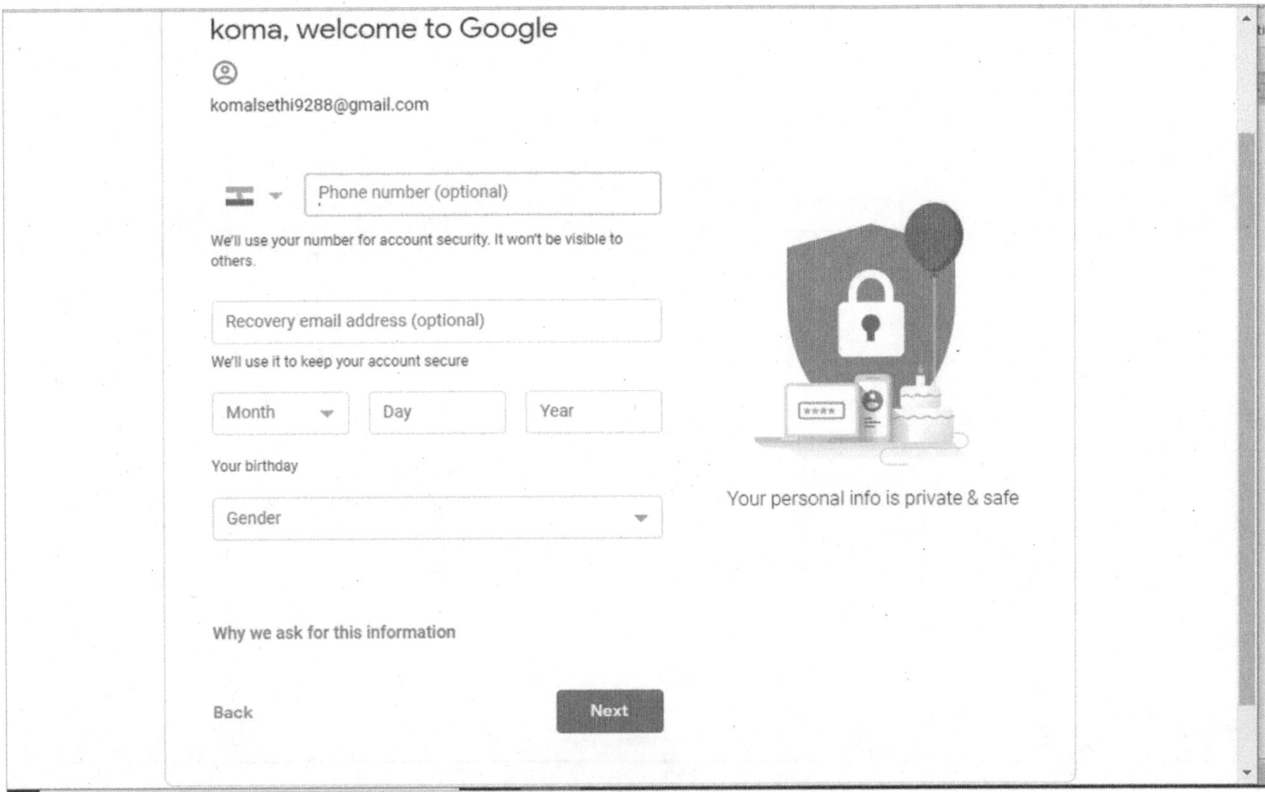

Figure 3.26: Registration form of Gmail

8. Fill the rest of the details and click on the **Next** button given in the bottom.
9. Verify your phone number by entering the verification code sent to your entered contact number.

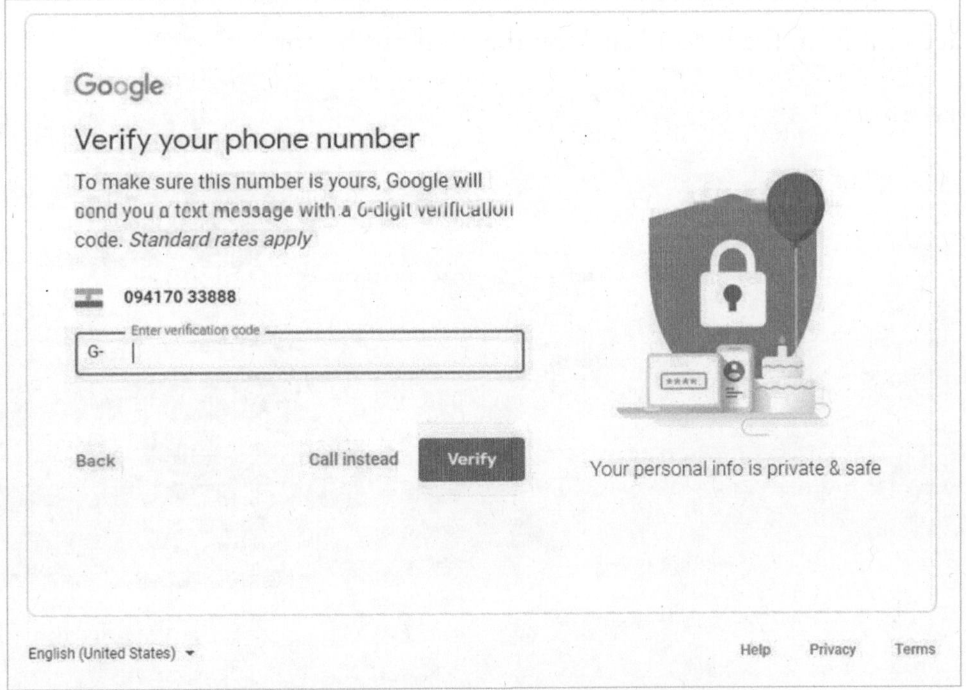

Figure 3.27: Phone verification window

10. If all the information entered by the user is correct, then your account will be created, and Gmail inbox screen will appear:

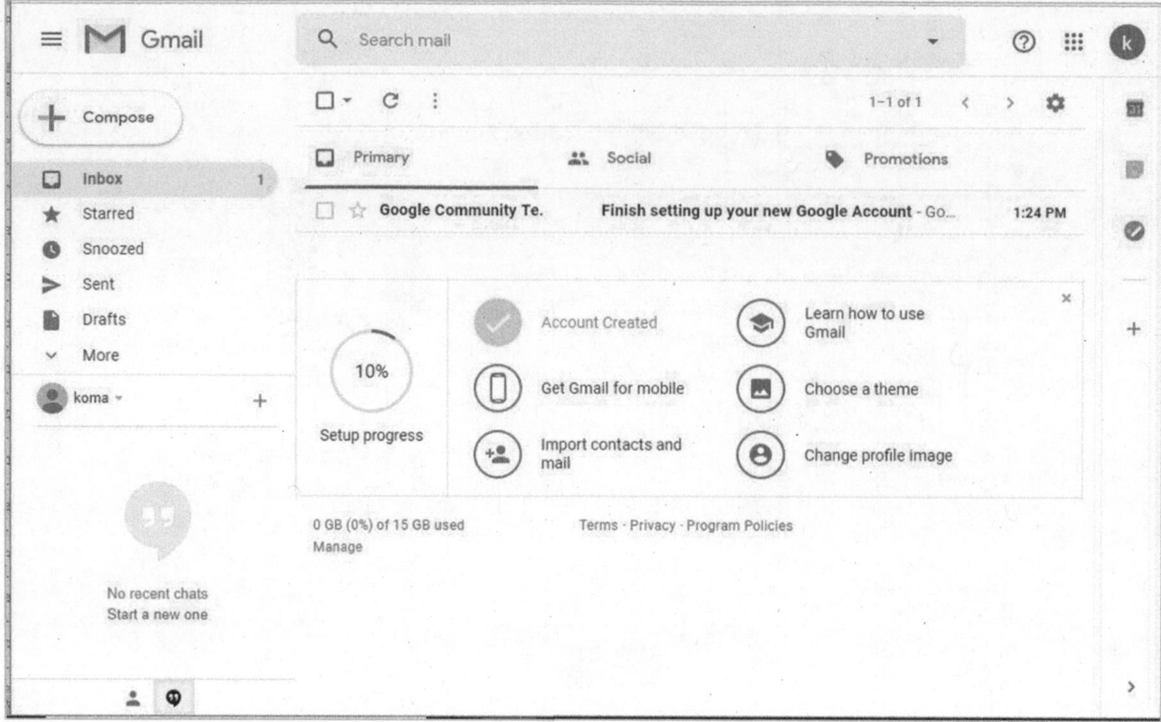

Figure 3.28: Gmail inbox window

Signing out from a Gmail account

The steps need to perform to sign out from Gmail account is:

1. Click on username drop-down arrow.
2. Select your account from the list and click on the **Sign out** button.

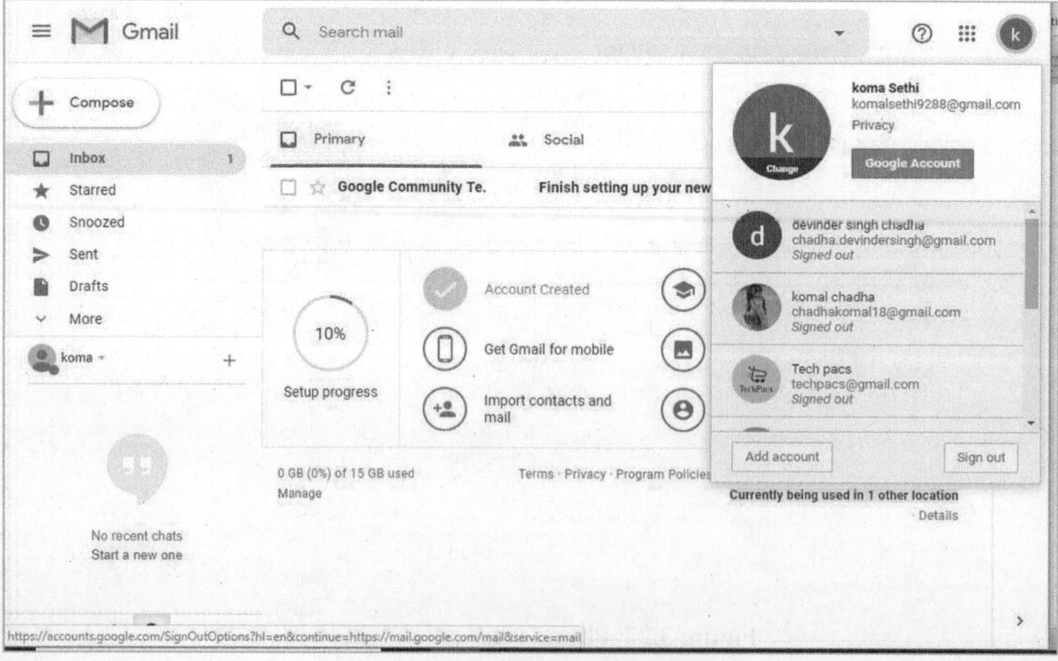

Figure 3.29: Sign out of Gmail

Compose an email message

To compose a mail performs the following steps:

Click on **Compose** button given on the upper left corner of default Gmail window | Fill different fields given in newly opened window:

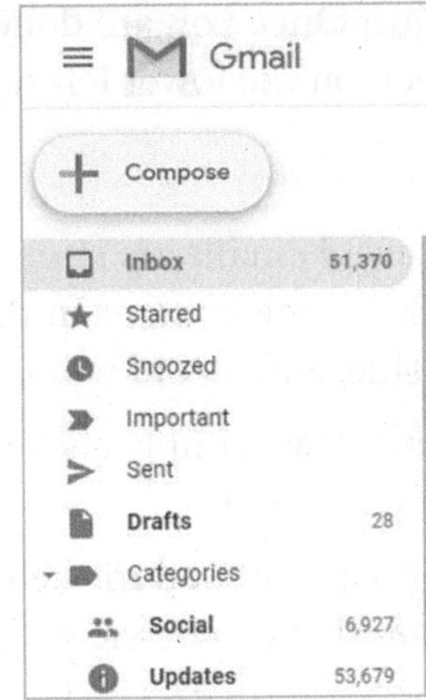

Figure 3.30: Composing a new email

Various fields are:

- **To:** Here user has to give the email address of recipients to whom you want to send the email. Users can also give multiple addresses separated by a comma.

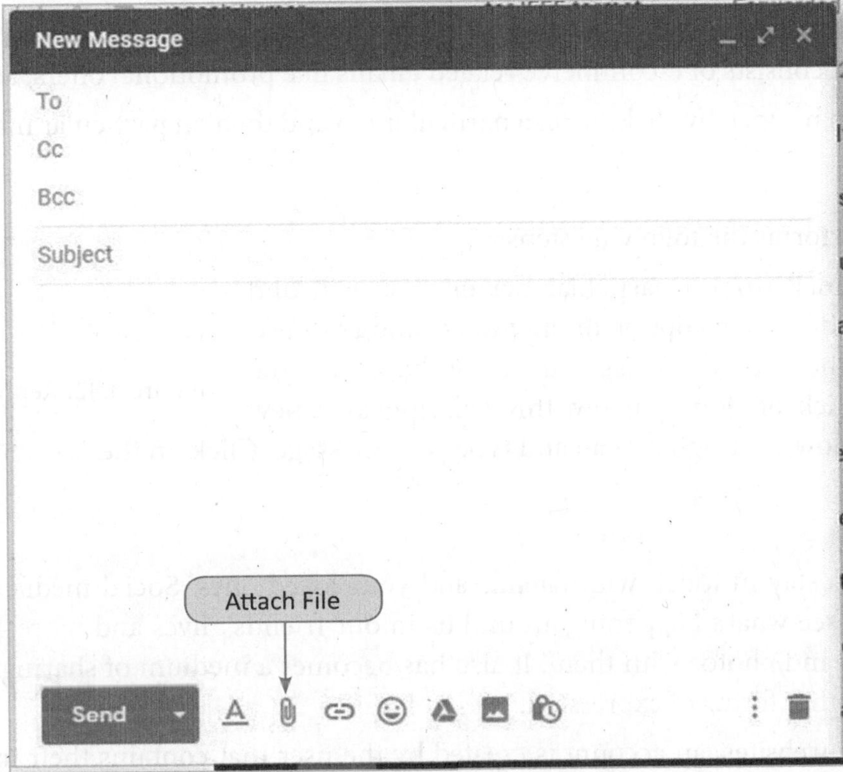

Figure 3.31: Composing mail window

- **Cc:** Cc stands for carbon copy, and multiple addresses can be given in this field to send the same mail to a number of persons. The address given in this field will be visible to all the recipients of the mail.
- **Bcc:** Bcc stands for Blind carbon copy. You can add multiple addresses in this field, but the other recipients are not visible to them.
- **Subject:** Here will write a concise one-line message to give an idea about the sent mail.
- **Body:** This will contain the main message. Here the user will write the message according to the type of mail, whether formal or informal. Try to keep your mail concise and meaningful. In case of having a message greater than one page, add a file in attachment.
- **Attach file:** In this user can add various files like audio, document, video, and more.

- **Send:** Once you are done with writing and attaching files, the next step is to click on the Send button given on the lower left side.

Receiving emails

All received emails are stored in the Inbox along with the details like the sender's name, subject line, time, date, and some content in the mail when we receive an email. By default, newer mails are stored on the upper side, and all old will start going downward on receiving any new mail. We can also arrange its order.

To open a mail, simply click on the **Inbox** button | Take the cursor on particular mail you want to open and double click on it.

It will open the mail in the message window. The received mail can also contain attachments along with messages that can be view by clicking on it, or one can also download these attachments.

There are mainly three tabs in the Inbox are:

- Primary tab: It consists of emails from your friends, family, colleagues, and more.
- Social tab: It consists of emails from social media like Facebook, Twitter, and more.
- Promotion tab: It consists of e-commerce related emails like promotional offers, adds, and more.

Any type of mails can be open by clicking on a particular tab and then on particular mail you want to open.

Reply to emails

To reply an email performs the following steps:

Click on received email from a particular person. You will find **Reply, Reply All,** and **Forward** option or only **Reply** and **Forward** option right below the opened message. Once you have read the received message, click on **Reply** arrow, this will appear a new compose window below the original mail and type your message. Click on the **Send** button.

Figure 3.32: Reply and Forward option

Introduction to social media

The Internet helps to stay in touch with friends and your loved ones. Social media sites like Facebook, Twitter enable us to see what's happening around us in our friends' lives and more. YouTube and Flickt allow sharing videos and photos with them. It also has becomes a medium of sharing information, ideas, career interest, and other forms of expression.

In social networking websites, an account is created by the user that contains their information and add some specific persons to whom they want to share their information and ideas. This section contains some brief detail about some of the social networking sites are.

Twitter

Twitter is an online news and social networking service on which users post and interacts with messages known as tweets. Before 7 Nov 2017, tweets were limited to only 140 words, but now its limits are increased and becomes double for all languages except Korean, Japanese, and Chinese. It is considered as 13th most visited websites worldwide, and some of its salient features are:

- **Tweets:** The short message broadcasted and communicated by a subscriber is known as tweets. As mentioned above, now its length becomes 280 characters except for some languages. The retweeting is the process of reposting someone's messages, and posting messages by yourself is known as Tweeting. Through twitter, one can send messages or news worldwide within a few seconds.

- **Twitter handle:** It is a term used for the user's account name on Twitter that is listed by putting @ symbol before the username.
- **Hashtags:** The topics or keywords are highlighted in it by putting the # hash symbol before it.
- **Follow:** By following people, one can get connected with them, and for not getting tweet of some specific person on your feed, you can unfollow them.
- **Timeline or Twitter feed:** It is an ongoing stream of tweets from the users that are followed by you.

Facebook

Facebook is the world's biggest social media website that covers around billion users worldwide. It provides user-friendly platform by creating your free account on it. When it comes in existence, it can only be used in PC, but now it becomes a default app in almost every mobile phone and tablet. Some of the common features used in it are:

- **Friend list:** Friend list is the list of people whom you are accepted to see your profile and information shared by you.
- **Walls:** It is the board or area where user posts their pictures, messages, videos, links, and more.
- **Virtual photo albums:** One can upload number of photos and also tag anyone in it. Further other connected person can comment or like the photos posted by you.
- **Status update:** These are the messages or any announcement one want to share with their friends
- **Facebook page:** One can also create a Facebook page to publish contents on public page and receive comments on it. Initially, it was created for business purpose.
- **Newsfeed:** It includes the status, updates, pictures, videos, and more shared by your friends or pages like by you.
- **Privacy controls:** One can put privacy by going in setting to protect their information from getting exposed to other person who are not in your friend list.

YouTube

It is a free online video sharing service that has now acquired by Google. One can search for video, songs, movies, exercise tips, comedy, and tutorial to learn something on it. Any person can upload their video on YouTube by creating user Id and password, and all other person can see it. One can also have access of some videos by subscribe it and give view, rate, share, like, add to favorite, comments on it.

- YouTube also earns advertising revenue from Google, AdSense, a program that targets ads according to the contents and audience on site.
- One can download YouTube videos and upload their videos by simply using their created user Id and password by this; you will create your own channel.
- One can check previously viewed videos by checking History option given on it.
- One can check their liked videos.
- You can use snip and combine like various editing tools to give professional look to your video.
- One can set privacy by choosing privacy settings of your channel and change the default public to private that restricts other than people who have subscribed you to view your videos.
- One can restrict some videos to be watch by your kids by employing parental control and safety mode features.

WhatsApp

It is a fireware and cross-platform messaging service that allows sending messages, pictures, and videos. One can also do voice or video call with other person across the world. This application runs from a mobile device, and some of its facts are:

- This App was created by Mountain view California based WhatsApp Inc., but in 2014 it was acquired by Facebook for approximately 19.3 billion US dollars.
- It is consider as most popular instant messaging apps by having more than 1.5 billion active users.
- Earlier it was developed only for text messages, but now one can share other documents with it and also do voice or video calls.
- One can also do group calling, group chatting, location sharing, that makes it more popular throughout the world.
- One can add various emojis and other things to make their text more innovative.

DIGITAL INDIA

'Digital India' is a program initiated by Prime Minister Mr. Narendra Modi. The motive behind the Digital India mission is to build participative, transparent, and responsive governance to reach out the citizens. It aims to provide all services electronically and promote digital literacy in India with the help of digital technologies, which includes the concept of cloud computing, and mobile applications have emerged as the catalysts for express economic growth and citizen empowerment.

In this perspective, companies all over the world desire to invest in digital India mission. Remarkably, global investors like Sundar Pichai, Satya Nadella, Elon Musk have supported Modi's Digital India initiative. It is a modest step to promote E-governance or m-governance.

The objectives of this program are as follows:

- To know how the e-governance process takes the help of technologies and connectivity to improve the quality of life.
- To find out how the government services can work effectively with practical solution projects and innovative ideas to translate the vision of a digital India.
- To find out how the benefits of exercise of digital India and its impact in economy.
- To draw out some necessary suggestion to make Digital India fruitful.
- To create job opportunities.
- To avail the government services to every citizen.

Aadhaar, Digilocker, Permanent Account Number (PAN), All India Council of Technical Education (AICTE), e-District, Passport, Central Board of Secondary Education (CBSE), Indian railway ticket booking, and many more are services provided by Digital India.

Summary

- In 15, Aug. 1995 Internet services were come in existence through Videsh Sanchar Nigam Limited (VSNL). Then it becomes available for Tata, Reliance, Airtel, and more private sectors in 1998.
- Around the world, internet is consider as a huge network of computers through which one can get any information stored in a web page on World Wide Web.

- Internet browser, Internet application software, and Web browser is important software for connecting to Internet. It is an interface between World Wide Web and user that can be GUI based like Google Chrome, Internet Explorer, Opera, Mozilla Firefox, and more, or it can text-based as Lynx.
- Webpage is a digital page that contains hyperlinks, audios, tables, text, images, and more. The Extensible Markup Language (XML), Hypertext Markup Language (HTML) and Hypertext Pre-processor (PHP), and more markup languages are used to write webpages.
- It is specially designed website that serves as a single point of access for information that can also be considered as personalized or categorized content library.
- Email stands for Electronic mail that is most popular internet application used to send or receive messages between various users.
- Internet helps to stay in touch with friends and your loved ones. The social media sites like Facebook, Twitter enable us to see what's happening around us in our friends' lives, and many more.
- Twitter is online news, and social networking service on which users post and interact with messages knows as Tweets.
- Facebook is the world's biggest social media website that covers around billion users worldwide. It provides user-friendly platform by creating your free account on it.
- YouTube is a free online video sharing service that has now acquired by Google
- WhatsApp is a fireware and cross-platform messaging service that allows sending messages, pictures, and videos.
- 'Digital India' is a program initiated by Prime Minister Mr. Narendra Modi. The motive behind the Digital India mission is to build participative, transparent, and responsive governance to reach out the citizens.
- Aadhaar, Digilocker, Permanent Account Number (PAN), All India Council of Technical Education (AICTE), e-District, Passport, Central Board of Secondary Education (CBSE), Indian railway ticket booking, and many more are services provided by Digital India

Self-Assessment

MULTIPLE CHOICE QUESTIONS.

1. Which of the following component of Internet is the interface between World wide web and user?

   a. Internal b. Internet Browser c. Web pages d. Web portal

2. _________ and _________ are two parts of email address

   a. Portal address and email address b. User name and domain name

   c. Portal address and domain name d. Email address and user name

3. In Twitter _________ term is used to handle user account name

   a. Tweets b. Twitter feed c. Twitter handle d. Hashtags

Answers

1. b 2. b 3. c

FILL IN THE BLANKS

1. _____________ is an online news and social networking service on which users post and interact with messages known as tweets.

2. ____________ in Facebook is a list of people whom you are accepted to see your profile and information shared by you.
3. ____________ tab contain emails from social media websites.
4. Full form of CC and BCC is ____________ and ____________.

Answers

1. Twitter 2. Friend list 3. Social Tab 4. Carbon copy and Blind carbon copy

TRUE FALSE

1. The motive of Digital India program is to build participative, transparent, and responsive government to reach out the citizen. (T/F)
2. Newsfeed is the an ongoing stream of tweets from the users that are followed by you (T/F)
3. Promotion tab contains the emails from your friends, family, and colleagues (T/F)

Answers

1. True 2. False 3. False

ANSWER THE FOLLOWING QUESTIONS:

1. Define Internet and its uses.
2. What is the full form of email? Write down the steps to compose an email message and send it.
3. Name various social networking sites. Explain any two.
4. Write a short note on Digital India.

PRACTICAL WORK

Create a new Gmail account and send email to one of your friend. Make one account on YouTube to upload one small video on it.

Exercise for Assessment

MULTIPLE CHOICE QUESTIONS.

1. Which of the following is not a learning app?

   a. Javatpoint b. Khan Academy c. WhatsApp d. Kindle books

3. ____________ company is not providing email service.

   a. Google b. Amazon c. Yahoo d. Microsoft

4. ____________ unit carries out the basic calculations and comparison operations on the data.

   a. CPU b. Control unit c. ALU d. ROM

5. ____________ is not an internal peripheral devices.

   a. Modem b. Wi-fi adaptor c. NIC d. Memory card reader

6. Operating system has two components used to perform and achieve the objectives

   a. System Software and Application software b. Software and hardware
   c. Kernel and Shell d. Software and technologies

7. __________ is not a feature of Linux.

a. Potable
b. Open-source
c. Single programming
d. Hierarchical File system

6. Which of the following component of Internet is the interface between World wide web and user?

a. Internal
b. Internet Browser
c. Web pages
d. Web portal

7. ________ and __________ are two parts of email address.

a. Portal address and email address
b. User name and domain name
c. Portal address and domain name
d. Email address and user name

8. The maximum length of tweet is:

a. 120 words
b. No limit
c. 140 words
d. 280 words

11. To avail government services to every citizen is the objective of ___________

a. Satya Nadella
b. Digital India
c. AICTE
d. All

12. In Twitter _________ term is used to handle user account name

a. Tweets
b. Twitter feed
c. Twitter handle
d. Hashtags

Answer

1. C	2. B	3. C	4. D	5. B	6. C
7. A	8. C	9. B	10. B	11. D	12. C

VERY SHORT QUESTIONS

1. Name any five Input and output devices.
2. Differentiate between volatile and non-volatile memory.
3. Define ICT?
4. Give full form of MODEM, CPU, ALU, NIC, and Wi-Fi
5. What is e-banking?
6. What do you mean by software?
7. What is the full form of DOS?
8. Name various common terms used in Internet?
9. What is the word limit of tweets?

SHORT QUESTIONS

1. Write down the steps to start computer?
2. What do you mean by peripheral? How peripheral helps in doing various task.
3. Briefly explain the role of ICT in medical science.
4. What is E-banking? How it has ease the life of human being.
5. How has ICT influenced the modern Education field?
6. Give advantages and disadvantages of DOS?
7. Differentiate CC and BCC.
8. What is the full form of email? Write down the steps to compose an Email message and send it.
9. What do you mean by computer? Name various basic components of computer system.

LONG QUESTIONS

1. Describe radio and mobile as ICT tools.
2. Give components of CPU and its functioning.
3. Give name of 5 each Internal and External peripheral devices and explain any 4 in detail.
4. Discuss any two applications of ICT in brief.
5. What was the name of Edubuntu when it was invented? Give various features and components of Edubuntu desktop?
6. Write a short note on Digital India?
7. Name various social networking sites? Explain any two in brief.

APPLICATION-BASED QUESTIONS

1. Komal mother want to book the two tickets for going to Ambala through train, but she doesn't have time to go to Railway station for booking advance tickets. Suggest her how she can help her mother in booking train tickets from home.
2. Simran gifted a computer system to her wife. Explain her how to start a computer and shutdown it.
3. Jaspreet father has gifted him a Memory card reader, Explain him the usage of memory card reader.
4. Rahul is working on DOS; explain him the steps to open DOS and start working on it.
5. Komal wants to share her wedding pictures with her friends and family via social media. Which platform should she use for sharing the pictures?

PROJECT WORK

1. Do a group discussion on importance of various tools of ICT and what i significance is in our daily life.
2. Check the hard disk and RAM size of your computer system. Check all input and output devices connected to your system and analyze its usage in it.
3. Make a presentation on various types of operating system. Open DOS and observe their various features.
4. Do group discussion on features and various components of Edubuntu and Linux.
5. Make a presentation on various social networking sites.
6. Do group discussion about Digital India program initiated by Prime Minister Mr. Narendra Modi after reading about it from various sources.

TEACHER NOTES

1. Tell your students to create a Gmail account and send mail on your mail ID.
2. Arrange a session in computer lab to show them various components of computers.

4 Entrepreneurial Skills

Learning Outcomes

After this chapter, you will have the knowledge of:

- Business
- What are entrepreneur skills
- Various types of business
- Types of business enterprises in our community
- Tell about entrepreneur
- Entrepreneurship development and various phases of entrepreneurship development
- Various factors that affect the growth of entrepreneurship
- Characteristics of entrepreneurship
- Role of entrepreneurship in various types of development
- The rewards or benefits of being an entrepreneur

INTRODUCTION

Everyone processes an inherent attitude and there is a need to identify our area of interest and inner strengths and develop our skills accordingly. We have to face various challenges and competition in every sphere of life and we should have different and optimistic thinking to nurture a winning attitude.

You should be clear that after completion of your education which career you want to opt for:

- Either you want to explore various job opportunities
- Prepare for further competition
- Want to appear for interviews
- Want to start something of your own and become an entrepreneur

SESSION 1: TYPES OF BUSINESS ACTIVITIES

Business is an economic activity that is related to regular and continuous production and distribution of services or goods that satisfy human needs. Businesses can be for non-profit or for profit organizations that cater to the society needs. Sometimes, there is a gap between our needs and availability and that is used as opportunity by some people who are ready to take a risk and fill that gap by providing necessary services and products. These people are known as Entrepreneurs.

Entrepreneur is a self-employed person who is willing to take a risk and start a business with a new idea. All self-employed persons, like shopkeepers, are not entrepreneurs until a new idea or method is not introduced by them in business.

Entrepreneur skills

An entrepreneur can be an educator, businessman, artist, restaurateur, inventor or professional. Employment opportunities are created in society and goods and services are provided by entrepreneurs who play an important role in it. They can be from any socio-economic background.

Some famous entrepreneurs among others are:

- Mark Zuckerberg, who has become one of the youngest billionaires with his skills and talent in computers. He first launched his website Facebook whilst attending Harvard University, the website was launched from his dormitory room, on 4 February 2004.
- William Bill Gates is the second richest man on the planet and one of the most recognized names in the world, as much a celebrity or movie star due to his highly public profile.
- Larry Page who is a Co-Founder of one of the most recognized search engines in the world, Google.
- Ariana Huffington, who was born in 1950 in Athens is one of the most influential, professional, and successful females in the blogging industry.

Some important skills required to be a successful entrepreneur are:

- Ambition
- Willingness to learn
- Ability to listen
- Creativity
- Courage and risk taking
- Team management
- Stress management and more

WHAT IS BUSINESS?

This is a very common question that comes in mind. Business can be understood through various means but its basic features remain the same. Some of these features are: business is an activity related to trade; it is done for earning profits or it is referred to as a source of income; it involves sales and purchase of services or goods; and it is mainly run to increase the profits by creating value for customers through services or goods.

Types of business

One should be aware about various types of business to become an entrepreneur. It is broadly classified into four types as given below:

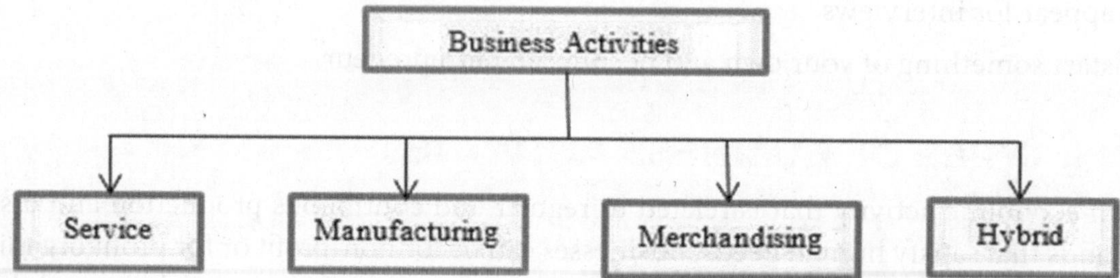

Figure 4.1: Types of business activities

- **Service:** It is a business that provides products with no physical form. These companies or firms provide expertise, professional skills, advice and other similar services. It involves the execution of specialized personal services on the basis of training, education and knowledge.

  This includes services given by:

  - Lawyers
  - Chartered accountant
  - Salons
  - Sports academic
  - Hotels
  - Doctors

  You pay these businesses for different services but you aren't buying any physical products.

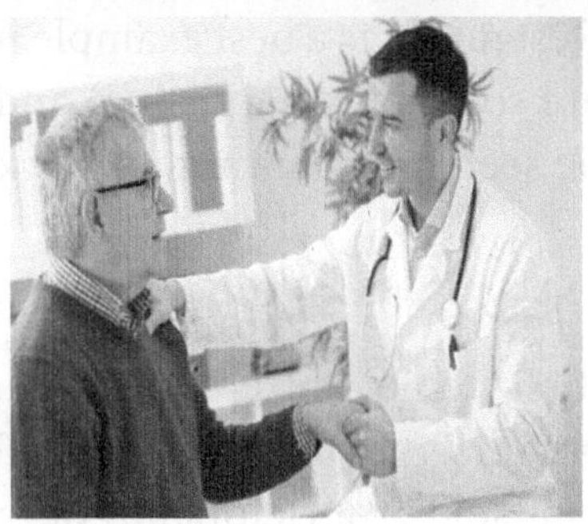

Figure 4.2: Service as a business activity

- **Manufacturing:** It is concerned with the transformation and manufacturing of raw materials, labor, and other production processes to manufacture goods. To make new products raw materials are bought by manufacturers.

  For example, to make steel, iron ore is used as a raw material. Yarn and wool are used as raw materials in cotton and wool/textile companies. Electronic parts, LCD screens, and batteries are used as raw materials by mobile phone manufacturing companies.

Figure 4.3: Manufacturing as a business activity

  Analytical, processing, and assembling are some more common types of manufacturing companies. They all mostly deal with wholesalers.

- **Merchandising:** It is also known as trading or buy and sell business. In this, merchandise business firms buy products at wholesale prices and further sell it at retail prices to other customers or retailers.

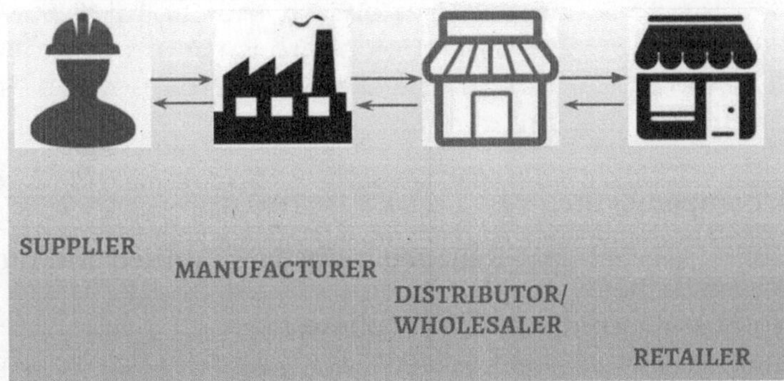

Figure 4.4: Merchandising as a business activity

- **Hybrid:** It is a company that is classified into more than one type of business or it is a mixed type of business.

Restaurant is a best example in which meals are prepared (manufacturing), bottled water or cold drinks are sold (merchandising) and food is served (service). All these three types of business functions can be seen in restaurant, this is known as hybrid type of business.

TYPES OF BUSINESS ENTERPRISES IN OUR COMMUNITY

The first step of entrepreneur is to choose the form of business he/she wants to start and these businesses are organized in different forms. It depends on the type of business ownership as it can be owned by single person (sole proprietorship) or by a group of persons.

Joint stock and cooperative society comes under co-operative form of business enterprises in which identity of the enterprise is separate from its owners. If the enterprise runs into obligations, the owners will not be personally liable for it.

On other hand, in case of non-cooperative form of ownership the identity of owners and enterprise is same and in case of any obligation owner is responsible for it.

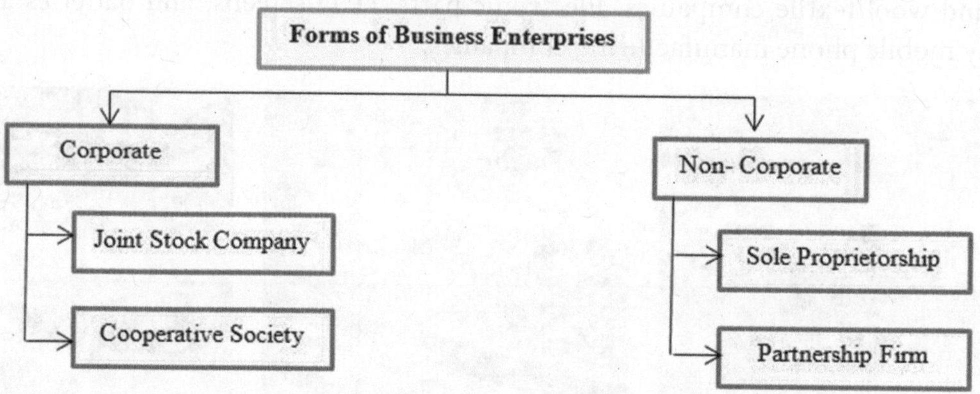

Figure 4.5: Forms of business enterprises

- **Joint stock company:** It forms a business organization as a voluntary association of persons to carry on business. It normally gives legal status and is subjected to certain legal regulations or association of persons who are contributing money for a common purpose. The board of directors handles the management of such companies.

A Joint stock company's money is the capital of the company; its members contribute money and their share is the proportion of the capital invested by them. Therefore, these members are known as shareholders and share capital is the share of each member.

Some of the joint stock companies are:

- Ponds India Limited
- Reliance Industries Limited and more

The advantages of the joint stock company are as follows:

- Limited liability
- Continuity of existence
- Benefits of large scale operations
- Professional management
- Social benefits and more

Figure 4.6: Joint stoke companies

- **Cooperative society:** It is a society whose purpose is to render services to its members and to the public. It is democratically operated and controlled on a non-profit basis as their basic motive is to meet social, economic and cultural needs of its members. It is organized on the principle of mutual self-help and has very less liability on its members.

The organization is run by managing committee elected by its members. A cooperative society needs to be registered by registrar of cooperative societies and financial grants or loans are offered to them by the government.

Some of the cooperative society forms of businesses are:

- o Amul
- o Shri Mahilla Griha Udyog Lijjat papad

Figure 4.7: Cooperative society

The advantages of the cooperative society are as follows:

- o Easy to form
- o Limited liability
- o Open membership
- o State assistance
- o Management

- **Sole proprietorship:** This business is owned by a single person who provides the entire capital, bears all the risks and independently manages it. This form is mainly adopted for small scale independent businesses, thus it is also known as one man business organization. It is seen everywhere in every state, country or locality.

  Examples of sole proprietorship are the grocery store, sweets shop, stationery store, chemist shops, and vegetable shops.

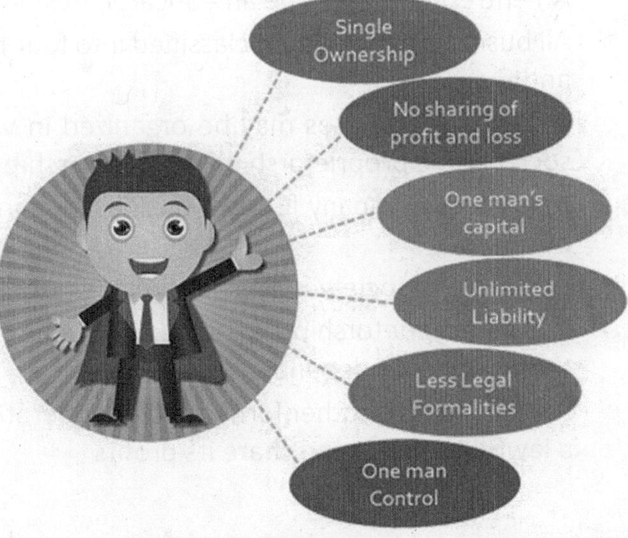

Figure 4.8: Sole proprietorship

In this entire capital for the business is provided by the owner. In addition to their own capital they may raise more funds from outside through borrowings from relatives, friends, taking loans from banks, etc.

The advantages of sole proprietorship are:

- o Easy formation
- o Better control
- o Prompt decision making
- o Flexibility in operations
- o Retention of business secrets and
- o Social benefits

✦ **Partnership:** It is another form of non-cooperative form of enterprise. In this more than one person carry a lawful business and share its profits. Even losses are borne equally by themselves. In this form of business, people from similar backgrounds or different skills join together to carry one business and they all are legally responsible for the business.

This type of ownership is often expected to have higher growth rates than sole proprietorship due to sharing of profits and losses equally between all members.

In this, each member of the group is known as partner and collectively all members are known as partnership firm.

The advantages of partnership are as follows:

- o Easy formation
- o Larger resources
- o Flexibility in operation
- o Better management
- o Sharing of risks
- o Better public relations

Figure 4.9: Partnership

Summary

- ⊙ Business is an economic activity that is related to regular and continuous production and distribution of services or goods that satisfy human needs.
- ⊙ An entrepreneur can be an educator, businessman, artist, restaurateur, inventor, or professional.
- ⊙ All business activities are classified into four broad categories: Service, Manufacturing, Merchandising, and Hybrid.
- ⊙ Business enterprises may be organized in various forms including joint stock company, cooperative society, sole proprietorship, and partnership firm.
- ⊙ Joint stock company forms a business organization as a voluntary association of persons to carry on business.
- ⊙ Cooperative society is a society whose purpose is to render services to its members and to the public.
- ⊙ In Sole proprietorship, business is owned by a single person who provides the entire capital, bears all the risks, and independently manages it.
- ⊙ Partnership is another form of non-cooperative form of enterprise. In this more than one person carry a lawful business and share its profits

Self-Assessment

MULTIPLE CHOICE QUESTIONS.

1. Which of the following skills are required to be a successful entrepreneur?

   a. Ambition b. Creativity

   c. Team management d. All

2. __________ is not a business activity.

   a. Service b. Manufacturing c. Creativity d. Merchandising

Answer

1. d 2. c

FILL IN THE BLANKS

1. ________________ is a person who takes risk to produce goods and services in search of profit.
2. ____________form of business enterprises form a business organization as a voluntary association of person to carry on business.
3. ____________ is a mixed type of business as it includes more than one business type.
4. Another name for merchandise business is __________.

Answer

1. Entrepreneur 2. Joint stock company
3. Hybrid 4. Trading or buy and sell business

TRUE FALSE

1. Restaurant is a good example of hybrid business activity. (T/F)
2. Joint stock company is a type of non-cooperative form of business enterprise. (T/F)
3. Entrepreneur is a self-employed person who is willing to take risk and start a business with new idea. (T/F)

Answer

1. True 2. False 3. True

QUESTIONS

1. Who is entrepreneur? Give a few important skills to become a successful entrepreneur.
2. Name four types of business activities. Explain any two of it.
3. Give types of business enterprises in our community.

PROJECT WORK

Make a poster on various business activities around you.

SESSION 2: CHARACTERISTICS OF ENTREPRENEURSHIP

The word "Entrepreneur" is derived from the French verb enterprendre that means to undertake and it is used to define a person who undertakes risk to start their own business. If there are any losses or profit then it will be borne by the entrepreneur only. There are a number of entrepreneurs who have become famous due to their necessary skills and talents that make them good entrepreneurs.

For example: founder of Apple Steve Jobs, founder of Microsoft Bill Gates, Founder of Facebook Mark Zuckerberg, and many more are famous entrepreneur but initially they were not very successful.

The story of Mark Zuckerberg

He has made one of the most famous social networking websites, Facebook. Mark Zuckerberg created it at the age of 19 in 2004; it made him as one of the most powerful entrepreneurs in the world. Facebook has strongly impacted the lives of people. He had interest in computers since he was 12 years old. At that time he had created Zucknet, a messaging program through which his father and family used to communicate with each other. Then, while he was in high school, he created Synapse, an early version of the music software Pandora and evoked interest from companies like Microsoft.

Mark had established himself as go-to software developer at Harvard campus and built a CourseMatch program that helped students choose their classes on the basis of course selections of other users. Another thing invented by him was Facemash that compared pictures of students on campus and allowed others to vote on more attractive one.

Facebook allows users to create profiles, upload photos and communicate with other users. Then he dropped out of college to devote himself completely to Facebook due to response of 1 million users he got by the end of 2004. With the success of Facebook, he made his mark as the chairman, chief executive officer and co-founder of Facebook with a net worth of US $58.6 billion and he became the fifth richest man in the world.

Definitions of entrepreneurs:

- An entrepreneur is a designer or creator who designs new businesses and ideas according to their own passion and requirements of market.
- Entrepreneurship is the art of starting a new company or business that makes creative products, process, and services.
- Entrepreneurship according to National Knowledge Commission is a set of activities performed by an entrepreneur.

Enterprise is a business organization that provides goods and services, create jobs, contributes to national income, exports, and imports.

In simple language, an entrepreneur is a person, entrepreneurship is the process and enterprise is the outcome of it.

Entrepreneurship development

It is the process of improving the skills and knowledge of entrepreneurs through various training and classroom programs.

For example: To score good in examinations, students go for extra classes or coaching and also to improve their communication skills they join various English communication courses and personality grooming institutes.

In the same way entrepreneurship development is the process to enhance one's personality and take them a step forward toward success. It is mainly concerned with the study of entrepreneurial behavior, the dynamics of business set-up, development and expansion of the enterprise. The main objective is to increase the number of entrepreneurs.

Phases of entrepreneurship development

- **Pre-training or initial phase:** This phase includes all the activities and preparation required to launch the training program. It involves designing course curriculum for training or selection and identification of potential entrepreneurs and providing initial motivation to them.

  Its objective is to provide information and knowledge about entrepreneurship, role of it and available facilities regarding establishment of enterprise to perspective entrepreneurs. To develop a right approach towards business, motivation training is provided to the prospective entrepreneurs. It also includes selection of faculty, advertisement and selection of potential entrepreneurs on the basis of various factors.

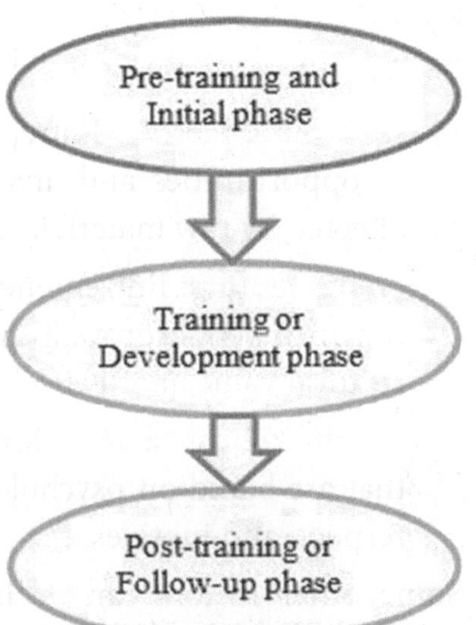

Figure 4.10: Flow of phases of entrepreneurship development

- **Training or development phase:** The training of potential entrepreneurs covers special inputs such as business opportunity guidance, technical and managerial inputs, behavioral inputs, and more. In this stage trainers have to judge how far trainees have moved in their entrepreneurial pursuits.

  Its objective is to bring desirable change in the behavior of trainees.

  Various methods that can be used to provide training are:

  - o Through lectures
  - o Written instructions method
  - o Conferences
  - o Practical
  - o Demonstration method
  - o Individual or group training

- **Post-training or follow-up phase:** As mentioned above, the main objective of entrepreneurship development program is to prepare the participants to start their enterprise. Its success can be judged from the achieved objectives, that is, by getting training how many participants have started their own enterprise. This last phase involves the assessment to judge how far the objectives of the program have been achieved.

  This is called Follow-up that includes three things:

  - o Was the program conducted as per plans
  - o If not then what were the deviation in the plan
  - o Taking corrective action to improve the weaknesses after identifying them

  The characteristics of entrepreneurship are as follows:

  - o It is a function of innovation.
  - o It is a function of leadership.

- It is an organization building function.
- It involves operation and creation of an enterprise.
- It is concerned with managing, developing, and employing the factors of production.
- It is a function of high achievement.
- It is concerned with unique combinations of resources that make existing products or methods obsolete.
- It is a positive and strong orientation towards growth in income, employment, sales, and assets.

Factors affecting the growth of entrepreneurship

The growth of Entrepreneurship gets affected by mainly three factors as given below:

- **Economic factors:** Entrepreneurship gets directly affected by economic factors as in case of absence of opportunities and unavailability of jobs people choose entrepreneurship. Entrepreneurship gets affected by raw material, capital, infrastructure, market and labor, and more.
- **Social factors:** Entrepreneurial behavior of people also gets affected by social factors or environment in which people grow. It shapes their basic values, norms and beliefs such as social mobility, education, cultural value, family background, and attitude of the society.
- **Psychological factors:** Many Entrepreneurial theorists have developed theories of entrepreneurship that are based on psychological factors. These factors are need of achievement, withdrawal of status, respect, and motives.

Some other factors can be individual who establish, expand, initiate, and maintain new enterprise, availability of industrial technology and state of the art and culture of business and trading.

Characteristics of entrepreneurship

Mature people in their fifties and youngsters in their teens can become an entrepreneur. They can be male, female, educated or self-educated; can be from any country or background. But they all have some common characteristics and they recognize business opportunities more quickly than other people.

Various other common characteristics of entrepreneurs are:

- **Systematic activity:** Entrepreneurship is not a mysterious thing and something that happens by chance as it is a step-by-step, systematic, and purposeful activity. It has certain skills and other requirements that can be learnt, developed and acquired by either vocational training or formal educational or by observing and work experience.
- **Purposeful and lawful activity:** Entrepreneurship is a goal oriented activity whose object is lawful business. Each and every enterprise is launched or created to either personal profit or social gain.
- **Creative activity:** Entrepreneurship is a creative response to changes in environment. It involves introduction of something better or new.
- **Organizing of production:** Production implying creation of place, form, time, requires combined utilization of diverse factors of land, capital, technology, and labor. In response to business opportunity, these resources are activated into a productive enterprise.
- **Risk bearing activity:** Risk is inseparable and inherent from entrepreneurship. Entrepreneurs usually do extraordinary things and take risks.
- **Gap filling:** An entrepreneur identifies and fills the gap between needs of society and availability for them.

- **Initiative taking:** Entrepreneurship should take initiative to take up new and challenging tasks.
- **Innovation:** Innovation not only includes new ideas in business but it also helps in cost saving and revenue enhancing. It should become a habit irrespective of results.

Role of entrepreneurship

Being an entrepreneur how do you think you will help your country? It has been found that countries who encourage entrepreneurship have grown fast. Due to this it becomes very important to broadly define the role of entrepreneurship. It is mainly classified into economic, social, and psychological development.

Role of entrepreneurship in economic development

The entrepreneur is the key to create new enterprises that energize the economy and rejuvenate the established enterprises that make up the economic structure. In the economic system an important role is played by entrepreneurship and nature and scope of it is determine by the economic system.

The entrepreneur or entrepreneurship initiate and sustain the process of economic development in the following ways:

- Capital information
- Generation of employment
- Improve per capital income
- Improve living standard
- Balanced regional development
- Improve economy of country
- Improve living standards of people

Role of entrepreneurship in social development

Business started by an entrepreneur is usually a very small business in the beginning. There is expansion of business if that small business becomes successful and grows. As it grows there is need for more work to be done, so it creates more jobs. Good quality jobs lead to more people earning money and having a good life.

Other important factors will be:

- Reduces unemployment
- Improves socio-economic status
- Satisfies needs of customers
- Improves standard of living
- More people will have good life
- Increase in social capital
- Innovation or new goods and services

Role of entrepreneurship in psychological development

The psychological development includes:

- Development of confidence
- Increase motivation
- Instils a drive for achievement

Rewards of entrepreneurship

- **Being the boss:** The most significant reward of entrepreneurship is working for your own. The entrepreneur becomes the decision maker and sole responsible person for all the activities of the business.
- **Freedom to do anything:** There is a saying that if you want to be happy with the profession, do what you love or love what you do. Entrepreneurs are the luckiest persons in the profession, who do the things they love to do.
- **Be creative:** The society is getting advanced day-by-day. Still, there are so many problems that need to be sorted out. The problems are old. The solution is also there. That is why creativity is required. The new ideas of the entrepreneurs bring new ways to solve the existing problems.

- **Building an enterprise:** Building an enterprise is itself a very rewarding achievement. The joy of being the creator is indescribable in words. The person who creates an enterprise on their own can better understand the glory of it.
- **Own schedule:** The rewarding achievement of being self-employed is that the entrepreneur can set his own schedule. The schedule of work is something which makes either energetic or tired. There is enough flexibility to set your own schedule. There is nobody to ask why you are late or why you are leaving early or why you are taking leave?
- **Business from home:** The greatest luxury probably anyone can think of is staying at home and work. Entrepreneurship allows that. Moreover, the atmosphere of home helps to keep up a certain desirable state of mind that is hardly expected from any other profession while working.
- **Excitement:** Entrepreneurship involves adventures and excitement; it is one of the reasons for people resigning from their current job and starting their business.

Summary

- The word "Entrepreneur" is derived from the French verb enterprendre that means to undertake and it is used to define a person who undertakes risk to start their own business.
- An Entrepreneur is a designer or creator who designs new businesses and ideas according to their own passion and requirements of market.
- Entrepreneurship development is the process of improvement the skills and knowledge of entrepreneurs through various training and classroom programs.
- Pre-training and initial phase, training or development phase and post-training or follow up phase are three phases of entrepreneurship development.
- Economic, social, and psychological factors are affecting the growth of entrepreneurship.
- Characteristics of entrepreneurship are systematic activity, powerful and lawful activity, creative activity, risk bearing activity, gap filling, initiative taking, and innovation.
- Role of entrepreneurship are classified into three categories: economic development, social development, and psychological development
- Rewards of entrepreneurship are: being the boss, freedom to do anything, building an enterprise, own schedule, business from home, and excitement.

Self-Assessment

MULTIPLE CHOICE QUESTIONS.

1. Entrepreneur is derived from French verb 'enterprendre' which means:
   a. To communicate b. To understand c. To take d. All
2. Which of the following factors is affects the growth of entrepreneurship?
   a. Economic factors b. Social factors
   c. Psychological factors d. All

Answer

1. b 2. d

FILL IN THE BLANKS

1. ________________ is a business organization that which provide goods and services, create jobs, contributes to national income, exports, imports or it is a business venture.
2. ____________ phase of entrepreneurship development includes all the activities and preparation required to launch a training program.
3. ____________ is the funds for investment to start a new business venture.
4. One of the psychological factors that helps entrepreneurship is that it increases __________.

Answer

1. Enterprise
2. Pre-training or Initial phase
3. Capital
4. Motivation

ANSWER THE FOLLOWING QUESTIONS

1. What is entrepreneurship?
2. Name and explain various phases of entrepreneurship development.
3. Give any five characteristics of entrepreneurship.
4. Give various rewards of entrepreneurship.

PROJECT WORK

Prepare a presentation on various factors affecting the growth of entrepreneurship.

Exercise for Assessment

MULTIPLE CHOICE QUESTIONS.

1. Services given by lawyers or doctors comes under which business activities
   a. Service b. Manufacturing c. Merchandising d. Hybrid
2. Grocery store, stationary store, vegetable shop, and more are examples of ________ form of business enterprises.
   a. Joint stock company b. Cooperative society
   c. Sole Proprietorship d. Partnership firm
3. An entrepreneur ____________
   a. Sets the interest rates of banks b. Manages financial investments
   c. Takes risks to earn profits d. Enforces government regulations
4. Which of the following is the non-cooperate type of business enterprise?
   a. Joint stock company b. Cooperative society
   c. Sole Proprietorship d. None
5. Which of the following skills are required to be a successful entrepreneur?
   a. Ambition b. Creativity c. Team management d. All

6. _________ is a process of improving skills and knowledge of entrepreneurs through various training and classroom programs
   a. Enterprise b. School
   c. Entrepreneurship development d. College
7. Which of the following factor is affecting the growth of entrepreneurship?
   a. Economic factors b. Social factors c. Psychological factors d. All
8. Which of the following does not come under the role of entrepreneurship in social development?
   a. Improves socio-economic status b. Increases social capital
   c. Develop confidence d. Reduces unemployment

Answer

1. a 2. c 3. c 4. c 5. d 6. c 7. b 8. c

VERY SHORT QUESTIONS

1. Name any four types of business activities.
2. Give any two examples of manufacturing business activity.
3. Define integrity.
4. Name the phases of entrepreneurship development.
5. Give various characteristics of entrepreneurship.
6. How Social factors affect the growth of entrepreneurship?
7. Define the role of entrepreneurship in economic development.

SHORT QUESTIONS

1. Who is an entrepreneur?
2. What do you mean by business?
3. Define hybrid type of business activity with an example.
4. What is the meaning of liability?
5. What are the types of enterprises in our community?
6. What is entrepreneurship?
7. Name the factors affecting the growth of entrepreneurship.

LONG QUESTIONS

1. Explain various types of business activities.
2. What are the various types of business enterprises in our community? Explain each form of business enterprises.
3. What do you mean by entrepreneur skills? Write down some of the important skills required to be a successful entrepreneur.
4. Briefly explain the various phases of entrepreneurship development.
5. Write a short note on various characteristics of entrepreneurship.

APPLICATION BASED QUESTIONS

1. Komal wants to start an organization to help needy people. Suggest the type of organization that she can start.
2. One of your neighbors wants to open their own clinic. She wants to choose an option that requires minimum investment and business regulations. So, which business ownership option should she choose and why?
3. Simran wants to be an entrepreneur, give her any five characteristics that you possess that can help her to become a successful entrepreneur.
4. Jasspreet is good in photography. What possible careers will you suggest him to pursue?
5. If you are thinking to open a venture, what are the four main phases of entrepreneur process for your venture?

PROJECT WORK

1. Make groups of two students and discuss 2 types of businesses each under various business activities.
2. Have a group discussion on various types of business enterprises in our community.
3. Prepare a chart on role of entrepreneurship in development.
4. Organize a group discussion on topic: entrepreneur vs salaried worker

TEACHER NOTES

1. Make a presentation on various forms of business enterprises along with practical examples of it.
2. Tell your students to make a report on various rewards entrepreneurs around their locality get.

5 Green Skills – I

Learning Outcomes

After this chapter, you will have the knowledge of:

- Categorization of environment
- Ecosystem and its three primary components
- Relationship between man and environment
- The effects of human activities on environment
- Ecological imbalance
- Greenhouse gas emission, habitat distinction, radioactive wastes, nuclear weapons, overexploitation of natural resources, environmental pollution, and biotechnological misuse
- Conservation of natural resources
- Concept of reduce, reuse and recycle
- Environment protection and conservation

INTRODUCTION

All aspects of our life get affected by environment around us and environment gets affected by our day to day activities. People who live in cities get their food from surrounding villages and in turn are dependent on forest, rivers, and grasslands, seashores for fodder, fuel, and water like resources. Environment is made by everything around us and our lives depend on the flora and fauna around us.

Similarly our school environment is made of socio-culture and physical environment. Physical environment includes the school building and the library, toilet, classrooms, kitchen, laboratories, and playground.

SESSION 1: ENVIRONMENT PROTECTION AND CONSERVATION

The word environment has been derived from French word environ which means to surround or encircle. Its dictionary meaning is: external condition influencing growth or development of people, surrounding and working or living conditions, and more.

Environment also refers to the sum total of conditions that surround us at a given point in time and space. In the beginning, the environment of early man comprised of non-living or abiotic aspects of earth like water, air, and land. It also includes living or biotic organisms like plants, animals, and time but by advancement in society, man extended and altered his environment through his economic, social and political functions.

Categorization of environment

Environment is categorized into two types as given below:

- **Natural environment:** It includes living and non-living things like air, animals, water, land and plants. Lithosphere is the solid crust or hard top layer of the earth that is made up of minerals and rocks and covered with thin layer of soil. It is an irregular surface with plateaus, valleys, plains and mountains. The forest, land for agriculture, human settlements, and grasslands for grazing are provided by lithosphere.

The natural environment is subdivided into biotic and abiotic components:

- o Biotic components: Biotic components are living components of an ecosystem. Some of these factors include animals, plants, bacteria, and fungus. On the basis of energy requirement source biotic component can be further classified.

  Three broad categories of biotic components are:

  - Decomposer
  - Consumers
  - Producers

  Examples of biotic components are fungi, birds, plants, animals, insects, and other living organisms.

- o Abiotic components: Abiotic components are physical or chemical factors that act on living organisms at any part of their life. Light, soil, air, water, and minerals are form of abiotic components of an ecosystem.

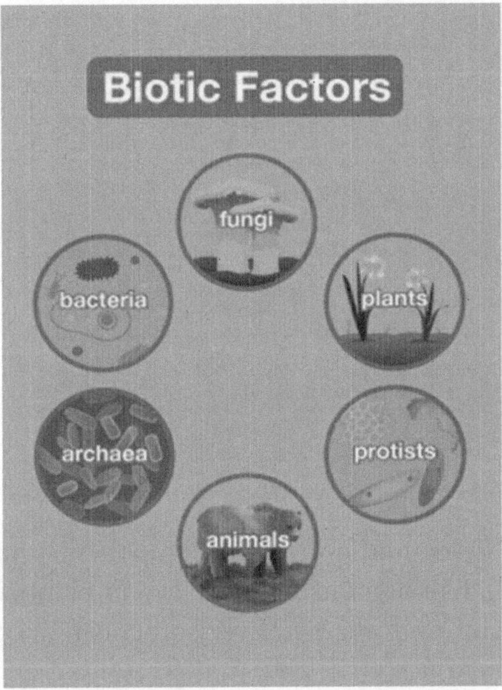

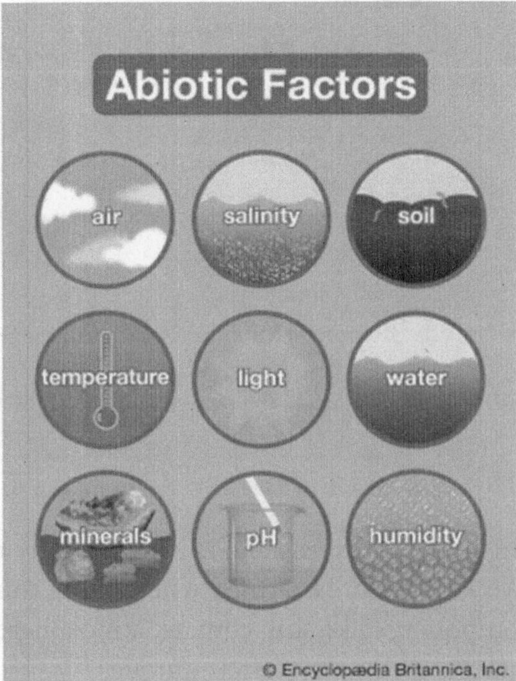

Figure 5.1: Biotic and Abiotic factors

Our environment provides platform for the interaction between these two factors. To grow, survive, and fulfil their requirements biotic factors depend on abiotic factors.

✦ **Human-made environment:** Human beings interact with the environment and modify it according to their needs. Early humans adapted themselves to the natural surroundings, led a simple life, and fulfilled their requirements from the nature around them. The needs grew with time and various new ways were learned by humans to change and use the environment.

The human-made environment includes human activities and their interaction with the abiotic components that consist of structures like:

o Bridges	o Markets	o Houses	o Dams
o Parks	o Factories	o Vehicles	o Building

Ecosystem

An ecosystem can be defined as a functional unit of nature in which living organisms interact with each other and also with surrounding physical environment. Ecosystem can be as small as pond or as large as sea or forest. In a pond you will find various living things from micro-organisms to insects and plants in it. These may be dependent on air, sunlight, water, and nutrients in the water.

Categories of ecosystem:

- Aquatic
- Terrestrial

Where terrestrial ecosystems are grasslands, deserts and forests; on other hand river, estuary, wetland, lake, and pond are examples of aquatic ecosystems:

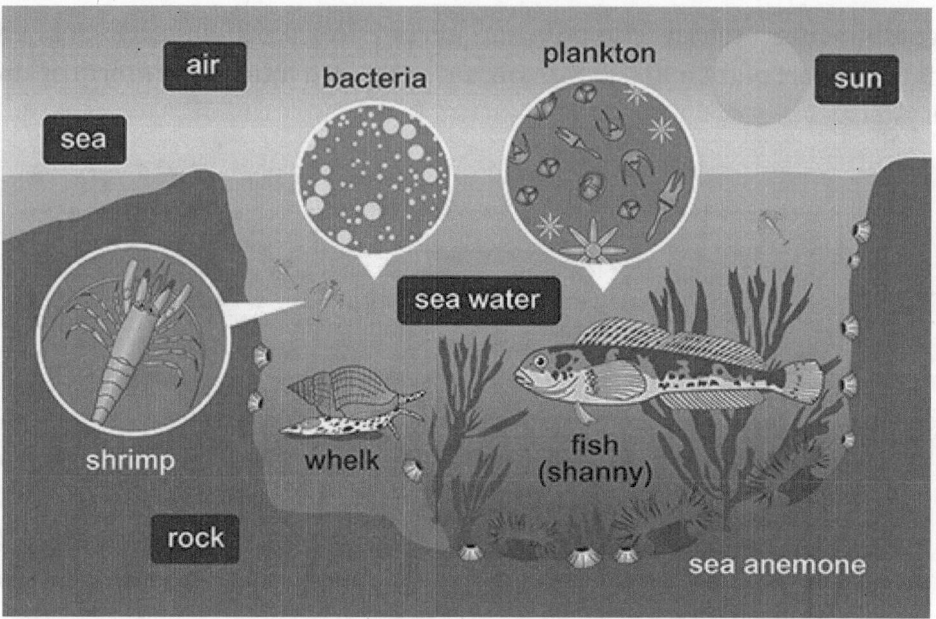

Figure 5.2: Ecosystem

As mentioned above, an ecosystem is a community of living and non-living components that depend on each other. An ecosystem is formed when living things like organisms, animals and plants interact with non-living components like sun, climate, atmosphere, soil, and weather. Every organism in ecosystem has its role to play and each ecosystem is unique.

The three primary components of all ecosystems are:

- **Autotrophs:** Autotrophs are producers of energy and majority of autotrophs in an ecosystem are made by plants as they convert energy from sun or other sources into food.
- **Heterotrophs:** Heterotrophs are the consumers of energy and these organisms directly or indirectly depend upon the autotrophs of their food. They are also known as consumers and most of the heterotrophs are animals.
- **Non-living matter:** It is leaf litter, soil, sediments and other organic matter found on ground or at the bottom of an aquatic system.

Relationship between man and environment

We know that behaviour is either directly or indirectly affected by physical environment. The interrelation between man and environment is established from the earliest times to the present day. However during different stages of the evolution of humans and their society there is variation in relation. In this relationship, a human being's life gets influenced by environment. The changing environment is adapted by humans but sometimes according to their requirements there is modification in natural environment.

Figure 5.3: Man and the environment

The survival of early humans depended on natural environment as their clothing, shelter and food all came from their natural habitat. Due to these reasons they lived in harmony with nature and devised various ways of preserving their natural environment. They also used to worship in different forms as a way to honor natural environment. There are five major components of human-environment interaction, such as:

- **Physical environment:** It includes aspects of natural environment like temperature, flora, terrain, climate, fauna, rainfall, and more.
- **Social-culture environment:** It includes all aspects of cultural environment such as customs, socialization, process and norms. It also includes all the aspects dealing with other people and their creations.
- **Environmental orientation:** It refers to the beliefs that people hold about their environment. For example, some people hold environment equivalent to God and therefore they perceive all its aspects with respect and try to maintain it in a perfect form without degrading it.
- **Environmental behavior:** It refers to the use of environment by people in the course of social interactions. For example considering the environment as personal space in which individuals identify themselves with it.
- **Product behavior:** It includes the outcomes of people's actions such as cities, schools, dams, homes, and more. This means these are outcomes or products dealing with the environment.

Effects of human activities on environment

Humans are only living organisms that can modify the environment according to their needs. Now a days, humans are exploiting natural resources for the development and comforts of human society. To fulfil the needs of increasing human population they have started overexploiting natural resources by deforestation, unplanned urbanization and rapid industrialization.

The environment gets affected by various activities done by human beings like:

- Driving scooter
- Car or motor cycle
- Use of pesticides
- Cooking food and more

Figure 5.4: Effects of human activities on environment

Environmental degradation has now become a global problem. Over the past few decades, millions of people have died due to natural disasters. The effect of human activities like air pollution is long term and irreversible that eventually affects the lives of generations.

Causes of environmental degradation:

- Earthquakes
- Volcanic eruption
- Forest fires
- Floods

Ecological imbalance

Ecosystems are balanced when species coexist with other species. If something happens in an ecosystem it becomes imbalance. Ecological imbalance takes place when a human or naturally caused disturbance disrupts the natural balance of an ecosystem. Disturbance can be any changes that cause disruption in the balance of an ecosystem.

The ecosystem gets imbalanced by:

- Volcanic eruptions
- Floods
- Natural fires like natural disturbances
- Pollution
- Logging a forest
- Overhunting of a species
- Introduction of new species are disturbances

Some other important factors are:

- **Greenhouse gas emission:** The greenhouse effect refers to circumstances where the short wavelength of visible light from the sun pass through a transparent medium, that is, CO, SO2, CO2, and get absorbed. But the longer wavelengths of the infrared radiation from the heated objects are unable to pass through that medium and are trapped causing more heat and a higher resultant temperature.

Figure 5.5: Greenhouse emissions

Figure 5.6: Habitat distinction

- **Habitat distinction:** 31% of land area in our planet is covered with forests that help people as they purify water and air, and provide jobs to people; 13.2 million of people are working in the forest section. There are number of animals like elephants, rhinos, etc. that rely on forests. Clearing forests to obtain timber and space for urban or agricultural zones, results in deforestation.

  Deforestation also greatly affects the soil that provides nutrients for vegetation in the ecosystems. It results in soil erosion and nutrients run-off by rainfall and reduces soil fertility.

- **Radioactive wastes:** Nuclear reactors generate nuclear wastes and are real threat to life on Earth. Exposures to radioactive elements can have severe health effects on human being that can result in irreparable DNA damage that lead to tumors, cancers and other life threatening conditions.

  Radioactive wastes can also destroy soil, air, water, and infuse harmful substances in the environment and affect wildlife, marine life, and vegetation.

- **Nuclear weapons:** A single thermonuclear weapon can be million times more destructive than the largest conventional weapon. Nuclear bombs are possessed by several countries so an extreme global and climate environmental change can take place if a major nuclear conflict happens. This will result in significant health implications and may destroy life on earth.

- **Overexploitation of natural resources:** This means overuse of natural resources to such extent that it almost reaches a stage off enervation. We can see this phenomenon in the exploitation of:
  - o Forest and natural vegetation
  - o Grazing pastures
  - o Medical plants
  - o Wildlife
  - o Fossil fuels
  - o Fish stock and water aquifers

Figure 5.7: Overexploitation of natural resources

There will be loss of forest lands by unplanned urbanization, oil drillings, and large scale mining.

- **Environmental pollution:** In health of our ecosystem, a major role is played by air, land, and water. Harmful chemicals are released in the environment due to any kind of pollution. Natural or human activities influence the balance which is manifested through changes occurring in air, water and land.

Figure 5.8 Environmental Pollution

Any disturbance in air, water and land is reflected in the deviation from natural balance in living beings. This undesirable change in the composition of air, water and land and the disturbed inter-relation (ecology) is called environmental pollution.

- **Biotechnological misuse:** Another threat to environment and mankind is production of disease producing bacteria, fungi, viruses for biological welfare. This can result in catastrophic epidemics to animals and human life as when super-powered pathogens are released there will be disseminate through water or air.

Conservation of natural resources

Figure 5.9: Conservation of natural resources

Conservation is the proper management of a natural resource to prevent its exploitation, destruction, or degradation.

Conservation is the sum total of activities, which can derive benefits from natural resources but at the same time prevent excessive use, which may lead to destruction or degradation. It means using them more efficiently and less wastefully.

There is abundance of natural resources on earth due to which humans don't think about their depletion. The consumption of resources is getting increased by urbanization and industrialization and due to increase in population. There will be no resources left for future if we human beings keep exploiting nature.

Various steps have been taken for soil conversation, water conservation, food conservation, and forest conservation.

- **Soil conservation:** It means checking soil erosion and improving the fertility of soil by adopting various methods that become useful in following:
  - o Maintenance of soil fertility
  - o Control on grazing
  - o Reforestation
  - o Terracing
  - o Contour ploughing
- **Water conservation:** For survival of plants, mankind and animals there is a need to conserve and manage water. To achieve water conservation use the following methods:
  - o Grow vegetation in the catchment area
  - o Constructing dams and reservoirs
  - o Sewage should be treated and only clear water should be released into the rivers
  - o Prevent throwing industrial wastes in water
  - o Judicious use of water in our day to day life
  - o Rainwater harvesting
  - o Watershed should be made
- **Food conservation:** Food conservation and storage have been practiced to feed mankind in times of shortage. Food is stored in warehouses on large scale and in refrigerators at home. Food is also preserved through various methods to prevent the spoilage due to harmful bacteria and other microorganisms.
- **Forest conservation:** Forest conservation means the retention of existing forests or the creation of new forests at the levels prescribed by the State or local authority. Participation of the community living in and around forests is important for the success of the forest conservation program.

Tips to conserve natural resources

The 3Rs can be applied in daily life to conserve natural resources. The 3Rs are Reduce, Reuse, and Recycle:

- **Reduce:** Do not use what is not required. If we reduce at source, there is a lesser chance of waste generation and the pressure on our already stretched natural resources is reduced.
- **Reuse:** Reuse the materials for other purposes, such as making pillow covers or rags out of used shirts or ladies suits.

Figure 5.10: Reduce, reuse and recycle circle of life

- **Recycle:** Recycling is reusing some components of waste that may have some economic value. Recycling has readily visible benefits, such as conservation of resources, reduction in energy used during manufacturing and reduction in pollution levels.

Example of recycling: Kitchen wet waste can be utilized to make compost that can be used as an organic fertilizer.

Environment protection and conservation

Conservation of environment means proper use and management of natural resources that can be water, air, land, wildlife, natural vegetation, earth deposits, and more. In India and other parts of world the conservation and protection of environment has become necessary.

Some of the essential steps for environment conservation are:

- Use less electricity by making sure appliances or fans are turned off when not in use or when no one is present in the room.
- Develop environment friendly habits by properly handling wastes and refrain from using polythene bags. Don't dump things in rivers, lakes and seas, and not even on land.
- Instead of using incandescent bulbs make use of CFL and LED bulbs. Use solar heaters, solar cookers like appliances that utilize renewable energy sources.
- For bathing, brushing teeth, drinking, cooking, and washing work use water sensibly.
- Buy air conditioners and refrigerators according to their energy star ratings. Less power consumption by these appliances result in reduction of global warming.
- Prefer to cover short distances by walking or through cycle as emission from vehicles are harmful to the environment.
- Start doing rainwater harvesting at home by encouraging the use of drip irrigation.
- Use biofuels and biogas at home.
- Raise awareness around you for protection and effective use of natural resources.
- In vehicles, try to use Compressed Natural Gas (CNG) like fuels instead of diesel and petrol.
- Avoid throwing industrial sewage and wastes in water or sea.
- Encourage afforestation by planting large number of trees in your surroundings.

Summary

- The word environment has been derived from French word environ which means to surround or encircle. Its dictionary meaning is: external condition influencing growth or development of people, surrounding and working or living conditions, and more.
- Natural and human-made environment are two types of environment.
- An ecosystem can be defined as a functional unit of nature in which living organisms interact with each other and also with surrounding physical environment.
- Ecosystems are balanced when species coexist with other species. If something happens in an ecosystem it becomes imbalanced. Ecological imbalance takes place when a human or natural caused disturbance disrupts the natural balance of an ecosystem.

- Greenhouse gas emission, habitat distinction, radioactive wastes, nuclear weapons, overexploitation of natural resources, environmental pollution and biotechnological misuse are some of the important factors of ecological imbalance.
- Conservation is the proper management of a natural resource to prevent its exploitation, destruction or degradation.
- The conservation of natural resources has become necessary because of rising greed and careless attitude towards nature.

Self-Assessment

MULTIPLE CHOICE QUESTIONS.

1. The word environment has been derived from the French word environ which means

   a. To protect b. To surround c. To circle d. None

2. Which of the following primary components of the ecosystem are producers of energy.

   a. Autotrophs b. Heterotrophs c. Non living matter d. All

Answer

1. B 2. A

FILL IN THE BLANKS

1. Examples of abiotic components are ______________.
2. All living organisms are included in ___________ components of ecosystem.
3. ___________ are the consumers of energy and these organisms directly or indirectly depend on the autotrophs of their food.
4. ______________ is a deep layer in earth's atmosphere that contains ozone which is naturally occurring molecule containing three oxygen atoms.
5. The full form of 3Rs that can be applied in daily life to conserve natural resources are ___________.

Answer

1. Light, air, soil, water, and minerals 2. Biotic 3. Heterotrophs
4. Ozone layer 5. Reduce, Reuse and Recycle

QUESTIONS

1. What do you mean by the word environment?
2. What is ecosystem? Name its three primary components.
3. Define the term ecological imbalance.
4. Give some essential steps for environment conservation.

PROJECT WORK

Prepare posters showing environment conservation.

SESSION 2: IMPORTANCE OF GREEN ECONOMY AND GREEN SKILLS

The current strategies of economic development are using up resources of the world so rapidly that our future generations would have serious environment problems. There is increase in consumption of natural resources with increase in population and income; this has led to increase in production and utilization of natural resources. The rapid increase in industrialization, commercialization and growing needs of people will lead to increase in number of power plants, use of chemical fertilizers, industries and vehicles. All this increases pollution in air, land, or water.

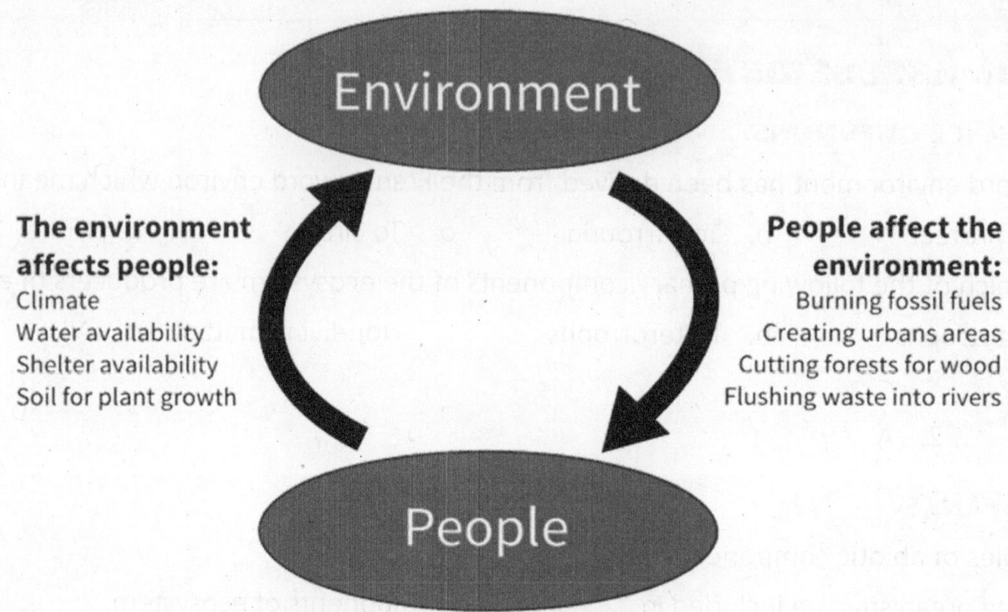

Figure 5.11: Cycle of green economy

Society has to change its unsustainable development strategy so that environment does not get destroyed by development. This form of sustainable development can only be brought about if each individual practices a sustainable lifestyle. Since most of the natural resources are scarce, judicious utilization of resources is necessary.

Green skills

Green skills are skills used for promoting green economy that are needed in areas like renewable energy, climate resilient cities, solid waste management, sewer water treatment and green construction. The green skills agreement defines skills for sustainability. Green skills are:

- Technical skills
- Technical values
- knowledge and attitudes needed in the workspace for supporting and development of sustainable economic,
- social and environment outcomes in industry,
- business and community

Some of the areas in which green skills has contributed to sustainable development are:

- Using solar, wind, and power renewable energy
- Management of waste and water
- Energy conservation
- Rain water harvesting
- Reducing pollution

According to environment scientists, environment can be protected from various ecological problems by adapting green economy.

Green economy

Green economy results in improved human well-being and social equity while reducing ecological scarcities and environmental risks. This system helps in economic growth along with taking care of environment. The economy is a system of institutions and organizations that either facilitate or play a role in the production and distribution of goods and services among the members of society.

The green economy required that economic development is decoupled from the use of resources and environmental degradation. Decoupling refers to reducing the environmental impact associated with any economic activity.

The causes of the climate change, food, social and economic crises that have unfolded during the last decade vary, but they all share one common feature- the gross misallocation of capital. During the past two decades, much capital was poured into property development, fossil fuels, and structured finance.

By comparison, relatively little was invested in:

- Development of renewable energy
- Improving energy efficiency
- Promoting and developing appropriate public transportation
- Sustainable agriculture
- Ecosystem and biodiversity protection
- Land and water conservation

The concept of green economy has become a global agenda and some of the important global events over the last few decades focusing on green economy are:

- 1972 Stockholm conference
- 1987 Brundtland Report
- 1992 Earth Summit and Agenda 21
- 2012 Rio+20Conference

A Three pronged approach has been proposed by United Nations Environment Programme (UNEP) for the attainment of green economy, these are:

- **Low carbon growth:** The concentration of CO2, Nitrogen oxide, methane like greenhouse gases in the environment is getting increased by burning fossil fuels. This prevents earth from cooling at night resulting in climate change and global warming.

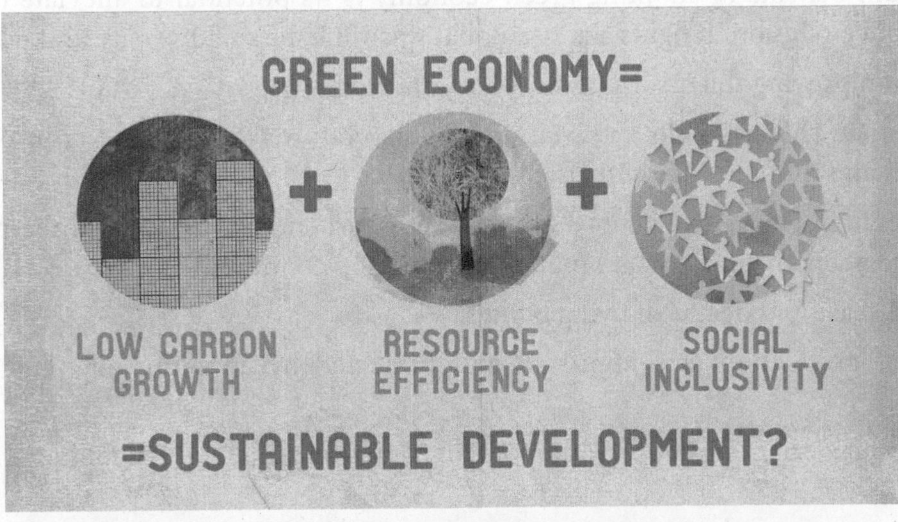

Figure 5.12: Green economy

- **Resource efficiency:** By overusing and exploiting the natural resources, they are getting depleted. These resources can be conserved by green economy as it involves increasing prosperity by using the resources economically without effecting the environment.
- **Social inclusion:** It essentially means sharing the responsibility and benefits of economic growth across all sections of society. There is need for investments from both private and public sectors that result in growth of income and employment through green jobs. Green job is the work in manufacturing, administrative, agriculture, research and development and service activities that contribute towards preserving the quality of the environment.

Importance of green economy

Given below are some of benefits of green economy:

Figure 5.13: Importance of green economy

- Green economy leads to economic growth as certain new markets have been created in renewable energy and bio-fuels areas.
- The emerging economies will be able to open a new market segment for export and production of green services and products by adopting green economy.
- It contributes in prevention of melting glaciers and resulting rise of sea levels.
- One of the main benefits of adopting green economy is its potential to alleviate the environmental impact caused by pollution. It fights against global warming, loss of diversity and desertification.
- It also helps in improving the quality of air, water, and soil.
- It prevents climate changes such as variation in temperature, rainfall, and crop production. It also prevents floods and droughts like climate disasters.
- With investments in alternative energy sources, access to energy services can be provided to create more social and economic advantages mainly in emerging countries.
- Reduction in disease and deaths of living beings.
- The agriculture production gets improved and protected by adopting new environment friendly technologies.
- Reduction in money spent on conservation of relief, environment, and rehabilitation of people.

- Increase in new areas of employment.
- Benefits in environmental and population health.

Summary

- The current strategies of economic development are using up resources of the world so rapidly that our future generations would have serious environment problems.
- Green skills are skills used for promoting green economy that are needed in areas like renewable energy, climate resilient cities, solid waste management, sewer water treatment, and green construction.
- The term Green economy was first devised in 1989 report for the Government of the United Kingdom by a group of leading environmental economists.
- Green economy will result in improved human well-being and social equity while reducing ecological scarcities and environmental risks.
- The three pronged approach has been proposed by United Nations Environment Programme (UNEP) for the attainment of green economy, these are low carbon growth, resource efficiency, social inclusion.
- One of the main benefits of adopting green economy is its potential to alleviate the environmental impact caused by pollution. It fights against global warming, loss of diversity and desertification.

Self-Assessment

MULTIPLE CHOICE QUESTIONS.

1. Green skills are the ability to ___________.

   a. Protect trees b. Plant trees

   c. Conserve the environment d. Identify trees

2. Green economy will not lead to ______________.

   a. More employment b. Energy efficiency

   c. Economic growth d. More pollution

Answer

1. c 2. d

FILL IN THE BLANKS

1. _________ building preserves precious natural resources and improves the quality of life.
2. Green economy is essential for _________ sustainability and future prosperity.
3. Green economy emphasizes on becoming more ____________ efficient.
4. Transition towards a _______________ can help us in countering the ecological problems.

Answer

1. Green economy 2. Resource 3. Environmental 4. Green

QUESTIONS

1. Define green skills.
2. What do you mean by Green Economy?

3. How do greenhouse gases affect our environment?
4. Give 5 benefits of Green economy.

PROJECT WORK

Arrange a discussion on the benefits of green skills and importance of green economy.

Exercise for Assessment

MULTIPLE CHOICE QUESTIONS.

1. The word environment has been derived from the French word environ which means
   a. To protect b. To surround c. To circle d. None
2. Biotic factors include:
   a. All non-living components b. All living components
   c. Both a and b d. None
3. Environment is categorized into:
   a. Biotic and abiotic components b. Natural and human-made environment
   c. Abiotic and natural environment d. None
4. Which of the following primary components of ecosystem are producers of energy?
   a. Autotrophs b. Heterotrophs c. Non-living matter d. All
5. What are the three aspects of humans in relation to the environment?
   a. Economical, social, and chemical b. Physical, chemical, and mental
   c. Physical, economical, and social d. None
6. Green skills is the ability to __________
   a. Protect trees b. Plant trees
   c. Conserve the environment d. Identify trees
7. Rain water harvesting is the example of __________.
   a. Social job b. Green job c. Hydel work d. Traffic job
8. Green economy will not lead to __________.
   a. More employment b. Energy efficiency
   c. Economic growth d. More pollution
9. Which of the following is not a pronged approach proposed by UNEP for attaining green economy?
   a. Low carbon growth b. Low oxygen growth
   c. Resource efficiency d. Social inclusivity

Answer

1. B 2. C 3. B 4. A 5. C 6. C 7. B 8. D 9. B

VERY SHORT QUESTIONS

1. Define the term ecological imbalance.
2. Define greenhouse gases?
3. What do you understand by overexploitation of natural resources?
4. Define habitat distinction.
5. List any three human activities that affect the environment.
6. How our environment gets affected by greenhouse gasses?
7. What are the aims of green economy?

SHORT QUESTIONS

1. What do you mean by the word environment?
2. What do you mean by conservation of environment?
3. Define the term ecosystem. Name its three primary components.
4. Why is conservation of environment important?
5. Define green economy.
6. What are green skills?
7. What do you mean by term the sustainable development?

LONG QUESTIONS

1. Write a short note on relationship between man and environment.
2. How can natural resources be conserve using the three Rs? What is the full form of three Rs?
3. What do you mean by environment protection and conservation? Give any five essential steps for environment conservation.
4. What is green skill and what is its importance in the present times?
5. Explain importance and benefits of green economy.

APPLICATION BASED QUESTIONS

1. Tell Simran about the importance of conservation of natural resources. Also give her various tips to conserve natural resources.
2. Imagine you are involved in a green skill development program. Some students have come to your office to know about some of the fields covered under this program. Suggest them some job opportunities involving green skills.
3. Explain how you are contributing towards green economy.

PROJECT WORK

1. Arrange a discussion on various factors that influences our environment.
2. Have a group discussion on hazards of deteriorating environment.
3. Prepare a poster showing the importance of green economy with the help of newspaper/magazine cuttings.

4. Have a group discussion on how banning diesel vehicles will help in reducing environmental pollution.

TEACHER NOTES

1. Give task to your students for making resourceful things using waste materials or the concept of Reduce, Reuse, and Recycle.
2. Make a presentation on various global events based on green economy.

Worksheet - 1 (Solved)

MULTIPLE-CHOICE QUESTIONS

1. Which of the following is not an example of written communication?

   a. Emails b. Reports c. Body language d. Letters

2. Which of the following is a Volatile memory?

   a. ROM b. Internal c. External d. RAM

3. Green skills is the ability to ____________

   a. Protect trees b. Plant trees
   c. Conserve the environment d. Identify trees

4. Which of the following skills are required to be a successful entrepreneur?

   a. Ambition b. Creativity c. Team management d. All

5. Which of the following shows the ability to participate as a team member?

   a. Interpersonal skills b. Communication skills
   c. Entrepreneur skills d. None

6. Perspective is an individual's

   a. Point of view b. Activity c. Body language d. None

7. _________ and __________ are two parts of email address

   a. Portal address and email address b. User name and domain name
   c. Portal address and domain name d. Email address and user name

8. ________ is a process of improving the skills and knowledge of entrepreneurs through various training and classroom programs

   a. Enterprise b. School
   c. Entrepreneurship development d. College

9. People with self-confidence have a____________ outlook:

   a. Negative b. Arrogant c. Outward d. Positive

10. ___________ is not an internal peripheral device.

    a. Modem b. Wi-Fi adaptor c. NIC d. Memory Card reader

Answers:

1. C 2. d 3. C 4. d 5. b
6. A 7. b 8. C 9. d 10. d

VERY SHORT TYPE QUESTIONS AND ANSWERS

1. Name 5 factors affecting perspective in communication
2. How our environment gets affected by greenhouse gasses.

3. Name various common terms used on the Internet?
4. How positive thinking helps in achieving self-confidence?
5. What do you mean by entrepreneurship development?
6. Write down the full form of SMART strategy.

Answers:

1. The factor affecting perspective in communication are:
    - Visual
    - Language
    - Past experience
    - Prejudices
    - Feelings
    - Environment
    - Attitude
2. The greenhouse effect refers to circumstances where the short wavelength of visible light from the sun passes through a transparent medium, i.e., CO, SO2, CO2, and many more and are absorbed. But the longer wavelengths of the infrared radiation from the heated objects are unable to pass through that medium and are trapped, causing more heating and a higher resultant temperature.
3. Various common items used on the Internet are:
    - Internet browser
    - Webpages or Websites
    - Web Portal
4. Positive thinking is nothing but focusing on the positives even in the time of adversity. Positive thinking is referred to your tendency to emphasize the positive aspects; on the other hand, negative thinking is emphasized on less optimistic aspects of the situation. By this, it helps in achieving the self-confidence.
5. Entrepreneurship development is the process of improving the skills and knowledge of entrepreneurs through various training and classroom programs. For example: To score well in the examination, the student goes for extra classes or coaching and also to improve their communication skills; they join various English communication courses and personality grooming institutes.
6. In SMART strategy,
    - S stands for specific
    - M stands for Measurable like divide your tasks whose completion gives the measurable outcome
    - A stands for Achievable that means set a task that can be achieved
    - R stands for Realistic
    - T stands for Time-bound

Worksheet - 2 (Solved)

MULTIPLE CHOICE QUESTIONS

1. R in SMART strategy stands for__________?
   a. Real b. Rate c. Realistic d. Required
2. Which of the following is not a type of phrase?
   a. Noun b. Adjective c. Adverbial d. Pronoun
3. Rainwater harvesting is the example of ____________.
   a. Social job b. Green job c. Hydel work d. Traffic job
4. Which of the following primary components of the ecosystem that are producers of energy.
   a. Autotrophs b. Heterotrophs c. Non-living matter d. All
5. People with self-confidence have a___________ outlook:
   a. Negative b. Arrogant c. Outward d. Positive
6. Which of the following is not a type of speech?
   a. Noun b. Pronoun c. Adverb d. Adjective
7. Which of the following is not a type of speech?
   a. Noun b. Pronoun c. Adverb d. Adjective
8. Green skills is the ability to ___________
   a. Protect trees b. Plant trees
   c. Conserve the environment d. Identify trees
9. Which of the following is not an example of written communication?
   a. Emails b. Reports c. Body language d. Letters
10. __________ is not the business activity.
   a. Service b. Manufacturing c. Creativity d. Merchandising

Answers:

1. c	2. d	3. b	4. a	5. d
6. b	7. b	8. c	9. c	10. c

VERY SHORT TYPE QUESTIONS AND ANSWERS

1. What is the page break?
2. What is the use of a cardiac screening machine?
3. What is the operating system?
4. Define the fill handle of a cell?
5. List any three human activities affecting the environment.
6. Give two characteristics of accountability.

Answers:

1. Page break is also known as a hard page break that is a code inserted by a software program like MS Word that tells the printing device were to end the current page and begin the next. It will move the text to a new page before reaching the end of the page.
2. The cardiac screening machine is used to displays the physiology of the heart and its inside movements. This machine is mainly used for diagnosis the problems related to heart like thinning of veins.
3. When you switch on the computer, OS is the first program that is a load on the computer. It is an interface between hardware and software of a computer that manages the overall functionality of the computer and its resources. It also monitors and controls the execution of other applications and programs by performing sending output to monitor, recognizing input from the keyboard, and controlling peripheral devices.
4. In the MS Excel Fill Handle tool, you can fill the next cells by dragging it with the next predefined value. For example, you want to fill the roll numbers, month, week, days, and many more, then you can input one or two in sequence, then select them and drag it to the next cell or till that you want to continue that series of sequence.
5. The environment gets affected by various activities done by human beings like:
   - Driving scooter
   - Car or motorcycle
   - Use of spray
   - Cooks food and more
6. Two characteristics of accountability are:
   - Avoid procrastination that means avoiding the important tasks that need to be completed. This includes choosing an easy task rather than doing the important, difficult task.
   - Adopting a problem-solving attitude is required in every area of work. Sometimes there can be a situation come when people have to face a difficult situation even after planning or prioritizing everything. In these cases, a problem-solving attitude helps in achieving the goal on time.

SECTION-B

1 Introduction to the IT-ITeS Industry

Learning Outcomes

After this chapter, you will have the knowledge of:

- The concept of IT-ITeS industry
- BPO services
- How BPM industry affecting India in a positive way
- What is the structure of the IT-BPM industry
- Categorization of BPM
- Applications of IT in various areas like health, business, communication, entertainment, education, workplace, and many more.

INTRODUCTION

Information and Communication Technology (ICT) that includes a set of technological resources and tools used for communication, creation, storing, managing, and disseminating information. ICT includes internet, computers, telephony, and broadcasting technologies that take knowledge about how a computer works and how different computers communicate with each other. It has become one of the basic requirements of basic society. In today's era, almost everyone uses mobile phones for performing their daily life tasks.

SESSION 1: INTRODUCTION TO IT AND ITES

The IT and ITeS industry in India has today become a growth engine for the economy, contributing substantially to increases in the GDP, urban employment and exports, to achieve the vision of a powerful and resilient India. Indian firms, across all other sectors, largely depend on the IT and ITeS service providers to make their business processes efficient and streamlined. The Indian manufacturing sector has the highest IT spending, followed by automotive, chemicals, and consumer products industries.

Information technology (IT)

IT is a study, design, development, implementation, storing, support, and management of all computer-based information systems, particularly software applications and computer hardware. IT is the use of any computer, networking devices, storage, and other physical devices, infrastructure, and processes for creating, storing, securing, processing, and exchanging all forms of electronic data.

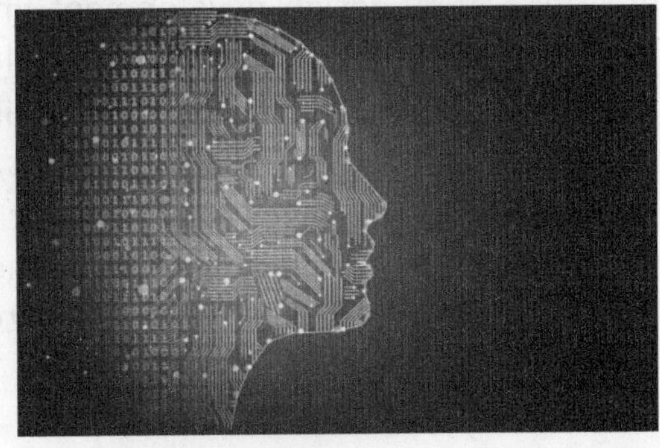

Figure 1.1: Information technology

Harvard Business Review has created the term information technology for making a distinction between purpose-built machines that are designed for performing the limited scope of general-purpose computing machines and functions.

This could be programmed for various tasks. The IT industry evolved from the mid-20th century, and computing capability advanced while device cost and energy consumption become less. Now IT has become an integrated part of business, and today in every business, a computer and information systems are an essential part. Some of the benefits of business are:

- Improve efficiency
- Increase in profit
- Minimize waste
- Reduce cost
- Improve the relationship with potential customers
- Provide better service to customers
- Allow customers to guide the business better
- Support good relationships with key partners

Information technology-enabled services (ITeS)

ITeS is an abbreviation for information technology-enabled services and also known as web-enabled services or teleworking that defined as outsourcing of processes that enabled with information technology and covered diverse areas like HR, healthcare, finance, administration, manufacturing, telecommunication, and many more. All services armed with manpower and technology is provided from e-enabled locations. This results in a reduction in costs and improves the standards of services.

Figure 1.2: ITeS

ITeS services provide a wide range of career options that include opportunities in medical transcription, back-office operations, legal databases, logistic management, medical billing and coding, call center, revenue claims processing, web services, Geographical information systems, content development, HR services, payrolls, and many more. The outcome of an ITeS is in two forms:

- Indirect benefits
- Direct improved service

Summary

- Information and Communication Technology that includes a set of technological resources and tools used for communication, creation, storing, managing, and disseminating information.
- IT is a study, design, development, implementation, storing, support, and management of all computer-based information systems, particularly software applications and computer hardware.
- Some of the benefits of business improve efficiency, increase profit, minimize waste, reduce cost, provide better service to customers, and many more.
- ITeS is an abbreviation for information technology-enabled services and also known as web-enabled services or teleworking that defined as outsourcing of processes that enabled with information technology and covered diverse areas like HR, healthcare, finance, administration, manufacturing, telecommunication, and more.

Self-Assessment

MULTIPLE CHOICE QUESTIONS.

1. ITeS is abbreviation of ____________
   a. Information technology end-to-end services
   b. Information tech and end-user services
   c. Information technology-enabled services
   d. Information tech enable services
2. _______________ is a study, design, development, implementation, storing, support and management of all computer-based information system.
   a. Communication b. Information Technology
   c. Process d. Technology

Answer

1. C 2. B

QUESTIONS

1. Give the full form of the following terms:
   a. IT b. ITeS
2. What do you understand by IT?
3. Write a short note on ITeS?
4. What are the benefits of using IT in business?

PROJECT WORK

Explore the impact of IT and ITeS in various areas in day to day life.

SESSION 2: BPO SERVICES AND BPM INDUSTRY

BPO services

BPO is the abbreviation of Business Process Outsourcing services that are meant to perform business operations through an outside service provider. In the BPO, complete transfer of the business process or the function to an external service provider takes place. BPO comes under the services of IT, and in business performance optimization, a very important role is played by IT.

Figure 1.3: BPO services

In India, various kinds of jobs are outsourced by a highly organized industry of BPO. Some of the BPO services included are:

- Taxation and insurance services
- Financial and accounting services
- Software testing services
- Healthcare services

- Web promotion and e-publishing
- Multimedia and design services
- Translation services
- Collection services
- Document management services
- Digital content development
- Customer care

BPM industry in India

BPM stands for Business Process Management that defines how a company creates, edits, and analyses the predictable processes that make up the core of its business.

In India, there is almost 36% of the global outsource Business Process management market, which was earlier referred to as the BPO market. BPM is not a one-time task, but rather an ongoing activity that involves persistent process re-engineering.

BPM is considered as the bridge between IT and business due to its focus and control over complex IT processes. In India, almost 8% of the Gross Domestic Product (GDP) is contributed by the IT-BPM sector.

The growth in the IT-BPM industry has provided India a wide range of social and economic benefits such as raised income levels, created employment, and promoted exports. It has also placed India on the world map with the advancement in technology and economy based on knowledge.

Some of the factors that are influencing the Indian IT-BPM industry till the year and time ahead are:

- **Revamped partnerships:** In recent years, a rapid increase has been seen in reliance of businesses on technology. With this, partnerships with IT players have become integral for the BPM industry, and there is also a fast growth in industries by partnerships with IT players.
- **Disruptive technologies:** In recent areas, robotics and artificial intelligence have opened the possibilities of the whole world. Healthcare, Retail, etc., sectors are looking to optimize a new level of technology for their benefits, and the IT-BPM industry has been fast to catch it.
- **Enhancement of skillsets:** According to a recent report of the National Association of Software and Services Companies (NASSCOM) and Federation of Indian Chambers of Commerce and Industry (FICCI) in collaboration with professional services, there will be several interesting insights on India's job scenario by 2022.

Structure of the IT-BPM industry

BPM defines how a company creates, edits, and analyses the predictable processes that make up the core of its business. BPM is considered as the bridge between IT and business due to its focus and control over complex IT processes.

The BPM can be categorized on the basis of the purpose that they serve. Three types of BPM are:

- **Integration-centric BPM:** It handles the processes of primarily jumping between HRMS, CRM like existing systems with much involvement of humans.
- **Human-centric BPM:** These are for humans executed processes. In this, a lot of approvals and tasks are performed by individuals.
- **Document-centric BPM:** These are required when document like an agreement is the main part of the process. They enable verifying, routing, getting, and formatting the document signed as the tasks pass along the workflow.

In the IT-BPM industry, organizations are categorized according to these parameters:

- Geographic spread of operations
- Sectoring serve by organization
- Revenues and size of operations

Types of companies according to the range:

- **Multinational companies (MNCs):** A multinational company is a business that operates in many different countries at the same time. Mainly their headquarters are outside India, but it is operated in multiple locations worldwide. They handle both domestic and global clients.
- **Indian Service Providers (ISPs):** These companies are started with their operations in India, and most of these organizations have their headquarters in India, but their offices can be in many international locations. They handle both global and domestic clients, but some of the ISP's companies serve only Indian clients.
- **Global In-house Centers (GIC):** These organizations gratify only the needs of their parent company and do not serve external clients. Or we can also say that thee organizations are offshore centers that perform designated functions for large organizations. This allows the organization to keep IT operations in-house and expand its global footprint by offering opportunities for innovation in a cost-effective manner.

Summary

- BPO is the abbreviation of Business Process Outsourcing services that are meant to perform business operations through an outside service provider.
- BPM stands for Business Process Management that defines how a company creates, edits, and analyses the predictable processes that make up the core of its business.
- Some of the factors that have influenced the Indian IT-BPM industry till the year are revamped partnership, disruptive technology, and enhancement of skillsets.
- A multinational company is a business that operates in many different countries at the same time.
- Indian Service Providers companies are started with their operations in India, and most of these organizations have their headquarters in India, but their offices can be in many international locations.
- Global In-house centers organizations gratify only the needs of their parent company and do not serve external clients.

MULTIPLE CHOICE QUESTIONS.

1. ____________ is a form of BPM that is a cost-saving technique which involves contracting business tasks to a third party.

   a. IT　　b. BPO　　c. ITeS　　d. None

2. Which of the following is not a type of BPM?

   a. Integration-centric BPM　　b. Human-centric BPO

   c. Human-centric BPM　　d. Document-centric BPM

Answer

1. b　2. b

QUESTIONS

1. Give various services of BPO?
2. Write a short note on the BPM industry in India?
3. What is the structure of the IT-BPM Industry? Give three parameters of the IT-BPM Industry.
4. What is the full form of the following terms:

   a. BPO   b. BPM   c. GDP

PROJECT WORK

Divide the class into two groups; first, with even roll numbers that will make a presentation on various BPO services and rest odd roll number, students will make a presentation on the IT-BPM industry.

SESSION 3: IT APPLICATIONS

IT is the use of any computers, storage, networking, and other physical devices or processes for creating, processing, exchanging, and storing all forms of electronic data. The commercial use of IT encompasses both telephony and computer technology. Nowadays in technology developed nations IT has become a part of everyday life and desired information is provided by a computer as a tool.

Figure 1.4: IT applications

Various application areas of IT are home computing, everyday life, library, workplace, education, entertainment, communication, business, science and engineering, banking, insurance, marketing, health, and agriculture.

IT in-home computing

For working at homes, a personal computer or PC is used for performing household work. It is used for surfing the web, creating and listening to music, playing games, doing household account, playing puzzles, and many more.

The aim of personal computers at home is to:

- Help families in need to use the internet and developing basic computer skills in their everyday lives that result in an increase in children's literacy rate.

Figure 1.5: IT in-home computing

IT in the library

Libraries are the main information center that has also started using IT and computers for the benefit of mankind as a whole.

Some of the features of the use of IT in the library are:

- The introduction of IT and computer in the library have made thing simple or can say that the mechanization of library operation that are of a routine and repetitive nature.

Figure 1.6: IT in the library

- There is a barcode in each book that makes it easier to keep track of books in the library and also to keep the status of the availability of a specific book.

Now, when anybody wants to either issue or return a book, then the complete system is computerized.

IT at workplace

Technology is such an integral part of the 21-st century workplace that any business without some level of technical knowledge will fail. In workplaces or offices, computers and their applications are used to perform work more effectively that makes computer use as prevalent. Some offices or companies may find functioning without them is virtually impossible.

Figure 1.7: IT at workplace

IT in education

Education and learning are lifetime processes that don't have any limit to start and stop. The speed of information delivery has been increased by information technology that results in the improvement of the education environment. Nowadays, computers and information technology are used in education for teaching, learning, and assessment.

Figure 1.8: IT in education

- **ICT in the classroom:** Nowadays, IC is used in the classroom for educational purposes in various ways such as:
  - o Interactive whiteboards or smartboards for presentations
  - o Educational games
  - o e-learning classrooms
  - o Use audio-visual education
  - o Online submission of assignments
  - o Learning using the CD-ROM media and many more
  - o Enable to gather information on the internet
  - o Videos for experiments
  - o Desktop publishing of magazines, letters, and documents
  - o Creation of images and video
- **Education — anywhere anytime:** Unlike in the past, when learning was limited to a physical classroom, students and teachers could only access academic information while at school. Nowadays, they can access information at any given the time of day. It doesn't matter where they are or the time of the day is. Online education is facilitated by information technology.
- **Teaching aids and media:** Information technology and computer makes it easy to access academic information at any time. Both students and teachers use information technology for acquiring and exchanging educational material.
  - o Teachers provide visual and audio classes to their students using computers and broadband internet
  - o Obtain subject-related information from the internet
  - o They use presentations for making lessons interesting
  - o To explain difficult lessons or subjects an animation, audio-visuals, and pictures are used
  - o Computers are used for organizing the lessons

IT in entertainment

Figure 1.10: IT in entertainment

Advancement in technology helps in improving every aspect of the home environment, including home entertainment systems. IT and the internet is a major source of entertainment. When we go back in years, then there were limited options for enjoying entertainment at home. However, this has been changed by the invention of cable and satellite TV as people are able to access a range of channels.

Other major sources of entertainment are:

- New games consoles
- Computer technology
- High-speed broadband that enables people to download and view movies, play games, chat, and use multimedia
- Incorporate visual and sound effects using computers or mobile systems

IT in communication

The use of technology in communication has become a necessity; it's now a part of our lives. The advancement in technology has made a great impact on the way we communicate. Over the years, communication methods have evolved from simple text messages and audio calls to more efficient video calls and chat platforms that offer other communication services. People communicate through:

- Faxes
- Video chat rooms
- Video conferencing
- Texting services
- Emails
- Social media channels

Figure 1.11: IT in communication

IT in business

Information technology drives innovation, and innovation is the path to business success. IT has become very important in the business world from your company's online store to enterprise software; there is a need to record the transactions and gather information. In every business organization, computers are used for payroll calculation, sales analysis, managing stocks, financial forecasting, budgeting, and maintaining stocks.

IT in business can help through:

- Communication
- Inventory management
- Management information systems
- Customer relationship management

Figure 1.12: IT in business

IT in science and engineering

Computers are also being used by scientists and engineers for performing complex scientific calculations, and drawing, designing, and testing or simulation of design is done using **Computer-Aided Manufacturing (CAM) and Computer-Aided Design (CAD) applications.**

IT in banking

IT also helps the banking industry to deal with the challenges poses by the new economy. To meet the needs of customers, financial institutions rely on gathering, processing, analyzing, and providing information. For the banking industry, a new service, new products, efficient delivery channels are opened by technology. Some of the examples of technology in banking are online electronics banking, internet banking, and mobile banking. The large paper hank accounts and huge account registers are diminished.

Figure 1.13: IT in banking

The e-bank that is known as easy bank offers the following services:

- Credit cards/debit cards
- DEMAT accounts banking
- E-chequ
- ATM
- Mobile banking
- Telephone banking

IT in insurance

Insurance companies also use computers to create a database that contains all records up to date. The demand for new insurance products is ever-growing from traditional life and health insurance to ensure against natural disasters and cyber-attacks. The insurance companies keep the data of their policies, starting date, date of next installment, maturity date, interest dues, survival benefits, and bonus are declared using computers in insurance companies.

IT in marketing

In the 21st century workplace, information technology or IT skills are essential for success in a marketing career. For planning, managing, and monitoring campaigns a computer technology is used by marketing professions. To increase the market campaign precision, prospect communications, personalize customer, data manipulation campaign, and improving customer relationship management, data is analyzed and manipulated on computers. The e-commerce websites have made it easy for people to purchase items, even sitting at home.

IT in healthcare

Information technology in healthcare is a broad term that describes the technology and infrastructure used for recording, analyzing, and sharing patient health data. The purpose of introducing IT in healthcare is to:

- Provide better care for patients and help them in achieving health equity.
- The patient's records and various activities pertaining to hospital administration are managed and maintain by the hospital management system.

IT in health improves:

- The quality of healthcare delivery.
- Decrease medical errors.
- Strengthens the interaction between patients and healthcare providers.
- Increase patient safety.

Use of ICT for diagnosis

The advancement in ICT and various high-tech machines results in the diagnosis and treatment of critical diseases. The use of advanced systems helps in the diagnosis of diseases at the early stages, and accordingly, treatment can be given to patients. Various medical images machines are:

- **Magnetic Resonance Imaging (MRI) machine:** MRI is a radiology technique scan that uses magnetism, radio waves, and computers to produce images of internal organs or structures. The digital images are very helpful in the detection of tiny changes within the body and also help in the detection of diseases then deciding treatment for it. It is most often used when other testing fails to provide sufficient information to confirm a patient's diagnosis.

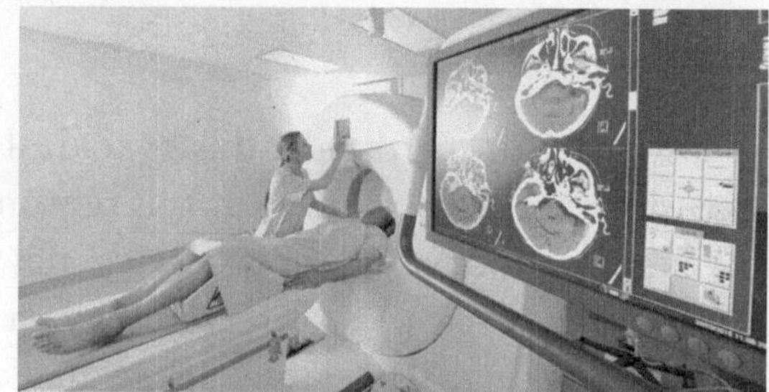

Figure 1.14: MRI machine

- **Computerized Axial Tomography (CAT) machine:** It uses a computer linked to an X-ray machine that makes a series of detailed pictures of areas inside the body. These pictures are taken from different angles and used to create 3-dimensional (3-D) views of tissues and organs. These images are helpful in the diagnosis of disease, plan treatment, or find out how well the treatment is working.

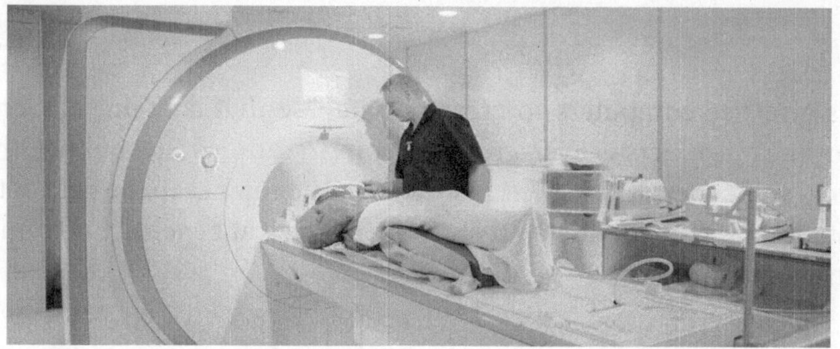

Figure 1.15: Computerized Axial Tomography (CAT) Machine

- **Cardiac screening machine:** Screening tests are used for finding the disease before symptoms begin, and the goal of screening is to detect disease at its earliest stage. The cardiac screening machine is used to displays the physiology of the heart and its inside movements. This machine is mainly used for diagnosis the problems related to heart like thinning of veins and then according to recommend treatment.

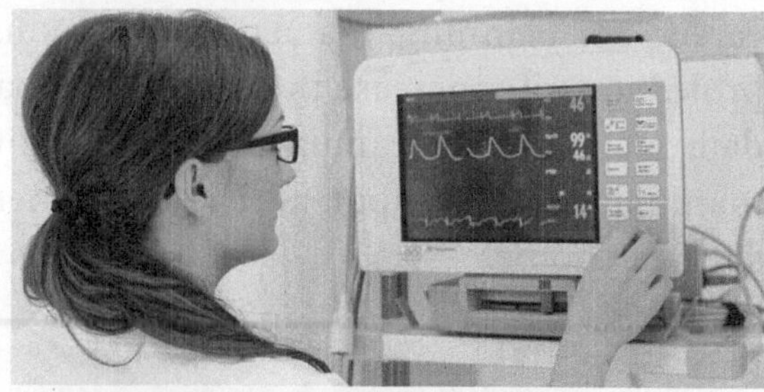

Figure 1.16: Cardiac screening machine

- **Electrocardiogram (ECG) machine:** The ECG is a diagnostic tool that is routinely used to assess the electrical and muscular functions of the heart. This machine monitors the heartbeat and detects electrical impulses produced when blood is pumped by the heart to different parts of the body. Then the recorded electrical impulses by machine are shown in the form of a graph. In the case of interrupted or misguided electrical activities, there are chances of heart diseases.

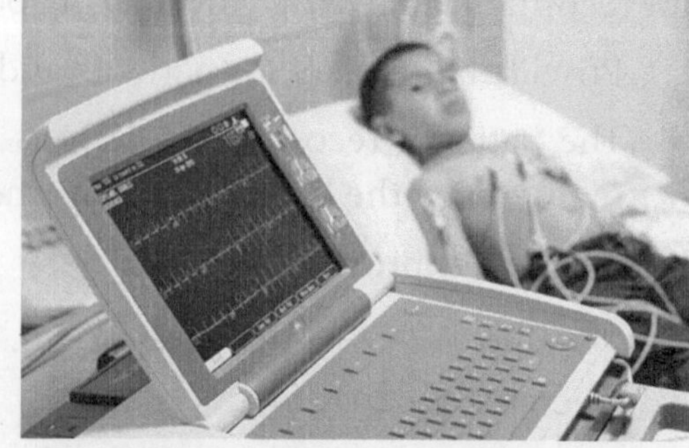

Figure 1.17: ECG machine

- **Electroencephalography (EEG) machine:** EEG is a test used to evaluate the electrical activity in the brain. Brain cells communicate with each other through electrical impulses. The potential problems associated with this activity can be detected by this machine. It also records and tracks the patterns of brain waves. The small electrical probes are attached to the head for receiving the electrical impulses of the brain and send signals to a computer for recording the results.

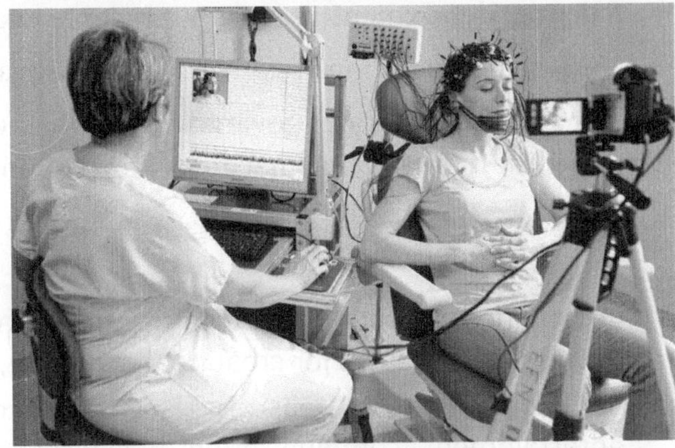

Figure 1.18: Electroencephalography (EEG) machine

- **Blood pressure measuring machine:** This device is worn on a wrist band for measuring the blood pressure of a person at rest or when a patient is involved in some physical activity. Now one can also monitor blood pressure at home by using digital blood pressure machines.

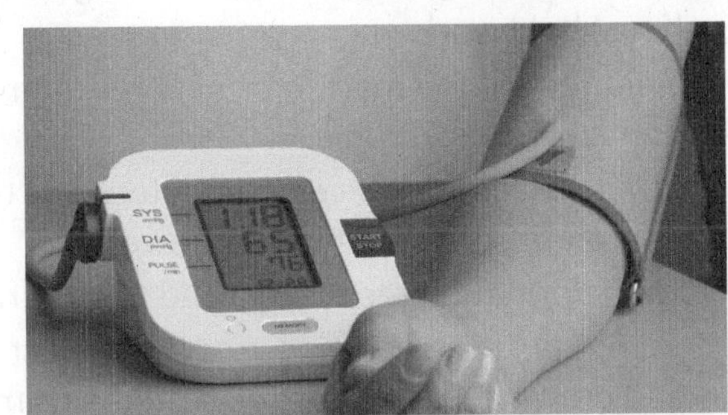

Figure 1.19: Blood pressuring measuring machine

- **Blood sugar testing machine:** This device is used to analyze a blood glucose level in your body. For this purpose, a sample of blood is taken then given to a device that gives the level of blood glucose in the body. Now one can also monitor the blood sugar level at home by using digital blood sugar testing machines.

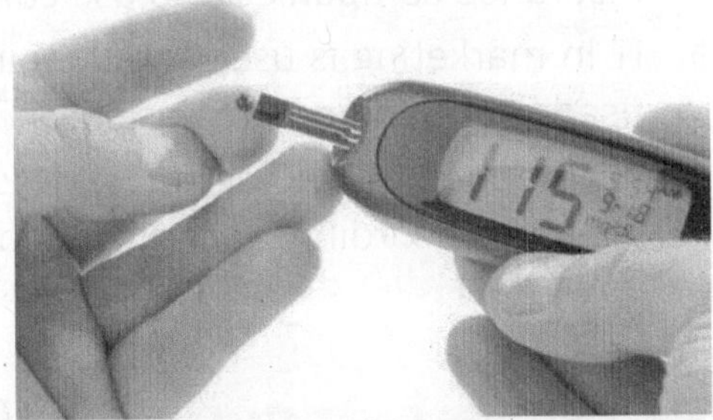

Figure 1.20: Blood sugar testing machine

IT in everyday life

Over the past few decades, it is a recognized fact that the application of IT in our daily life has changed dramatically. IT is used in every sphere of life like microwave oven, washing machines, OTG, television, printers, refrigerators, and many more products using which have embedded software in it.

Figure 1.21: IT in everyday Life

IT in government and public services

Nowadays, in daily operations, a computer application is used by the government on large-scale that actively encourages e-governance practices. The best example of this is Digital India and the e-governance initiative of the Government of India. Digital government is a powerful tool for enabling the provision of better public services to citizens and businesses. The computer system is used by:

- Sales tax department
- Income tax department
- Voter list preparations
- ADHAR card and PAN card preparations

We can also access various government services online, like paying electricity bills, phone bills, and more. Even the traditional voting machines for elections have been replaced by electronic voting.

Summary

- Information technology or IT is the use of any computers, storage, networking, and other physical devices or processes for creating, processing, exchanging, and storing all forms of electronic data.
- Various application areas of IT are home computing, everyday life, Library, workplace, education, entertainment, communication, business, science and engineering, banking, insurance, marketing, health, and agriculture. For working at homes, a personal computer or PC is used for performing household work.
- Libraries are the main information center that has also started using IT and computers for the benefit of mankind as a whole.
- In workplaces or offices, computers and their applications are used to perform work more effectively that makes computer use as prevalent.
- The information technology and the Internet have become a major source of entertainment.
- Computers are also being used by scientists and engineers for performing complex scientific calculations and drawing, designing, and testing or simulation of design.
- IT also helps the banking industry to deal with the challenges poses by the new economy.
- Insurance companies also use computers to create a database that contains all records up to date.
- IT in marketing is used for planning, managing, and monitoring campaigns a computer technology is used by marketing professions.
- Information technology in Healthcare is a broad term that describes the technology and infrastructure used for recording, analyzing, and sharing patient health data,

Self-Assessment

MULTIPLE CHOICE QUESTIONS.

1. Out of the given options, which one is not an application area of IT?

   a. Education b. Health c. Banking d. None

2. What is the full form of EEG?

   a. Electricagram b. Electroencepalogy
   c. Electroencephalography d. Electrocardiogram

Answer

1. d 2. c

QUESTIONS

1. Give various services of BPO?
2. Write a short note on the BPM industry in India?
3. What is the structure of the IT-BPM Industry? Give three parameters of the IT-BPM Industry.

4. What is the full form of the following terms:

   a. BPO   b. BPM   c. GDP

PROJECT WORK

Explore the use of IT in various areas inside and outside your school and home area.

Exercise for Assessment

MULTIPLE CHOICE QUESTIONS.

1. _______________ is a study, design, development, implementation, storing, support and management of all computer-based information system

   a. Communication   b. Information Technology

   c. Process   d. Technology

2. Which of the following is the benefits of the use of IT in business:

   a. Improve efficiency   b. Minimize waste

   c. Increase in profit   d. All

3. ITeS is abbreviation of ____________

   a. Information technology end-to-end services   b. Information tech and end user services

   c. Information technology enabled services   d. Information tech enable services

4. BPO stands for:

   a. Business portal organization   b. Business Process Outsourcing

   c. Business Process organization   d. Business portal outsourcing

5. Which of the following are not the services of BPO?

   a. Software testing services   b. Health care services

   c. Customer services   d. Multimedia and design services

6. Which of the following defines how a company creates, edits, and analyses the predictable processes that make up the core of its business?

   a. Government   b. BPO   c. IT   d. BPM

7. Which of the following organization gratify only the needs of their parent company and do not serve external clients?

   a. Multinational Companies   b. Indian Service Providers

   c. Global In-house Centers   d. All

8. Out of the given options which one is not an application areas of IT

   a. Education   b. Health   c. Banking   d. None

9. What is the full form of ECG?

   a. Electricagram   b. Electroncardiogram

   c. Electrocardiogram   d. Electrocardiograin

Answer

1. b	2. d	3. c	4. b	5. c	6. d
7. c	8. d	9. c			

VERY SHORT QUESTIONS

1. What is the full form of IT?
2. What is the full form of ITeS?
3. What is the full form of BPO?
4. What is the full form of BPM?
5. Define BPO services.
6. What is the full form of GDP?
7. Which are the different areas of healthcare in which IT is used?
8. What is the use of cardiac screening machine?
9. What is the purpose of EEG machine?

SHORT QUESTIONS

1. What do you understand by IT?
2. Define ITeS?
3. Gives advantages and disadvantages of using ICT?
4. Gives three factors that influence the Indian IT-BPM industry?
5. How IT is used in Home computing?
6. Give examples of use of IT in everyday life?
7. Give various processes of workplace where IT is used.
8. Define LMS in education.
9. What is MRI machine?
10. Define EEH machine and what is its purpose?

LONG QUESTIONS

1. Write a short note on BPM industry in India?
2. What is the structure of the IT-BPM industry? Give three parameters of IT-BPM industry.
3. Give in detail various processes of use of IT in education.
4. Give in detail about any four areas in which IT is used.
5. For what purpose IT is used in business. Explain in detail
6. Briefly describe the use of IT in healthcare and use of it for diagnosis.

APPLICATION BASED QUESTIONS

1. Komal have her own medical industry in which she want to introduce the concept of IT. Help her in outlining the areas where she can do improvement by introducing IT.
2. Doctor has suggested Simran uncle for taking the test of ECG; tell him the purpose of ECG test.

3. Rahul have to give presentation on various applications areas of IT, Help him in preparing presentation on at least main five application areas in which IT have proven to be efficient.
4. Priya is preparing for interview in BPO sector; help her in differentiating BPO and BPM.
5. Simran is opening a new smart school, suggest him the benefits of adapting IT in education.

PROJECT WORK

1. Identify and list the various IT enabled services
2. Observe the application of IT in various areas.
3. Identify the advantages of using ICT over conventional method in various areas.

TEACHER NOTES:

1. Arrange a visit for students in BPO office, so that they can see the BPO services practically.
2. Show them practical usage of IT around them.

2 Data Entry and Keyboarding Skills

Learning Outcomes

After this chapter, you will have the knowledge of:

- Keyboarding skills
- Brief about home row keys
- What is typing ergonomics
- Various types of keys and their functioning
- How to type and delete number, symbols, and sentences
- Positioning and allocations of keys to fingers
- What is the mouse, its operation and various pointers associated with it
- Rapid touch tutor, various components and its stages
- Various rules and interface of rapid touch typing
- Interpretation of rapid typing software results

INTRODUCTION

The use of a keyboard reduces the paperwork and increases the speed of typing a text. The type's text on a computer can be used many times that reduce the need to rewrite the same text. You can master keyboarding skills and acquire high speed with consistent, sincere efforts and controlled environment. This unit focus on various types of keys, typing economics and positioning of fingers on the keyboard according to touch method of typewriting and use of typing software for learning various keyboarding skills.

SESSION 1: USE DATA ENTRY TOOLS KEYBOARD AND MOUSE

Keyboarding skills

The keyboard is an input device used to enter characters and functions into the computer system. Both computer keyboards and electronic typewriter keyboards are the same with some additional keys. It is a primary device with more than 100 keys used to enter text, and each key corresponds to a single symbol. A keyboard typically contains keys for an individual letter, numbers, and special characters as well as keys for special functions. A keyboard is connected to a computer system using a cable or a wireless connection.

Computer commands or actions are produced by simultaneously pressing the key. In touch method of typewriting:

- You type without using the sense of sight to fund the keys
- There is no need for searching the keys while typing as one has only to move their fingers to strike a correct key.
- Through muscle memory, a touch typist gets to know the location on the keyboard.
- Touch typing involves the placing of eight fingers in a horizontal row along with the middle of the keyboard.
- You can do touch typing either by using both hands or a single hand.

Figure 2.1: Keyboard

By practice, a touch typist keeps their fingers on the start position, which is in the middle row, and knows which finger to move and how much to move it for reaching and pressing the required key.

Keyboarding skills are very important in that:

- They can impact a person's ability to communicate with others in the future, both in social and professional realms.
- The practice improves the speed of typing, and by it, one can achieve a speed of 60 WPM or even higher.
- The rate of speed not necessary to be the same for everyone.

For learning touch typing, there is the availability of various websites and software products, and most of them are free. Rapid typing tutor is one of the free software products that are available for practice the touch typing. Some people also use the keyboard for gaming purposes by using either regular keyboard or keyboard with special gaming features.

Types of keys

There are various input devices of computers such as:

- Mouse
- Mic
- Keyboard
- Joystick
- Touchscreen
- Scanner, and many more, that are used for giving input to the computer.

Out of all these input devices, the keyboard is considered as the most common method for input the data into a computer. Electric contact is formed by pressing a key, and then these electric signals are transmitted to a microcontroller in a coded form to the computer that describes the character corresponds to that key. There are customized keyboards with special buttons, features, and standard keyboards that have a fixed layout of 104 keys. Detail of various keys on keyboards are:

- **Alphabetic keys:** There are 26 alphabets keys on the keyboard from A to Z. But these keys are not present in the alphabetic order. You can use these keys for typing words, sentences, or paragraphs.
- **Alt key:** Alt key stands for Alternate that is press together with another ley so that the other key does something different from what it usually does. It is like a second control key.
- **Arrow keys:** There are four arrow keys for moving the cursor up, down, left, or right, and these are used for moving the cursor in the respective direction.
- **Backspace key:** Backspace key is similar to the delete key that removes texts in a word. It deletes the text in the left of the cursor and moves the cursor to that position.
- **Caps lock key:** It is a toggle key, on pressing it every alphabetic character will be in uppercase.

- **Ctrl key:** The Ctrl key stands for the control key that is used in combination with other keys for doing a particular operation. It is the keyboard shortcut key.
- **Delete key:** It deletes or removes the characters at the current position of the cursor or also the selected object or text. The difference between backspace and delete is that the backspace key will delete the text and move the cursor; on the other hand, by deleting a text, the cursor will not move. Sometimes this key is simply referred to as del.
- **Enter key or Return key:** It is used to makes the computer perform an action or start a new line of writing, or it move the cursor to the beginning of the next line.
- **Esc key:** The Esc key in the computer stands for the Escape key that is used to send special codes to devices and exit from the programs and tasks and return to a previous menu.
- **Function keys:** It is a special button on a keyboard that is used for a particular operation in a program. The special keys on the computer keyboard are labeled as F1 to F12.
- **Home key:** It returns us at the beginning of the line, document, page, or screen.
- **Insert key:** It toggles how text is inserted.
- **Numlock key:** It enables or disables the numeric keypad given on the right side of the computer keyboard.
- **Page up key:** It will move you up one page from the currently viewed page.
- **Page down key:** It will move you down from the currently viewed page.
- **Punctuation keys:** There are various keys on the computer keyboard that are associated with punctuation, such as:
  - The comma (,)
  - Period (.)
  - Semicolon (;)
  - Brackets ([])
  - Parenthesis ({})

  There are some mathematical operators such as:
  - Plus sign (+)
  - Minus sign (-)
  - Equal sign (=)
  - Multiplication sign (*)
- **Shift or Alt keys:** This key is used to move the cursor in more than one position at a time.
- **Spacebar:** This key is press for creating an empty space to separate words.
- **Tab key:** The Tab key is used to begin a line of text.

Numeric keypad

Sometimes the numeric keypad is a separate device but not built into a keyboard. This keyboard is usually connected to a computer with either a USB cable or serial connector. This keypad is used when you have to enter massive numeric data. This is the same as a simple calculator that is now also available on the right-hand side of the computer keyboard. It contains:

- The numbers 0 through 9
- Decimal point (.)
- Addition (+)
- Subtraction (-)
- Multiplication (*)
- Division (/) along
- Num lock
- Enter key

Figure 2.2: Numeric keypad or keys

Frequently these keys serve as cursor control keys that decide the mode of the numeric keypad. It can also word on dual-mode in one mode; it represents numbers, and on another mode, it acts as various keys like page up, page down, Home, End, and more.

Home row keys

The home keys are the row of keys on the computer keyboard; your fingers rest on when not typing. The Alphabets ASDF are home keys for left hand and LKJ along with semi-colon (;) are for the right hand. For both hands, the thumb rests on the spacebar.

By positioning your hands correctly on the home row keys, you can memorize where all other keys on the keyboard are located. By positioning your hands correctly on the home row keys, you can memorize the location of all other keys. If your fingers are trained to make the correct movement to other keys, and after that, it returns to their respective home key, then you will be able to type in fast speed.

Guide keys

The guide keys are those keys that help in moving the cursor using the keyboard. On a computer keyboard, the F key for the left hand and J key for the right hand are guide keys. This helps touch typists in placing the fingers correctly on home keys.

Keyboard finger position

Left hand | Right hand

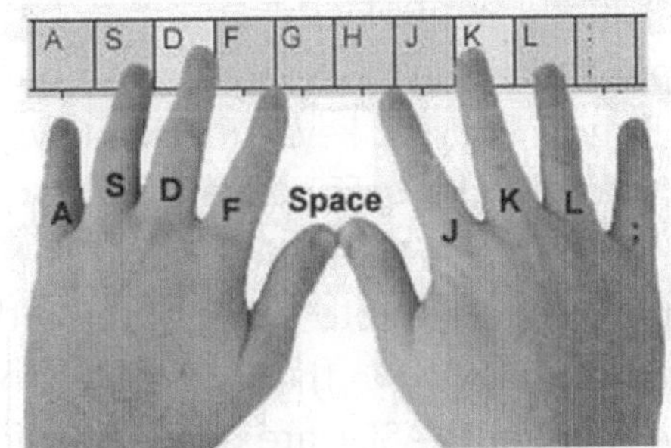

Figure 2.3: Home row keys

Typing and deleting text

To type text in a document, there is a need to click on the position from where you want to start writing then press letters or keys on the keyword for typing a text.

To delete a text in a document, there is a need to select the text or click on the end of the text you want to delete then use the delete key. Another option is using a backspace key that will delete the text from behind that means to the left of the position of your cursor.

- **Typing numbers:** To type numbers in a document, you have to use either the numbers keys available on the second top row of keys on the keyboard or enable Num lock of numeric keypad given on the right side.
- **Typing capital letters:** To type capital letters, you first have to click on the Caps Lock key available on the left side of the keyboard, and you will observe light on its top right side corner that shows it is on. Now whatever key you will press will come in the capital on the computer. To turn it off, again, click on the Caps lock key.
- **Typing symbols:** To type symbols given on the keyboard, you have to press the shift key along with the key with the required symbol. There are two shift keys on the keyboard; the first one is present on the left bottom side and second on the right bottom side of the keyboard. By pressing the shift key, you can access the top symbols given on keys with two characters.
- **Typing sentences:** For making sentences, you have to add space between words, to get space, press the space bar after typing one word and typing the next word.

- **Guide for typing:** For typing in a document, cursor keys are act as a guide. The cursor is a small downward indicator on the screen that flickers in a sentence while typing.
- **Creation of new lines and spaces between paragraphs:** For creating new lines and spaces between paragraphs, you have to press either Enter key given on the keyboard. This moves the cursor to a new line.

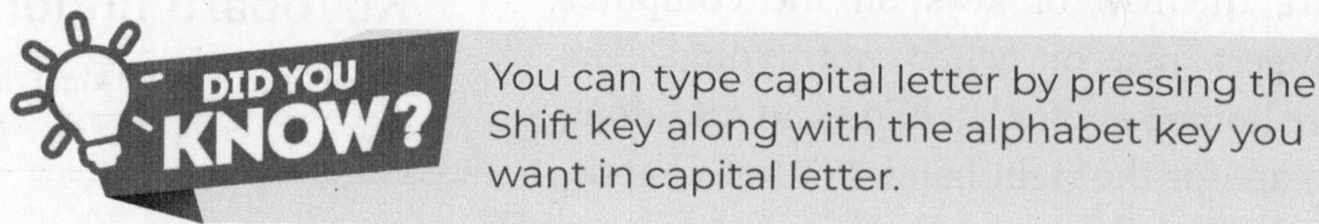

Summary

- The keyboard is an input device used to enter characters and functions into the computer system.
- The keyboard is a primary device with more than 100 keys used to enter text, and each key corresponds to a single symbol.
- Types of keys in Keyboard are Alphabetic keys, Alt key, Arrow key, Caps lock key, Delete key, Enter key or Return key, Esc key, Function keys, Home key, Insert key, Numlock key, Page up key, Page down key, Punctuation keys, Spacebar, Tab key and Shift or Alt keys.
- Sometimes the numeric keypad is a separate device but not built into a keyboard. This keyboard is usually connected to a computer with either a USB cable or serial connector.
- The home keys are the row of keys on the computer keyboard; your fingers rest on when not typing. The Alphabets ASDF are home keys for left hand and LKJ along with semi-colon (;) are for a right hand.
- For both hands, the thumb rests on the spacebar.
- The guide keys are those keys that help in moving the cursor using the keyboard.

Self-Assessment

MULTIPLE CHOICE QUESTIONS.

1. Which of the following is not a punctuation key?

   a. Comma (,) b. Semicolon (;) c. Parenthesis ({}) d. Equal sign (=)

2. Number of keys on Window keyboard are:

   a. 98 b. 110 c. 104 d. 106

Answer

1. d 2. c

QUESTIONS

1. What do you mean by keyboarding skills?
2. Name any five types of keys on the keyboard along with their function?
3. Define numeric keypad?
4. Name all home row keys.
5. How to type and delete text.

PROJECT WORK

Explore various keys of the keyboard along with their functioning.

SESSION 2: TYPING ERGONOMICS

Typing ergonomics is used to reduce the stress, strain, and wear and tear of your joints as you repeatedly type away. This also helps in maintaining effective typewriting, along with maintaining accuracy and speed. Some of the factors that come under typing ergonomics are given below:

- **Sitting posture:** To avoid any back pain and other problems, sit straight, slightly bending your neck forward while operating the computer keyboard. In ideal typing posture, your keyboard is below your elbow height when seated, with your wrists straight and not planted on the surface of the desk, touch both the feet to the floor. The key positions to achieve the most ergonomic and comfortable typing position are:

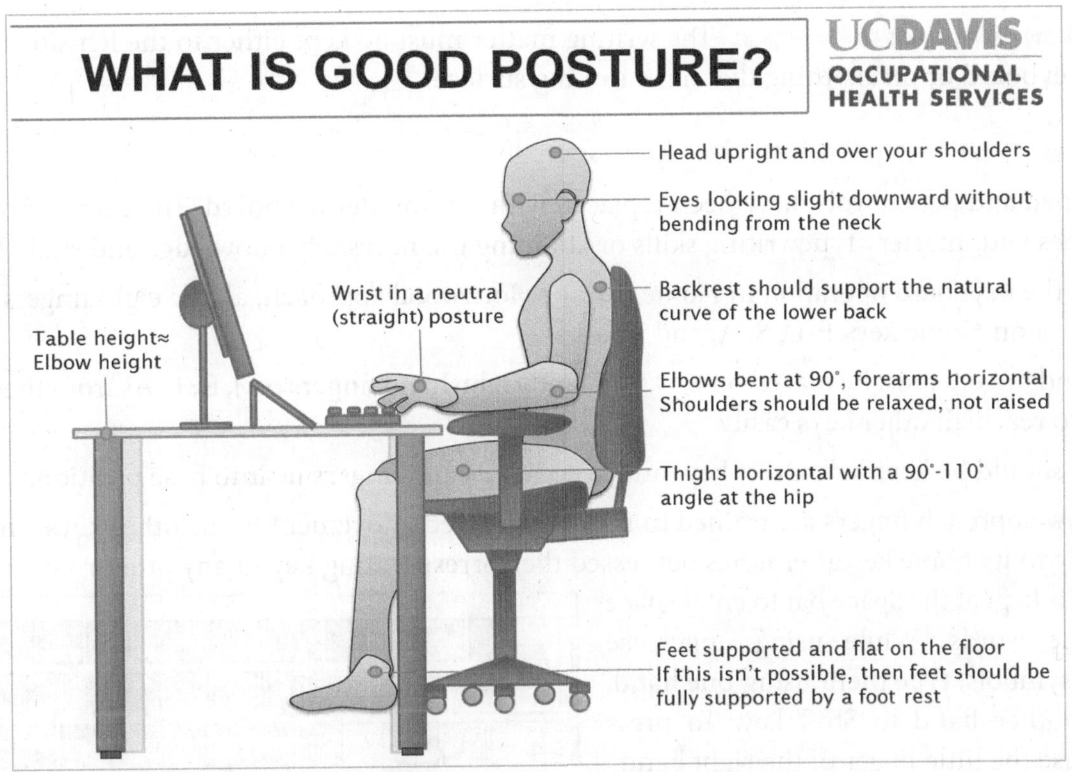

Figure 2.4: Sitting posture while working on the computer

- **Position of hands:** Your forearms should be at level with the keyboard, and palms should be down. Make sure you keep your wrists straight and naturally hang your elbows. Your elbows must not touch your body, and it must also not be too far away from it. Elbows should be at an open angle of 90 to 110 degrees that relax your forearms and shoulder.

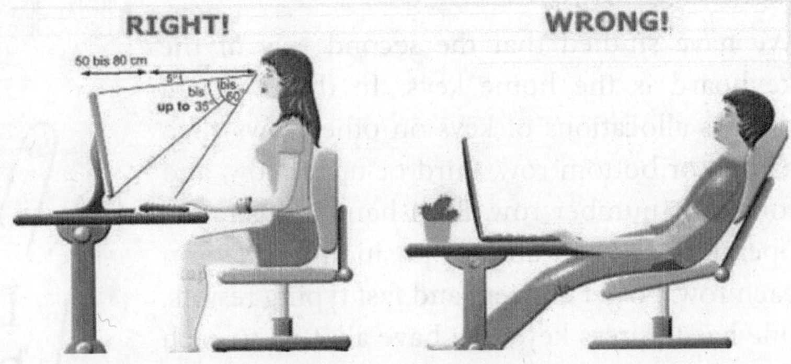

Figure 2.5: Right and wrong posture or position of hands, foot, and back

- **Position of feet:** Keep your both the feet flat on the floor, and you can also use a footstool if required.
- **Placement of mouse and keyboard:** Your mouse and keyboard should be near to each other around in the distance of 20 cms that helps in operating the keyboard smoothly and effortlessly. The keyboard should be flat on the desk or sloping gently away from you.
- **Placement of monitor:** Do not bend your neck while working on the monitor as bending forward will create too much pressure on your discs. Keep your upper border of the screen at eye level or slightly below it, and its distance depends on the screen size. If your screen is of 17 inches, then keep an approximate distance of 50 to 80 cms.
- **Placement of chair and table:** The height of the chair and table should be chosen so as to expose the shoulder, wrist, and arm muscles to the least possible strain. The wrist can touch the tabletop in front of the keyboard. Keep keyboard and printers like vibrating devices on separate tables. From the floor, the height of the under-desk keyboard drawer or tabletop must be 68 to 73 cm. Make sure there is enough space in the table for your legs.
- **Placement of matter to be typed:** The writing matter must be kept either to the left side or right side of the keyboard or on anything that has a sloping surface.

Positioning of fingers on the keyboard

Nowadays pen and pencil work have been replaced with a computer keyboard. The correct positioning of fingers comes with mastery typewriting skills or attaining the necessary knowledge and skill of keyboard.

- During the keyboard operation in Home Row or Horizontal approach, all the eight fingers of both the hands rest on Home keys F, D, S, A, and J, K, L.
- Left-hand fingers must be placed on F, D, S, A, and right-hand fingers on J, K, L. As from these keys user is able to reach all other keys easily.
- Fingers should be kept on correct keys and keep hands and fingers near to base position.

In-home row approach fingers are trained to make the correct movement to the other keys, and it returns immediately to its home key after it has depressed the corresponding key in any other row. The thumb of both hands is kept at the Space bar to enter space between the words. While using uppercase letters and symbols, type them using one hand, and use another hand to Shift key. To press Enter key, use the little finger of the right hand.

Allocation of keys to fingers

We have studied that the second row of the keyboard is the home keys. In this, we will discuss allocations of keys on other rows such as first or bottom row, third or upper row, and fourth or number row. Both hand's fingers are operating on their allotted position to them on each row. To get efficient and fast typing results, one has to press keys that have allotted to each finger.

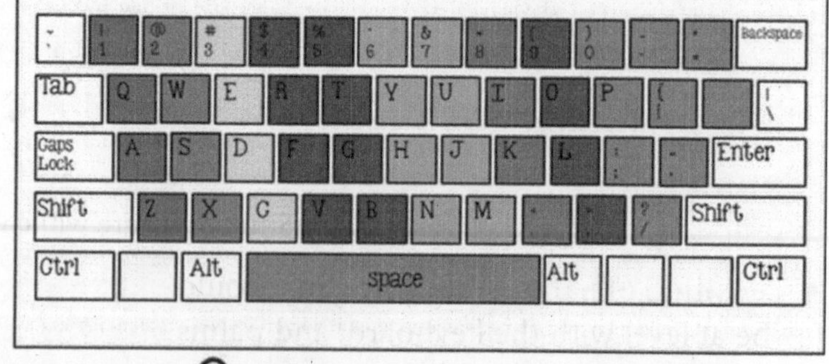

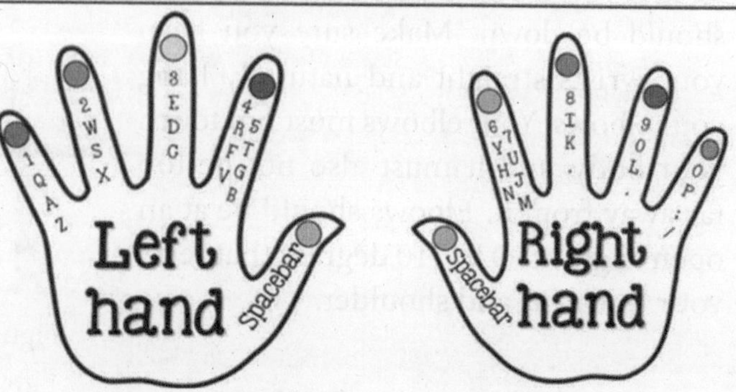

Figure 2.6: Allocations of keys to fingers

- **Allocation of keys to fingers on the second or home row:** To operate the second row, you have to place your fingers of each hand on the allotted keys. Now you will leave with key g and h that is operated by the forefingers of the left and right hand, respectively.
- **Allotion of keys to fingers on the first or lower row:** To operate or press keys on the first row thcaat contains Z, X, C, V, B, N, M, Comma, Full Stop, and / sign. To work on these keys, simply take your pinky finger off to key A and move it up to the below first key Z. Use the middle finger of the left hand to type C key then again take that finger back to home key D. Rest keys are also pressed in the same way by using fingers used for corresponding keys in Home or second row.
- **Allocation of keys to fingers on the third or upper row:** To operate or press any key on the third or upper row, you have to take your finger from a to q by little left-hand finger and from (;) top by the little right-hand finger. Then the third finger is placed to the adjoining keys w and o, so on.
- While typing on the upper row, firstly, keep your fingers on the home row. Now take your left-hand pinky finger off the A key and move it up to the top row first key Q. Use the middle finger of your left hand from D up to E key then again come back to the home key. The left-hand index finger is used to type R then return to the F key. Now lift the fingers of the right hand and strike upper row keys one after another and type p, o, I, u, and y.

  Make sure that at a time, only one finger should move and keep the rest of the fingers on the home row at their respective position.
- **Allocation of keys to fingers on the fourth or number row:** To operate or press a key on the fourth or number row, you have to use a little finger to type 1, ring finger to type 2 and middle finger to type 3 and 4 and 5 number is press using index or forefinger. Similarly, the little finger of the right hand is used to press 0, ring finger to type 9, and 8 number is press using middle fingers of right hand and index or forefingers are used to press number 7 and 6.

Summary

- Typing ergonomics is used to reduce the stress, strain, and wear and tear of your joints as you repeatedly type away.
- Keep both your feet flat on the floor, and you can also use a footstool if required.
- Your mouse and keyboard should be near to each other around in the distance of 20 cms that helps in operating the keyboard smoothly and effortlessly.
- Do not bend your neck while working on the monitor, as bending forward will create too much pressure on your discs.
- From the floor, the height of the under-desk keyboard drawer or tabletop must be 68 to 73 cm.
- The writing matter must be kept either to the left side or right side of the keyboard or on anything that has a sloping surface.
- The correct positioning of fingers comes with mastery typewriting skills or attaining the necessary knowledge and skill of keyboard.
- During the keyboard operation in a home row or horizontal approach, all the eight fingers of both the hands rest on Home keys F, D, S, A, and J, K, L.
- Left-hand fingers must be placed on F, D, S, A, and right-hand fingers on J, K, L.
- To operate the second row, you have to place your fingers of each hand on the allotted keys. Now you will be left with key g and h that is operated by the forefingers of the left and right hand, respectively.
- To operate or press any key on the third or upper row, you have to take your finger from a to q by little left-hand finger and from ;) top by the little right-hand finger.

Self-Assessment

MULTIPLE CHOICE QUESTIONS.

1. Your mouse and keyboard should be near to each other around in the distance of _______ cms.
   a. 12 b. 15 c. 17 d. 20
2. To operate or press a key on the fourth or number row.
   a. Ring finger type 1 b. Ring finger type 2 c. Ring finger type 3 d. Ring finger type 4

Answer

1. d 2. b

QUESTIONS

1. What is the role of typing ergonomics?
2. What is the correct sitting posture while working on a computer?
3. Give the correct position of fingers on the keyboard to increase the typing speed?
4. What is the right way to press the keys of other than home row?

PROJECT WORK

Practice typing of one paragraph using correct ergonomics.

SESSION 3: POINTING DEVICE: MOUSE

The mouse is a pointing device that consists of two or three buttons. One button is present on the left side, one on the right side and one in the middle. It can be used to perform more than one actions like:

- Selecting menu commands
- Resize windows
- Selecting actions from screen icons and more

The left side button is used most commonly to select or activate the application. In order to check the list of commands on the screen, a right button of the mouse is used. Its use has been found in various applications like designing to drag the pictures, etc. Through mouse, one is able to delete, copy, cut, and move files on the screen. The middle scroll wheels or button is used to scroll down the page, folders, documents, and more.

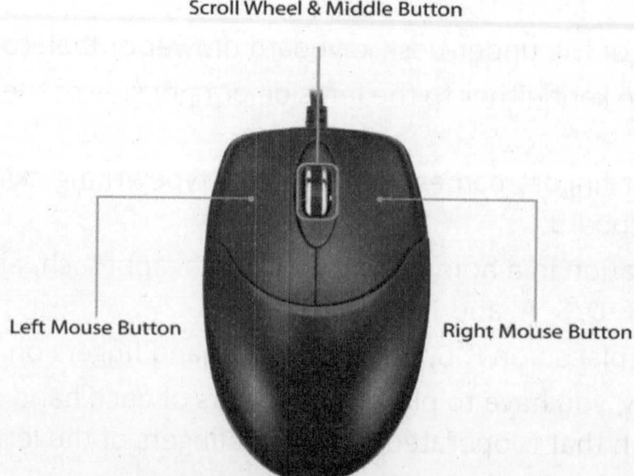

Figure 2.7: Mouse and its buttons

Various types of the mouse are:

- Mechanical mouse
- Opto-Mechanical mouse
- Optical mouse

There is a rubber or metal ball on its lower side that can roll in all the directions in case of a mechanical mouse. The mechanism as used in mechanical mouse in case of the optomechanical mouse, but an optical sensor is used in it to detect movement of the ball. There is no moving part in the case of an optical mouse as it detects the movement of the mouse through laser technology.

Mouse pointer

The mouse pointer is also known as mouse arrow, mouse cursor that is a graphical image that is used to control or activate certain elements in a graphical user interface. It also indicates where your mouse should perform its next action by following the path of the user's hand as they move their mouse. The mouse pointer gets changes according to the action.

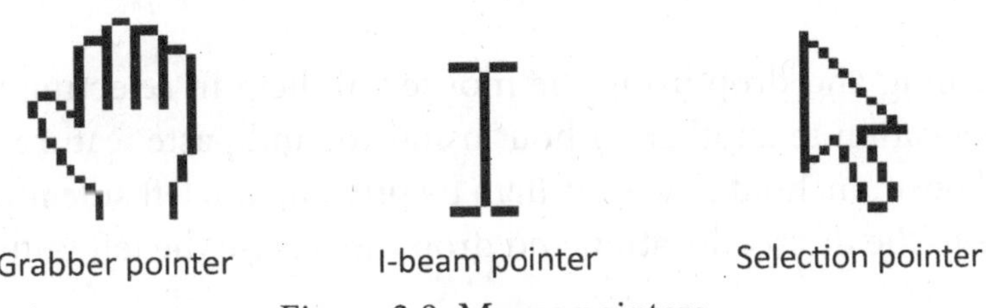

Figure 2.8: Mouse pointers

- There is grabber pointer while working on a web browser that changes to the pointing finger symbol as it moves over the page. This identifies a hyperlink.
- The I-beam pointer is used in graphical-based text processing applications. This is used in word processors or various desktop publishing systems for marking the blocks of text and moves the insertion point.
- The Selection pointer appears when you move it around the screen that particularly consists of text. This also appears while typing text.

Mouse operations

All mouse have their own mechanism operation according to their types, but all of them accomplish the same task. In some of the mice, there is a light beam at the bottom of the mouse that tracks the motion or mouse; on the other hand, some use a tracking ball for the same purpose. For performing the same job on laptops, there is either a very short stick or small flat surface.

In the most common type of mouse, there are either two or three buttons on its top that are used for different actions. The left side button is used most commonly to select or activate, drag, move, and paste the application; on the other hand, the context menu is open for an item with the right button of the mouse.

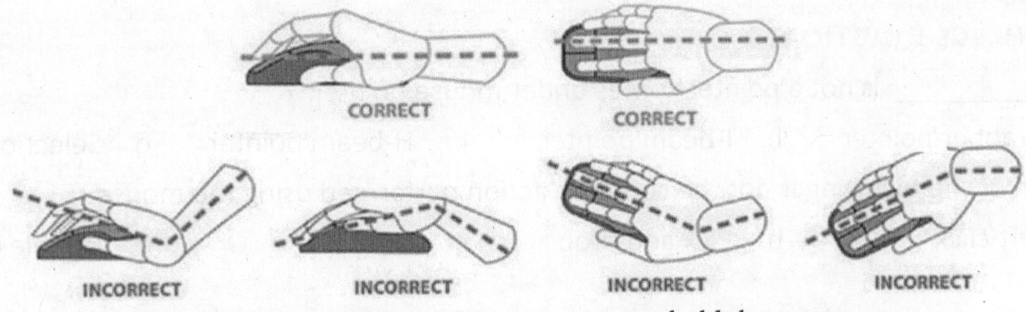

Figure 2.9: Correct and incorrect way to hold the mouse

Some common actions of the mouse are:

- **Click or left click:** As mentioned above, the left click of the mouse is used to select an item. To do it, simply press the left button with your index finger.
- **Double click:** A double click on element or file will open, or it displays a dialog for editing its properties. Sometimes double click is also used to start some program or application.
- **Right-click:** The right-click anywhere in the interface will display a context-sensitive menu or displays a set of commands and available options. The contents of a context menu depend on the position of the cursor when you click. To do it takes the mouse of the desired position then press the right button with your middle finger.
- **Scroll:** The scroll wheel or wheel mouse is a rubber or plastic wheel located between the left and right buttons. In various applications, there are scrollbars on the right side of the screen in case of having more page length than the screen or monitor length. The scroll wheel on the mouse is used to scroll the page up or down.
- **Drag and drop:** The drag and drop using the mouse will help in selecting then moving the item or document from one location to another without using cut and paste feature. To do it, simply take the mouse of the desired position, hold down the item by pressing the left side mouse, then drag the object and move the mouse to the desired location and drop the release the left button of the mouse.

Summary

- The mouse is a pointing device that consists of two or three buttons. One button is present on the left side, one on the right side and one in the middle.
- Various types of the mouse are mechanical mouse, optomechanical mouse, and optical mouse.
- The mouse pointer is also known as mouse arrow, mouse cursor that is a graphical image that is used to control or activate certain elements in a graphical user interface.
- In the most common type of mouse, there are either two or three buttons on its top that are used for different actions.
- Some actions of the mouse are left click, Double click, right-click, scroll and drag and drop.
- Then right-click anywhere in the interface will display a context-sensitive menu or displays a set of commands and available options.
- The scroll wheel or wheel mouse is a rubber or plastic wheel located between the left and right buttons.
- The drag and drop using the mouse will help in selecting then moving the item or document from one location to another without using cut and paste feature.

MULTIPLE CHOICE QUESTIONS.

1. ______________ is not a pointer comes under mouse pointer.

   a. Grabber pointer b. I-beam pointer c. H-beam pointer d. Selection pointer

2. Which of the following is not the common action performed using the mouse?

   a. Left-click b. Pick and drop c. Scroll d. Double click

Answer

1. c 2. b

QUESTIONS

1. Write a short note on Mouse?
2. Mouse can be used to perform some actions. Name them.
3. What is Mouse Pointer?
4. Explain in brief the operation of Mouse?

PROJECT WORK

Practice various mouse options.

SESSION 4: USING TYPING SOFTWARE

There are many software available that is free of cost and are customized to learn to type efficiently and effectively.

What is Rapid Touch Tutor?

Rapid Typing Tutor is a free and open-source software that is designed for learning typing skills on the computer. Learning to type with a rapid typing tutor is a fun and typing game. To use a computer more efficiently by kids and adults, a rapid touch-typing tutor is used. There is a number of games, exercises, and training sessions that sharpen the skills of users and help them to work efficiently in a short time. According to the level of difficulty, various courses are provided by Rapid typing are:

- **Introduction:** It covers all the characters typed on a keyboard
- **Beginner course:** It helps in knowing the positions of various keys like uppercase, lowercase, and special characters on a keyboard and helps in knowing the keys without looking at the keyboard.
- **Experience course:** The frequently used words and syllabus are memorized, and improve the speed of typing comes under this.
- **Advanced skills:** The user learns to type the actual text that comes with an improvement in typing skills.
- **Testing:** There are advanced typing tests in the testing part of the course that helps in knowing the accuracy and typing speed of the user.

Various techniques or stages of touch typing

As mentioned above, various benefits of Touch Typing is Increase in speed, accuracy, and more. A touch typist never looks at the keyboard while typing and hits the right keys with practice. This is a fast way of typing as typist has to only focus on text being typed, reading the words and phrases as the fingers type the text. To learn touch typing, various stages are:

- **Stage one:** From this stage process of touch typing starts from where the user learns the home row on the keyboard. In this touch, the typist is restricted from viewing the keyboard while the whole typing focus should be on reading the words, the text being typed. In this user, learn about the lower row, upper rows, number row, uppercase letters, and special symbols.
- **Stage two:** In this stage, remembering of the frequently used syllabus and typing words containing this syllabus is done.
- **Stage third:** In this stage, the user will type the actual text with the acquired skills.

Components of rapid typing software

There are various components of Rapid Typing software as given below: (Figure 2.10):

- **Title bar:** It consists of program modes, option buttons, and three control buttons.
- The Option buttons are available on the top right corner of Title bar that helps in changing the background, themes, help, logout, sound, text color, font, and more.
- There are three program buttons available on the top left corner of the title bar. Click on the current lesson button given in the very first position from left to check the current lesson. Click on student statics next to the current lesson button gives the current statics of the students typing. The last one is the Lesson editor that is used to edit the lesson settings.
- On the extreme right side, there are three control buttons Minimize, Maximize and Close that is used to reduce the size of RapidTyping window, maximize the size, and to close the window, respectively.
- **Toolbar:** Current course and current lesson control come under this section that helps the user to select the current course from the above-given list Introduction, beginner, experienced, advanced and testing modes. On the other hand, current lesson control consists of going back to the beginning, pause/resume current lesson, checking accuracy, elapsed lesson time, and current speed.
- **Text Area:** Text area or text panel is an area where the user sees the text typed by them.
- **Status bar:** This bar is present on the bottom of the text area that consists of tips, progress bar, and volume control. The length of the lesson, metronome to help a user to know about the lesson details, comes under the progress bar. The sound is increased or decreased through the volume button given above the virtual keyboard.
- **Virtual keyboard:** This is the keyboard of RapidTyping software that helps the user to learn touch typing with all your fingers.

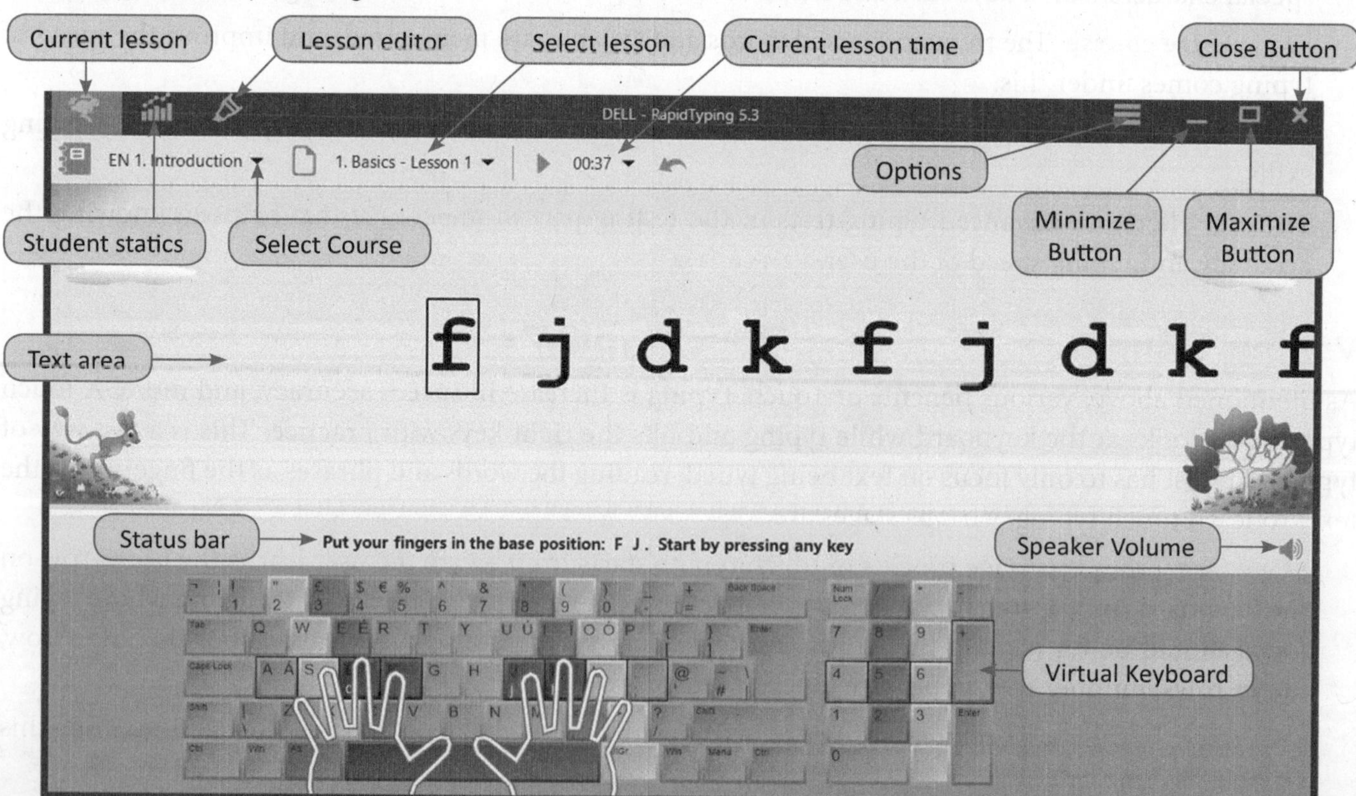

Figure 2.10: Rapid Typing 5 software main window

Various rules of touch typing

While learning Touchtyping user has to keep some of the rules, which are:

- Users must use all the fingers of two hands while typing and keep a thumb on the space bar.
- Fingers should be kept on correct keys and keep hands and fingers near to base position. To start typing fingers should be kept on base position or home keys F, D, S, A, and J, K, L. After every keystroke, try to bring fingers back on base position.
- Left-hand fingers must be placed on F, D, S, A, and right-hand fingers on J, K, L. As from these keys user is able to reach all other keys easily.
- While using uppercase letters and symbols, type them using one hand, and use another hand to Shift key.
- To press Enter key, use the little finger of the right hand.
- Do lots of exercises given in the software regularly that will increase the speed and accuracy of typing the right words.

The interface of rapid typing software

This section will learn in brief about the various interface of RapidTyping Software. Perform the following steps to start practicing on RapidTyping software.

Current lesson: The user has to click on the **Current lesson** tab given on the top left corner of the title bar. From drop-down arrow of course and lesson given below the title bar, the user can choose the required one. (Figure 2.11)

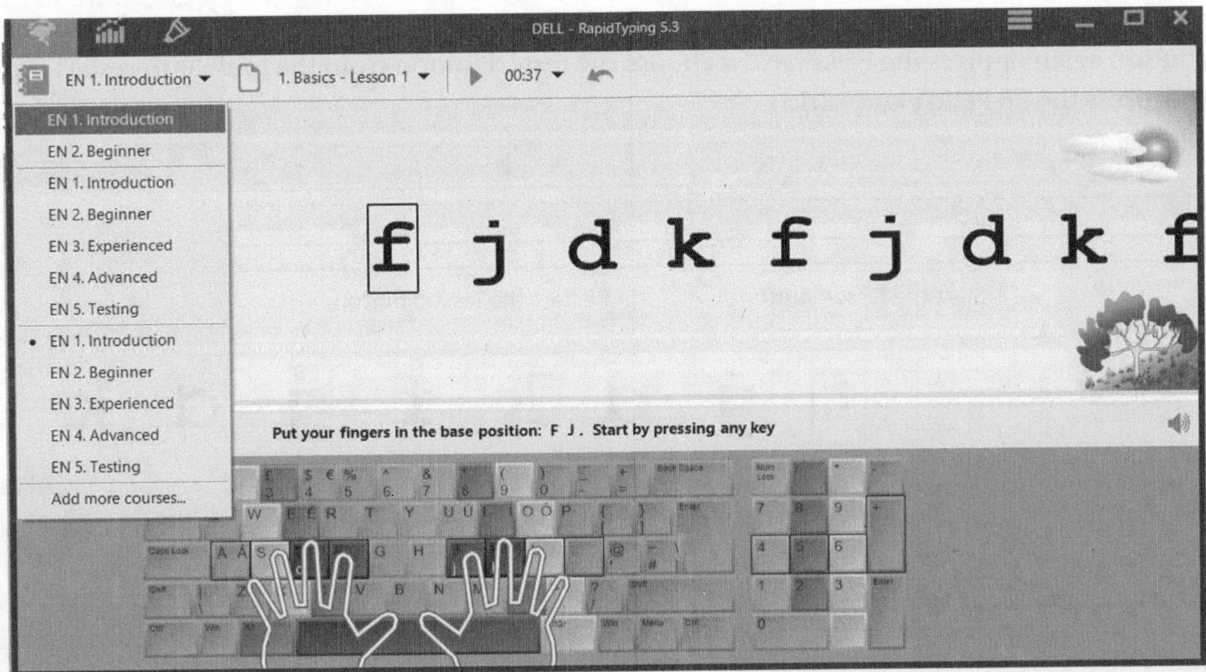

Figure 2.11: Choosing a course

After selecting the course, the next step is to select the lesson on which the user wants to work on. The lessons are categorized by the types as introduction and beginner courses have basics, shift keys, digits keys, and number pad sections. Other course lessons are categorized into different lessons. As you have done with selecting the course now, you can select a lesson from the next drop-down arrow of the current course. (Figure 2.12)

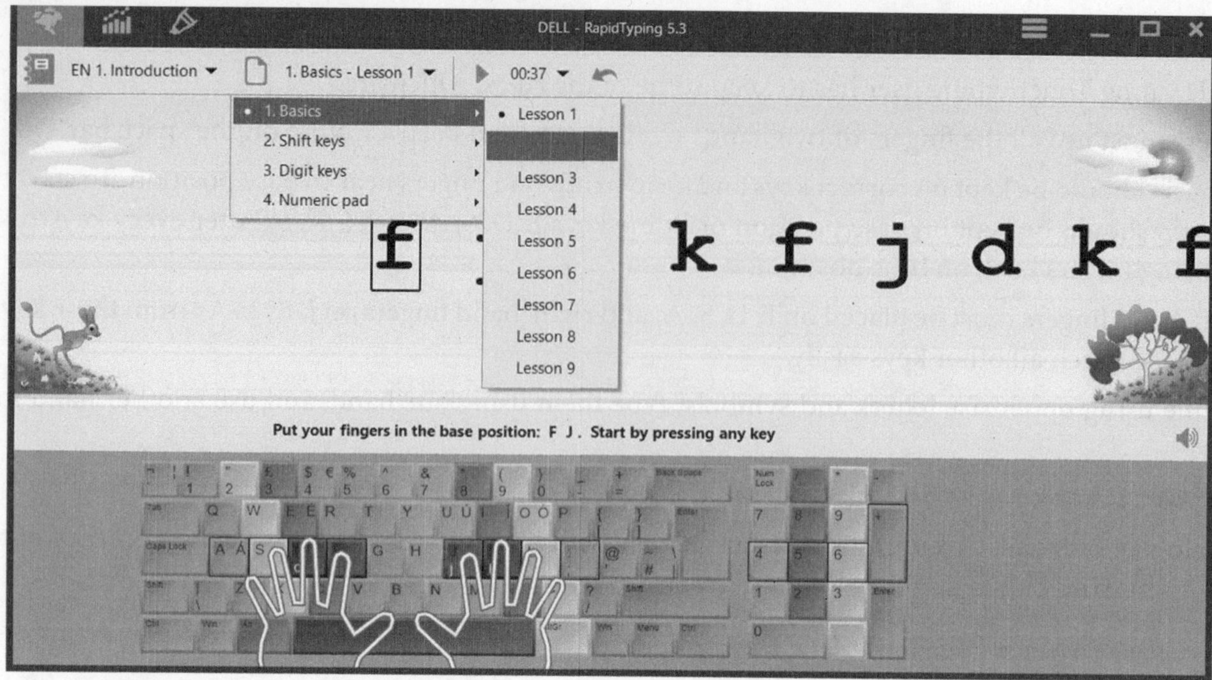

Figure 2.12: Choosing a lesson

To write a text for practice, a virtual keyboard is used. To start typing first, keep your left-hand fingers on F,D,S,A keys, and right-hand fingers on J, K, L. Now start typing the alphabets from the virtual keyboard given on the Text area of the RapidTyping software window.

While you are typing, the current lesson time is display on the current lesson time button given on the toolbar. You can pause the time if you want to stop the lesson in between. To pause it, click on start the lesson button again or press the F5 key. Now choose the restart button from the toolbar to restart the lesson or simply press the F8 key. (Figure 2.13)

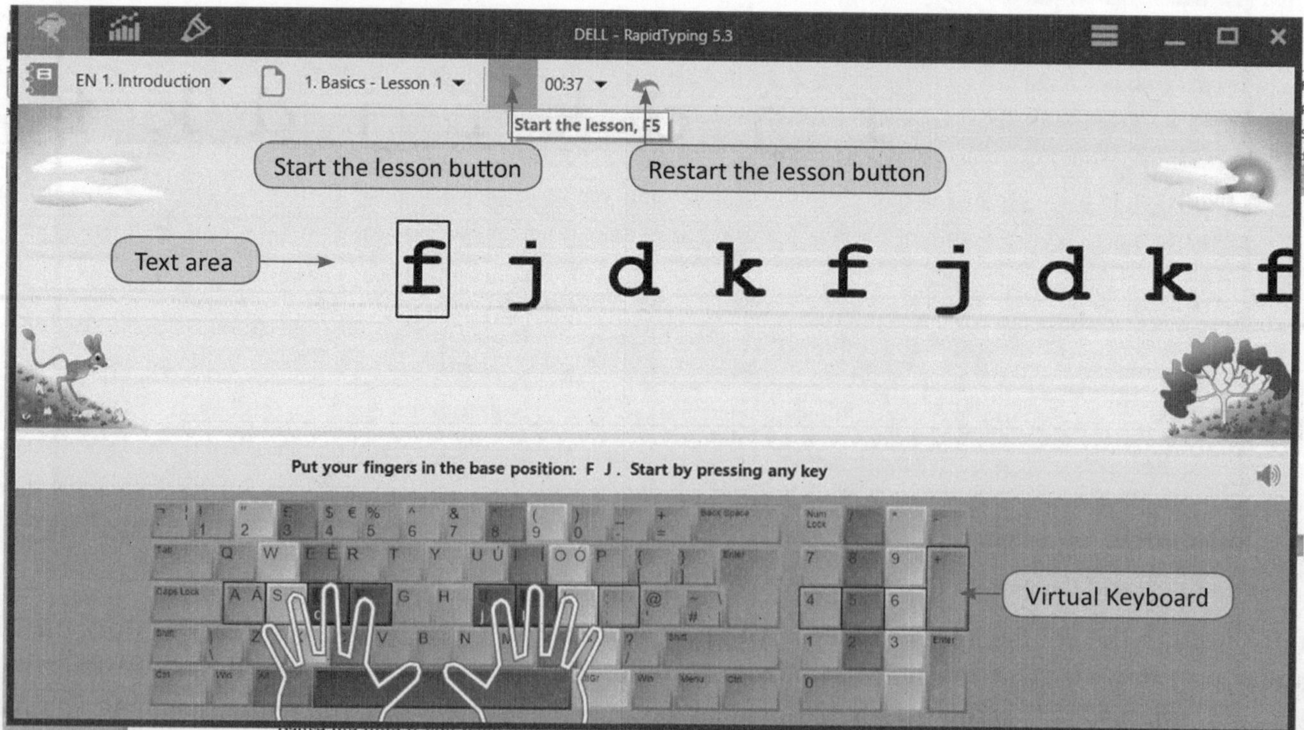

Figure 2.13: Start typing and controlling lessons

Instructions and two progress bars are given on the status bar. The percentage of completion of the lesson is displayed by the; the acceptable time for typing a single character is display by the yellow progress bar. (Figure 2.14)

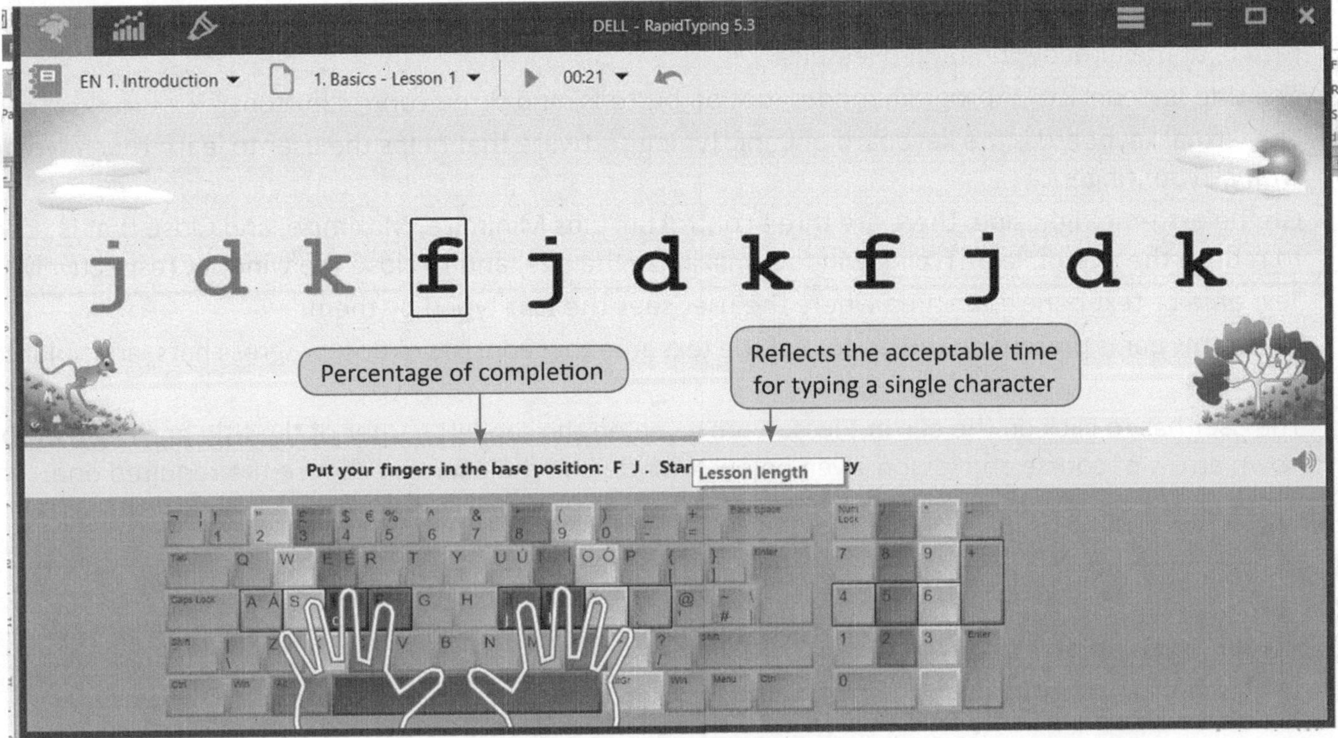

Figure 2.14: Progress bar

After finishing off each lesson, a result window will appear through which you can analyze your progress report. (Figure 2.15)

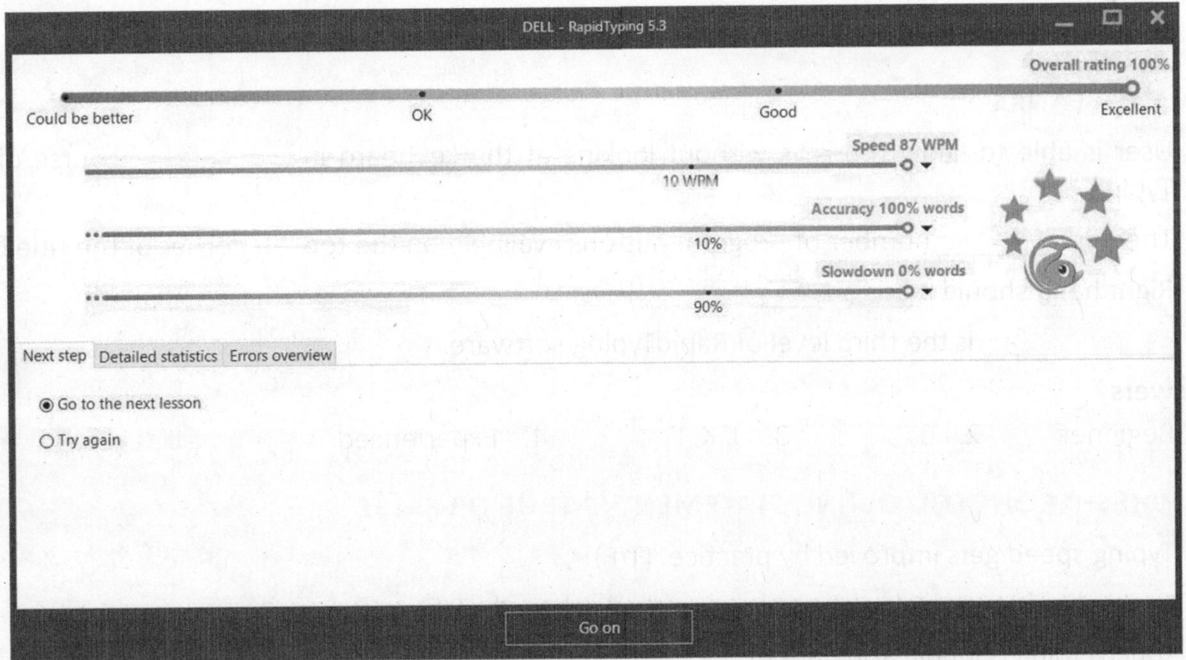

Figure 2.15: Interpreting the results after completion of the lesson

Summary

- Rapid Typing Tutor is a free and open-source software that is designed for learning typing skills on the computer.
- The progress results are displayed after every lesson. You can use the statistics window to view the results of the already completed lessons.
- The title bar consists of program modes, option buttons, and three control buttons.
- The virtual keyboard is the keyboard of RapidTyping software that helps the user to learn touch typing with all your fingers.
- On the extreme right side, there are three control buttons Minimize, Maximize, and Close that is used to reduce the size of RapidTyping window, maximize the size, and to close the window, respectively.
- Text area or text panel is an area where the user sees the text typed by them.
- The status bar is present on the bottom of the text area that consists of tips, progress bars, and volume control.
- The user has to click on the current lesson tab given on the top left corner of the title bar. From drop-down arrow of course and lesson given below the title bar, the user can choose the required one.

Self-Assessment

MULTIPLE CHOICE QUESTIONS.

1. ______________ are the number of fingers used while typing.

   a. 4 b. 5 c. 10 d. 2

2. Which of the following is not a stage of TouchTyping?

   a. Stage introductory b. Stage one c. Stage practice d. Both a and c

Answers

1. c 2. c

FILL IN THE BLANKS

1. User is able to know the keys without looking at the keyboard in __________ course of Rapid Typing.
2. There is ________ number of program buttons available on the top left corner of the title bar.
3. Right hand should place on ___________ keys.
4. _____________ is the third level of RapidTyping software.

Answers

1. Beginner 2. 3 3. J, K, L 4. Experienced

STATE WHETHER THE FOLLOWING STATEMENT IS TRUE OR FALSE

1. Typing speed gets improved by practice. (T/F)
2. Users should type by looking at keys on the keyboard. (T/F)
3. TouchTyping is inbuilt software of the computer system. (T/F)

Answers

1. True 2. False 3. False

QUESTIONS

1. What is Touch typing?
2. What do you mean by RapidTyping software?
3. Name four benefits of Touch Typing?
4. Name various courses of RapidTyping along with their purpose.
5. Write down the steps to open RapidTyping software.
6. Name various stages to learn TouchTyping.

PROJECT WORK

Open RapidTyping software and review all components and try typing by following various rules of TouchTyping and identify the user interface of a typing tutor.

SESSION 5: VIEWING AND ANALYZING STATISTICS

The progress results are displayed after every lesson. You can use the statistics window to view the results of the already completed lessons. After completion of course interpretation of results is necessary to know your overall performance. The results window is divided into **Rating** pane and three tabs. The **Next step**, **Detailed statistics**, and **Errors overview** are three tabs of the results window. This helps in evaluating your performance by tracking the progress at any time. (Figure 2.16)

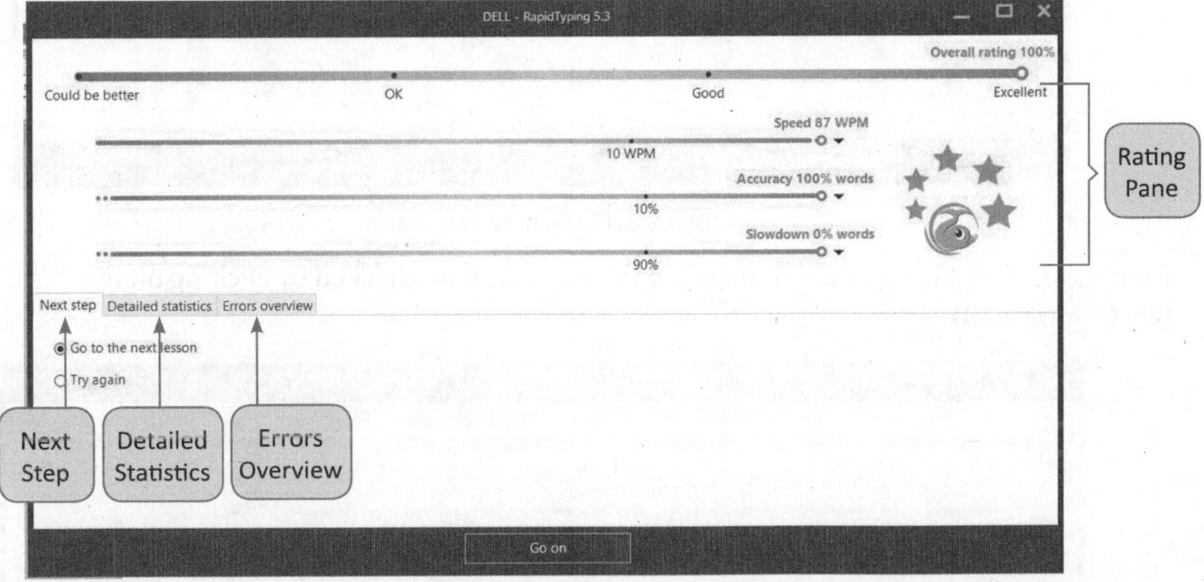

Figure 2.16: Interpreting the Results

Figure 2.16 reflects the typing statistics by giving typing speed, accuracy, slowdown strokes, and a summary is given at the end of each lesson.

The different colors in the above Figure 2.16 indicate as follows:

- **Red:** The red color indicates the wrong inputs within the acceptable timeframe.
- **Green:** The green color indicates the right inputs.
- **Yellow:** The yellow color indicates the right inputs exceeding the acceptable timeframe.
- **Orange:** The orange color indicates the wrong inputs that exceed the acceptable timeframe.
- **Next step:** Users can click on the **Next step** tab to go on the next lesson.

- **Error Window:** The detailed statistics for the current lesson can be seen on the **Error** tab that shows your errors and delays percentage both in the table and graphical view. This helps in understanding the hard letters to type for you. You can switch between errors in percent chart and delay in percent chart. In bar charts, the letters used in the lesson are given on X-axis, and delays or errors related to each letter are shown on Y-axis. The chart will not be shown for no errors and delays for a certain character.
- **Detailed statistics:** The detailed lesson statistics display the details like typing speed, errors, and slowdown for each chapter. Mistakes done in the text can be check as they get highlighted with different colors. Where the green line indicates the good results, red color indicates bad results, and the time span exceeded by the user is indicated by yellow color. The incorrect characters and time for typing a character exceeded by users are depicted by orange color. (Figure 2.17)

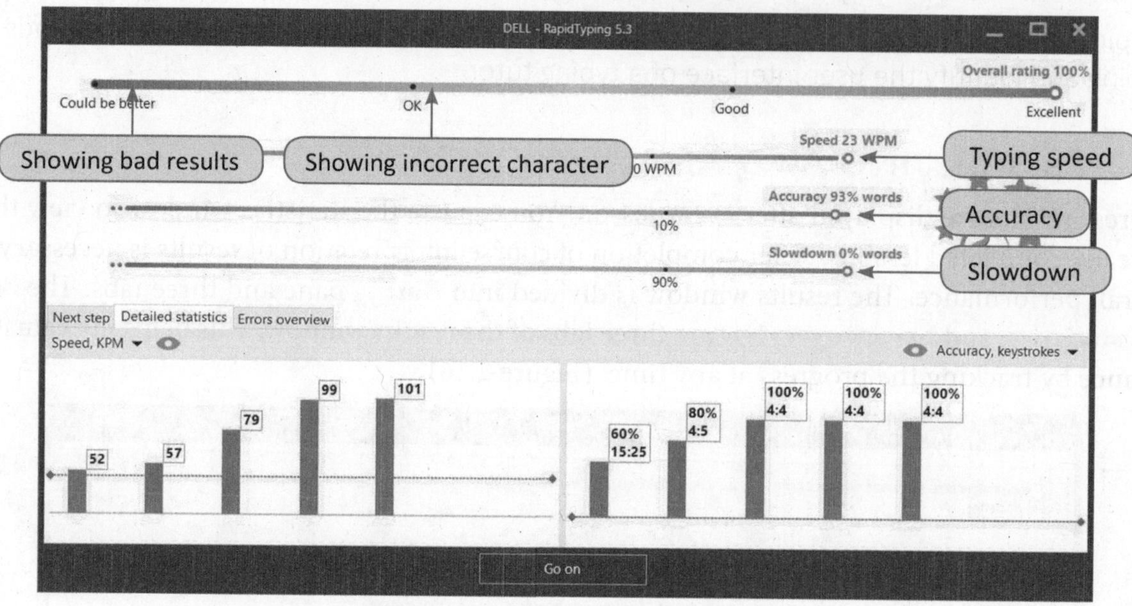

Figure 2.17: Detailed statistics

- **Errors overview:** Errors occurred during the lesson can be checked by clicking on the **Errors overview** tab. (Figure 2.18)

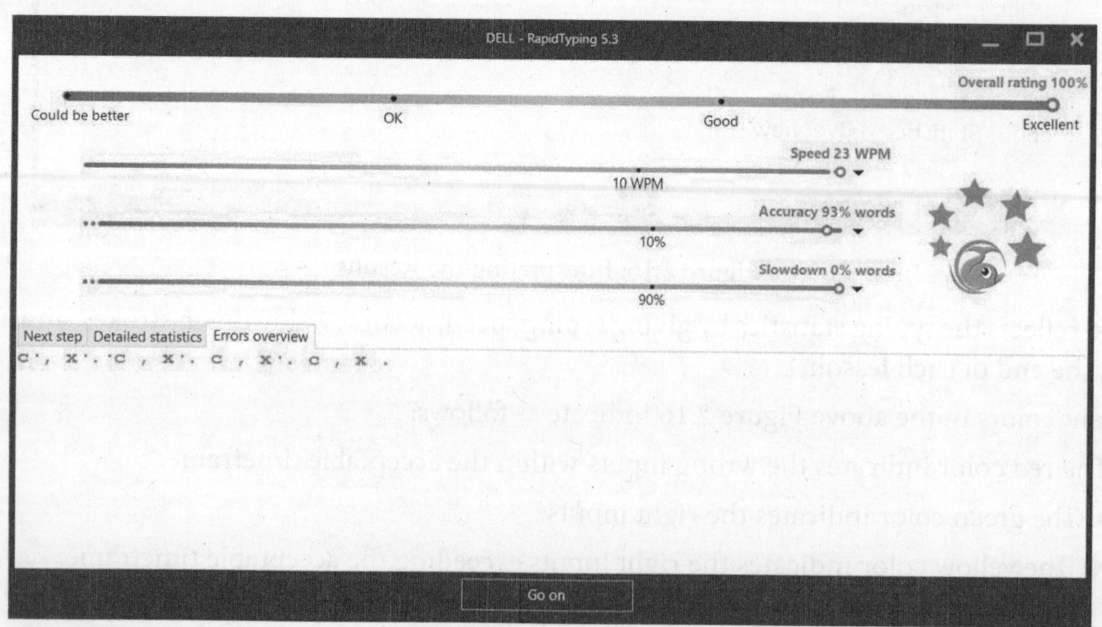

Figure 2.18: Error overview

Analyzing student statistics in Rapid typing software

In the last section, we have worked on viewing the statistics. Now, we will learn to add students or student groups and preview their statistics. Click on the student statics tab given on the top right corner of the title bar after the current lesson tab. The opened student statistics window consists of Student accounts/groups and Statistics panel/session statistics controls.

- **Student accounts/groups:** It consists of three parts name as student toolbar, student account, and property panel.
  - o The student toolbar is used to add, remove, insert, and save existing student accounts and student groups. It also gives the option of downloading the student's statistics in PDF, HTML, and CSV like formats.
  - o The current student account or group is selected from the student accounts.
  - o In the navigation tree, student properties and a group of selected items can be edited.
- **Student panel/session Statistics:** It consists of statistics toolbar, course diagram/statistics, lesson diagram/statistics and lesson statistics table.
  - o Choosing a course, removing the selected statistics, and customizing the statistics display options is chosen from the statistics toolbar.
  - o For all lessons of the current course, a common statistic is given in the course diagram/statistics.
  - o In the course diagram, a selected lesson, each keystroke or character, is shown in lesson diagram/statistics.
  - o In the course diagram, a full statistic of the selected lesson is shown in the lesson statistics table. (Figure 2.19)

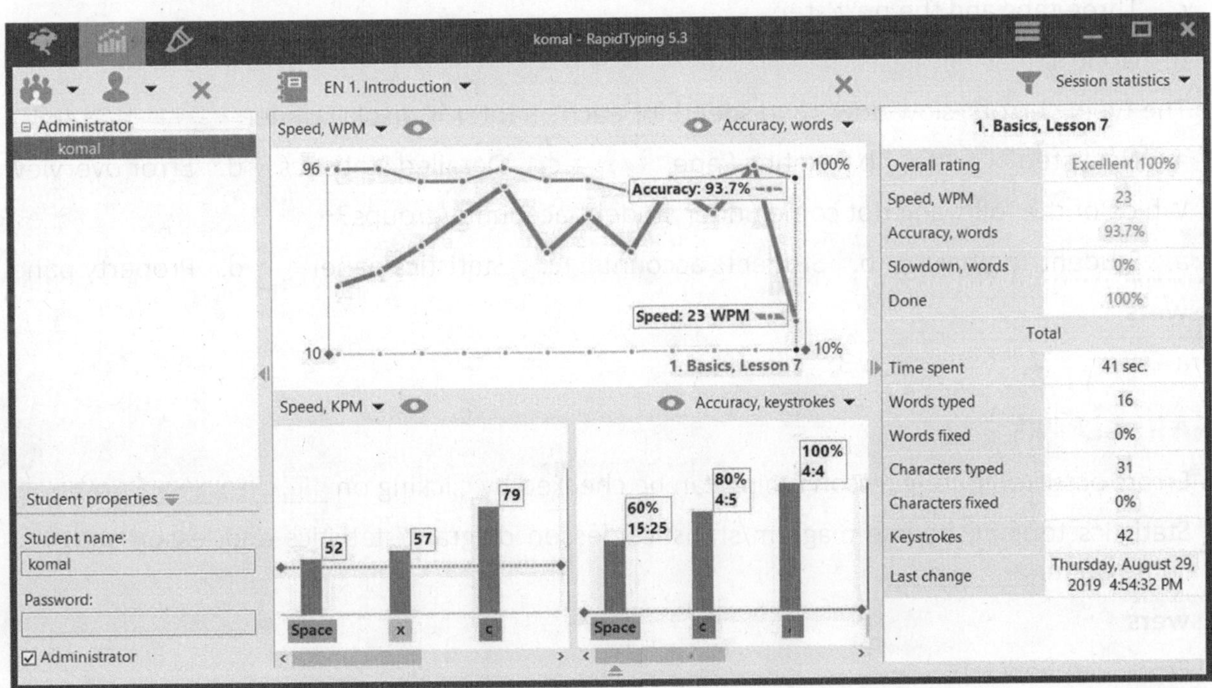

Figure 2.19: Student statistics screen

Summary

- You can use the Statistics window to view the results of the already completed lessons.
- After completion of course interpretation of results is necessary to know your overall performance.
- In the statistics window, the red color indicates the wrong inputs within the acceptable timeframe.
- In the statistics window, the green color indicates the right inputs.
- In the statistics window, the yellow color indicates the right inputs exceeding the acceptable timeframe.
- In the statistics window, the orange color indicates the wrong inputs that exceed the acceptable timeframe.
- Users can start the same lesson again if the better score is not achieved by them, or they can click on the next step tab to go on the next lesson.
- The detailed statistics for the current lesson can be seen on the error tab that shows your errors and delays percentage both in the table and graphical view.
- The detailed lesson statistics display the details like typing speed, errors, and slowdown for each chapter.

Self-Assessment

MULTIPLE CHOICE QUESTIONS.

1. Result window consists of:
   a. Rating pane and three tabs
   b. Next step, Detailed statistics and Errors overview
   c. Three tabs and the next step
   d. None
2. The typing errors, slow down and speed for each chapter is display under__________ tab?
   a. Next step   b. Rating Pane   c. Detailed statistics   d. Error overview
3. Which of the following not come under student accounts/groups?
   a. Student Toolbar   b. Students account   c. Statistics panel   d. Property panel

Answers

1. a   2. c   3. c

FILL IN THE BLANKS

1. Errors occurred during lesson typing can be checked by clicking on ____________ tab.
2. Statistics toolbar, Course diagram/statistics, lesson diagram/statistics and lesson statistics table come under __________.

Answers

1. Error overview tab
2. Student panel/session statistics

TRUE OR FALSE

1. Yellow color gives an acceptable time for typing a single character. (T/F)

2. To add, remove, insert, and save existing student accounts, a student toolbar is used. (T/F)
3. Student statistics can be downloaded in XML format. (T/F)

Answers

1. True 2. True 3. False

QUESTIONS

1. What is display in a detailed statistics screen display?
2. What is indicated by different colors in the detailed statistics tab?
3. What does the lesson statistics table show?
4. Explain student panel/session statistics.
5. Differentiate different colors line displayed on the statistics screen.

PROJECT WORK

Open RapidTyping software and do the practice of three exercises under the beginner's level course and then analyze your performance from statistics students view.

SESSION 6: WORKING WITH LESSON EDITOR

On the left side of the title bar, there is a button of Lesson editor after the student statistics. By clicking on the lesson editor button, a lesson editor window will appear. (Figure 2.20)

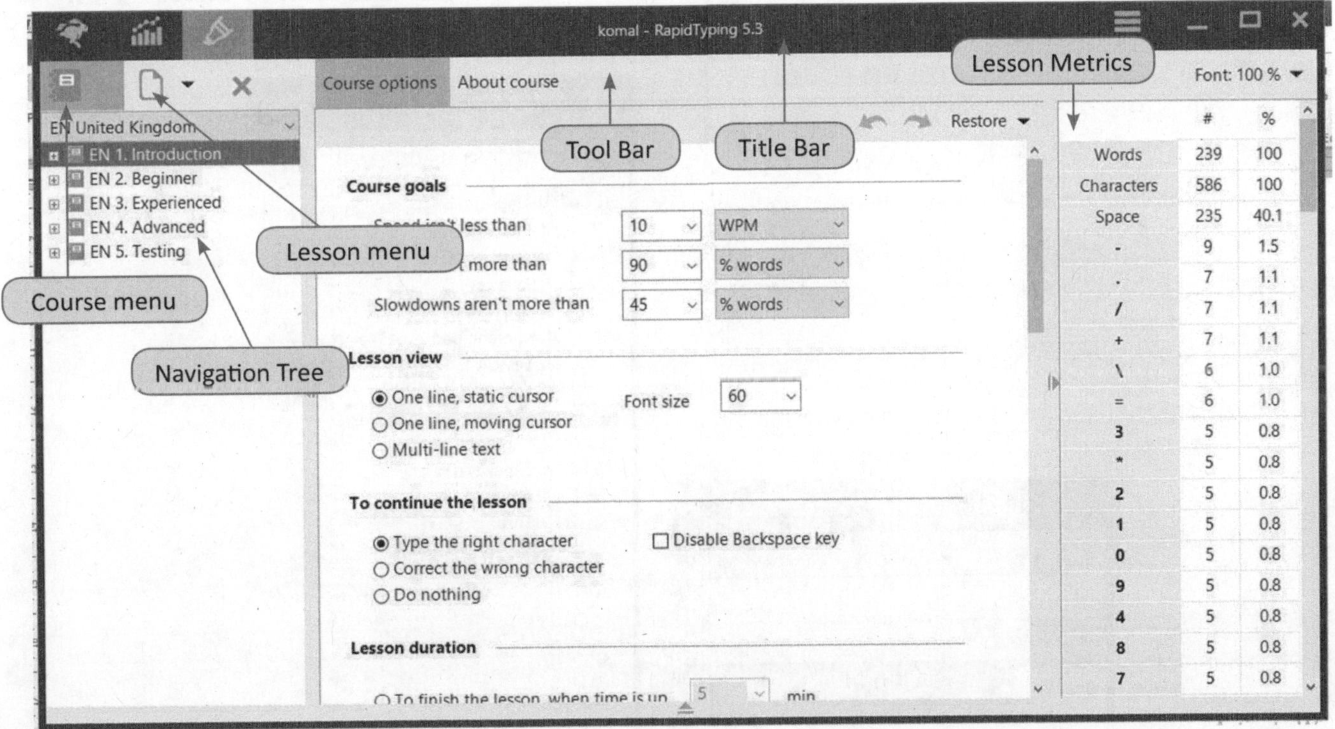

Figure 2.20: Lesson editor window

This window allows us to customize lessons that means you can add, change, import/export, and remove lessons and courses. You can also review the statistics for each lesson:

- The number and percentage of words, spaces, characters, and specific characters in the lesson are displayed in the lesson metrics section given in the lesson editor window.

- The title bar displays the title, lesson editor tab button along with the current lesson, and student statistic buttons. It also consists of control buttons given on the right corner.
- Adding, removing, inserting, and saving the existing courses and lessons command is given in the toolbar.
- The list currently was chosen keyboard, current course, section, and the lesson green progress barare displayed in the navigation tree.

Properties let the user modify the course, section, and properties like the current lesson name along with a section of the current lesson. Other Interfaces of the lesson editor are:

- **Editing panel:** It is the area where changes can be done in the existing course option or text of a lesson such as a navigation tree. A long text session can be split into many smaller lessons using the split lesson dialog box.
- **Table analysis text:** It displays the percentage and number of characters, words, spaces, and specific characters in the lesson.
- **Virtual keyboard:** It gives constant feedback that shows the finger or key to press that keeps us not looking down at our hands while typing the characters of the selected lesson.

Creating a new lesson plan

Following steps are performed to create a new lesson of your choice:

Click on the Lesson menu option. Select the course level in which you want to add a new lesson and select create new lesson option from the **Lesson** menu or right-click on any course level or select **Create new lesson** option from the pop-up menu. Enter the name and title for a chapter in a given box. (Figure 2.21)

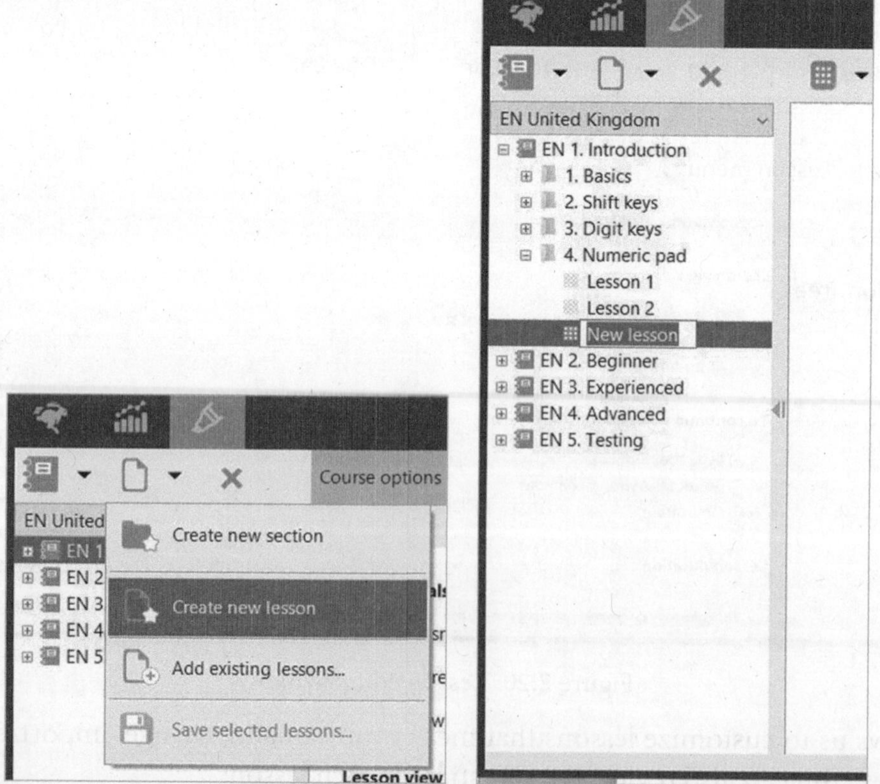

Figure 2.21: Create a new lesson

Deleting a lesson

You can delete the lesson by simply selecting it from the navigation tree and click on the delete button given on the toolbar.

Another option is to press Delete key given on the keyboard after selecting it from the Navigation tree. (Figure 2.15)

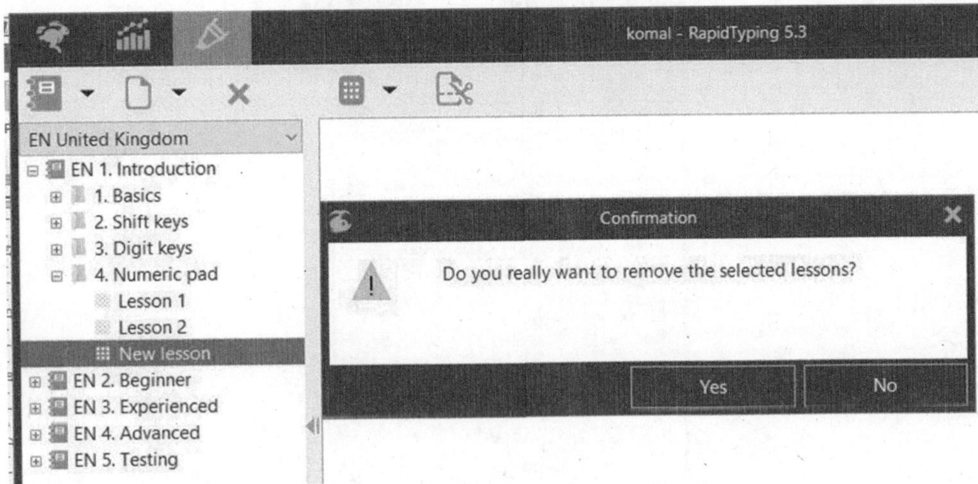

Figure 2.22: Deleting the selected lesson

Inserting a lesson from an external file

Use any of the given options to insert a lesson from an external file:

- Press Ctrl + I and choose the corresponding text file or select Add existing lesson option from **Lesson** menu dropdown
- Click on Insert key given on keyboard in case of inserting a text from multiple files into a multi-section lesson. In the new dialog box, you can specify a length, section of each subsection, and lesson type. RTF files are not supported by this function. (Figure 2.23)

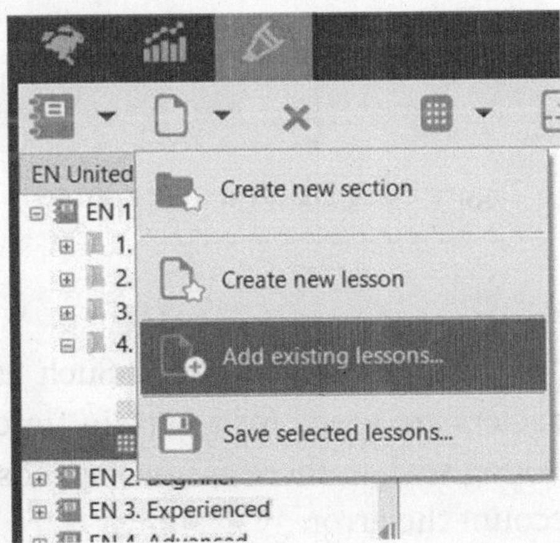

Figure 2.23: Insert a lesson from External File

Creating a new course

In the above section, we have learned to create a new lesson, and here we will learn to create a new course. To create a new course, performs the following steps:

1. Select the Lesson editor option given on the title bar and select **Create a new course** from the **Course** menu option.
2. After this, a new course has been added in the navigation tree, enter the name and title of your course, and press Enter. (Figure 2.24)

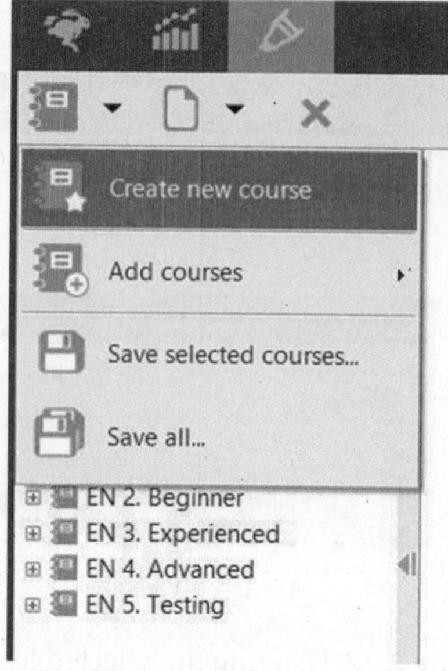

Figure 2.24: Create a new course

Delete a new course

To delete a newly created course, select the course and click on the delete button, or press delete key given on the keyboard. (Figure 2.25)

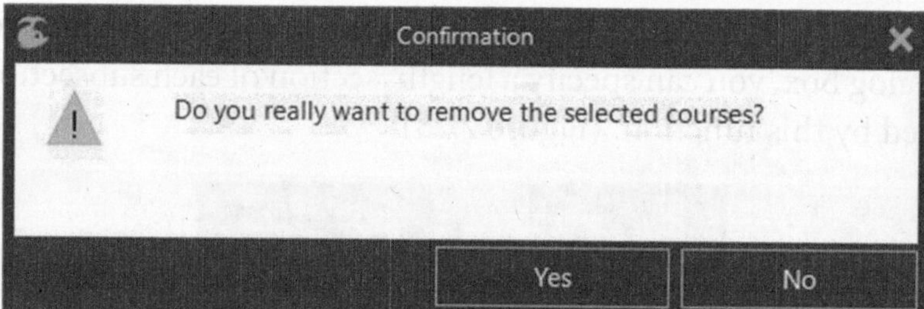

Figure 2.25: Delete a new course

Calculating the typing speed

The typing speed can be measured with different accuracies. Such as how many words are typed for a certain time period, how many characters are typed for a certain time period, and how many keystrokes are made for a certain time period. Along with it, there are two speeds one is simple speed or gross speed and net speed or which takes into account the error.

Various typing measurements of speed rates:

- **CPM:** CPM stands for characters per minute that are used to view the character per minute speed progress.
- **Net CPM:** Net CPM is the CPM without characters with errors.
- **KPS:** KPS stands for Keystroke per second.

- **CPS:** CPS stands for characters per second that are used to view the character per second speed progress.
- **KPM:** KPM stands for keystrokes per minute, and it defines the number of keystrokes in a one minute period of time.
- **Net KPM:** It is the KPM without keystrokes with errors.
- **WPS:** WPS stands for words per second that are used to view the word per second speed progress.
- **WPM:** WPM stands for Word per minute that is used to view the word per minute speed progress.

Formulas for various typing measurements of speed are:

- CPM = (Characters without errors + Characters with errors) / Time spent in minutes
- Net CPM = CPM - (Characters with errors / Time spent in minutes)
- KPM = (Keystrokes without errors + Keystrokes with errors) / Time spent in minutes
- Net KPM = KPM - (Keystrokes with errors / Time spent in minutes)
- WPM = (Words without errors + Words with errors) / Time spent in minutes
- Net WPM = WPM - (Words with errors / Time spent in minutes)

Typing accuracy

It defined as the percentage of correct entries out of total entries typed. Different formulas for typing accuracy calculation are:

- Accuracy in words = (100% - Words with errors* 100%)/Total number of words
- Accuracy in characters = (100% - Characters with errors* 100%)/Total number of characters
- Accuracy in keystrokes = (100% - Incorrect keystrokes * 100%)/Total number of keystrokes

Sometimes typing accuracy is evaluated by considering errors.

- Errors in words = (Words with errors * 100% / Total number of words
- Errors in characters = (Characters with errors* 100%)/Total number of characters
- Errors in keystrokes = (Incorrect keystrokes * 100%)/Total number of keystrokes

Typing rhythm

In touch typing techniques, the typing rhythm defines that the keystrokes should come at equal intervals. In this, a slowdown indicator is used for controlling the constant speed of typing. Various formulas for calculating the slowdown in percentage are:

- Slowdown in words = (Words with delay * 100% / Total number of words
- Slowdown in characters = (Characters with delay* 100%)/Total number of characters
- Slowdown in keystrokes = (delay in keystrokes * 100%)/Total number of keystrokes

Summary

- On the left side of the title bar, there is a button of Lesson editor after the student statistics. By clicking on the lesson editor button, a lesson editor window will appear.
- The lesson editor window allows us to customize lessons that means you can add, change, import/export, and remove lessons and courses.

- In Rapid typing software, you can create a new lesson, delete a lesson, and more.
- Editor panel is the area where changes can be done in existing course options or text of a lesson such as a navigation tree.
- You can delete the lesson by simply selecting it from the navigation tree and click on the delete button given on the toolbar.
- To create a new course, Select Lesson editor options are given on the title bar and select **Create a new course** from the **Course** menu option.
- To delete a newly created course, select the course and click on the delete button, or press delete key given on the keyboard.
- The typing speed can be measured with different accuracies.
- Typing accuracy is defined as the percentage of correct entries out of total entries typed.

In touch typing techniques, the typing rhythm defines that the keystrokes should come at equal intervals.

Self-Assessment

MULTIPLE CHOICE QUESTIONS.

1. The title, lesson editor, current lesson, and student statistics tab buttons are available in _____:
   a. Title bar b. Toolbar c. Navigation tree d. Table Analysis Text
2. Commands for adding lesson from external file is present in __________.
   a. Title bar b. Toolbar c. Text panel d. Navigation panel
3. CPM stands for?
   a. Character per minute b. Component per minute
   c. Character cases per minute d. None

Answers

1. A 2. B 3. B

FILL IN THE BLANKS

1. There is __________ keyboard in RapidTyping.
2. In ______________ display a list of currently chosen keyboard, current course, section and lesson.
3. ____________ is the full form of KPM.

Answers

1. Virtual keyboard 2. Navigation tree 3. Keystroke per minute

TRUE OR FALSE

1. The add lesson command is available in Lesson Editor. (T/F)
2. Users cannot delete the newly created lesson using the Delete key of a keyboard. (T/F)
3. CPS in typing measurement of speed rats gives character written per second. (T/F)
4. Weight per minute is the full form of WPM. (T/F)

Answers

1. True 2. False 3. True 4. False

QUESTIONS

1. Write down the steps to add a lesson in RapidTyping?
2. Explain the role of the navigation tree in the Lesson editor.
3. Write the steps to add a new course in Rapid Typing?
4. Give various interfaces available in RapidTyping software with their purpose.

PROJECT WORK

Open RapidTyping software and add two lessons in it; one of them should be from an external file. Then add a new course and 2 lessons in it, delete all the added sources and lessons.

MULTIPLE CHOICE QUESTIONS.

1. Caps lock key is used to ____________
   a. Type text in uppercase
   b. Type text in lower case
   c. Type numeric data
   d. All
2. Which of the following keys are not available on Numeric keypad?
   a. Numbers 0 through 9
   b. Addition
   c. Spacebar
   d. Enter
3. ______________ are Home row keys for left hand.
   a. SDFG
   b. LKJ
   c. ASDF
   d. HJK
4. Which of the following key is pressed to add a space between paragraphs?
   a. Space bar
   b. Shift
   c. Insert
   d. Enter
5. From floor the height of under-desk keyboard drawer or tabletop must be ________ to ________ cm.
   a. 20 to 25
   b. 50 to 60
   c. 68 to 73
   d. 40-45
6. Selection pointer in word processors represents:
   a. Typing text
   b. Make blocks of text
   c. Moving over the page
   d. Moving the insertion point
7. Which of the following is not the benefit given by Touch Typing software?
   a. Accuracy
   b. Speed
   c. Good handwriting
   d. Focus
8. The typing errors, slow down and speed for each chapter is display under__________ tab?
   a. Next step
   b. Rating pane
   c. Detailed statistics
   d. Error overview
9. Which of the following color display the percentage of completion of the lesson?
   a. Red
   b. Green
   c. Blue
   d. Yellow
10. CPM stands for?
    a. Character per minute
    b. Component per minute
    c. Character cases per minute
    d. None

Answer

1. a	2. c	3. c	4. d	5. c
6. a	7. c	8. c	9. b	10. a

VERY SHORT QUESTIONS

1. What is the function of the backspace key in the keyboard?
2. Name the home row keys.
3. What is the guide keys?
4. What is the usage of typing ergonomics?
5. Define mouse?
6. Define the I-beam mouse pointer on the document.
7. Give various stages of Touch Typing?
8. What are the other names of Touch Typing?
9. What different colors in typing statistics show?

SHORT QUESTIONS

1. What is keyboarding skills?
2. Define the usage of the numeric keypad.
3. What are the various actions performed by the mouse?
4. Write a short note on mouse operations?
5. Define touch typing?
6. Write down the steps to open Rapid Touch Typing software on your computer?
7. What is the purpose of the statistics window?
8. What is the purpose of the error window?
9. What is the purpose of the drag and drop action of a mouse?

LONG QUESTIONS

1. How can you type and delete text in a document that includes numbers, capital letters, symbols, sentences, and more?
2. What is the usage of any 7 keys of a computer keyboard?
3. What are the typing Ergonomics that users must keep in mind while working on a computer or laptop?
4. Mention the finger allocation of keys for typing to third or upper row, second or home row, first or lower row, and fourth or number row?
5. Give components of Rapid Typing Software?
6. Write a short note on analyzing the student statistics in Rapid Typing?

APPLICATION-BASED QUESTIONS

1. Your father wants to train their new data entry operator. Which tool or software will you suggest?
2. Office HR wants to judge the level of typing of persons who comes for a job interview. Help her to judge and select one.
3. One of your classmates wants to delete a lesson using Lesson Editor. Where should he go?

4. While analyzing your results in Touch Typing, how will you identify the speed rates identified using KPM, WPS, CPS, KPS, CPM, and WPM?
5. Your teacher wants to send your statistics. In what form should she send.

PROJECT WORK

1. Demonstrate various keys on the keyboard and to type the text, numbers, and special character using appropriate keys on the keyboard.
2. Practice placing fingers on the correct key in four different rows of the keyboard.
3. Practice to type text in typing tutor software and interpret the results.
4. Calculate the typing speed.
5. Practice improving typing using typing tutor software.

TEACHER NOTES

1. Arrange one week class in the computer lab and practice students to work using Typing tutor that improves their typing speed
2. Practically show students the correct typing ergonomics.

3 Digital documentation

Learning Outcomes

After this chapter, you will have the knowledge of:

- Introduction to Word processor
- Basic features of Word processor
- Word processor applications
- Various operations in MS Word 2010 such as opening, closing, creating or saving a document, etc.
- Edit and save a document
- Various User Interface elements
- Formatting of document such as setting text fonts, change the type, size of font, effect of fonts, etc.
- Checking and correction of errors in the document
- Copy paste and cut paste of text or data
- Find and replace the text
- Use of bullet and numbering in text
- Text alignment
- Various types of layout for view a document
- Print a document
- Creating a table
- Table formatting
- Conversion of text to table
- Setting borders and shadings
- Adjust margins and orientation

INTRODUCTION

In 19th century, for the purpose of writing a document manual typewriter were used. After that computer comes in existence. Some of the most common activities performed in office are communication, Word processing, presentation and data processing. To perform these activities an office productivity software is used.

To create any kind of text documents on the computer use of Word processing is one of the most popular applications. By the use of Word processor, you can write, edit, save, format, retrieve, and print the document. The document can be any novel, paper, report, business data, etc.

The purpose of this chapter is to aware user about Word processor and its various applications. Word processor and its various features are explained which will help user to create different types of documents.

Resource Requirements:

- A multimedia computer system is used as hardware
- A Word processing application MS Office-2010 Software is required

SESSION 1: START THE WORD PROCESSING APPLICATION

Introduction to Word Processor

Through Word processing programs user is able to manipulate text and images. Word processor allows us to create, save, edit, and print a document. The Notepad and other text editor are not same as Word processor. As Notepad allow user to only create and edit the plain text. On other hand text can be illustrated and changed by using word processor. It also allows user to use images in the documents.

What is Word processor?

Word processor allow user to organize and present text on a page or several pages. The text organized in this way is referred to as a document.

According to Encyclopaedia of Business and Finance, 2nd Edition

Word processing refers to creating, editing, formatting, storage, and output of both printed and online or electronic documents. Word processing is the most-used business application for personal computers, perhaps alongside World Wide Web browsers and electronic-mail (e-mail) applications.

Definition Box

According to Vangie Beal, A word processor is software or a device that allows users to create, edit, and print documents. It enables you to write, store, display text on a screen, modify it by entering commands and characters from the keyboard, and prints it.

Basic features of Word processor

Feature	Explanation
Formatting	Italic, Font name, Boldface, WordArt, Font Color, etc. are some of the formatting features.
Graphic	Charts, drawing, pictures can be added in your documents. This results in overall document presentation enhancement.
Ease and Speed	For text typing a faster and easier method is provided by Word processor.
Printing	Printout of documents can be easily taken, and a printed version of document can be seen in Word processor.
Storage	All documents can be stored for future use.
Mail merge	Through this feature a piece of text can be sent to multiple addresses. Example: Mail merge feature will change the invited guest names, address and send the same document to multiple guests. This results in time and effort saving
Vocabulary and Spell Check	Spell check feature in word processor that keeps your documents free from errors. There is Vocabulary feature of synonyms that gives multiple alternate to same word.

Fact box: The first version of Microsoft Word was developed by Charles Simonyi and Richard Brodie, former Xerox programmers hired by Bill Gates and Paul Allen in 1981.

Skill Test Box

Select the best option from following given options.

1. Which of the following is not a basic feature of Word processor?
   a. Graphic b. Mail Merge c. Printing d. Time consuming
2. The MS Word document is known by:
   a. Open Word b. Word c. Writer d. None of these

Word processing applications

By the use of Word processing any kind of text document can be written and its overall performance can be enhance by using various features of Word processor.

Various word processing applications are:

- ✦ WordPad
- ✦ Notepad
- ✦ Microsoft Word
- ✦ OpenOffice Writer
- ✦ Google Docs
- ✦ LibreOffice Writer

Notepad and WordPad are the basic text editors and they are desktop-based application that comes with windows. On the other hand advanced word processing applications are Microsoft word, LibreOffice Writer and Open Office. OpenOffice is available online on www.openoffice.org website and it is a part of OpenOffice suite. Microsoft office is a part of Microsoft Office suite.

Definition bot

Notepad: Notepad is a generic text editor included with all versions of the file contains special formatting or is not a plaintext file, it cannot be read in Microsoft Notepad. The image is a small example of what the Microsoft Notepad may look like while running.

WordPad: WordPad is a basic word processor available in every version of Microsoft's operating systems since Windows 95. It can be used to create and modify documents. Although slower to load than Notepad, it can handle graphics and rich formatting, unlike notepad, along with handling larger files. WordPad is well preferred for taking quick notes and text-based writing.

Introduction to MS Word 2010

In this chapter will give brief detail about MS word 2010. After this chapter you will be able to create their own document in MS Word 2010, Further you will learn to edit, save, reopen, format and close the document.

Some of the major functioning's of MS Word given in this session are:

- ✦ Opening MS Word 2010
- ✦ Creating a Document
- ✦ Saving a document
- ✦ Closing a Document

Opening MS Word 2010

Launch a Document: To open a MS Word 2010 step:

Click on Start > Click on All Programs > Microsoft Office > Microsoft Word 2010 (Figure 3.1)

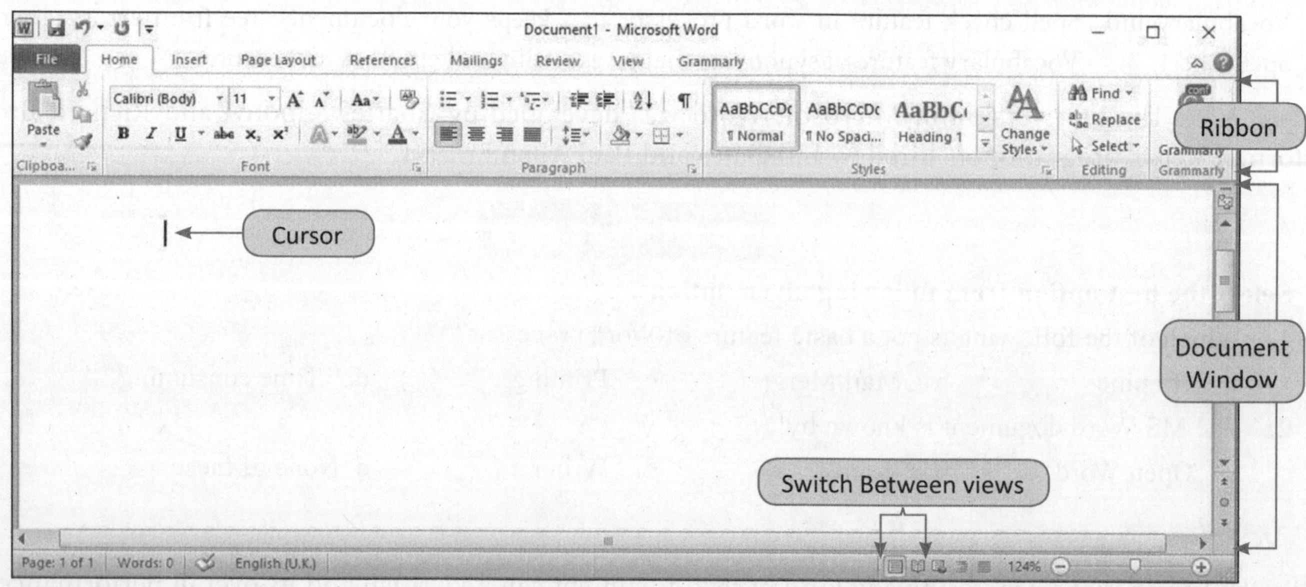

Figure 3.1: Opening MS Word 2010

The above figure or blank document comes on screen after opening MS Word 2010. The temporary name of this blank document is **Documnet1**. One small blinking cursor appears on the screen and it is also known as **insertion point**. The components are shown in the figure 3.1. The open application of MS Word displays document window, Ribbon bar, Cursor and switch between views icon. The formatting, editing, typing part is done in document window. The typing part start from cursor and ribbon bar contains various functionality buttons that can be used.

Knowledge Box

In case if above shown blank document is not visible in MS Word. Then you can open it by: Clicking on File > New > Blank Document.
Shortcut to create a new document is Ctrl + N keys.

MEMORY BOX

It is estimated that more than 10 million people worldwide use the MS Office Suite on either Windows or macOS X, and 15 million use it on Linux.

Creating a Document

We have learnt to open a document either by default when you open MS Word or by creating it by performing the following steps: (Figure 3.2).

1. Click on **File** Tab.
2. Click on **New** option.
3. Click on **Blank document**.
4. Click on **Create** button.

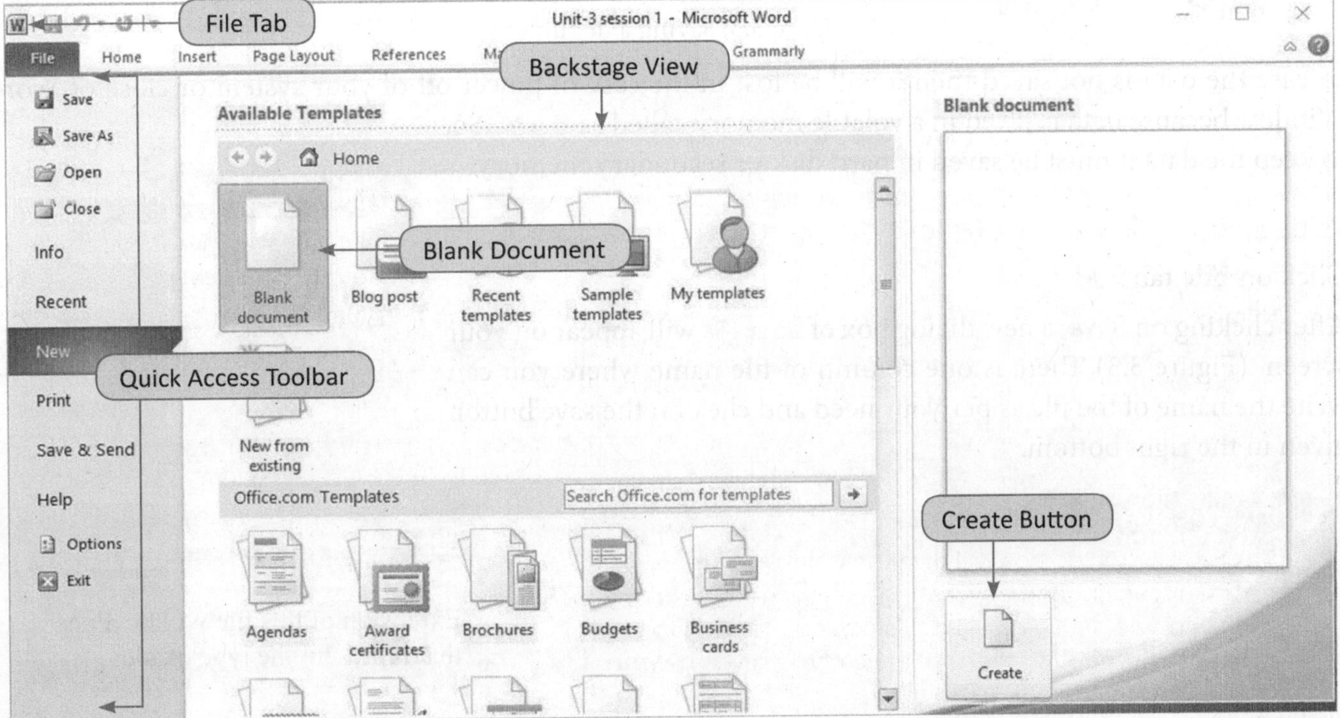

Figure 3.2: Creating a document

Once you are done with creating a new document then you can type the data you want to enter in it. The typing will start from cursor position. The cursor will move horizontally from left to right while typing a text.

Knowledge Box

Google Docs, Office 365 Word, and Microsoft OneDrive Word are Web-based word processor.

Saving a Document

The written data in the document is temporarily available in the **Random Access Memory (RAM)** or internal memory of your system. This can be saved permanently on the hard disk for future use. (Figure 3.3)

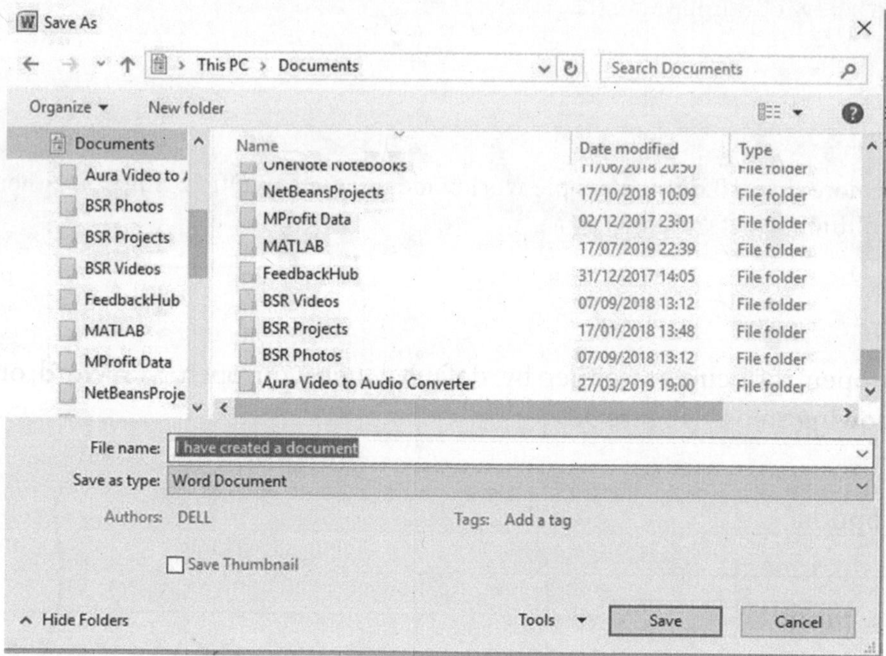

Figure 3.3: Saving a document

In case the data is not saved then it will be lost in the case of power off of your system or close of Word Window because data is saved in a volatile memory called as **RAM**. So, to keep the data it must be saved in hard disk or secondary memory.

Shortcut

You can also save it by pressing both Ctrl + S keys.

By Clicking on Save As, you can save your existing file with another name.

For saving a document follow these steps:

Click on **File** tab > **Save.**

After clicking on **Save**, a new dialog box of **Save As** will appear on your screen. (Figure 3.3) There is one column of file name where you can write the name of the file as per your need and click on the save button given in the right bottom.

Knowledge Box

The Save As dialog box will give the default location, further it can change by creating a folder and put name in the file name dialog box and click on save button to save it. Now document is saved with the name given by you and in the location chosen by you.

Memory Box

Extension of this file will be .docx that represent the type of file.

Closing a Document

Once you are done with your work, you can close the document by following the step:

Click on **File** > **Close** (Figure 3.4)

After clicking on close icon your document will be close or one new Window will be pop up for asking to save the document if you have not saved in before. (Figure 3.5)

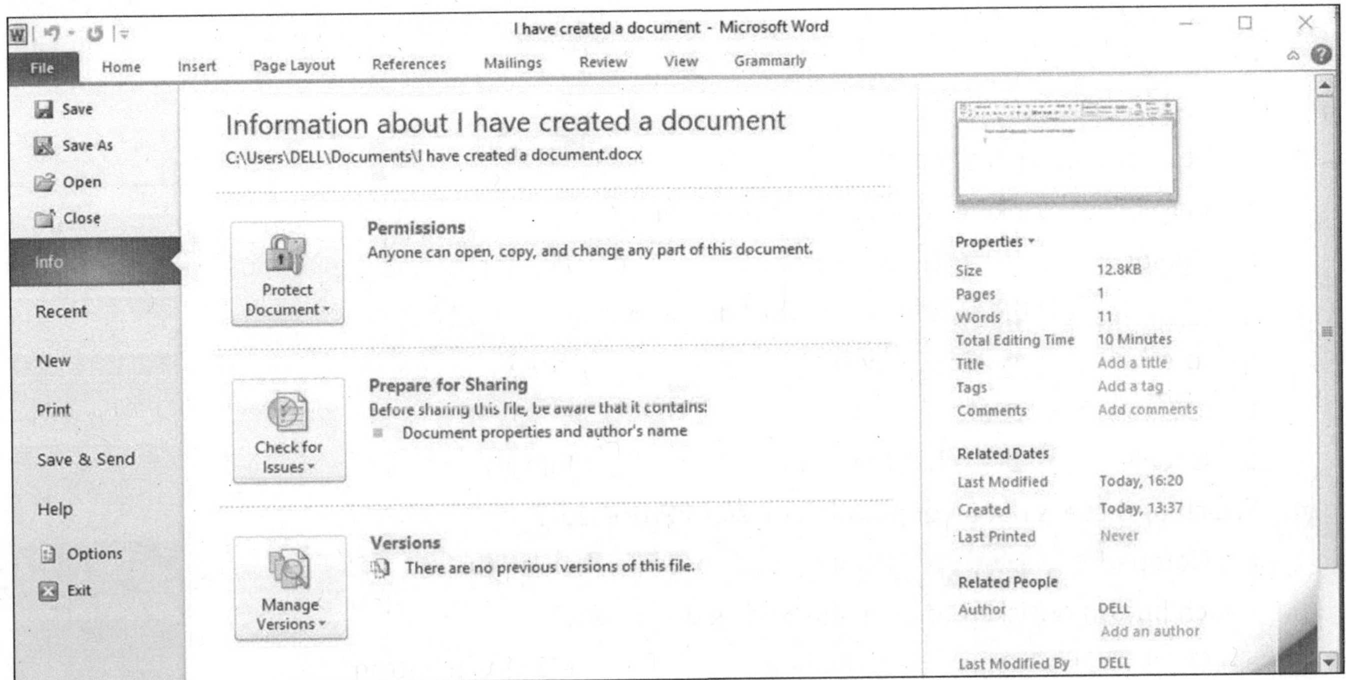

Figure 3.4: Closing a Document

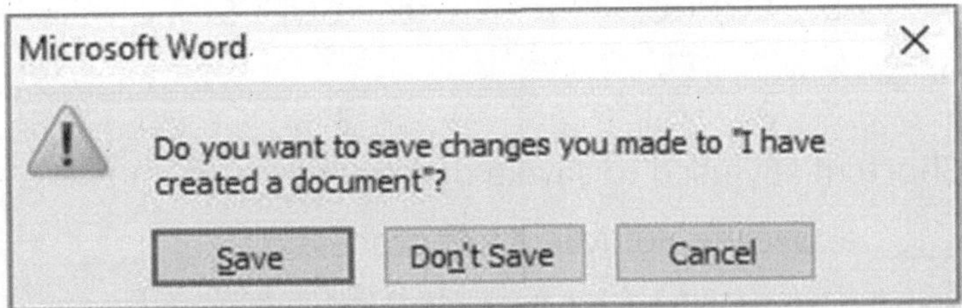

Figure 3.5: New pop up window for saving the alteration before closing the document

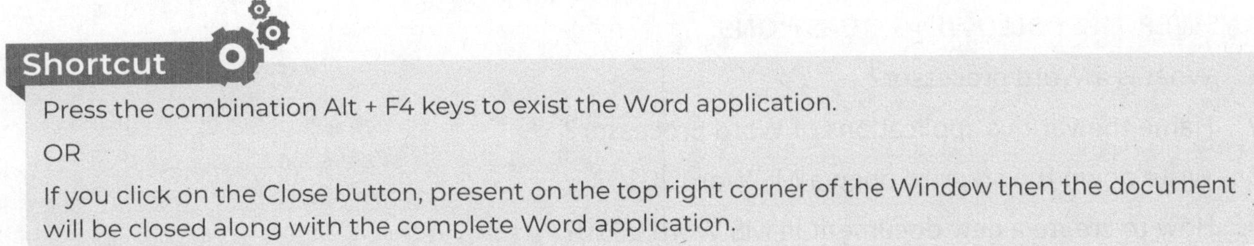

Shortcut

Press the combination Alt + F4 keys to exist the Word application.

OR

If you click on the Close button, present on the top right corner of the Window then the document will be closed along with the complete Word application.

Summary

- Word processor allows user to organize and present text on a page or several pages. The text organized in this way is referred to as a document.
- Formatting, graphic, ease and speed, printing, storage, mail merge, vocabulary and spell check are the basic features of Microsoft word 2010.

- Notepad and WordPad are the desktop based applications.
- To open MS word 2010, Click on Start > Click on all programs > Microsoft Office > Microsoft Word 2010.
- To save a Document, click on File tab > Save.
- By Clicking on Save As, you can save your existing file with another name.
- To close a Document, Click on File > Close.

Self-Assessment

A. MULTIPLE CHOICE QUESTIONS.

1. A small vertical blinking line in a Word is known as:
   a. Cursor b. Indicator c. Pointer
2. ____________ is the extension of Word document.
   a. .doc b. .dob c. .docx
3. Word is the product of:
   a. Google b. Microsoft c. Infosys
4. Which of these is not an application of Word Processor?
   a. Notepad b. Paint c. Open Office
5. Which button is clicked to open an existing document?
   a. Quick access Toolbar b. Ribbon c. MS Office button
6. Shortcut key used to Save a document
   a. Ctrl + A b. Ctrl + C c. Ctrl + S

B. FILL IN THE BLANKS.

1. _________ is the Shortcut key used to save a document
2. Notepad is a ________ application of Microsoft processing.
3. MS Word is a _________ application of Microsoft programming
4. __________ is used to save the existing file with another name

C. ANSWER THE FOLLOWING QUESTIONS.

1. What is a Word processor?
2. Name the various applications of Word processor?
3. Write down the steps to open a MS Word 2010?
4. How to create a new document in MS Word 2010?
5. What are the steps to save a file in MS Word 2010?

D. PRACTICAL WORK

Open a MS Word and write one paragraph in it, then save it with your name, close the document and reopen it.

ANSWERS

A. Multiple choice question.

1. c 2. c 3. b 4. b 5. a 6. c

B. Fill in the blanks.

1. Ctrl + S
2. Desktop based applications
3. Advanced word processing
4. Save As

SESSION 2: PARTS OF A WORD PROCESSOR WINDOW

Window Parts of a Word Processor

Various parts of Word processor Window are:

Title Bar: On the top and middle of word window there is title bar. Both the name of program and its currently used document name is display on it. (Figure 3.6)

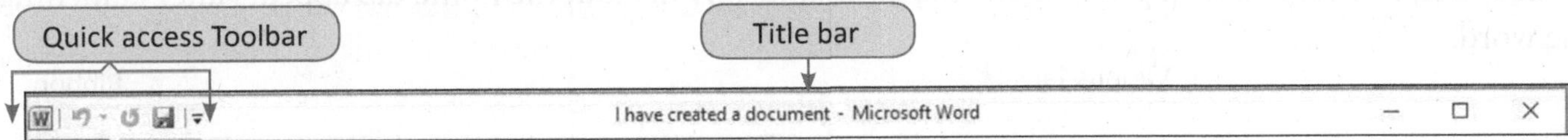

Figure 3.6: Title Bar and Quick access toolbar

Quick access toolbar: It is located on the top left side of the title bar. The frequently used common buttons are present on it. Redo, Undo, and Save are the three buttons that are present by default on it. We can remove or add another button through the drop-down arrow present on it.

Window control buttons: The window control buttons consist of three buttons named as minimize, restore or maximize and close button. Each have their own functioning as to reduce the size of the word window a minimize button is clicked. To get back to the default size of word window a restore or maximize button is used and to close or exit the word a close button is used. (figure 3.7)

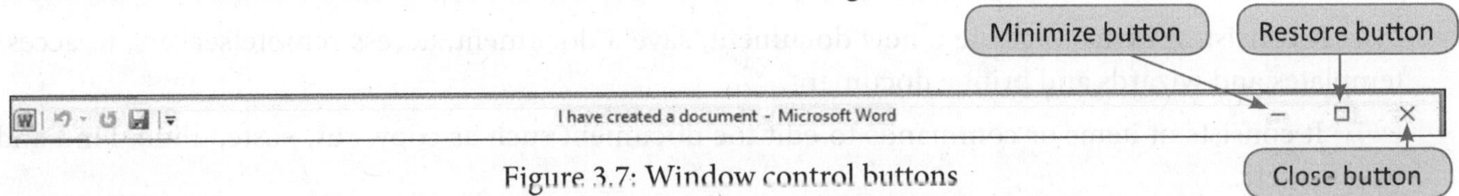

Figure 3.7: Window control buttons

Tabs: Below the title bar there is tabs that contains various group of command used to work in word. Some of the tabs in word are home, insert, page layout, references, mailing, review, view and Grammarly. (Figure 3.8)

Figure 3.8: Tabs

There are various group of tabs and each contain functioning related to it. Like home tab contains clipboard, font, paragraph, styles, editing.

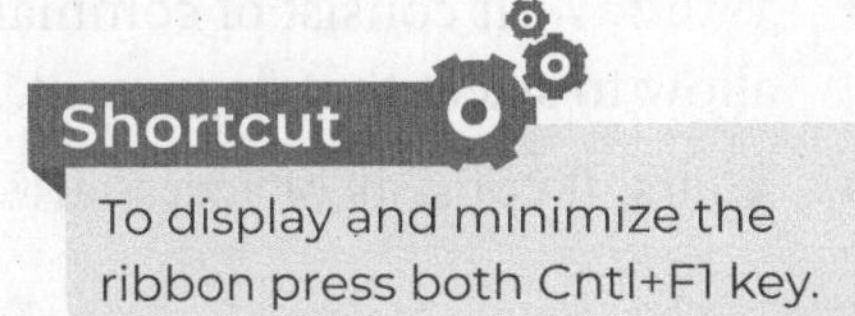

File Tab: In word 2010 there is file tab in the place of office button in word 2007. By clicking on it you will get various options like opening a File, New, Save, Save as, Print, etc. (figure 3.9)

Knowledge Box

Press Alt and first character of the tab name to select the tabs using keyboard.

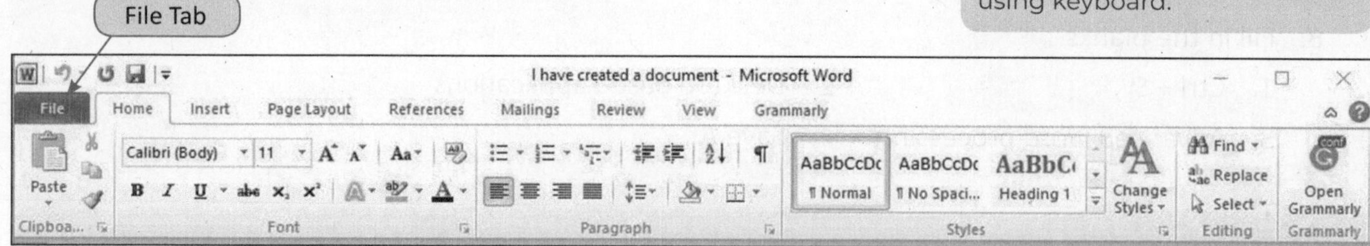

Figure 3.9: File Tab

Ribbon: On clicking on any tab a ribbon appears. It contains tab, groups, and commands. On top of ribbon button there are eight tabs present which contains groups of related commands which are organized in groups. As shown in the figure 3.10 the font contains its group of commands, clipboard contains commands related to it, etc. Within each group there are commands. By default, the home tab appears after launching the word.

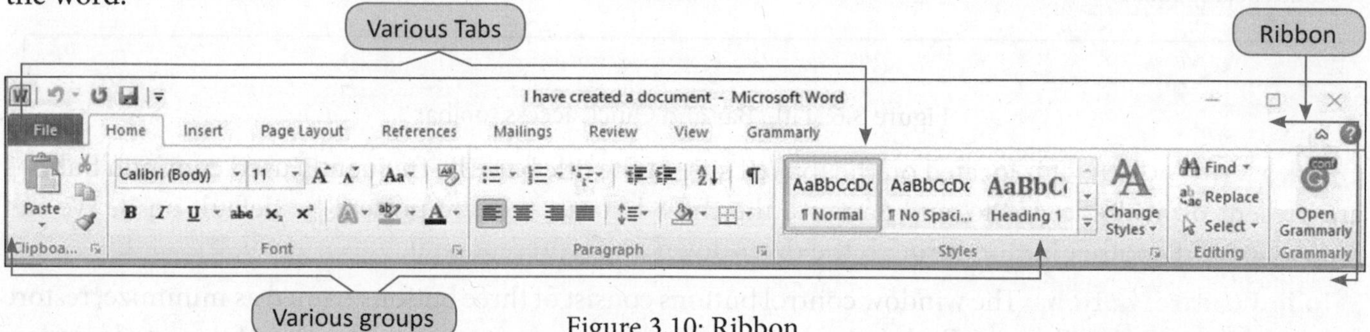

Figure 3.10: Ribbon

Menu Bar: Menu bar is located below the Title bar. On selecting any menus from menu bar, a submenu drops down to show further options or commands.

- **File:** It consist of items to create a new document, save a document, access remote servers, to access templates and wizards and print a document.
- **Edit:** It consists of items or commands to edit the document such as copy, cut, paste, undo, Find and Replace, etc.
- **View:** It consists of items for controlling the display of the document, such as Open or close the sidebar, access the data resources, Zoom and Web layout.
- **Insert:** It consists of commands to insert images, charts and shapes or Header and Footer.
- **Format:** It consist of commands to format rows, columns, sheets and images.
- **Styles:** It consists of commands to quickly apply common styles for editing, loading, creating new styles and for accessing the styles and formatting section of the Slidebar.
- **Table:** It consists of commands to insert and edit a table in a text document.
- **Tools:** It consists of access to spelling, grammar, autocorrect, customize and language tools.
- **Window:** It consist of command for display window that helps in see which documents are open and allow to select that document.
- **Tools:** It consists of access articles about different features of the Microsoft Office and Excel Help file.

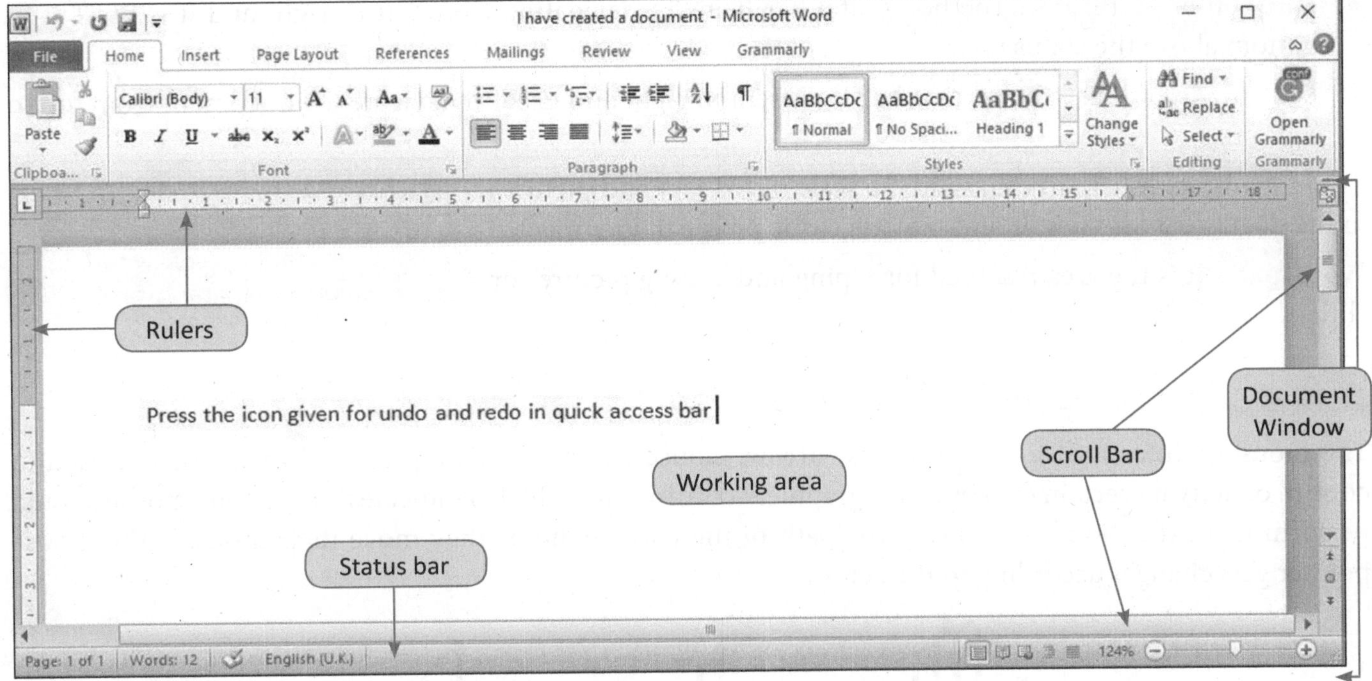

Figure 3.11: Microsoft Word Window

Rulers: There are two types of ruler bars name as vertical and horizontal bars present. The horizontal bar is present on the top that is used to set tab stops and margins on other hand the vertical alignment of text is formatted by using vertical ruler bar present on the left side of the Word Window.

Document or work area: This is the blank area where user type, edit, and format the text. User start writing from vertical line called insertion point or cursor. (Figure 3.11)

Tool Bar: Tool bar appears below the Menu bar. In Microsoft Word there are two types of Tool bar, Standards toolbar and Floating toolbar.

- **Standard Toolbar:** The standard toolbar is just under the Menu bar and it is also known as docked or fixed toolbar. It consists of command in the form of icons and is consistent across the Microsoft Word applications.
- **Floating Toolbar:** The floating toolbar is just below the Standard Toolbar. It is context sensitive that shows the tools relevant to the current position of the cursor or the selected object.

Definition Box

Toolbar: The toolbar, also called bar or standard toolbar, is a row of boxes, often at the top of an application window, that control various functions of the software.

Status Bar: The status bar is on the left bottom of the Window that displays the number of pages, word count, language used and zooming function, etc.

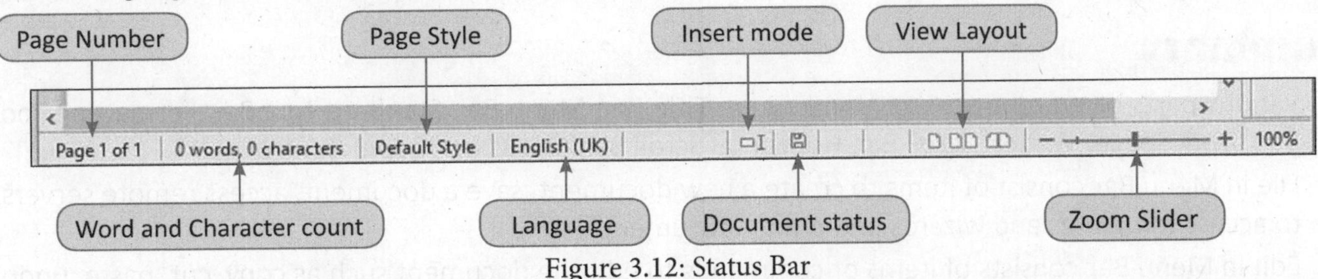

Figure 3.12: Status Bar

Scroll Bar: It helps to move the work window down or up and left or right by which we can check the non-visible part on the Window. There are two types of scrollbars name as horizontal and vertical.

- **Horizontal Scroll bar:** The horizontal bar helps in navigating from left to right and it is present in bottom above the status bar.
- **Vertical Scroll bar:** The vertical bar is present in right and used to navigate the document from top to bottom.

Zoom Control: It help in changing the scale of the text and pictures in the document for view. It does not affect the physical document.

Workspace: It is the area reserved for typing and adding pictures or clipart.

Knowledge Box

The workspace area is also available in software development, graphical interface, software as a service.

CURSOR AND MOUSE POINTER

The mouse pointer is also known mouse arrow, mouse cursor that is a graphical image that is used to control or activate certain elements in a graphical user interface. It also indicates where your mouse should perform its next action by following the path of the user's hand as they move their mouse. The mouse pointer gets changes according to the action.

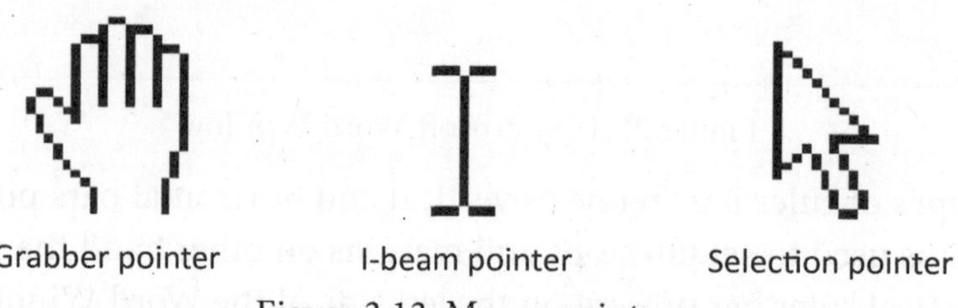

Figure 3.13: Mouse pointers

- You will observe the grabber pointer while working on a web browser that changes to the pointing finger symbol as it move over the page. This identifies a hyperlink.
- The I-beam pointer is used in graphical based text processing applications. This is used in word processors or various desktop publishing systems for marking the blocks of text and moves the insertion point.
- The Selection pointer appears when you move it around the screen that particularly consists of text. This also appears while typing text.

MEMORY BOX

There is Text cursor that has flashing vertical line in the body of the text. The four arrows on the keyboard are called as cursor control keys.

Definition Box

The mouse, sometimes called a pointer, is a hand-operated input device used to manipulate objects on a computer screen.

Summary

- Various parts of Word processor Window are Title Bar, Menu Bar, Standard Tool Bar, Formatting Tool Bar, Work Space, Vertical Scroll Bar, Horizontal Scroll Bar, Status Bar, Zoom Control.
- File in Menu Bar consist of items to create a new document, save a document, access remote servers, to access templates and wizards and print a document.
- Edit in Menu Bar consists of items or commands to edit the document such as copy, cut, paste, undo, Find and Replace, etc.

- View in Menu Bar consists of items for controlling the display of the document, such as Open or close the sidebar, access the data resources, Zoom and Web layout.
- Insert in Menu Bar consists of commands to insert images, charts and shapes or Header and Footer.
- The standard toolbar is just under the Menu bar and it is also known as docked or fixed toolbar.
- The floating toolbar is just below the Standard Toolbar. It is context sensitive that shows the tools relevant to the current position of the cursor or the selected object.
- The Status Bar displays the number of pages, word count, language used and zooming function, etc.
- Scroll Bar helps to move the work window down or up and left or right by which we can check the non-visible part on the window.
- Zoom Control help in changing the scale of the text and pictures in the document for view.
- The mouse pointer is also known mouse arrow, mouse cursor that is a graphical image that is used to control or activate certain elements in a graphical user interface.

Self-Assessment

A. MULTIPLE CHOICE QUESTIONS

1. Which of the following button reduce the size of window from its standard size?

   a. Maximize b. Reduce c. Minimize

2. The default tab of Word is:

   a. Home b. View c. File

3. Shortcut key to open an existing document?

   a. Ctrl + E b. Ctrl + S c. Ctrl + O

4. Which of the following is a not a default buttons present in quick access toolbar?

   a. Undo b. Open c. Save

B. FILL IN THE BLANKS.

1. Title bar contains _______ and __________.
2. To cancel the last editing _______ button is used.
3. The text is set according to the margins using ________.
4. User type in __________ area.

C. ANSWER THE FOLLOWING QUESTIONS.

1. What do you mean by quick access toolbar?
2. Name the three window control buttons in Word?
3. What do you mean by title bar?
4. What do you mean by groups and commands?
5. Explain the commands in status bar?
6. List the various views present in word?

E. PRACTICAL WORK

1. Check the operation of various tabs available on the menu bar.
2. Open a Word, Make a new report on Taj Mahal of 2 pages, Insert 1-2 beautiful Taj mahal photo in the same (Take from Internet). For this use various features of Word processor.

Answers:

A. Multiple choice question.

1. c 2. a 3. c 4. b

B. Fill in the blanks.

1. Name and type of document
2. Undo
3. MAX
4. Document or Work

SESSION 3: EDIT AND SAVE A DOCUMENT

Opening an Existing Document

In previous session we have learnt to open, write, save or close the document. What if you want to do some changes in the existing saved document, this can be done in MS Word 2010. For editing in existing document, you have to open it from the location where you have saved it. The steps to open the existing document are:

Click on **File** tab > **Open.**

Or

Click on **Quick access toolbar > Open.**

In both cases after clicking the **Open** button a new dialog box will appear. After that go to the desired location where you have saved the file which you want to open and then select that particular file and click on open button present in the bottom right corner. (Figure 3.14, 3.15)

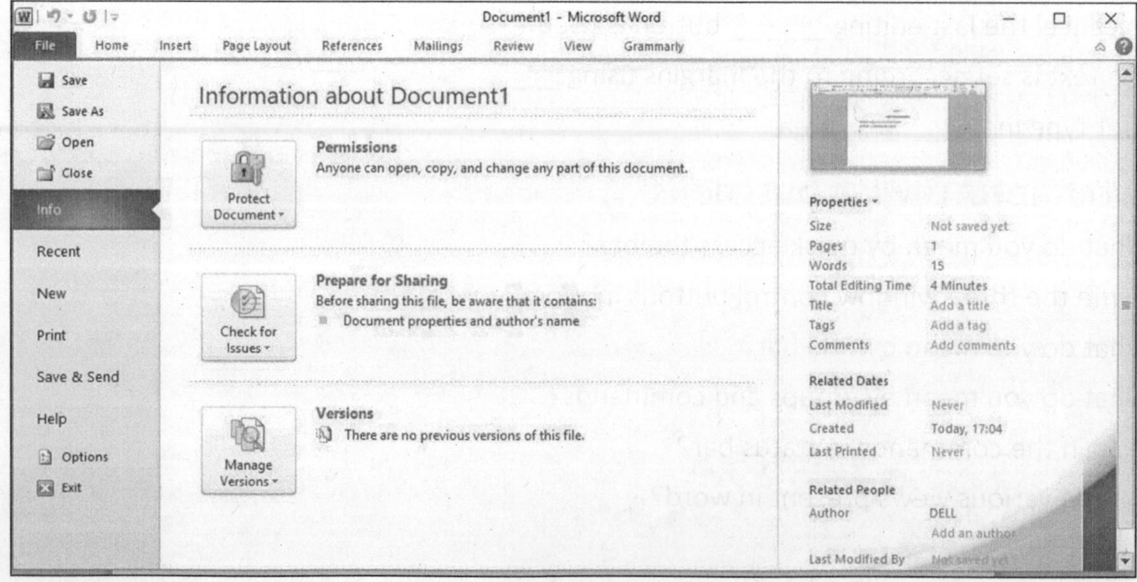

Figure 3.14: Opening a Document

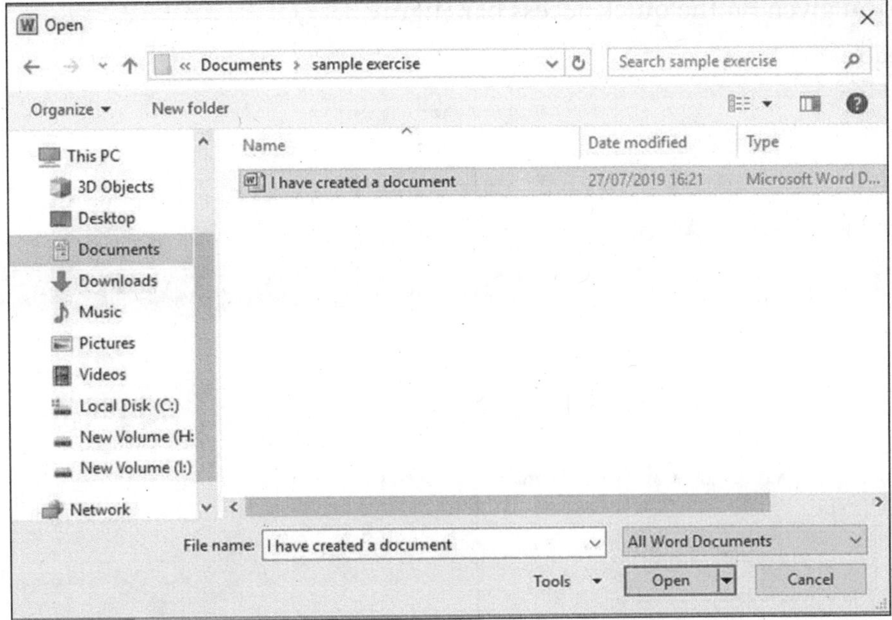

Figure 3.15: Opening the existing saved file

Editiing in Existing Document

The existing document is open by following the steps given for opening an existing document. Now next step is to do the needful changes by either adding some new data or editing the existing data written earlier in that document. (Figure 3.16)

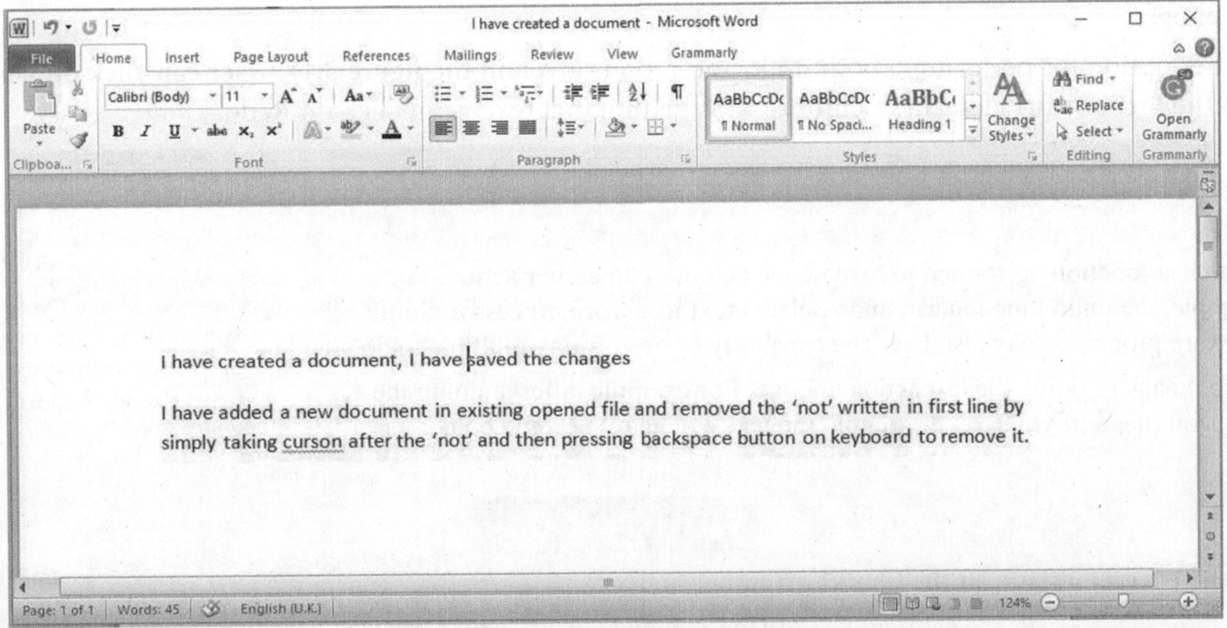

Figure 3.16: Editing an existing document

Undo and Redo The Text

If you have done some changes in the existing document or in new document that is not required than you can use undo to remove it from your document. To do this you have to follow the following steps:

Click on Undo button given on the quick access bar (figure 3.17)

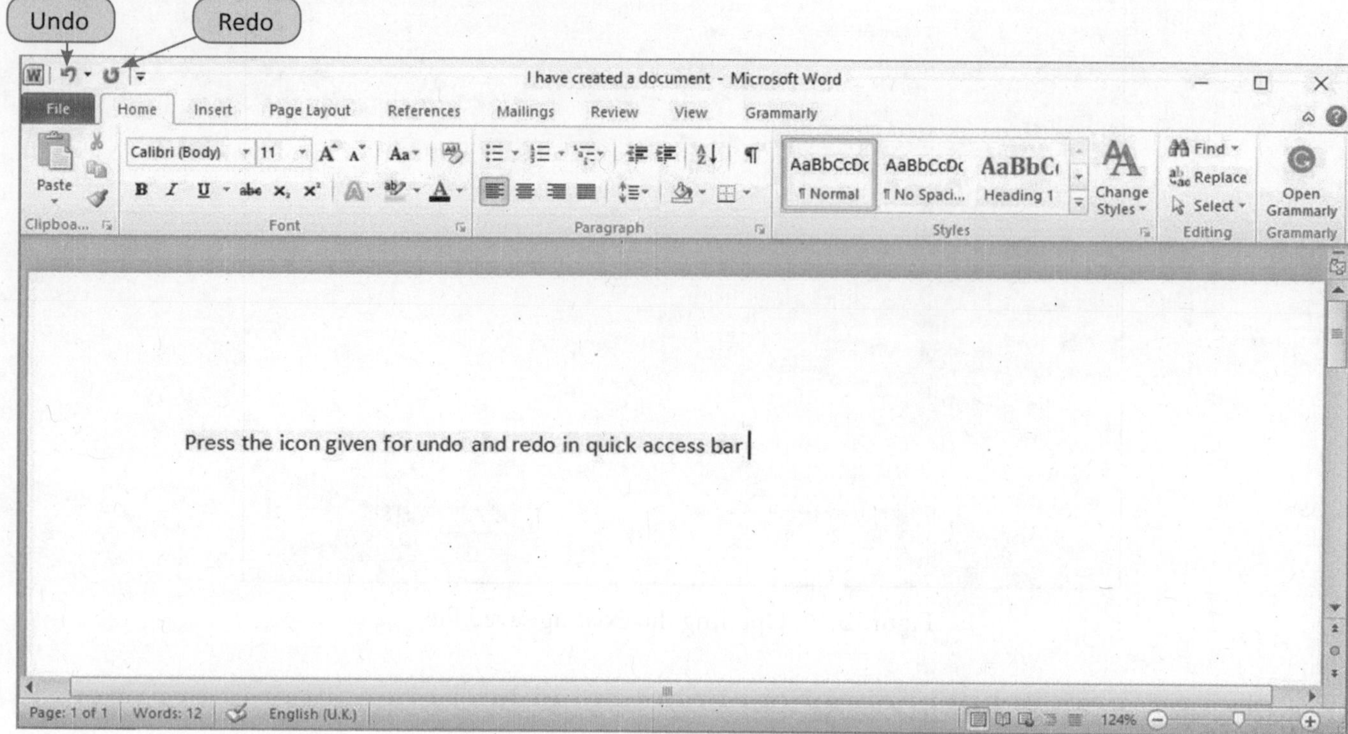

Figure 3.17: Undo and Redo a Text

There can be cases in which you want to delete the text again in your document to do it you can use the redo functioning of MS Word. To perform redo simply click on Redo button given in the quick access bar on the top.

Another option for performing both undo and redo is given in the figure 3.17. User can click on Undo to undo the text or work done in document or to getting that text again click on Redo.

Definition Box

Undo is a function performed to reverse the action of an earlier action. For example, the undo function can undo deleted text in a word processor. Some software programs may also have the capability of performing multiple undo's.

Redo means re-doing the last action undone. For example, after undoing the bold command, if you redo the action, the text will again become bold.

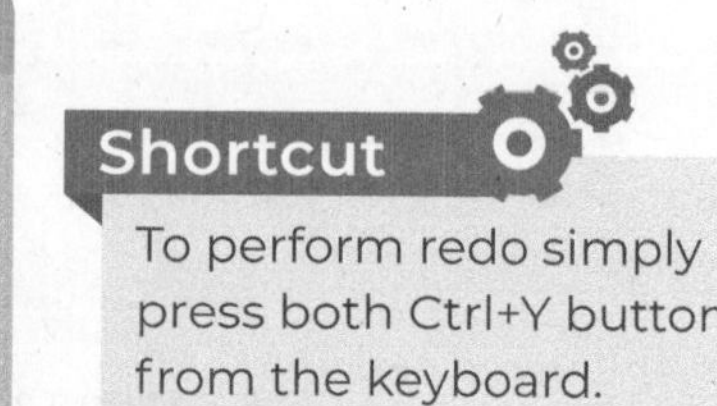

Skill Test Box

Fill the correct answer in the blanks given below.

1. ______________ is the shortcut key of Undo the document.
2. ______________ is the shortcut key of Redo a document.

Save Changes Done in The Document

After performing the required changes in the existing document, next step is to save it. One can save the changes by clicking on File tab then click on Save. This will save the changes and the updated file in the existing location or folder.

In case, if you want to rename the document or save it in another location then perform the following steps:

Click on **File** tab > **Save As.**

Click on Save As after clicking on File tab. By this one new dialog box will appear, select the location and file name and click on save button. (0046fygvüigure 3.18)

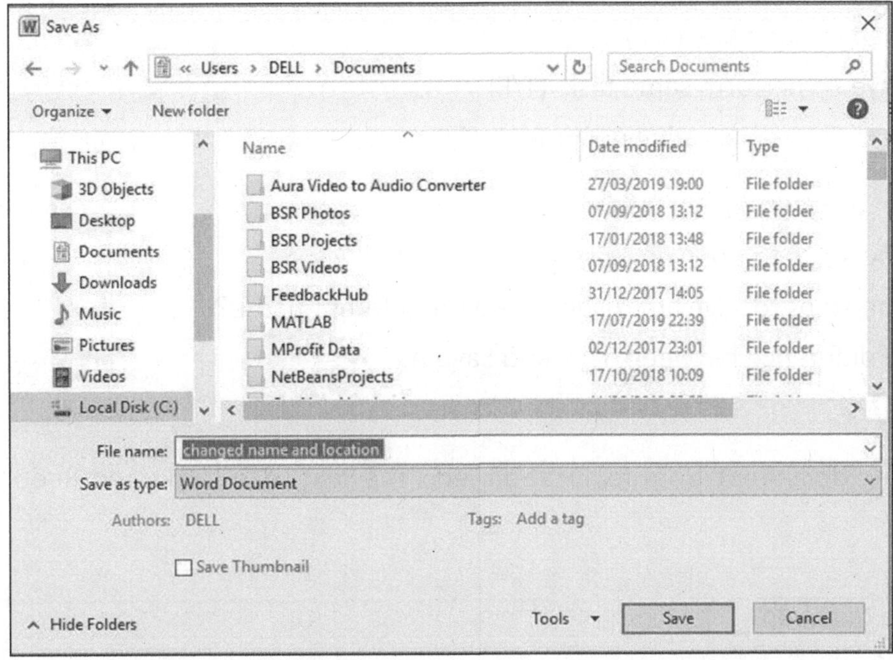

Figure 3.18: Saving the document in different location

Summary

- To open an existing document, Click on File tab > Open or Click on Quick access toolbar > Open
- To perform Undo action, click on Undo button given in Quick Access Bar
- To perform Redo action, click on Redo button given in Quick Access Bar
- To save changes done in the document, click on the file tab > Save

Keywords: Opening an existing document, Open, write, close, Editing in existing document, Undo, Redo the text, Save changes.

Self-Assessment

A. MULTIPLE CHOICE QUESTIONS

1. To save an existing file with another name which command will be used?

   a. Save b. Save New c. Save As

2. Open, New and Save option is present in which tab?

   a. Home b. View c. File d. Insert

3. Shortcut key to Open an existing document?

   a. Ctrl + E b. Ctrl + S c. Ctrl + C d. Ctrl + O

B. FILL IN THE BLANKS

1. __________ is the Shortcut key used to Save a document
2. __________ is the shortcut key to open an existing document

C. STATE WHETHER THE FOLLOWING STATEMENTS ARE TRUE OR FALSE

1. One can open existing file. (T/F)
2. Save and Save As perform same task. (T/F)
3. One can do changes in existing document. (T/F)

D. ANSWER THE FOLLOWING QUESTIONS

1. What are the steps to open an existing document?
2. What are the steps to save an existing file with different name?
3. What is the difference between Save and Save As?

E. PRACTICAL WORK

Open an existing document from its location, edit the text, Use Undo and Redo, then Save it with different name.

Answers:

A. Multiple choice question.

1. c 2. a 3. d

B. Fill in the blanks.

1. Ctrl + S
2. Ctrl + O

C. True or False

1. True
2. False
3. True

SESSION 4: FORMATTING A DOCUMENT

Copy The Data

If you want to create or use the same data, then copy command of MS Word 2010 can be used. Either single or multiple copies of data can be created by using single command without affecting the existing data. This will save time and efforts that user has to put in writing the same data again in different location. The copy operation can be done by performing following steps:

Select the text > Right click on it > Select copy command (figure 3.19)

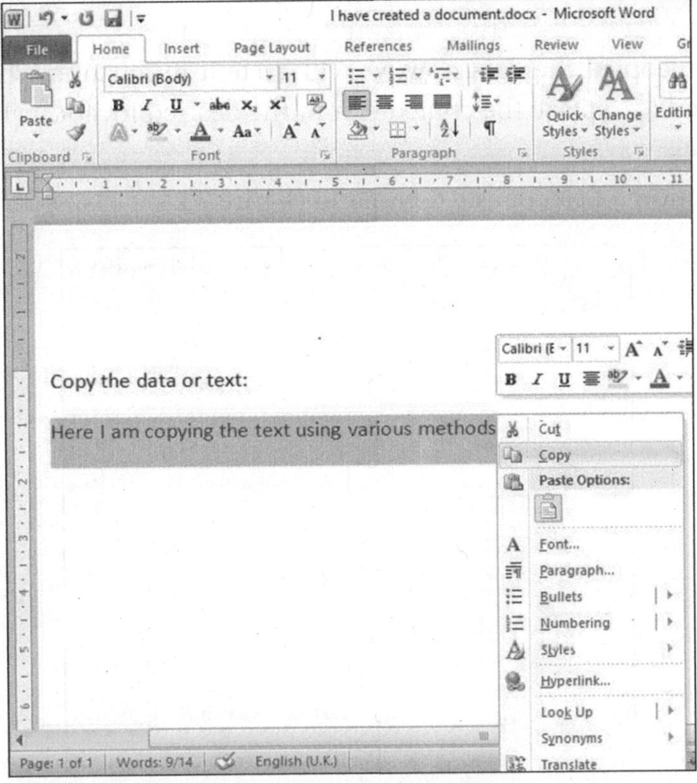

Figure 3.19: Copy the Data

This will make the copy of that data, now you can use it anywhere in the text. Another option is:

Select the text > click on the copy command from the clipboard group of Home tab

Now it is ready to use anywhere in whole document. You have copied the data now next step is to use it by pasting it in another location. (figure 3.20)

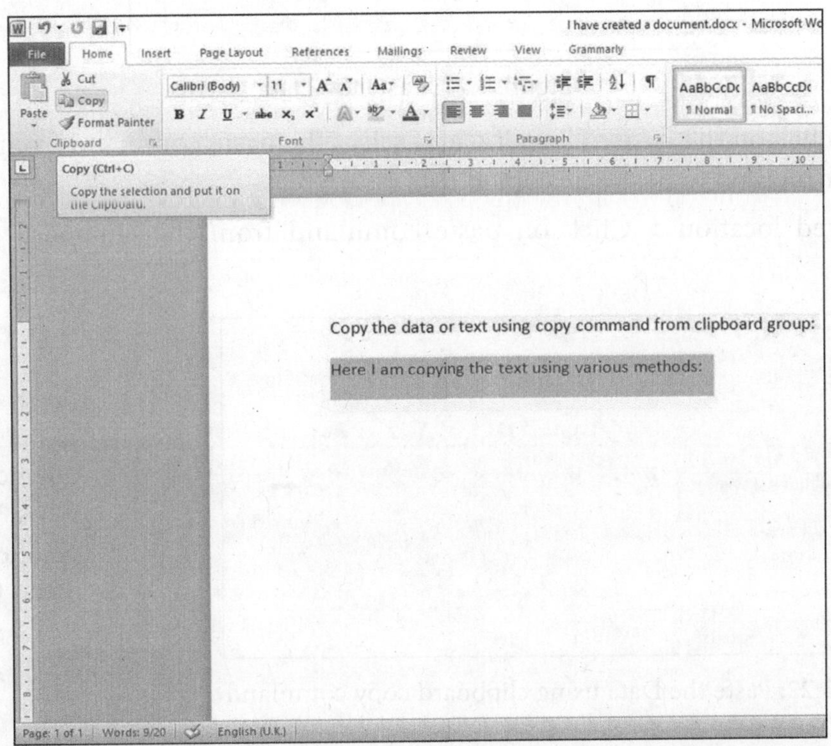

Figure 3.20: Copy the Data using Copy command from Clipboard group

Paste The Data

In the last section we have copied the data now we will paste it in location where we want to use it. The work of the paste command is to place the copied text in the desired location. The task of pasting the data can be performed in various ways:

Right click on desired location > Select paste command (figure 3.21)

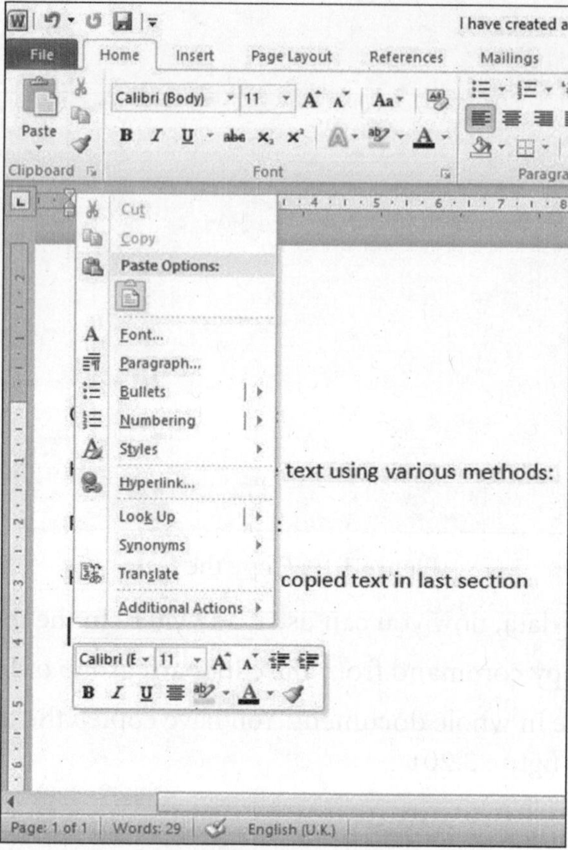

Figure 3.21: Paste the Data

In this we will right click on the desired location and select the paste command from it that will paste the copied data. Another method to paste the copied data is:

Put cursor on desired location > Click on paste command from the clipboard group of home tab. (figure 3.22)

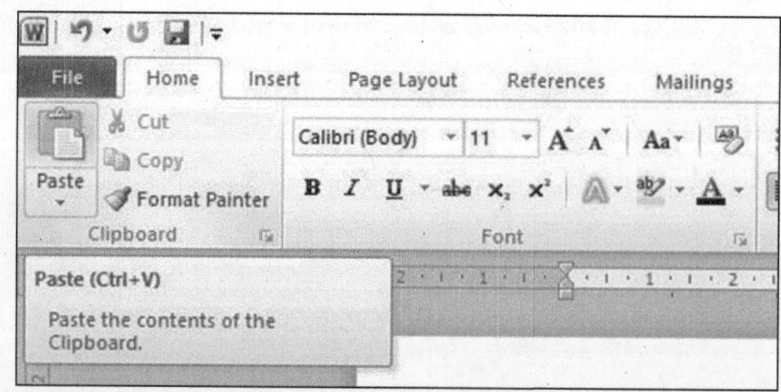

Figure 3.22: Paste the Data using clipboard copy command

LETS KNOW MORE

Shortcut to copy the text: Press Ctrl + C key.

Shortcut to paste the text: Press Ctrl + V key.

Cut The Data

In case of copy command, we will get the copy of that data which is further being pasted on different locations. On the other hand, the cut command will remove that data from the particular location, and it will paste the text in another location. Steps to perform cut task are:

Select the desired text > Right click on it > Select the cut command

Or

Select the desired text > Click on Cut command from Clipboard group of Home tab. (figure 3.23, 3.24)

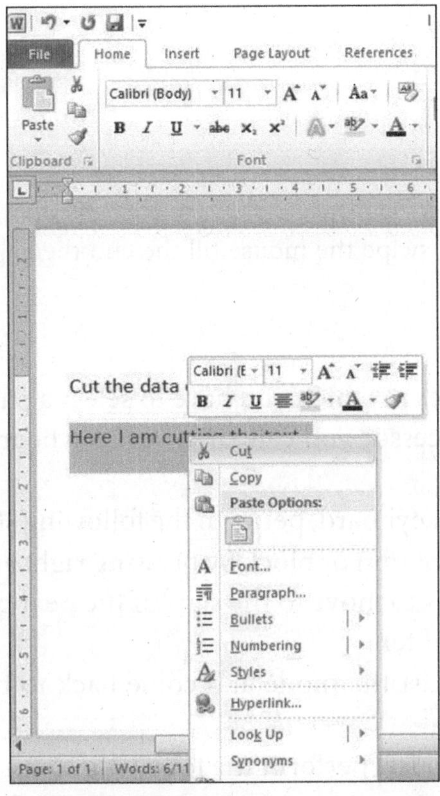

Figure 3.23: Cut the Data

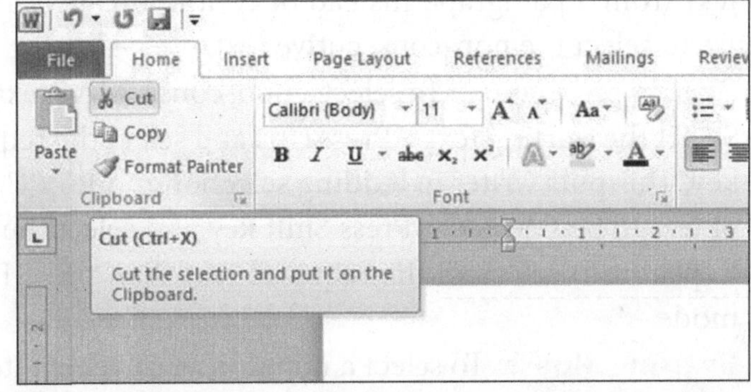

Figure 3.24: Cut the Data using Cut command of Clipboard

Then the data which has been cut from one location can be pasted in another location by same way as given in the previous section of pasting the copied data.

LETS KNOW MORE

Shortcut to cut the text:
Press Ctrl + X key.

In case of copy command, we will get a copy of that data, which is further being pasted on different locations. The cut command is almost same but in this the data is remove from exiting location and past in another location. It is just like change in location of data.

Skill Test Box

Select the best option from following given options under the questions.

1. If you want to remove any particular text from a particular location, and paste the text in another location the which of the following option will be used:

   a. Copy and paste   b. Cut and paste

Selecting Text

To perform the operation of copy and paste or cut and paste operation, you have to select the text that will be highlighted after selection. Firstly text is selected before editing the text. As you can do editing part of selected text.

Selection Criteria: There are various ways of selecting the text according to the part of text you want to select. In general to select the text, you just have to swipe the mouse cursor over the text. Various tricks of selection for increasing speed are:

Table 3.1: Various selection techniques

Technique	Action
Single Word	Double click on single word
Sentence	Triple click
Paragraph	Click four times in a row
Multiple selection	Press Ctrl key while clicking
Continuous selection	Click at the beginning then press Shift key and swipe the mouse till the end then again click at the end
All text	Ctrl +A

Selecting Non-consecutive text items: Sometimes there can be cases in which you have to select a part of the text from a paragraph instead of continuous text. In Word processor you can either use keyboard or mouse to select the non-consecutive text.

- **By using Keyboard:** To select a non-consecutive text item using keyboard, perform the following steps:
  Select the starting text > Press Ctrl and select the required text, column or block by pressing right arroq key, This puts writer in 'Adding selection mode' > Use arrow keys to move to the start of the next piece of text to be selected > Press Shift key and select the next piece of text
  Repeat it to select all the required text then press Esc key to exist the mode and come back to basic mode
- **By using Mouse:** To select a non-consecutive text item using mouse, perform the following steps:
  Select the starting text > Hold down or press Ctrl key and move the mouse to select next piece of text
  Repeat it to select all the required text

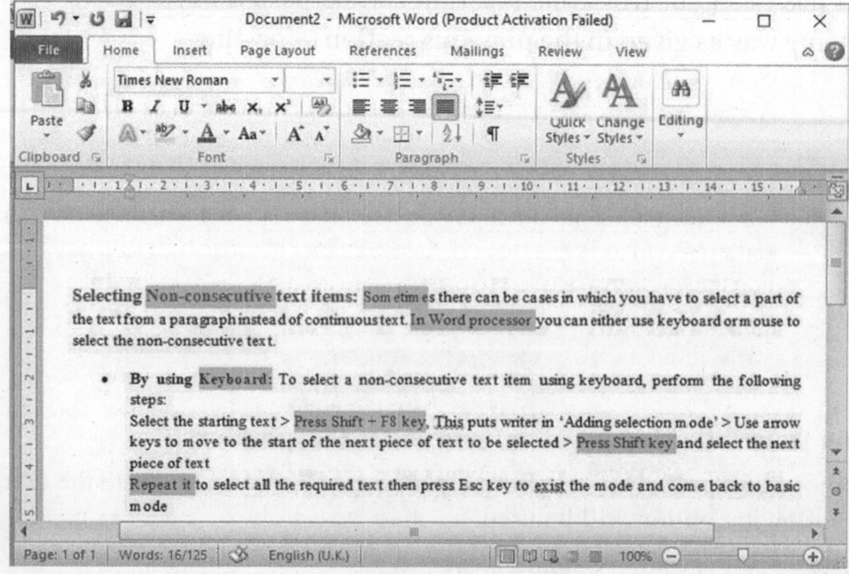

Figure 3.25: Selection of Non-consecutive text

Selecting Vertical block of text: Sometimes there are cases where you have to select a vertical block or column of text separated by tabs. To select the vertical block of text, perform the following steps:

Select the vertical block or column by mouse by simply taking mouse to starting point and then taking it towards rest of the block that you want to select.

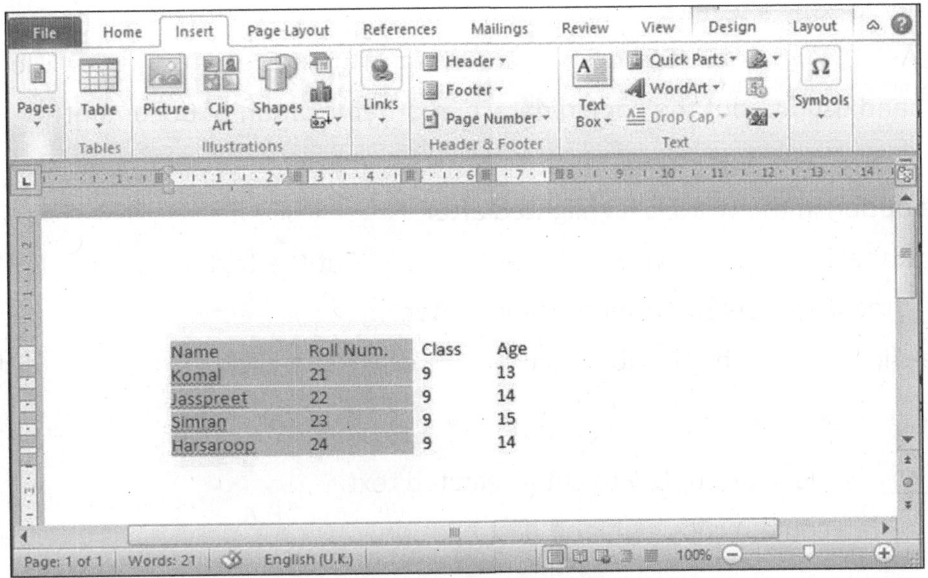

Figure 3.26: Selection of Vertical block of text

Skill Test Box

Solve the Multiple choice question with the knowledge you have gained about the topic.

1. ____________ is the selection criteria of selection a complete sentence.
   a. Single click on it b. Double click on it c. Triple click d. Four time click
2. Which of the following is not a Non-printing characters in Microsoft Word?
   a. Paragraph marks b. Line marks c. Tab stops d. Punctuation marks

Summary

- If we want to create or use the same data, then copy command of MS Word 2010 can be used.
- To copy a data, Select the text > Right click on it > Select copy command.
- Shortcut key to copy the text is Ctrl + C.
- The work of paste command is to place the copied text in the desired location.
- After copying a data to paste it, Right click on desired location > Select paste command.
- Shortcut key to paste a copy is Ctrl + V.
- The cut command will remove that data from the particular location and now it can be pasted in another location.
- To select a non-consecutive text item using mouse, select the starting text then hold down the mouse to select next piece of text
- To select a vertical block of text item using mouse, Select the vertical block or column by mouse by simply taking mouse to starting point and then taking it towards rest of the block that you want to select.

Keywords: Undo, Redo, Edit the document, Moving and copying text, copy and paste, cut and paste, Selecting text, Selection criteria

Self-Assessment

A. MULTIPLE CHOICE QUESTIONS

1. Shortcut key to copy a text:

   a. Ctrl + A b. Ctrl + B c. Ctrl + C d. None of the above

2. The command used to put the copied data in another location of document:

   a. Copy b. Cut c. Paste d. None of the above

3. The paste option in the word is highlighted after:

   a. Copy the text b. Writing the text c. Cut the text d. Both a and c

4. __________ technique selects a sentence in writer.

   a. Single-click b. Double click c. Triple-click d. Click four times

B. FILL IN THE BLANKS

1. ___________ is the shortcut key to cut a selected text.
2. ___________ tab contain copy, cut, and paste option.

C. STATE WHETHER THE FOLLOWING STATEMENTS ARE TRUE OR FALSE

1. You can paste the text of document by copying the document from its location. (T/F)
2. There is no shortcut key to cut a text. (T/F)
3. Ctrl + X is the shortcut key to paste the text.

D. ANSWER THE FOLLOWING QUESTIONS

1. What is the need of copying a text?
2. Explain the concept of copy a data and its steps?
3. How to remove a text from one location and put it into another location?
4. Give various techniques to perform different selection action on the document in Word processor?

E. PRACTICAL WORK

Open a MS Word, create a document and give it heading 1, then create a second heading name as heading 2 and insert the same text in it without rewriting it, Then create one more heading with the name of heading 3, change the location of data from heading 2 to heading 3.

Answers:

Multiple choice question answers:

1. c 2. c 3. d 4. c

Fill in the blanks answers:

1. Cut 2. Home

State whether the following statements are True or False:

1. False 2. False 3. False

SESSION 5: FIND AND REPLACE THE TEXT

Find The Text

In MS Word 2010, we have command that help in finding the occurrence of particular word in the whole document. This task can be performed by:

Click on drop down button "Find" given in the editing group of home tab > Select find > type the word in dialog box open in left side of document. (figure 3.27, 3.28)

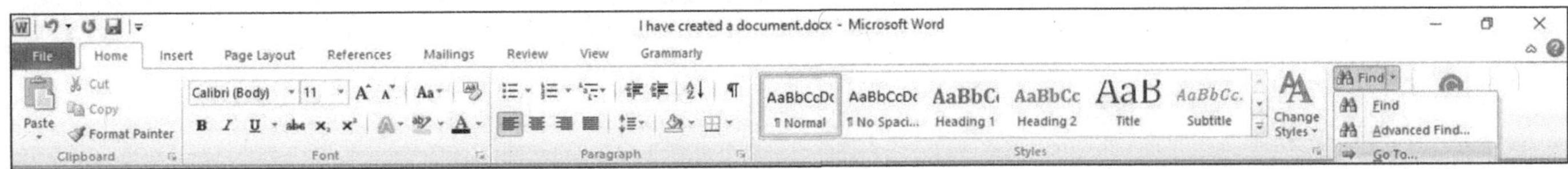

Figure 3.27: Find command in Editing group

When you type the word, it will highlight that word in the whole document. Press enter again and again to go through each word search by find command.

Another way to find the word is:

Click on the drop down button "Find" given in the editing group of home tab > Select Advanced Find > New dialog box with the name of Find and Replace will open > Type the word in column of "Find what" and press Find Next to go on the position of that word in whole document. (figure 3.29)

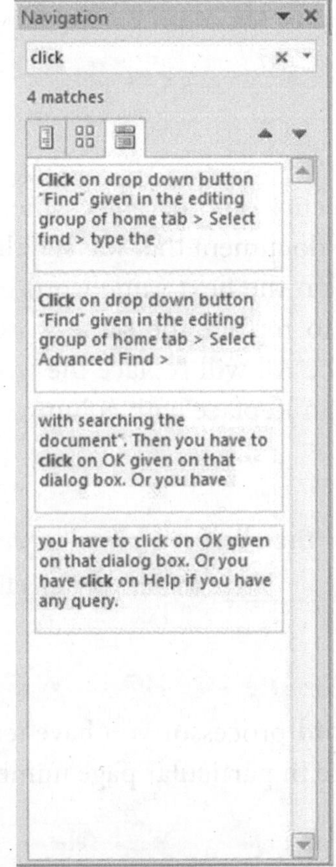

Figure 3.28: Dialog box of searching a Word using Find Tool

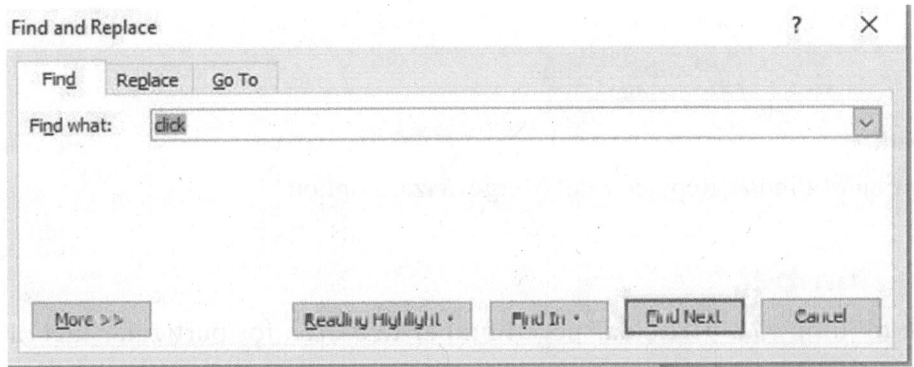

Figure 3.29: Dialog box of searching a Word using Advanced Find Tool

Once word will be done with find task it will display message "Word has finished with searching the document". Then you have to click on OK given on that dialog box. Or you have can click on Help if you have any query. (figure 3.30)

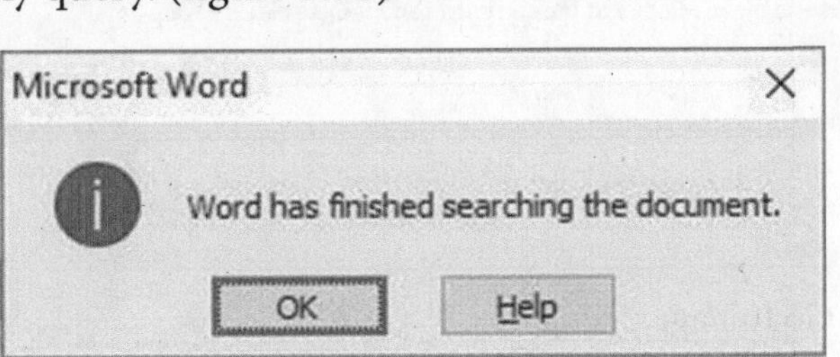

Figure 3.30: Dialog box of searching a Word using Advanced Find

LETS KNOW MORE

Shortcut to open Find command: Press both Ctrl + F key

Replace The Text

In the last section we have learnt to find the text in particular document. Now, we will work on replacing the text with another text. To replace the text user, have to perform the following steps:

Click on the Replace command given in Editing group of Home tab > A new dialog box will appear > Write the word which you want to replace in "Find What" column > Write the new word you want to add > Click on either Replace or Replace All. (figure 3.31)

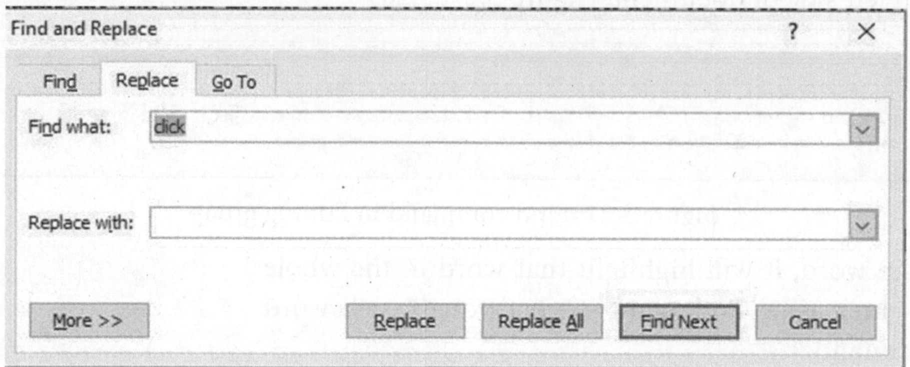

Figure 3.31: Dialog box of Replace Command

If you click on the Replace, then word will replace that particular word in the document that was highlighted, and you have to press Find Next to go on the next same word in the document. This is used when we want to replace the same word with different word. On other hand Replace All will replace the word in whole document with new word given in Replace with column.

LETS KNOW MORE

Shortcut to open Find command: Press both Ctrl + H key.

Skill Test Box

Enter the correct answer in the blank.

1. __________ Menu contains the option of Find & Replace Mail Merge Wizard option?

Jumping to the new page number

In Word processor you have feature to jump to a particular page number to search for particular text or picture in particular page number.

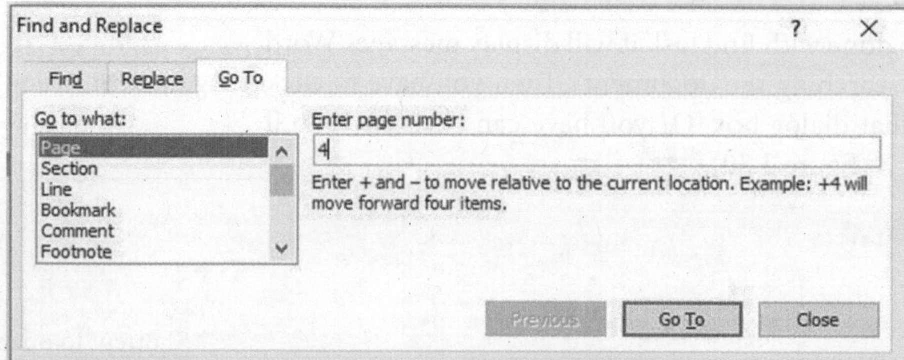

Figure 3.32: Go to Page dialog box

In dialog box you can specify the required page number then click on Ok button. It will take the cursor to the first character of the specified page number.

LETS KNOW MORE

Shortcut to open Go to Page dialog box: Press Ctrl + G

Non-printing characters

Non-printing characters are such paragraph marks, line breaks, tab stops, spaces, etc. that do not appear on the screen. Other characters that are visible on the screen are alphabet, numbers, punctuation marks, etc. In Word processor you have feature to see these non-printing characters on the screen that helps in exact formatting the document.

In Word processor, you have a feature to see these non-printing characters on the screen that helps in exact formatting the document.

Summary

- Find command in word will find the particular text for user.
- Find command is available in Editing group of Home tab.
- To find a text or word, click on drop down button "Find" given in the editing group of home tab > Select find > type the word in dialog box open in left side of document.
- Shortcut key to open a navigation bar is Ctrl + F.
- In word we can also replace the particular word with another word.
- To replace the text, Click on Replace command given in Editing group of Home tab > A new dialog box will come > Write the word which you want to replace in "Find What" column > Write the new word you want to add > Click on either Replace or Replace All.
- Shortcut to open Go to Page dialog box: Press Ctrl +G
- Non-printing characters are such paragraph marks, line breaks, tab stops, spaces, etc. that do not appear on the screen.

Keywords: MS Word 2010, Find text, Dialog box, Find tool, Advanced Find, Replace text, Home tab, Replace command, Go To page, Non-printing character.

Self-Assessment

A. MULTIPLE CHOICE QUESTIONS

1. Shortcut key to open a navigation bar is:

   a. Ctrl + O　　b. Ctrl + F　　c. Ctrl + P　　d. None of the above

2. The searched word can be replaced with another word by using:

   a. Replace command　　b. Replace All command

   c. Find Next　　d. Find

3. The Tab contains Find, replace command is:

   a. File　　b. Home　　c. Insert　　d. Page layout

B. FILL IN THE BLANKS

1. __________ is the shortcut key to open a Find and Replace dialog box.
2. Find command is available in __________ group

C. STATE WHETHER THE FOLLOWING STATEMENTS ARE TRUE OR FALSE

1. Replace and Replace All command do the same task. (T/F)
2. At one time only single word can be replaced. (T/F)

D. ANSWER THE FOLLOWING QUESTIONS

1. Differentiate between Replace and Replace All?
2. Explain the concept of copying a text and various steps involved in it?
3. What is the difference between cut and copy command?
4. Give in brief the concept of copy and paste command in word 2010.
5. Define Non-printing character.

E. PRACTICAL WORK

1. Open a document in any exiting word file then search for any particular text and replace it with another text.
2. Open a document in any exiting word file, go in last page by single click.

Answers:

Multiple choice question:

1. b   2. a   3. b

Fill in the blanks:

1. Ctrl + H
2. Editing

State whether the following statements are True or False

1. False
2. False

SESSION 6: CHECKING AND CORRECTION OF ERRORS IN THE DOCUMENT

Checking Spelling And Grammer

Errors are related to spelling and grammar mistakes. In MS word 2010 there is built in feature of checking and correcting the errors. When you write a text in word you must have seen some words or lines get underline with red, green, and blue wavy lines. These underlines are highlighting the spelling mistake, grammatical error, and contextual spelling error, respectively.

In review tab there is proofing group that have Spelling & Grammar command used for checking various errors.

Red wavy line or Spelling mistake

The red wavy line highlights the errors related to spelling mistakes. In case, if you found red line under your text then:

Right click on then text that have red wavy line > Select the matching word.

Or

Click on the Review tab > Select Spelling and Grammar command from Proofing group. After selecting it a new dialog box will open then select the matching word (figure 3.33)

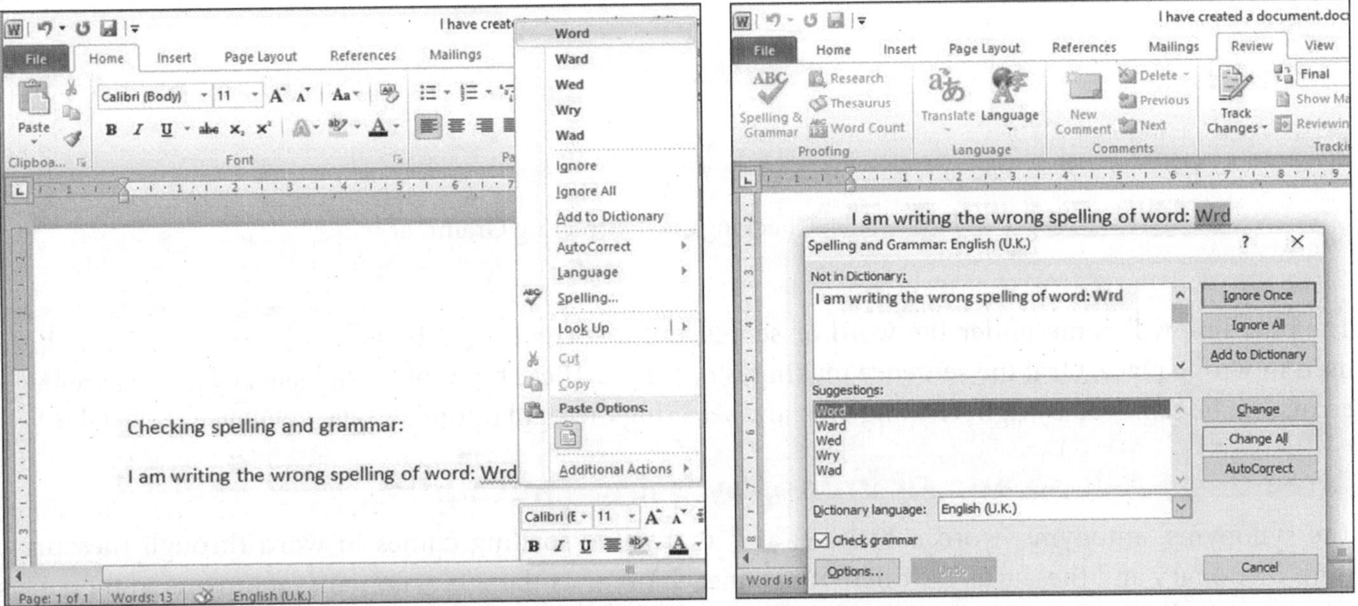

Figure 3.33: Checking and Correcting Spelling

Green wavy line or Grammatical mistake

The green line under the text shows the grammatical mistake. In those cases, simply right click on the text and you will get suggestions for writing the correct word. Another option is to select the Grammar icon on dialog box, which appears once you click on the text having green line. Or click on review tab and then select the spelling and grammar command in proofing group as shown in the figure 3.34 for spelling checking.

The new window comes after clicking on spelling and grammar command contains:

- **Ignore once:** After clicking this button the current error will be ignore for that particular word.
- **Ignore All:** After clicking on it all the same error words are ignored.
- **Add to Dictionary:** This will add that particular word in the dictionary of word.
- **Change:** This will replace the wrong word with the selected word.
- **Change All:** This will change all the same wrong words with the right or selected word.
- **AutoCorrect:** This will automatically replace the wrong word with the right one.
- **Cancel:** It will close the opened dialog box when user click on spelling and grammar command.

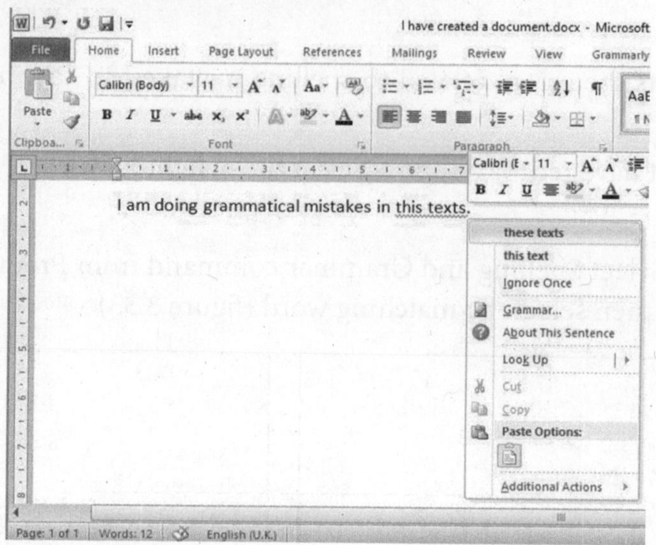

Figure 3.34: Checking and Correcting Grammar

Blue wavy line or Contextual mistake

The blue line will come under the word or sentence if a correct word is used in wrong place. Or if the sentence making is not right. These types of errors can be removed by right clicking on it and selecting the right option.

> **LETS KNOW MORE**
>
> Shortcut key to open spelling and grammar command is F7

Checking Spelling and Grammer by Using Thesaurus

The synonyms, antonyms, word substitute, and alternative spelling comes in word through thesaurus. Both dictionary and thesaurus are different from each other as there is synonyms, antonyms in thesaurus on other hand dictionary contains pronunciation and definitions. Thesaurus help users while writing by giving suggestions to make them to better understand their words. To use thesaurus, follow the steps:

Select the word > right click on it > click on synonyms

Here you will get same meaning word for selected word. Or

Click on review > select Thesaurus command from proofing group > a new research pane will appear on the right of your document that displays the antonyms and synonyms for selected word. (figure 3.35)

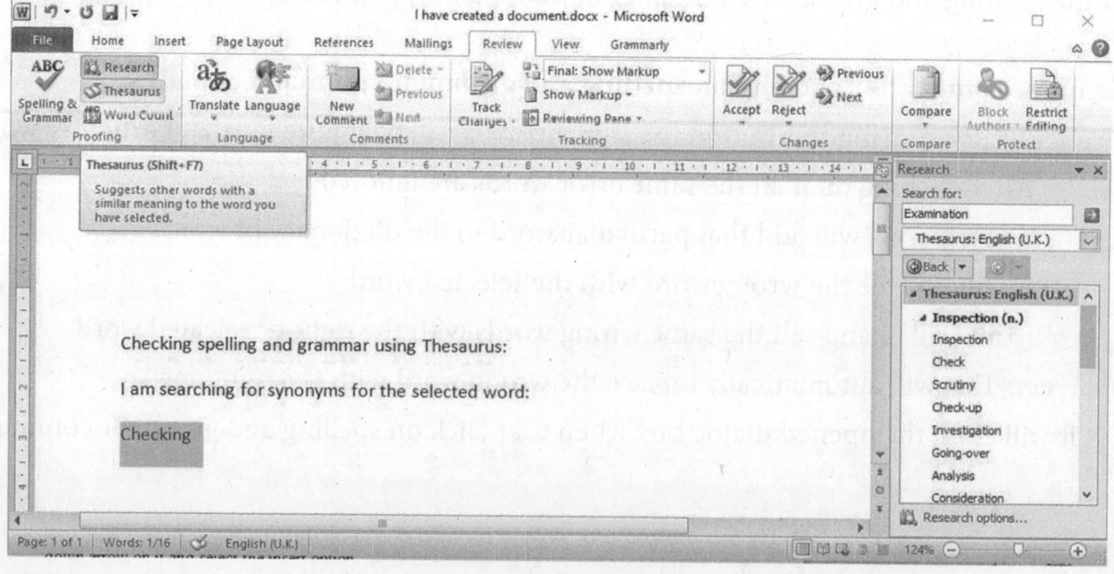

Figure 3.35: Checking and Correcting Grammar using Thesaurus

From that dialog box take you cursor on the specified most suitable word and use drop down arrow on it and select the insert option. (figure 3.36)

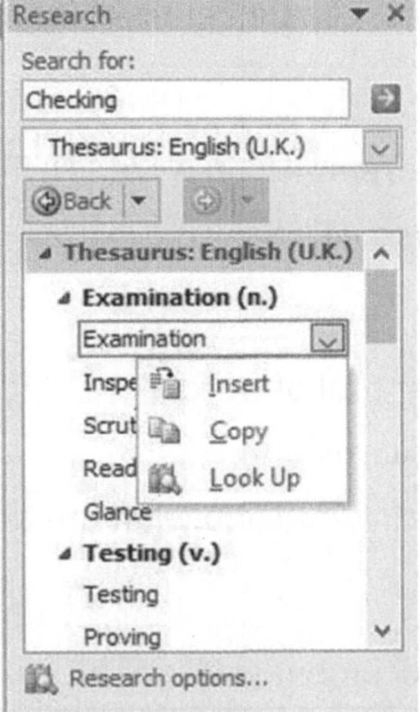

Figure 3.36: Thesaurus dialog box

> **LETS KNOW MORE**
>
> Shift + F7 is a shortcut key to open Thesaurus in the document

Summary

- In MS word 2010 there is built-in feature of checking and correcting the errors.
- The red wavy line highlights the errors related to spelling mistakes.
- To remove these errors, Right click on text that have red wavy line > Select the match word.
- The green line under the text shows the grammatical mistake.
- Blue wavy line will come under the word or sentence if a correct work is used in wrong place.
- The synonyms, antonyms, word substitute, and alternative spelling comes in word through thesaurus.
- F7 key is a shortcut to use Spelling and Grammar tool.
- Shift + F7 is a shortcut key to open Thesaurus in the document

Keywords: Checking spelling and grammar, Red wavy line or Spelling mistake, Green wavy line or Grammatical mistake, Blue wavy line or Contextual mistake, Using Synonyms and thesaurus.

Self-Assessment

A. MULTIPLE CHOICE QUESTIONS

1. Red wavy lines highlight the error related to:
   a. Grammar b. Mismatch word c. Spelling d. None of the above
2. Spelling and Grammar tool is present in:
   a. File Tab b. Page Layout Tab c. Review Tab d. View Tab
3. Green wavy line indicate which type of error:
   a. Grammar b. Mismatch word c. Spelling d. None of the above
4. Which of the following is the shortcut key to use "Spelling and Grammar" tool:
   a. F5 b. F6 c. F7 d. F8

B. FILL IN THE BLANKS

1. ____________ is the shortcut key to open a Thesaurus tool.
2. There are ________ types of errors can be detected in word?

C. STATE WHETHER THE FOLLOWING STATEMENTS ARE TRUE OR FALSE

1. Errors related to grammar can be removed in word. (T/F)
2. Dictionary and Thesaurus are same. (T/F)

D. ANSWER THE FOLLOWING QUESTIONS

1. Explain the Spelling and Grammar tool of word?
2. Differentiate dictionary and Thesaurus?
3. Name the various types of errors in word and what are the steps to remove it?

E. PRACTICAL WORK

Open the word document; write a document given in the below screenshot:

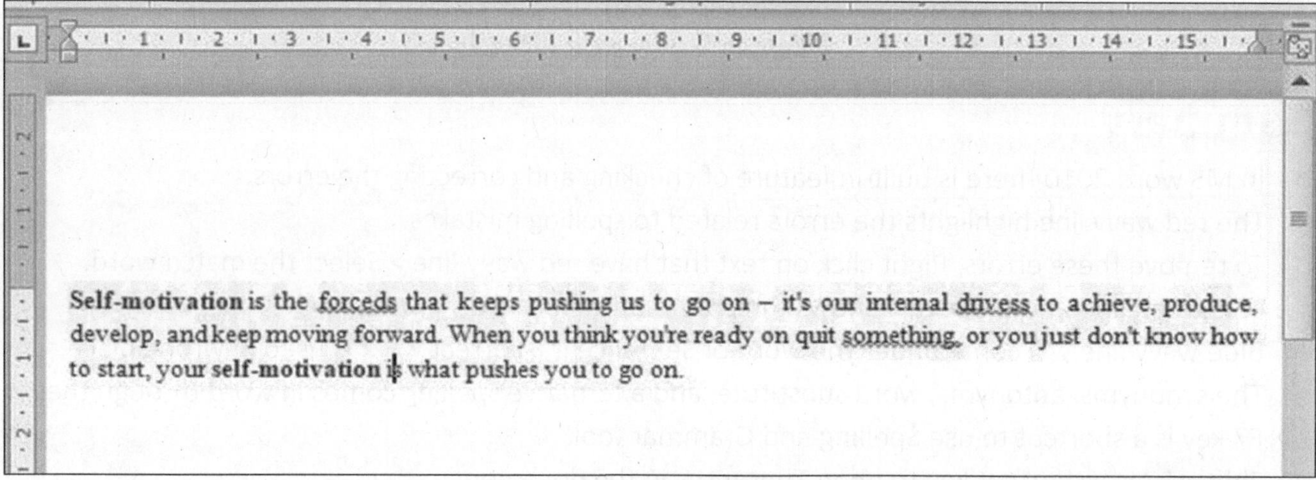

Self-motivation is the forceds that keeps pushing us to go on – it's our internal drivess to achieve, produce, develop, andkeep moving forward. When you think you're ready on quit something, or you just don't know how to start, your self-motivation is what pushes you to go on.

Check for mistakes and do the required changes by using Spelling and Grammar tool and then use thesaurus to remove or replace the words with other synonyms.

Answers:

Multiple choice question:

1. c 2. c 3. a 4. c

Fill in the blanks:

1. Shift + F7
2. Three

State whether the following statements are True or False:

1. True
2. False

SESSION 7: FORMATTING A DOCUMENT

In this session we will focus on formatting a document in which we will deal with setting the text fonts. This cover how to catch the eye of reader by applying various font effects by changing their type and size, text positioning, text attributes, etc. We have an option of bold, italic and underlying the text that catches the eye of users to focus on it.

Setting Text Fonts

How to set text font and its size is covered in this section. There are various types of fonts available in MS Word 2010 along with the various sizes. Mainly it is used while giving heading, etc., that differentiates it with the other text available in that document.

Change the type and size of font

To change the type and size of font by using keyboard, Home tab and shortcut menu are used. The font type of the below given document is shown in figure 3.37 is Calibri and its size is 11. The font changing function is available in font group of home tab.

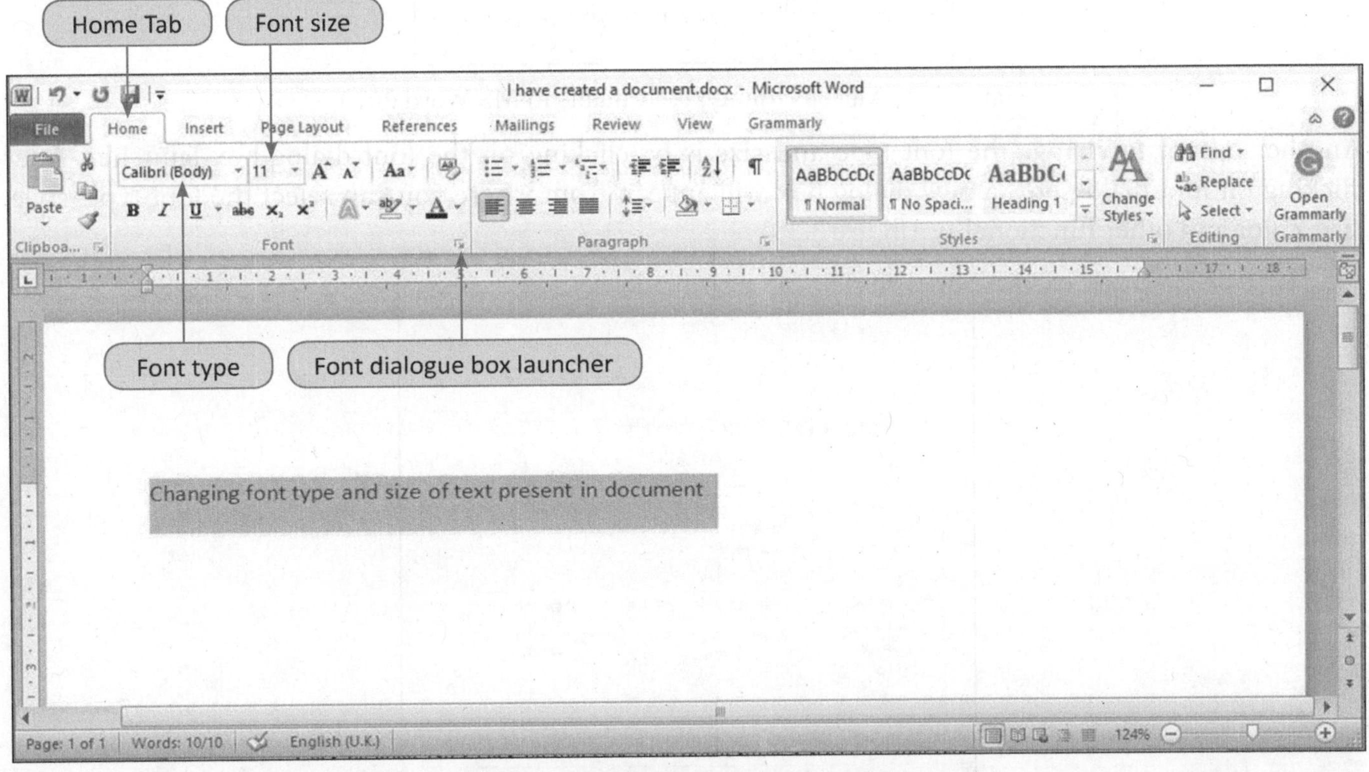

Figure 3.37: Font type and size setting

To perform the change in font types, follow the following steps:

Click on home tab > click on font type drop down arrow > select the font type

You can apply this on the whole document by selecting it or on specific paragraph or line of the document. Same is applicable for changing the font size of document. (figure 3.38)

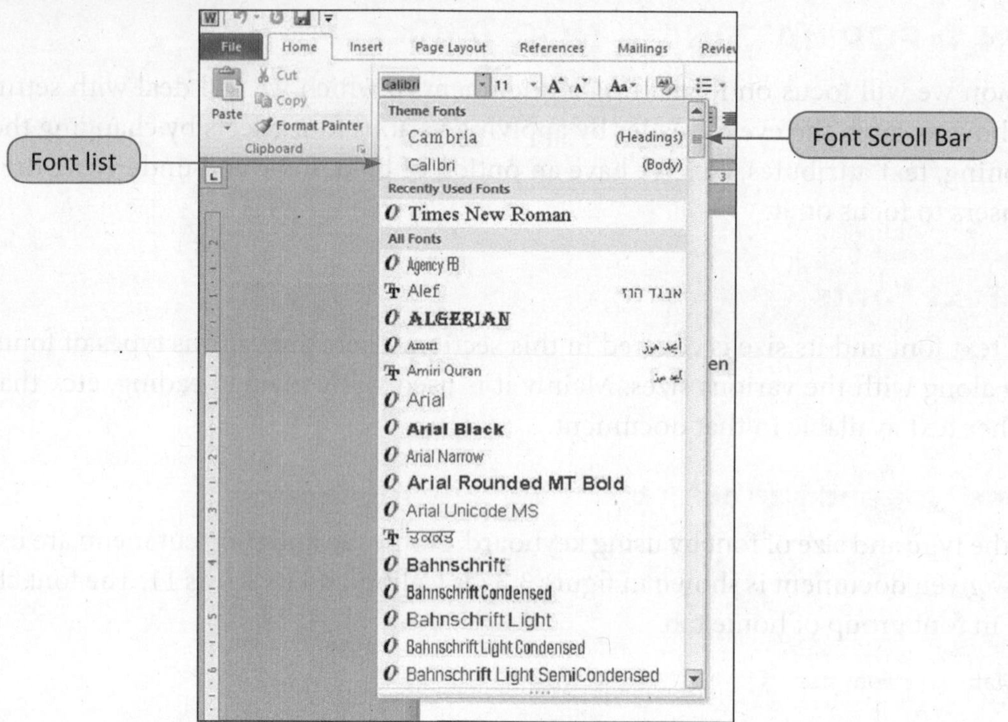

Figure 3.38: Various font types available in MS Word 2010

Another option to change the font type and size is by clicking on the font dialog box launcher. After clicking on font dialog box, a new dialog box will appear, from where you can select the font type, style, size, color and other functionality. (figure 3.39)

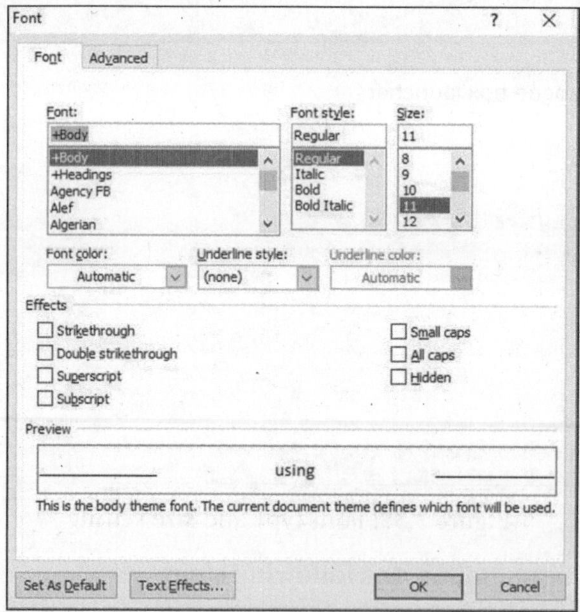

Figure 3.39: Font dialogue box

Effects of Font

In Home tab various font effects are available that can be used to highlight the text or to make your document more attractive. First functionality comes under this is font color that changes the color of the selected text. You can see in the figure 3.40, given below; it shows that the color of selected text gets changed by selecting the red color from drop down arrow of font color. Another color can be chosen from it.

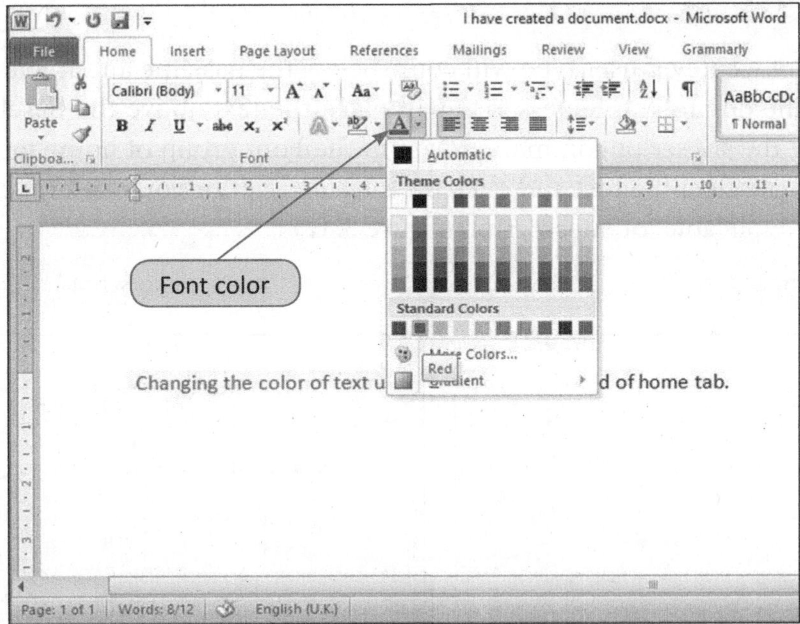

Figure 3.40: Font color

Next command comes under this is Text highlight color. This will make your text to look like it is highlighted by using marker pens. (figure 3.41)

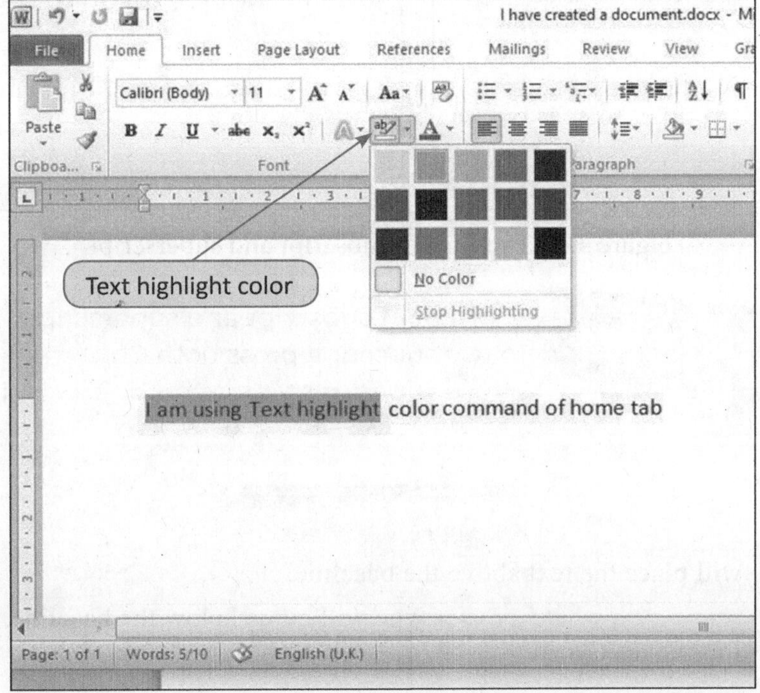

Figure 3.41: Text Highlight Color

Change case

Using this command user can change the selected text into Sentence case, lowercase, UPPERCASE, Capitalize each word and Toggle case. To perform it selects the text then:

Click on Change case > Select the required type from drop down bar.

Then the action will be performed according to the type of font case selected.

Subscript and Superscript effect

After selecting subscript whatever user type will come below the baseline and it will look smaller than the other normal text in the document. Superscript will place the text above the baseline. To make the text appear subscript select the subscript command given in the Font group of home tab. You can either write the normal text and then select the text and click on the subscript or you can first click on subscript then write the text. Same is applicable for superscript. (figure 3.42)

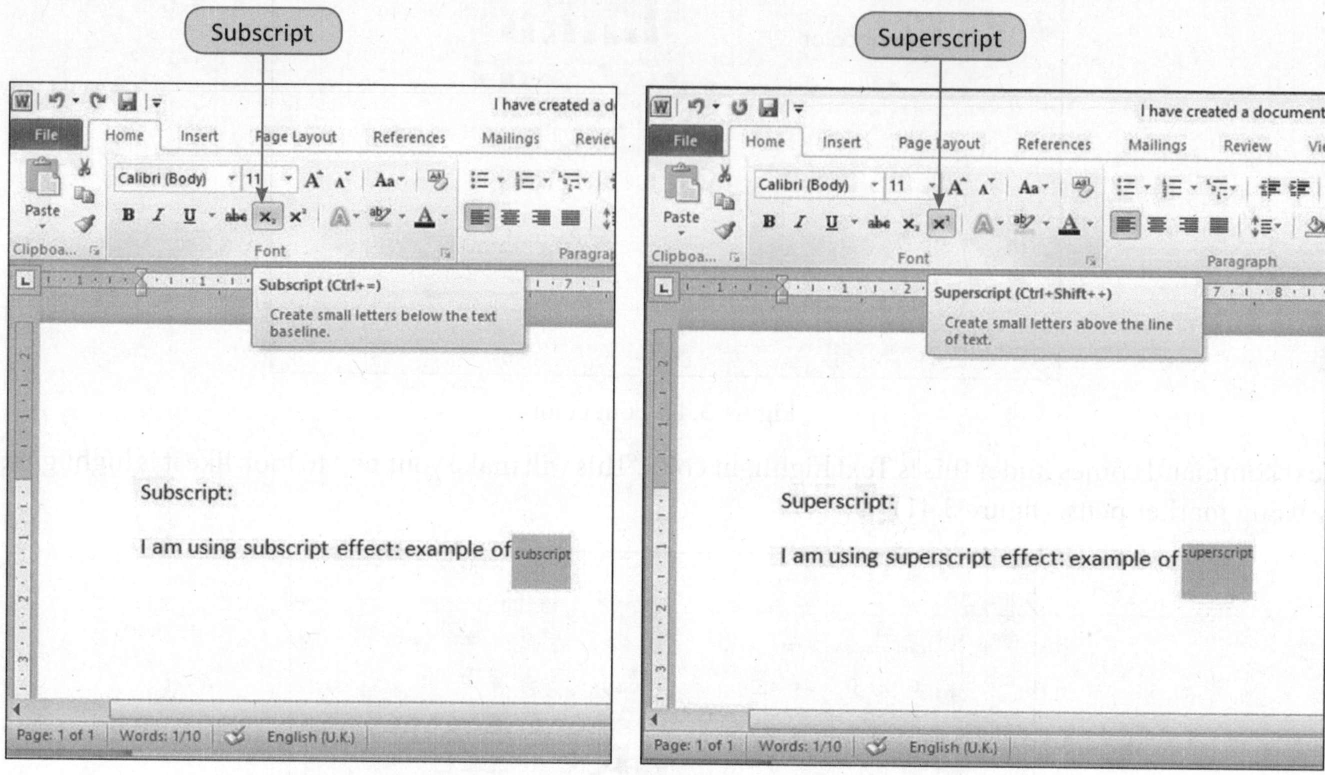

Figure 3.42: Example of subscript and superscript

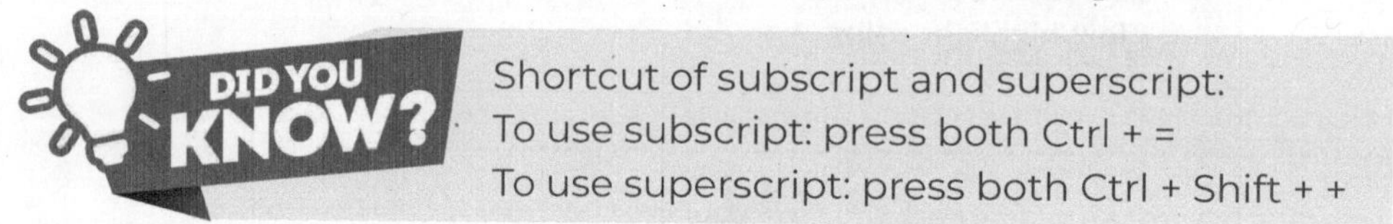

Shortcut of subscript and superscript:
To use subscript: press both Ctrl + =
To use superscript: press both Ctrl + Shift + +

Skill Test Box

1. The ______________ will place the text above the baseline.
2. After selecting ______________, whatever user type will come below the baseline, and it will look smaller than other normal text in the document.

BOLD, ITALIC AND UNDERLINE THE TEXT

This section will help user to decorate their text by using bold, italic, and underline commands of font group. In Font group of home tab there is command written as B in capital. To highlight the text by using Bold command: Select the text > Click on Bold 'B' command or another option is click on Bold 'B' command and then write the text. (figure 3.43)

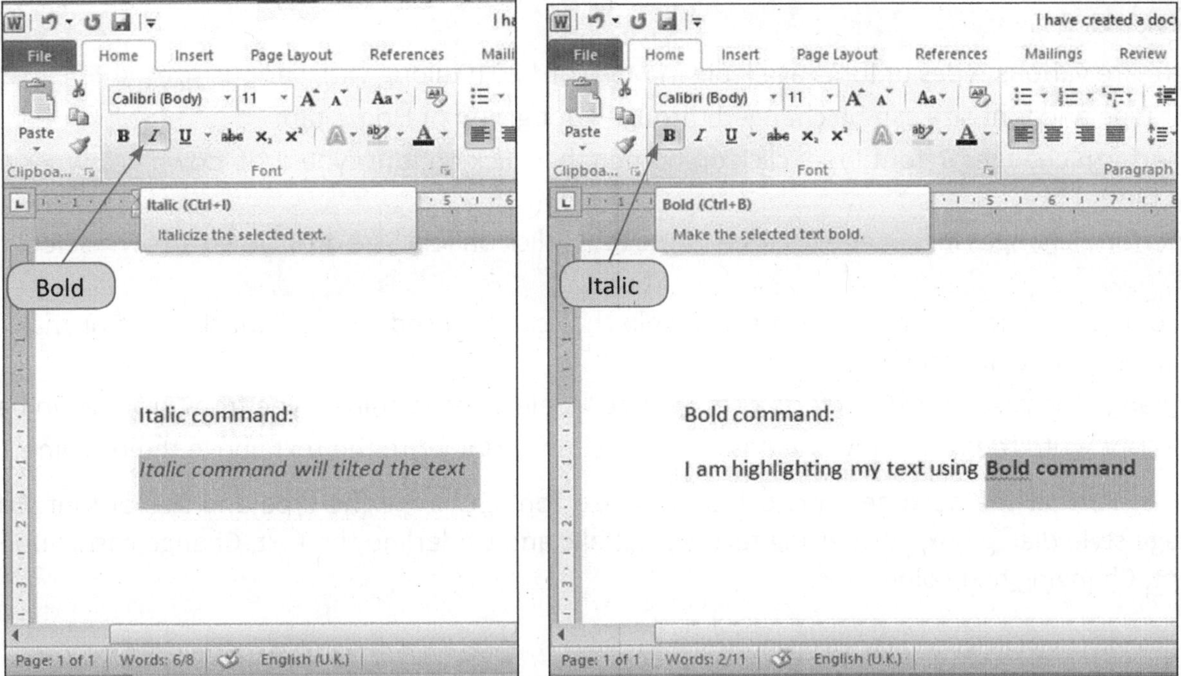

Figure 3.43: Bold and Italic command

To perform italic command press italic and write the text or select the text which you want to make to appear italics then click on Italic command.

Another command is underline that will highlight the text by putting underline below the text. In MS word 2010 we have different style options of underlying the text. (figure 3.44)

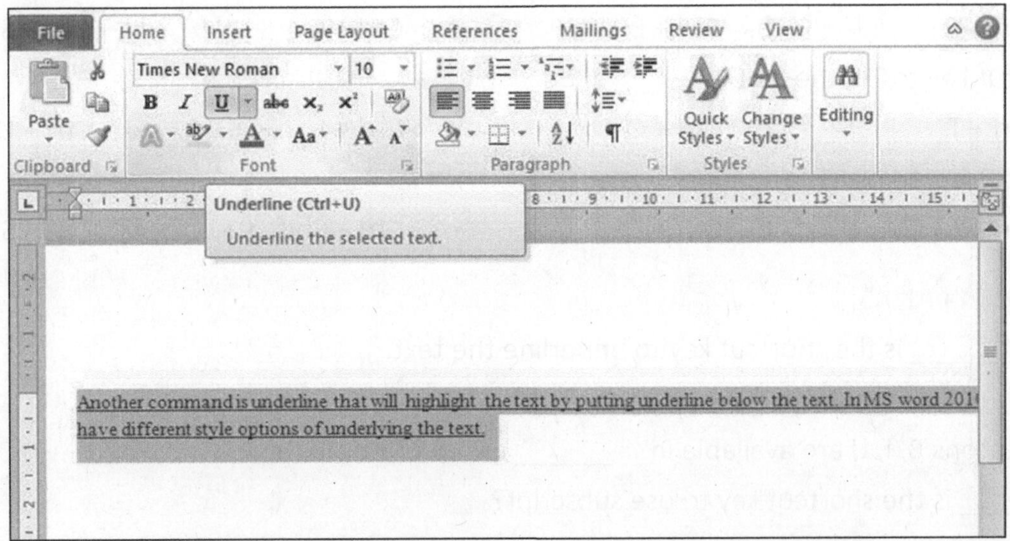

Figure 3.44: Underline command and its various styles

LETS KNOW MORE

- Keyboard shortcut for bold is: Press Ctrl + B keys
- Keyboard shortcut for Italic is: Press Ctrl + I keys
- Keyboard shortcut for Underline is: Press Ctrl + U keys

Summary

- There are various types of fonts available in MS Word 2010 along with various sizes.
- Font type and font size can be changed through Font group of Home tab.
- To perform changes in font type, click on home tab > click on font type drop down arrow > select the font type.
- To perform changes in font size, click on home tab > click on font size drop down arrow > select the font size.
- In Home tab various font effects are available that can be used to highlight the text or making your document more attractive.
- To change the case of text, Click on Change case > Select the required type from drop down bar.
- Subscript write the text below the baseline and superscript write the text above the baseline.

Keywords: Format the document or text, Setting text fonts, Change the type and size of font, Effects of Font, Page style dialog box, Formatting text, Bold, Italic and Underline the text, Change case, Superscript, subscript, Changing text colors.

Self-Assessment

A. MULTIPLE CHOICE QUESTIONS

1. Font type, Font size, Font color is the commands of
   a. Clipboard group b. Styles group c. Font group d. Editing group
2. Shortcut key to Bold the text?
   a. Ctrl + E b. Ctrl + B c. Ctrl + C d. Ctrl + S
3. Shortcut key to Tilt the text?
   a. Ctrl + T b. Ctrl + O c. Ctrl + I d. Ctrl + U
4. Shortcut key to use Superscript?
   a. Ctrl + + b. Ctrl + - c. Ctrl + Shift + + d. Ctrl + Shift + =

B. FILL IN THE BLANKS

1. ____________ is the shortcut key to underline the text.
2. __________ will change the case of the text.
3. The buttons B, I, U are available in ________ group of Home tab.
4. ________ is the shortcut key to use subscript?

C. STATE WHETHER THE FOLLOWING STATEMENTS ARE TRUE OR FALSE

1. Whether we can change the type and size of font or text. (T/F)
2. Whether you can change the color of limited text. (T/F)
3. Font dialog box launcher can't be used to change the font type, style and size. (T/F)

D. ANSWER THE FOLLOWING QUESTIONS

1. How to change the type and size of font?

2. How we can change the type and size of font?
3. Explain Font dialog box launcher?
4. Name the effects of font?
5. Write how to perform Bold, Underline and Tilt of text?

E. PRACTICAL WORK

Open a word, write a text same as given in below screenshot:

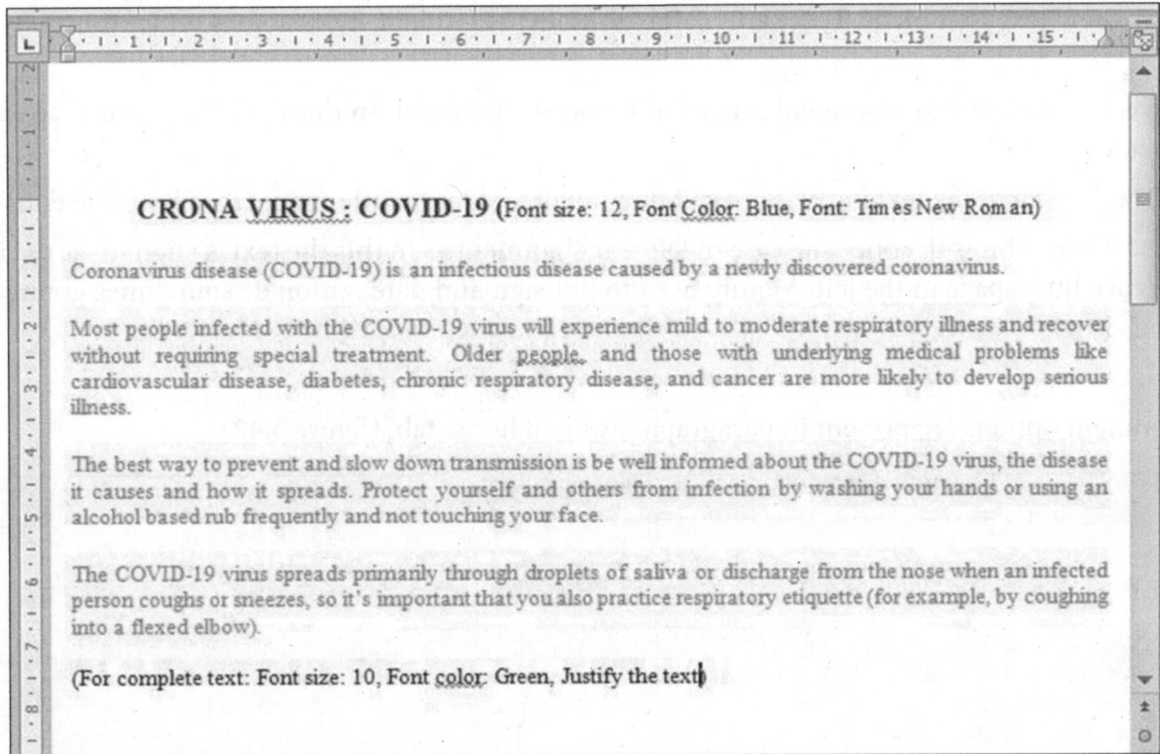

CRONA VIRUS : COVID-19 (Font size: 12, Font Color: Blue, Font: Times New Roman)

Coronavirus disease (COVID-19) is an infectious disease caused by a newly discovered coronavirus.

Most people infected with the COVID-19 virus will experience mild to moderate respiratory illness and recover without requiring special treatment. Older people, and those with underlying medical problems like cardiovascular disease, diabetes, chronic respiratory disease, and cancer are more likely to develop serious illness.

The best way to prevent and slow down transmission is be well informed about the COVID-19 virus, the disease it causes and how it spreads. Protect yourself and others from infection by washing your hands or using an alcohol based rub frequently and not touching your face.

The COVID-19 virus spreads primarily through droplets of saliva or discharge from the nose when an infected person coughs or sneezes, so it's important that you also practice respiratory etiquette (for example, by coughing into a flexed elbow).

(For complete text: Font size: 10, Font color: Green, Justify the text)

Change its font size and type, Write more data select half of it and use font color button, and in other half of text select it and use text highlight color. Use subscript and superscript effect to check its output.

Answers:

Multiple choice question:

1. C 2. b 3. c 4. c

Fill in the blanks:

1. Ctrl + U
2. Change case
3. Font group
4. Ctrl + =

State whether the following statements are True or False

1. True
2. True
3. False

SESSION 8: TEXT ALIGNMENT

The position of text between the page margins is known as text alignment. Horizontal and vertical are the two types of text alignment present in word. This session will help reader to make their text look synchronized.

Horizontal Text Alignment

By default, the text is aligned on the left side of the document and the right margins in the document is known as horizontal text alignment. There are mainly four text alignment styles comes under this category are:

- **Align Text left:** The left text alignment is a default type of alignment. In this case there is little space in the right side.
- **Center:** This will align the text in the center of document and leave little space from both the ends.
- **Align Text Right:** This is the opposite case of left text alignment as in this the text is align towards right side and leave little space in the left. Mainly used to put sign and date option or sometimes giving the chapter heading.
- **Justify:** In this case text is evenly aligned between the left and right side.

All these alignment options are present in paragraph group of home tab. (figure 3.42)

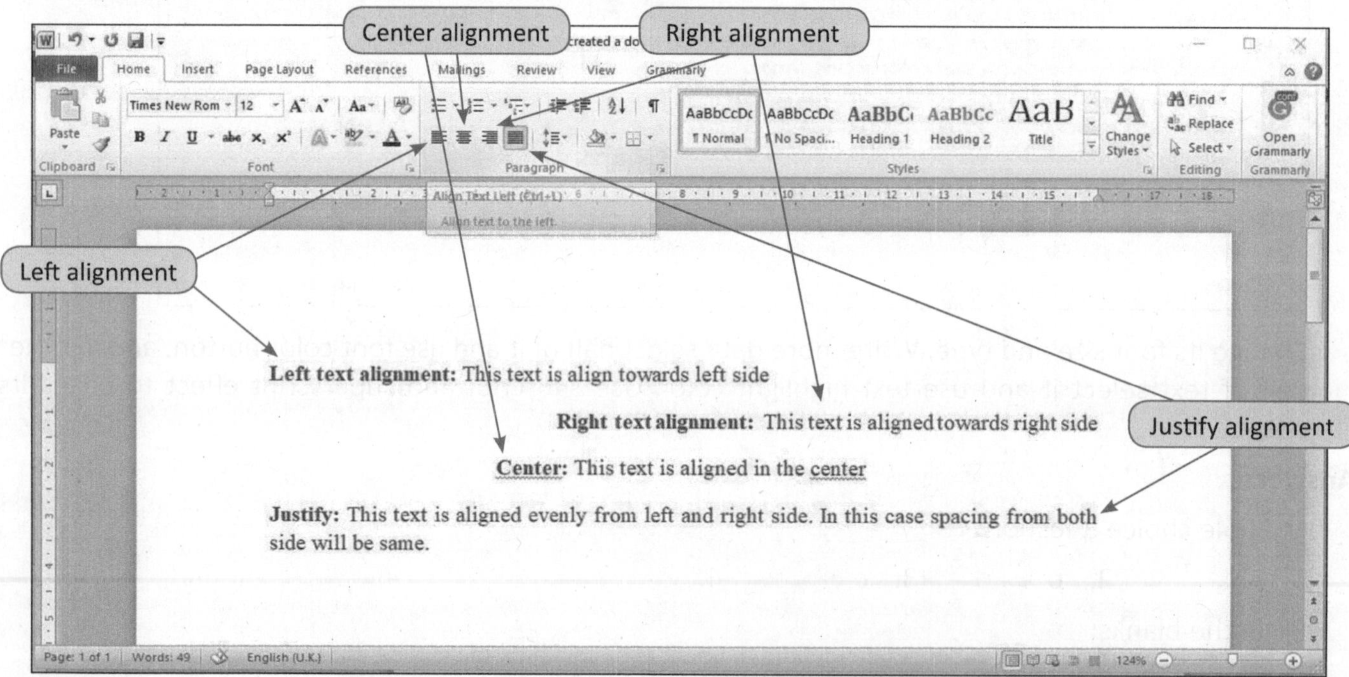

Figure 3.42: Various style of Horizontal text alignment

In the figure 3.42 orange line shows the command and output of left alignment, Blue arrow show the center alignment command and output, Black shows for Right alignment and Justify is shown using Green color arrow.

LETS KNOW MORE

Keyboard shortcut for aligning the paragraph:

- Align left: Press Ctrl + L key
- Align right: Press Ctrl + R key
- Center: Press Ctrl + E key
- Justify: Press Ctrl + J key

Vertical Text Alignment

This will align the text by considering the margins in top and bottom of text. To perform vertical text alignment:

Click on the Page Layout tab > Page setup dialog box > Layout tabs

This will open new dialog box, select the desired option from the vertical alignment drop down arrow. We can also select the option to either apply the changes to whole document or document written after the selection. Once done with it, click on Ok. (figure 3.43)

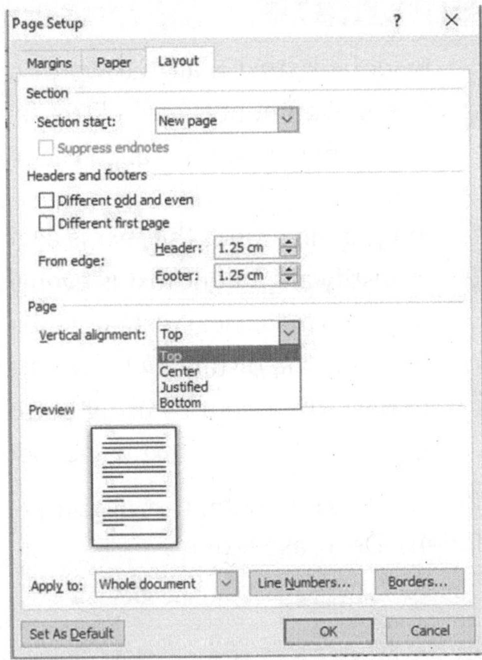

Figure 3.43: Page setup dialog box

Indent

Indent is the distance of page margins and text boundaries. Tab key are mostly used to indent the text and it is mainly use in indenting a single line of text rather than for multiple lines or paragraphs. To perform this simply take mouse in front of first line of text and press Tab key.

The other option is the use of Indent buttons given in the paragraph group. This will help in moving the complete paragraph. This is mainly used to make the text look in structured and organized form. To perform the task of indent by using buttons:

Select the text > Click on Decrease or Increase Indent (figure 3.44)

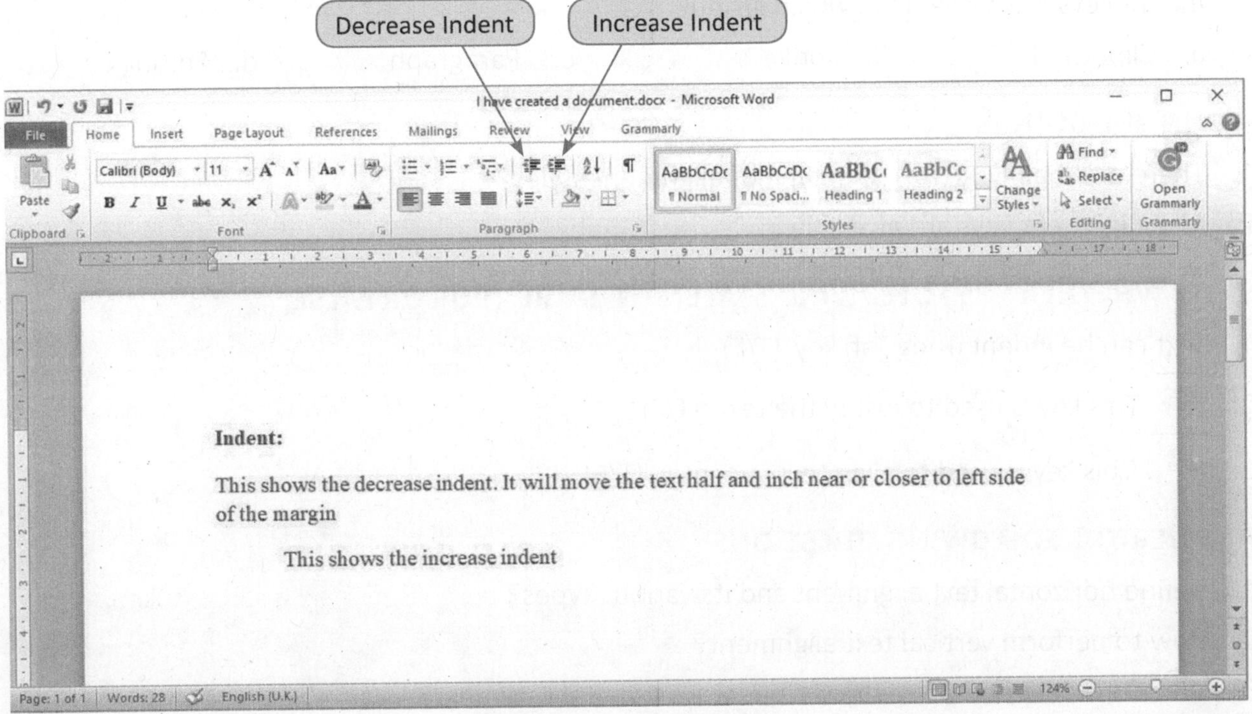

Figure 3:44: Indent Button

The decrease indent will bring your text half an inch near to left margin and vice a versa for increase indent.

Summary

- By default, text is align towards left side.
- In left alignment there is little space in the right side.
- Center alignment will align the text in the center of the document and leave little space from both the ends.
- In right alignment the text is align towards right side and leave little space in the left.
- In Justify alignment text is evenly aligned between the left and right side.
- To perform vertical text alignment, Click on the Page Layout tab > Page setup dialog box > Layout tabs.
- Indent is the distance of page margins and text boundaries.
- To perform Indent by using buttons. Select the text > Click on Decrease or Increase Indent.
- We can indent the text using indent marker given on the ruler.

Keywords: Horizontal text alignment, Left, center, Right, Justify, Vertical text alignment, Indent, Increase Indent, Decrease Indent.

Self-Assessment

A. MULTIPLE CHOICE QUESTIONS

1. Default position of text is?

   a. Right b. Middle c. Left d. Justify

2. Indent keys are available in which group?

   a. Clipboard b. Font c. Paragraph d. Editing

B. FILL IN THE BLANKS

1. There are mainly __________type of alignment styles?
2. The alignment keys are available in ________ Tab?

C. STATE WHETHER THE FOLLOWING STATEMENTS ARE TRUE OR FALSE

1. Text can be indent using Tab key. (T/F)
2. This key is used to justify the text. (T/F)
3. This key is used to align text in center. (T/F)

D. ANSWER THE FOLLOWING QUESTIONS

1. Define horizontal text alignment and its various types?
2. How to perform vertical text alignment?
3. What is Indent and write the various ways to Indent the text?

E. PRACTICAL WORK

Open a word document, write six paragraphs in it, apply left, right, center, justify, Decrease and increase indent on each paragraph as given in below screenshot. Donot write the text written in bracket Blue font color.

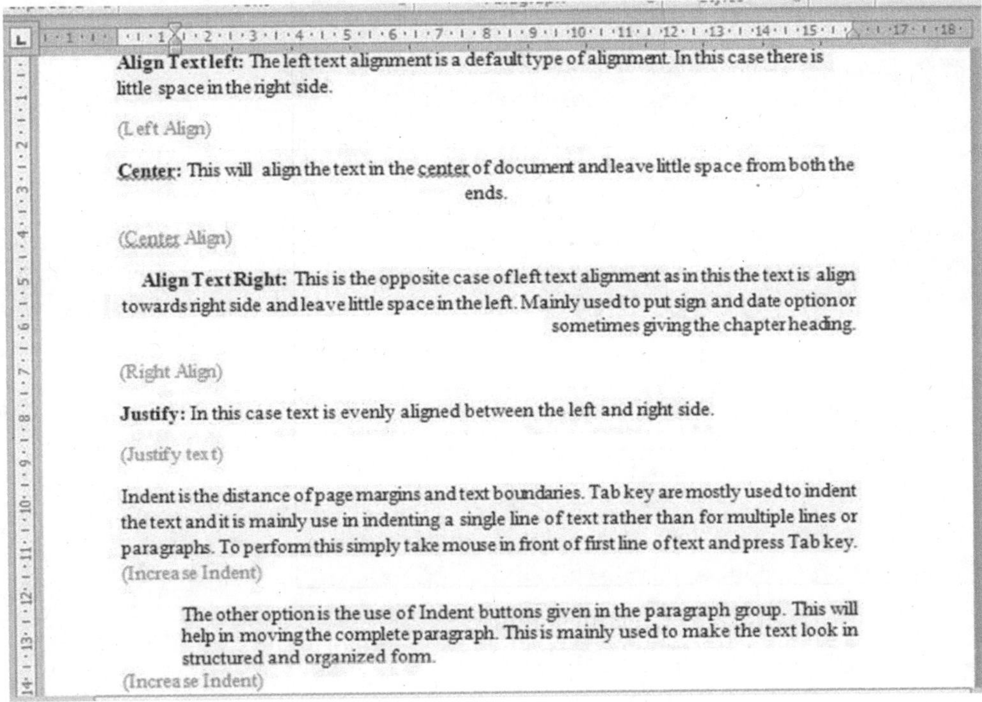

Align Text left: The left text alignment is a default type of alignment. In this case there is little space in the right side.

(Left Align)

Center: This will align the text in the center of document and leave little space from both the ends.

(Center Align)

Align Text Right: This is the opposite case of left text alignment as in this the text is align towards right side and leave little space in the left. Mainly used to put sign and date option or sometimes giving the chapter heading.

(Right Align)

Justify: In this case text is evenly aligned between the left and right side.

(Justify text)

Indent is the distance of page margins and text boundaries. Tab key are mostly used to indent the text and it is mainly use in indenting a single line of text rather than for multiple lines or paragraphs. To perform this simply take mouse in front of first line of text and press Tab key.
(Increase Indent)

The other option is the use of Indent buttons given in the paragraph group. This will help in moving the complete paragraph. This is mainly used to make the text look in structured and organized form.
(Increase Indent)

Answers:

Multiple choice question:

1. c 2. c

Fill in the blanks:

1. FourHome

State whether the following statements are True or False:

1. True 2. False 3. False

SESSION 9: USE OF BULLET AND NUMBERING IN TEXT

To put the list of items in a well manner format there is option of bullet and numbering in word. These both will arrange the content in the form of lists. These both options are there in paragraph group of Home tab. There are various style of bullet and number available in word. This session will make user understand the use of it.

Bullets

Mainly unordered list are created by using bullet as there is no sequence of items in it. There are various styles of bullets available in Word.

Steps to create a bullet list:

Create a list > select it > click on drop down button on Bullets command from paragraph group > select the style

When you select the style of bullet it will appear on the selected text in the document. Now if you want to use bullet on other typed document then simply take cursor on last text with bullet, press enter and write the text or list.

To stop bullet option simply again click on it and start typing. (figure 3.39)

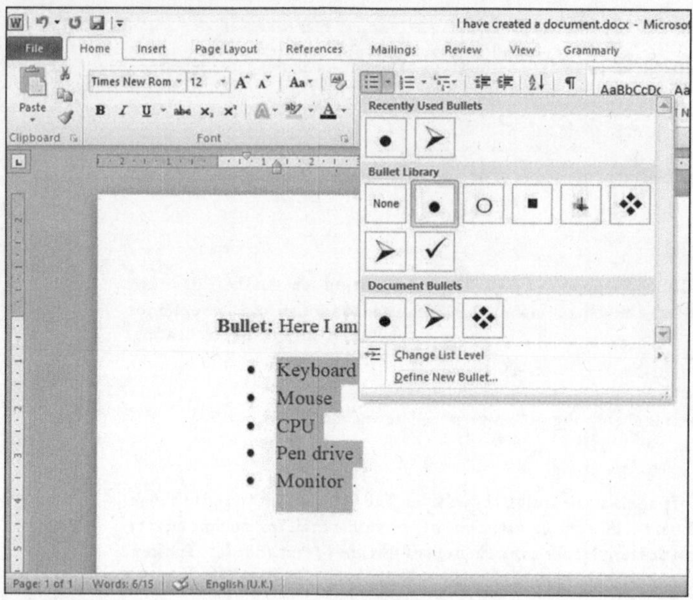

Figure 3.39:Creating a Bullet

Numbering

Ordered list are created by using number as there is sequence of items in it. There are various styles of numbering available in Word.

Steps to create a numbered list:

Create a list > select it > click on the drop-down button on Numbered command from paragraph group > select the style.

When you select the style of number it will appear on the selected text in the document. Now if you want to continue with count on other typed document then simply take the cursor on the last numbered text, press enter key and write the text or list.

To stop Numbering option simply again click on it and start typing. (figure 3.40)

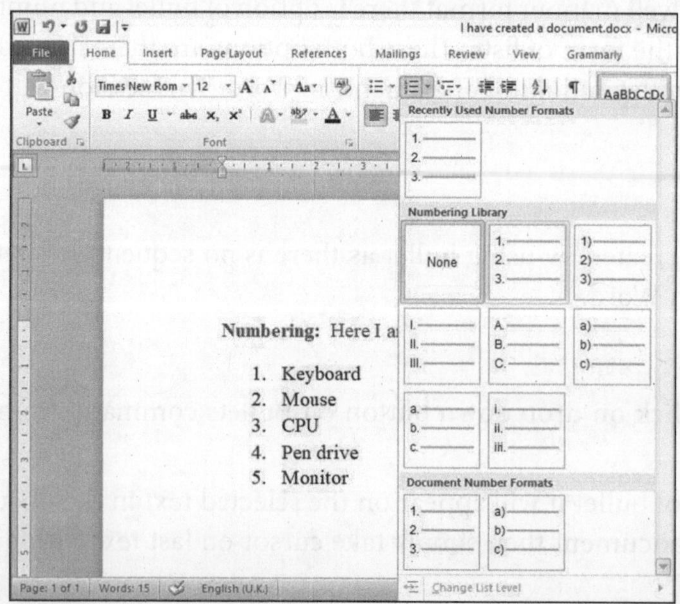

Figure 3.40: Creating a Number list

Skill Test Box

Write the correct answer in the blank given below:

1. To put a list of items in a good manner format, there is an option of _________.

Defining Your Own Bullet and Numering Style

Instead of using the already given style of options of bullet and numbering you can create your own style of bullet and numbers by following the steps as:

Click on the Bullet drop down arrow given in the paragraph group > Define New bullets.

Now a new dialog box will appear as given in figure 3.41 where you can create it by using symbols, pictures, font, etc.

In the same way you can also define a new style formatting of numbering. To create it:

Click on the Numbering drop down arrow given in the paragraph group > Define New Number Format.

A new dialog box will be open here you can create a new style by using number style drop down, Font style, Number format, etc.

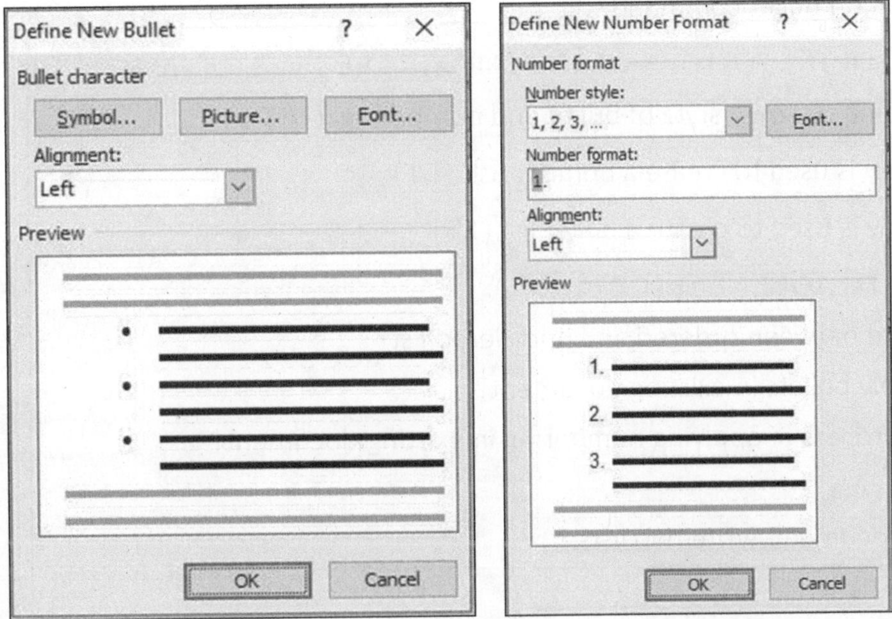

Figure 3.41: Defining new bullet and number style

Once you are done with the creating part click on Ok given on the dialog box and symbol of bullet or numbering will appear on your selected text in the document.

Summary

- There are two types of list name as Ordered and Unordered.
- Bullets is used to create an unordered list.
- To create a list by using bullet, create a list > select it > click on the drop-down button on Bullets command from paragraph group > select the style.
- Numbering is used to create an ordered list.
- To create a list using numbering, create a list > select it > click on the drop-down button on Numbering command from paragraph group > select the style.

- We can also create our own style of numbering and bullet by using define a new bullet and new numbering style given in drop-down of both bullet and numbering command.

Keywords: Bullets, Numbering, Bullet style, Numbering style.

Self-Assessment

A. MULTIPLE CHOICE QUESTIONS

1. What is the group of Bullets and numbering options?

a. 1. Clipboard	b. * Font	c. > Paragraph	d. $ Editing
2. Notebook	* Style	> Graph	$ Texting
3. Paper	* Option	> Text	$ Writing

2. Which of the following is the group of Bullet and Numbering?

a. Clipboard b. Font c. Paragraph d. Editing

B. FILL IN THE BLANKS

1. Double click on Bullet command will ___________.

C. STATE WHETHER THE FOLLOWING STATEMENTS ARE TRUE OR FALSE

1. Can we define our own style of bullet and numbering. (T/F)
2. This key is used to create a number list. (T/F)
3. This key is used to create a bullet list (T/F)

D. ANSWER THE FOLLOWING QUESTIONS:

1. Differentiate between ordered and unordered list?
2. How to apply bullets in existing document?
3. Write the process of applying numbering in existing document?

E. PRACTICAL WORK

Open a word document, write two lists:

Name of states and UT in India

India comprises 28 States and 8 Union Territories. They are: Andhra Pradesh, Assam, Arunachal Pradesh, Bihar, Chhattisgarh, Goa, Gujarat, Haryana, Himachal Pradesh, Jharkhand, Karnataka, Kerala, Madhya Pradesh, Maharashtra, Manipur, Meghalaya, Mizoram, Nagaland, Odisha, Punjab, Rajasthan, Sikkim, Tamil Nadu, Telangana, Tripura, Uttarakhand, Uttar Pradesh and West Bengal. Union Territories are: Andaman and Nicobar Islands, Chandigarh, Dadra and Nagar Haveli and Daman and Diu, National Capital Territory of Delhi, Jammu and Kashmir, Lakshadweep, Ladakh and Puducherry.

Separate the states and UTs from screenshot, Insert bullet in UTs and Numbering in States

Answers:

Multiple choice question:

1. a 2. c

Fill in the blanks:

1. Remove bullet from text

State whether the following statements are True or False:

1. True 2. True 3. False

SESSION 10: CREATING A TABLE

In some cases normal text or organizing a text with bullets or numbering will not work, suppose you want to make mark sheet, progress report, datasheet, etc, then you have to make tables. We can enter text, number, value, and image in the tables. Like in case of datasheet made for survey done on type of house people are living in particular village will contains the row of name of person, contact number or numeric data, number of persons in house and type of house.

Definition Box

A table is an arrangement of information in cells that make comparing and contrasting information easier. As you can see in the following example, the data are much easier to read than they would be in a list containing that same data.

LETS KNOW MORE

Tables is a combination of row and column where texts are arranged. The cell is the term used for the combination of row and column.

Creating A Table

There are two methods to create or insert a table in the document. One is by using a grid option and other is using a dialog box.

When we have to organize or present a large amount of data then the use of tables makes it more efficient.

Method 1: Using Grid option

To create a table by using grid option follow the following steps:

Click on Insert Tab > Table command Drop down arrow > Drag the mouse pointer over the grid on number of rows and columns required by you

Once you have selected the number of rows and columns from grid; a table will appear on your document. There is 10 x 8 block of table out of which user can select the count according to their requirements. (figure 3.42)

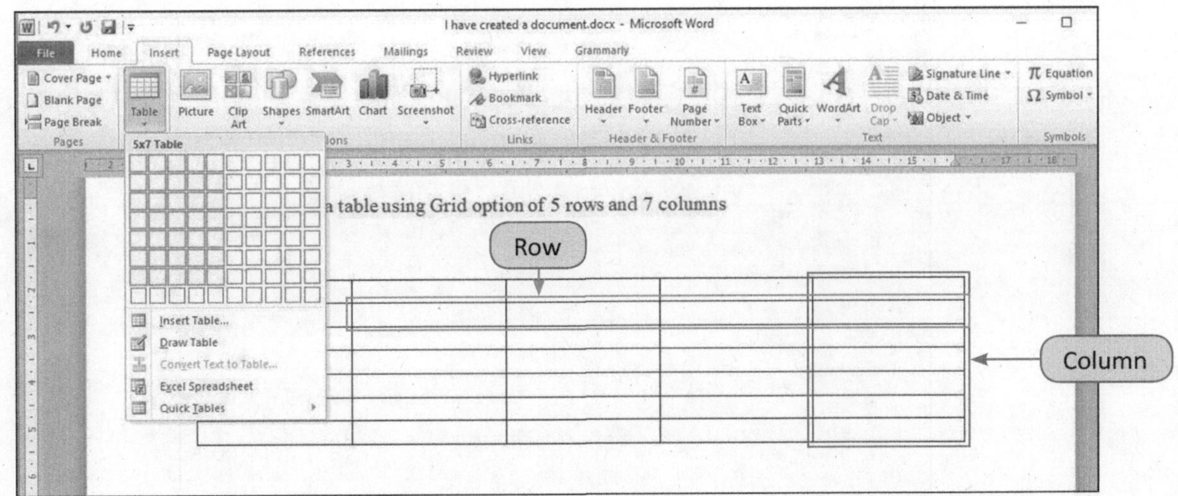

Figure 3:42: Creating table using Grid

Method 2: Using Dialog box

Another option to create a table in word document is by using a dialog box. To create a table by using dialog box perform the following steps:

Click on Insert Tab > Select the table drop down arrow > Select Insert Table option.

When you click on Insert Table command given in the drop-down arrow, a new dialog box will appear on the document. Here you can select or enter the required number of rows and columns. Then press Ok, this will give a table on document as per your requirements. This is used when you want to create a table of large number of rows and columns. (figure 3.43, 3.44)

DID YOU KNOW? You can also select the desired option and the width of table.

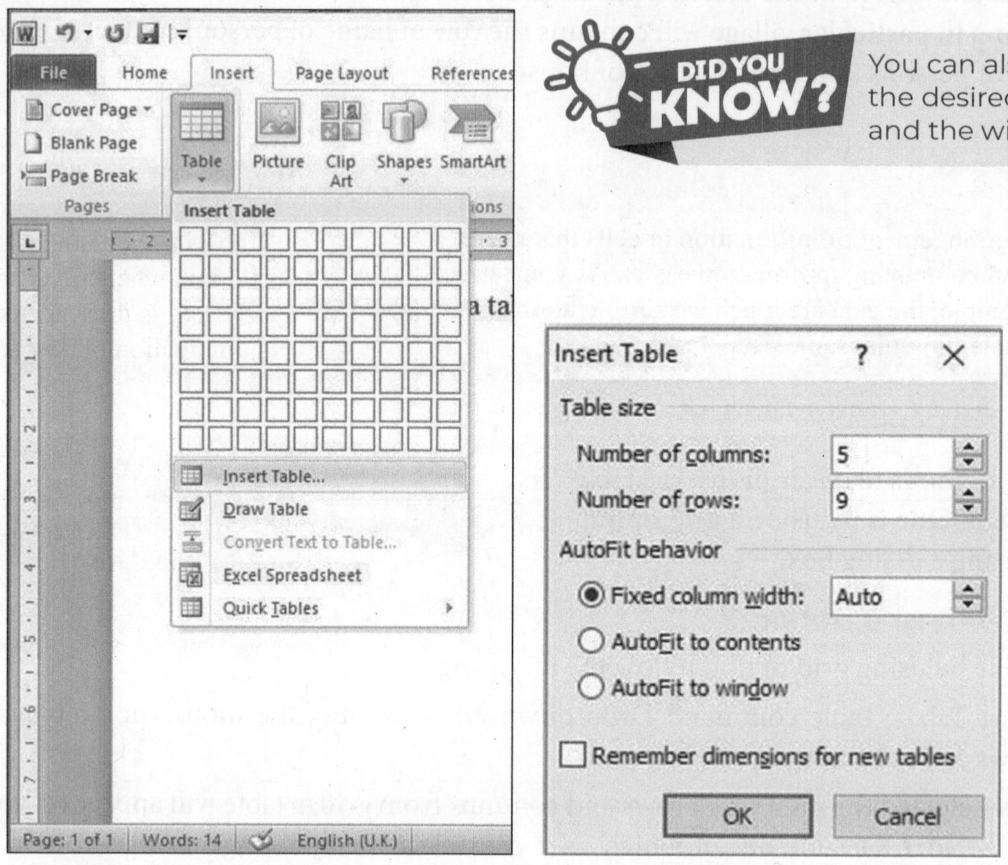

Figure 3:43: Creating table using Insert option

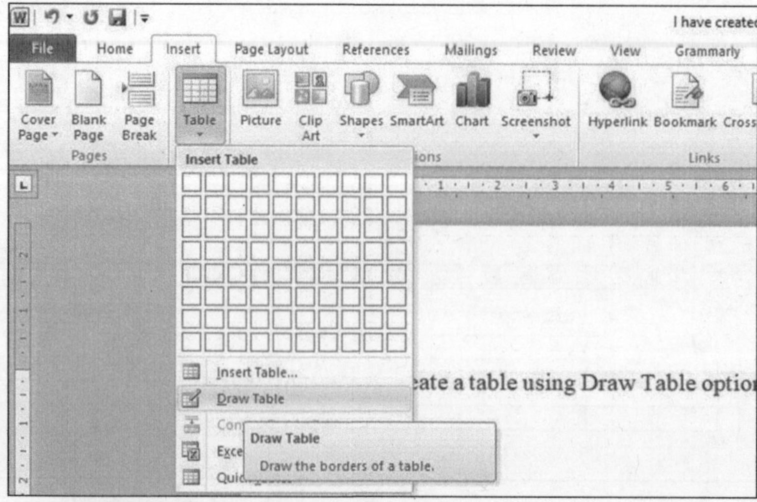

Figure 3.44: Creating table using Draw table option

We can also create a table by using draw table option given in the Table drop down. In this case a pointer is replaced by pencil. To draw a table, drag the pencil from left to right by using left button of mouse. Write a data in tables and use Tab key to move from one row or column to another

LETS KNOW MORE

Example: In the case of datasheet made for a survey done on the type of house people are living in particular village will contain the row of the name of a person, contact number or numeric data, Number of persons in house and type of house. In Word processor, we have a tool to create and manage tables.

Inserting Rows and Columns

After creating a table, sometimes there can be needed to insert more rows and columns. In order to insert any number of rows or columns before or after the rows and columns of table, place the cursor before or after the column on which you want to add new rows or columns.

Inserting rows: To insert row, perform the following steps:

1. Right click on Table, click on the Insert command from menu, Select Rows above or Row below icons.
2. This will insert one row, either above or below the selected cell.

Inserting columns: To insert a column, perform the following steps:

1. Right click on Table, click on the Insert command from menu, Select Columns before or Column after icons.
2. This will insert one column either before or after the selected cell.

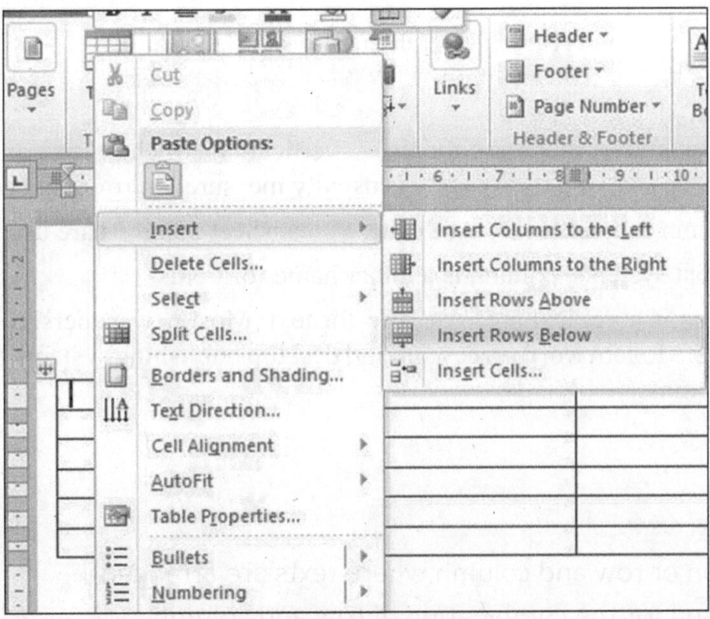

Figure 3.45: Inserting Row and Column

Skill Test Box

Check whether the given statement is true or false:

1. Once you have added rows in a Table, you can't edit the count.
2. One can add number of tables in a document.

Deleting Rows and Columns

Sometimes there can be needed to delete the extra rows or columns. To delete rows and columns, perform the following steps:

1. Place the cursor in the row or column you want to delete. Click on the Delete option.
2. Alternatively, click on row or column you want to delete and right-click on it. Choose either delete rows or delete columns option:

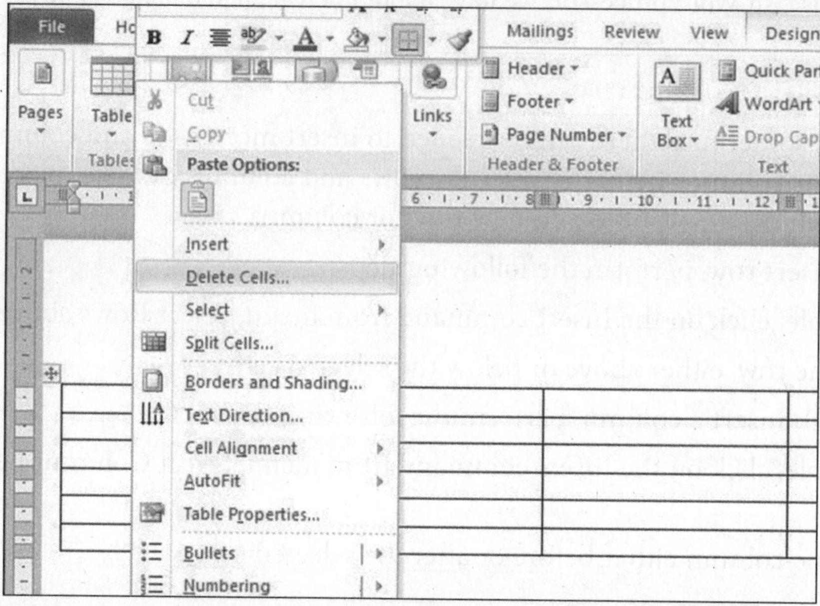

Figure 3.46: Deleting Row and Column

LETS KNOW MORE

1. On a display screen in character mode, a column is a vertical line of characters extending from the top to the bottom of the screen. The size of a text display is usually measured in rows and columns.
2. In spreadsheets, a column is a vertical row of cells. Spreadsheet columns are usually identified by letters.
3. In database management systems, column is another name for field.
4. In documents, a column is a vertical area reserved for text. Most newspapers, for example, contain four or more columns per page. Modern word processors and desktop publishing systems enable you to automatically divide a page into columns.

Summary

- Tables is a combination or row and column where texts are arranged.
- The cell is the term used for the combination of row and column.
- Tables can be created by two methods: Grid and dialog box.
- To create a table by using grid, Click on Insert Tab > Table command Drop down arrow > Drag the mouse pointer over the grid on number of rows and columns required by you.
- To create a table by using Dialog box, Click on the Insert Tab > Select the table drop down arrow > Select Insert Table option.
- User can also create their own table by using Draw table option given in the table drop down arrow.
- Tab key can be used to move from one row or column to another.

Keywords: Table, Creating a Table, Grid option, Using dialog box, Inserting Row, Inserting Column, Deleting Row, Deleting Column.

Self-Assessment

A. MULTIPLE CHOICE QUESTIONS

1. Horizontal sections in table represent a:

   a. Rows b. Columns c. Cell d. Nothing

2. The number of row and columns can be drawn using grid are?

   a. 5 row and 7 columns b. 7 rows and 5 columns
   c. 10 rows and 8 columns d. 8 rows and 10 columns

3. The intersection of rows and column is a:

   a. Grid b. Intersection c. Cells d. Sections

B. FILL IN THE BLANKS

1. The intersection of row and column is known as _____________.
2. To draw a big table of large number of rows and columns __________ option of creating a table is used.

C. ANSWER THE FOLLOWING QUESTIONS

1. Define a table?
2. Explain Grid method of creating a table?
3. Explain dialog box option of creating a table?

D. PRACTICAL WORK

Open a word document, create two tables of 6 rows and 6 columns, one by using grid method and other by using dialog box, Add same data in it

Answers:

A. Multiple choice question.

1. b 2. c 3. c

B. Fill in the blanks.

1. Cell 2. Insert table

SESSION 11: TABLE FORMATTING

In the last session we have created a table. Now in this session, we will discuss the various options available for formatting it. The complete appearance of the table can be changed according to our requirement that comes as more attractive and presentative. The formatting is done to catch the eye of the reader and when we create a table a design and layout label is appears in the Table tools written on the Title tab.

Changing Table Style

The overall appearance of the table can be change by using design label given in the Table tools. There are inbuilt styles of tables in word that contains option of changing the color, appearance and borders of a table. User can fill the cells or create a border of table by using various colors. (figure 3.47)

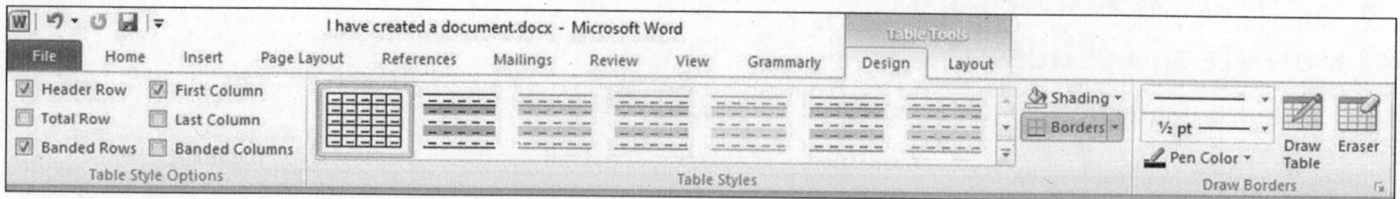

Figure 3.47: Design Tab View

To perform the task of changing the style of table, select the table under a Table Tools tab, after this a Design and Layout label will start appearing. From Design label we can use various styles or color of tables. (figure 3.48)

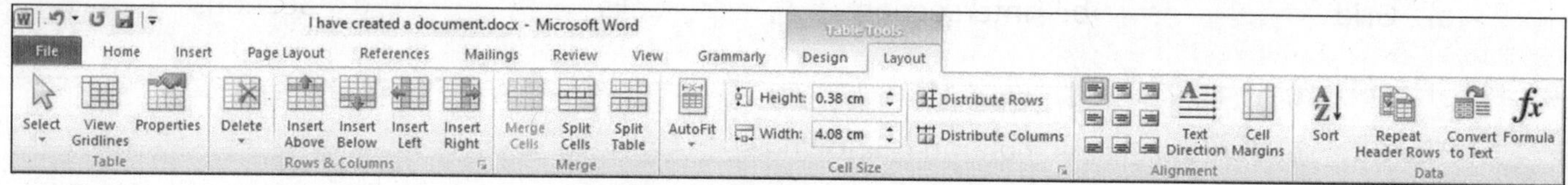

Figure 3.48: Layout Tab View

Table

Table group contains select, View gridlines and properties commands. Current row, column, cell or entire table can be selected by using select command. Then within the tables a gridline can be shown and hide by using view gridlines command. Last command under this group is Properties this is used for advanced settings like text wrapping and indentation.

Rows and Columns Group

Rows and Columns group contains the command of delete that can be used to delete the row, columns or table. Then Insert above, insert below is used to insert a row in above and below the cell or Insert left and right is used for inserting a columns.

- You can also copy the table by Press Ctrl + C keys.
- You can also paste the table by Press Ctrl + V keys.

Merge Group

Merge group contains merge cells, split cells, split tables commands. The selected cells are merge into single cell by using merge command. The selected cells can be split into various cell using split cells. The split tables will split the table into two tables. Next group contains Autofit, Alignment and Text direction commands. The Autofit command will resizes the columns according to the text written in it and different alignments on cells can be apply by using Alignment command. In the selected cells the direction of text can be changed.

Skill Test Box

1. ____________ option one can perform in Table.

   a. Insert b. Split c. Merge d. All of these

Summary

- Using Formatting the complete appearance of table can be changed according to our requirement that comes as more attractive and presentative style of table.
- Two label of Table tools are Design and Layout.
- The overall appearance of the table can be change by using design label given in the Table tools. There are inbuilt styles of tables in word that contains option of changing the color, appearance and borders of a table.
- When you click on Layout label various groups of changing the table style will come in the ribbon bar.

Keywords: Table Formatting, Changing Table Style, Design Tab view, Layout Tab view, Table group, Row and Column group, Merge group.

Self-Assessment

A. MULTIPLE CHOICE QUESTIONS

1. Multiple cells can be combined by using:
   a. Split tables b. Split cells c. Merge cells d. Combine cell
2. After selecting a table two labels appear under the Table tools?
   a. Layout and Format b. Design and Format
   c. Design and Layout d. Format and Table tools
3. Which of the following is a part of Table group in Layout label?
   a. View gridlines b. Insert Above c. Merge cells d. AutoFit

B. FILL IN THE BLANKS

1. __________ is used to split the cells.
2. There are ________ number of labels under Table tools.

C. STATE WHETHER THE FOLLOWING STATEMENTS ARE TRUE OR FALSE

1. A table can be split into two parts using split cell command. (T/F)
2. A row can be inserted using Insert right command (T/F)

D. ANSWER THE FOLLOWING QUESTIONS

1. Explain the concept of formatting?
2. Name the formatting labels of Table tools?
3. Explain the Layout label and groups contain in it?

E. PRACTICAL WORK

Open a MS Word, create a table with same columns as given below:

Roll No.	Name of Student	Class	Grade

Roll No.	Name of Student	Class	Grade

Fill the table and apply various styles comes under Design label.

Answers:

Multiple choice question:

1. c 2. c 3. a

Fill in the blanks:

1. Split cells 2. Two

State whether the following statements are True or False

1. True 2. False

SESSION 12: CONVERSION OF TEXT TO TABLE AND TABLE TO TEXT

In word 2010, the process of making tables is very easy but things become little complex when text have to convert into table format. In word we can perform both the conversion of text to table and from table to text in very less time.

Converting Text to Table

To convert text into table: Select the Text > Click on Insert Tab > Tables drop down arrow > Select Convert Text to Table

Make sure the selected text is separated by comas for entering data in different columns. Once you select the "Convert text to Table" a new dialog box will come and do the needful changes in it according to your requirements. (figure 3.49)

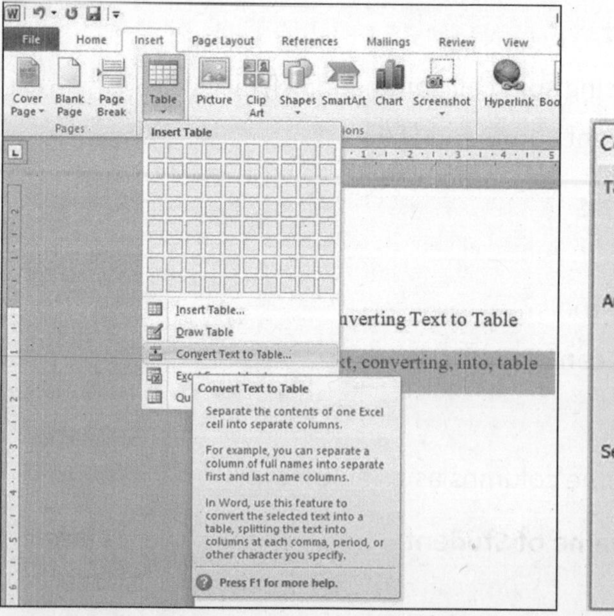

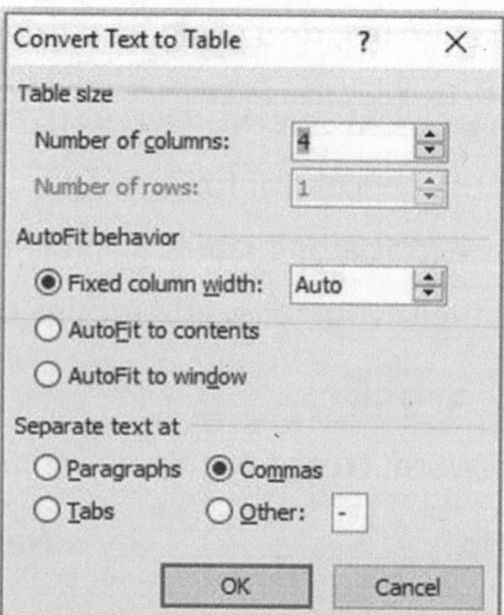

Figure 3.49: Selection of converting Text to Table and its dialog box

In dialog box press OK, once you are done with the required changes. After that a selected text separated with comma is converted into Table.

Converting Table to Text

In the last section we have learnt to convert the text into a table. Now, in this session will learn to convert a table back into a text format. To convert table into a text:

Place cursor on any cell of table > click on layout label from Table tools > Select Convert to Text command from Data group

By selecting it a new dialog box will appear then do the needful changes and press Ok. (figure 3.50, 3.51)

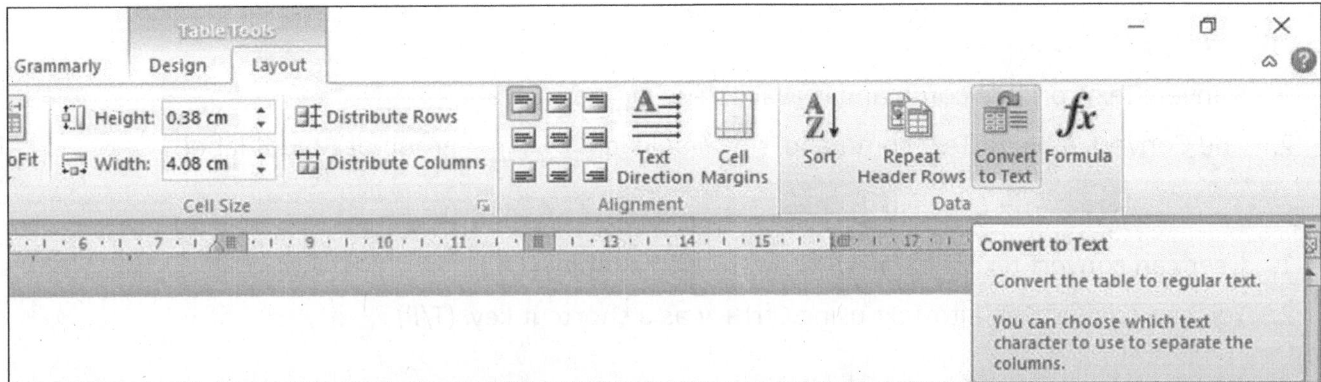

Figure 3.50: Selection of converting Table to Text

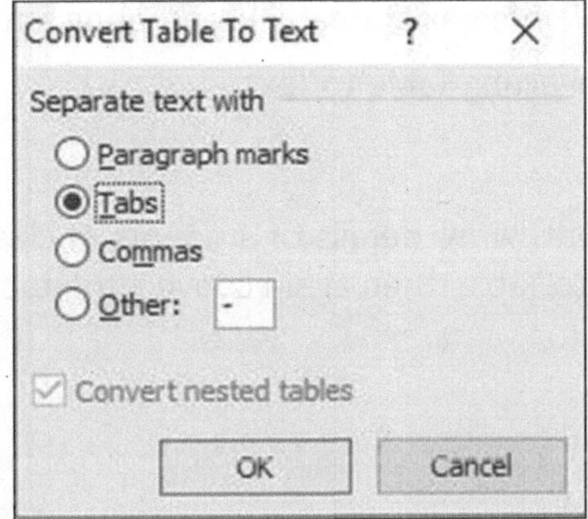

Figure 3.51: Convert Table to Text dialog box

This command will convert the table to text by differentiating it either by paragraph marks, Tabs, Commas and Other.

Summary

- Text can be converted into Table by using Convert Text to Table command in Table drop down.
- The text must be either separated by commas or tabs.
- The table can be converted into a text using Convert Table to Text command of Data group in Layout label.
- The text converted from table can be separated by Tabs, Paragraph marks and commas.

Keywords: Conversion of text to table, Conversion of table to text, Dialog box, MS Word 2010

A. MULTIPLE CHOICE QUESTIONS

1. Convert Text to Table command is available in which group:

   a. Tables b. Illustrations

   c. Header and Footer d. None of the above

2. The option Convert Table to Text is available in which label:

   a. Design label b. Layout c. Table tools d. None of the above

B. FILL IN THE BLANKS

1. Convert Text to Table command is available in _________ Tab.
2. The Convert Table to Text command is available in _________ group of Layout label.

C. STATE WHETHER THE FOLLOWING STATEMENTS ARE TRUE OR FALSE

1. User can convert text separated with tabs into a table. (T/F)
2. You can convert Table to Text using Ctrl + V as a shortcut key. (T/F)

D. ANSWER THE FOLLOWING QUESTIONS

1. Explain the concept of converting the text to a table.
2. Tell in brief about the role of commas and tab in separating a text.
3. Describe the concept of converting Table to Text.

E. PRACTICAL WORK

Open a word, create a document, write details of students in class separated by tabs and commas, Select the text and convert it into Table, then again convert the table into previous text form.

Answers:

Multiple choice question:

1. a 2. b

Fill in the blanks:

1. Insert 2. Data

State whether the following statements are True or False:

1. True 2. False

SESSION 13: SETTING BORDERS AND SHADINGS

In general case, pages, text or paragraph are highlighted by using border. As people gets more attracted towards your document when it is highlighted by using borders and shadings. This session will help user to learn about adding borders and shades as an outline to their document or paragraph.

Adding Border to A Page

To add border to a page, perform the following steps:

Open a document > Write a text > Click on page Layout tab >select Page Borders from Page Background group > Border and shading dialog box will appear > Select box option or style of border as per your requirements

User can also select Art, Width, Color and Style option as per their needs. Once you are done with the required changes click on OK button. This will add borders in every page of document. If you want to add border in one particular page, then select the option from Apply to drop down arrow and then click on OK. (figure 3.52)

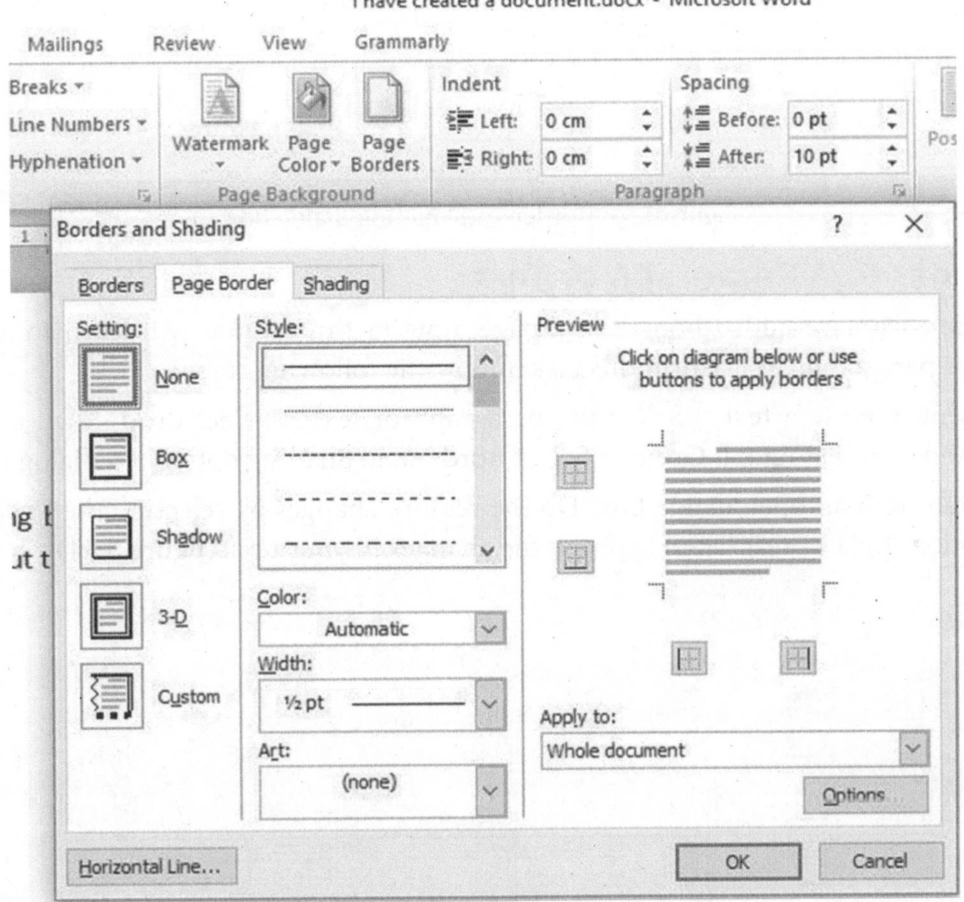

Figure 3.52: Page Border Dialog Box dialog box

Apply Shading On A Page

To apply shading on the page, perform the following steps:

Select the text of a page > Click on Page Layout > Page and Border command from Page Background group > Shading tab > Do needful changes in Fill and Patterns section

In Fill and Patterns section, select the colour you want to use and patterns in pattern section. After this click on OK button to apply the changes on a page. (figure 3.53)

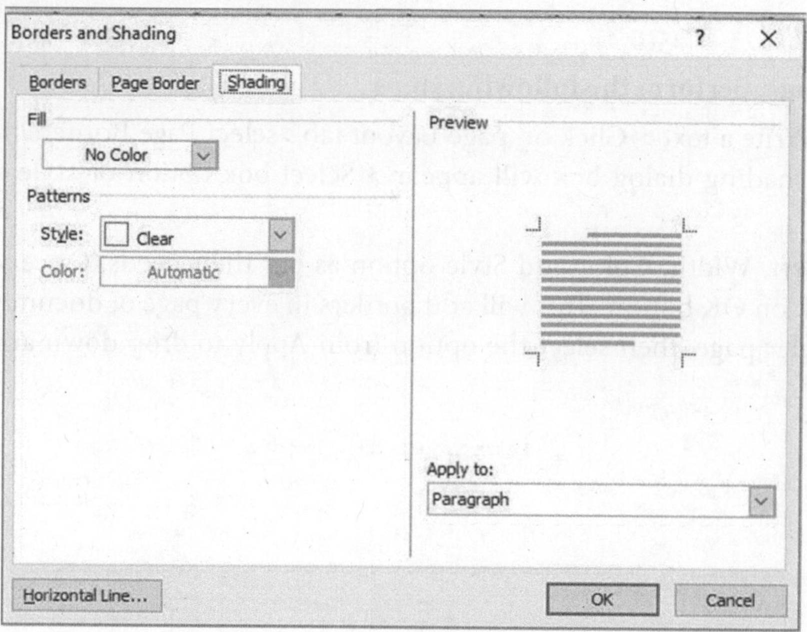

Figure 3.53: Border and Shading dialog box

Adding Border to A Paragraph or Text

In the last section we have added border to a page, now in this section will learn to add border to a particular text or paragraph. To perform this task, follow the following steps:

Open a document > Write a text > Select the paragraph or text > Select drop down arrow of Bottom Borders command from Paragraph Group > Select Border and Shading option > a dialog box will appear. Select Borders tab from an open dialog box, Do the require changes by selecting the Style, Color, Width from Setting option. In last press Ok to apply all the changes in your text. (figure 3.54)

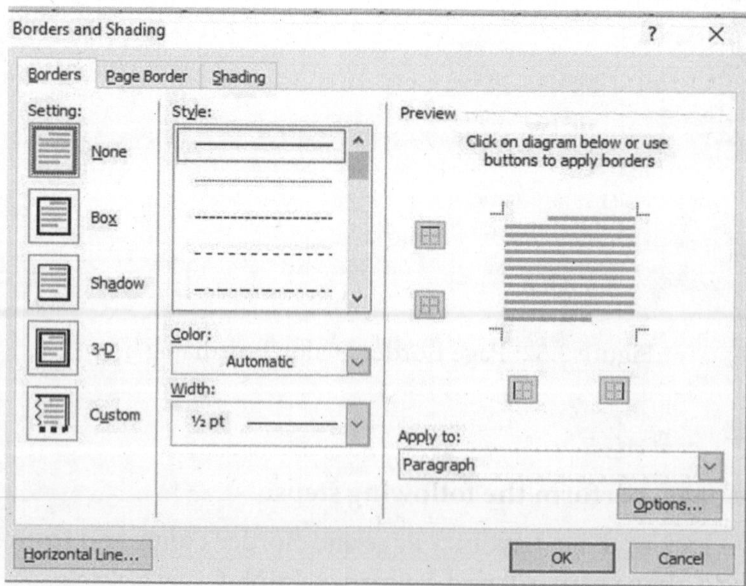

Figure 3.54: Borders and Shading dialog box

Apply Shading on A Paragraph or Text

To apply shading on a particular text or paragraph perform:

Select the paragraph or text > click on the Shading command from Paragraph group of Home tab > Click on the colour you want to use to shade your paragraph or text. (figure 3.55)

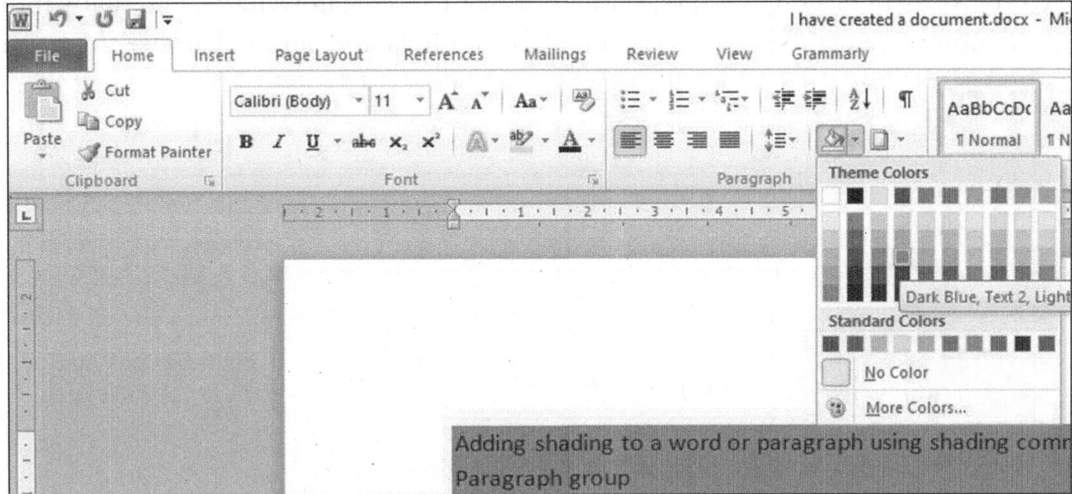

Figure 3.55: Using Shading colour

If you want to remove the existing colour of shading, click on "No Color" option

Inserting images, shapes, and special characters in a document

To make a regular document more attractive and presentable, Word processor gives the option to add various elements like image, shapes, and special characters to the document.

Inserting image: To insert any image or picture in any document, the first, foremost important thing is image or picture should be present either in hard disk or external storage like pen drive, and many more. To insert image in a document, perform the following steps:

- Select the **Insert** tab and click on **Clip Art** option, then go to the desired location and select an image from it. Click on the **Open** button or double click on it.

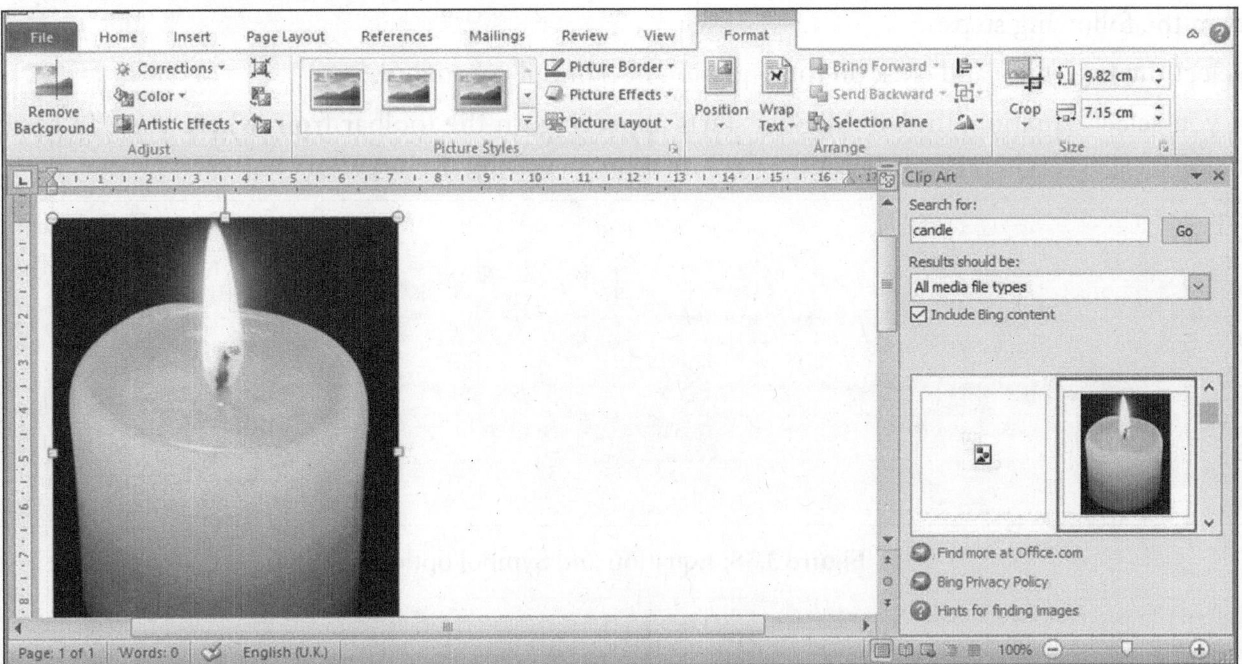

Figure 3.56: Inserted image

Further one can do other operation on t from the command gin under Format of Picture toolbar.

Inserting shapes: Like images, you can also insert various shapes in your document. The variety of shapes available in Word processor is a line, arrows, symbols, stars, callouts, flowcharts, and many more. To insert a shape in the document, select the Insert tab, and click on the Shape option. Choose the required shape:

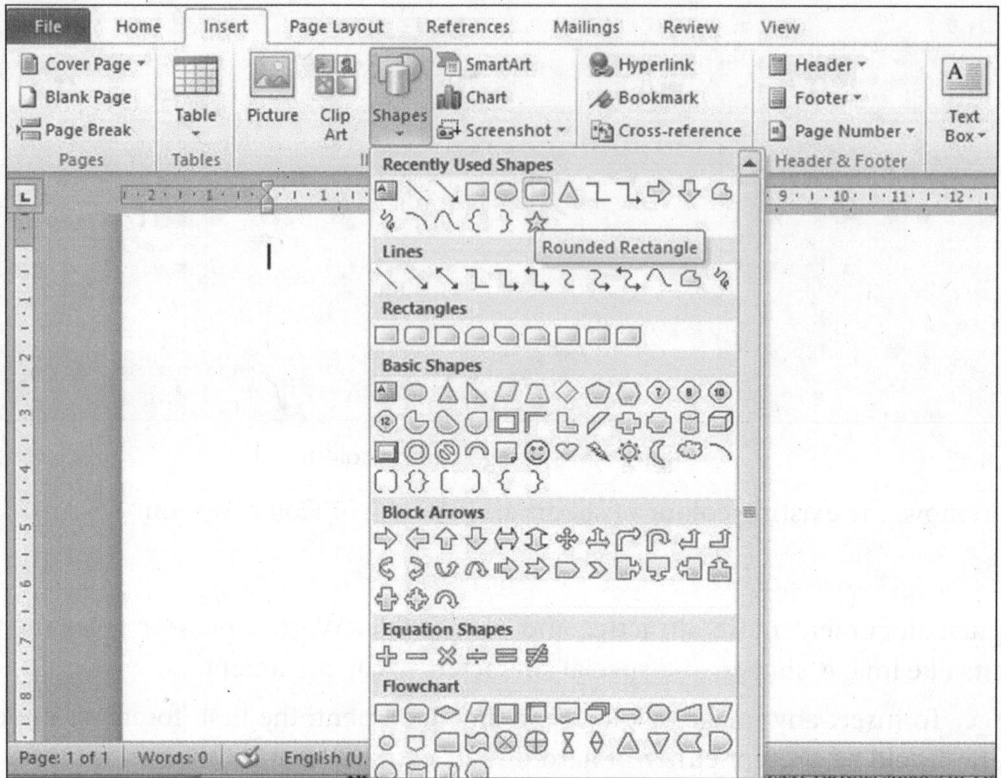

Figure 3.57: Inserting shapes

Inserting special characters: Sometimes, there is a need to write some equations and adding special characters that can't be typed using the keys of the keyboard. To insert special characters in Word processor, perform the following steps:

1. Select the Insert tab and click on the Equation or Symbol command.
2. If you select equation, then its symbol starts appearing on the toolbar from where you can select the required special character by simply selecting it then clicking on the Insert button.

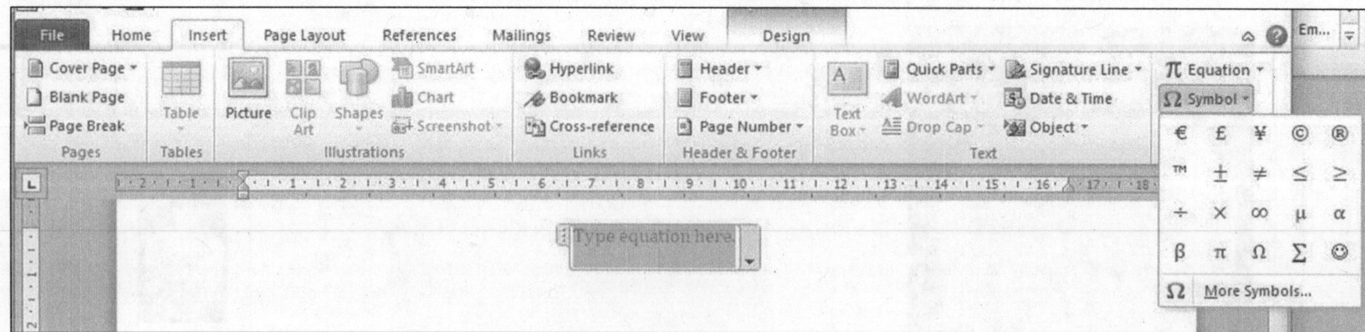

Figure 3.58: Equation and Symbol option

Dividing the document page into columns

Sometimes you must have observed that pages are divided into two or three columns in some books, magazines, newspapers, and novels. Word processor also gives you an option or feature to divide the regular text into one or more than one column before or after adding the text. To divide the page into columns, perform the following steps:

1. Select the **Page Layout** tab and click on Column option, and you will observe a column dialog box:

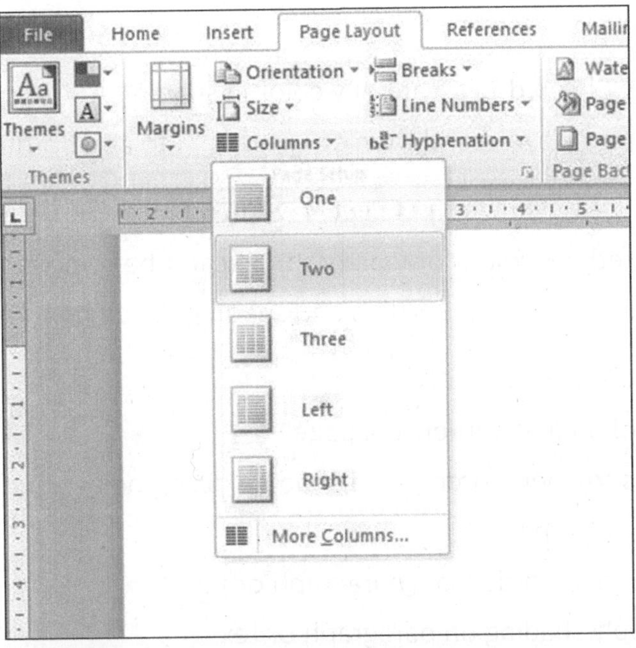

Figure 3.59: Dividing Page into Columns

2. In the dialog box, you can enter the count for columns under settings. In **Columns** dialog box, you can also enter the spacing between the columns. Click the **OK** button on the screen.

Summary

- To add border to a page, open a document > Write a text > Click on the page Layout tab >select Page Borders from Page Background group > Border and shading dialog box will appear > Select box option or style of border as per your requirements.
- To apply shading on the page, Select the text of a page > Click on Page Layout > Page and Border command from Page Background group > Shading tab > Do needful changes in Fill and Patterns section.
- To apply border to a Paragraph or text, open a document > Write a text > Select the paragraph or text > Select drop down arrow of Bottom Borders command from Paragraph Group > Select Border and Shading option > a dialog box will appear.
- To add border to a paragraph or text, open a document > Write a text > Select the paragraph or text > Select drop down arrow of Bottom Borders command from Paragraph Group > Select Border and Shading option > a dialog box will appear.

Keywords: Adding Border to a page, Art, Width, Color, Style, Apply shading on a page, Border and shading dialog box, Adding border to a paragraph or text, Apply shading on a paragraph or text, Shading color.

Self-Assessment

A. MULTIPLE CHOICE QUESTIONS

1. Shading option is present in which group of home tab:

   a. Clipboard b. Illustrations c. Paragraph d. Grammarly

2. Which of the following is a Tab of border and shading dialog box:

   a. Borders
   b. Page Background
   c. Border and shading
   d. None of the above

B. FILL IN THE BLANKS

1. Click on ____________ if you don't want any color in shading.
2. You have to click on page Layout and then on _________ to add border on your text.

C. STATE WHETHER THE FOLLOWING STATEMENTS ARE TRUE OR FALSE

1. Once you have selected the colour on paragraph, it can't be removed. (T/F)
2. There are three number of tabs in Borders and shading dialog box. (T/F)

D. ANSWER THE FOLLOWING QUESTIONS

1. Explain the concept of adding border to a page.
2. Write down the steps to open Borders and Shading dialog box.
3. How to apply shading on a page?
4. What are the steps to add border to a paragraph or text?
5. Write the steps to apply shading on paragraph or text.

E. PRACTICAL WORK

Open a word, create a document, add border to a page, then add shading in it, create new document then apply border on particular paragraph or text, add shading in that paragraph.

Answers

Multiple choice question:

1. c 2. a

Fill in the blanks:

1. No Color 2. Page Borders

State whether the following statements are True or False:

1. False 2. True

SESSION 14: ADJUST MARGINS AND ORIENTATION

To print a document in desired manner, you need to set the margins and orientation of document.

Page Margins

Around the edges of a document there is blank space known as margins. The header, footer, and page number or extra information like items can be written in the margins. There are two ways to set a margin:

a. Using Ruler Bars
b. Using Page Setup dialog box

Setting Page margin using Ruler Bars:

To set the page margin by using ruler bars perform the following steps:

On left Horizontal ruler bar there is indent marker place pointer on it > Drag the mouse pointer towards right or left to increase or decrease the margin respectively.

When you place the pointer on ruler bar a double headed arrow will appear in the place of pointer and drag it left or right according to your requirements then release and observe the changes. Similarly, you can change the right, bottom and top margins. (figure 3.60)

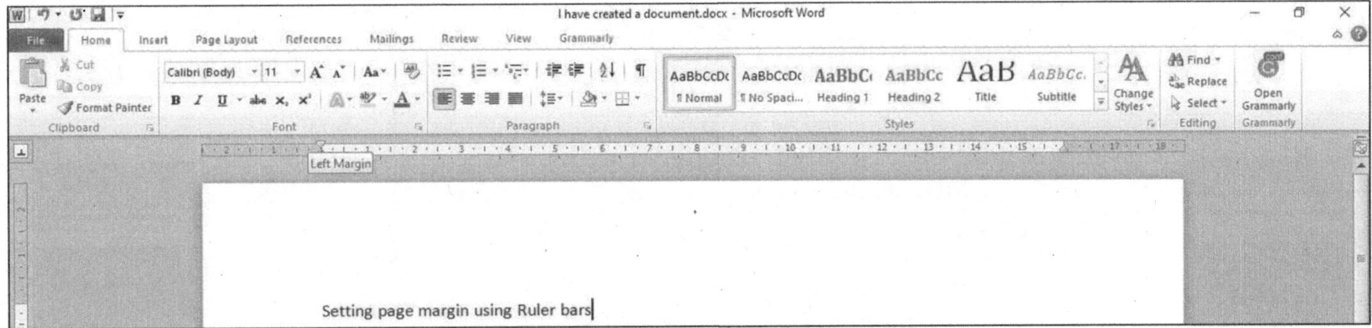

Figure 3.60: Setting left margin using Ruler bar

Setting Page margin by using Page setup dialog box:

To perform the page setting by using page setup dialog box perform the following steps:

Open the document > click on Page Layout tab > Margin drop down arrow > Select the required margin option

First thing is to either open an existing or create a new document. Then click on Page Layout tab and on drop down arrow of margins. A list will appear and select a required margin from that list. (figure 3.61)

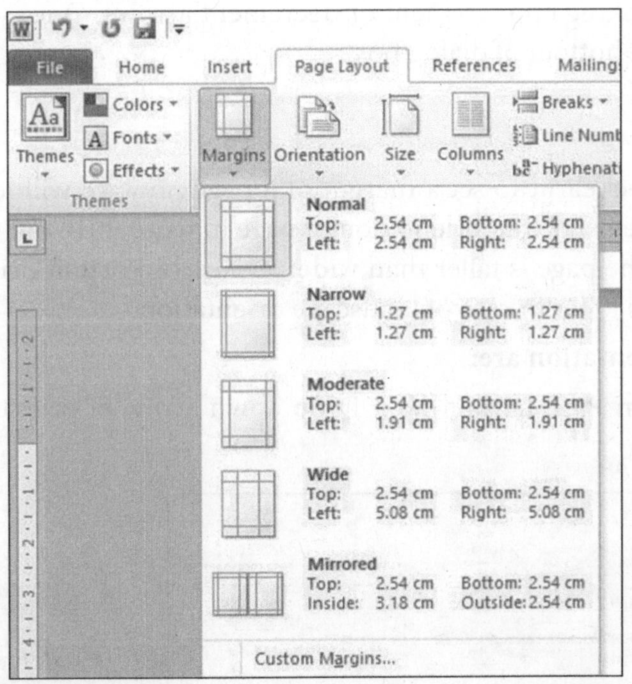

Figure 3.61: Setting margin using Page setup dialog box

Or

You can also specify your own margins by using Custom Margins option given in the end of the Margins drop down arrow. When you click on it a Page Setup dialog box will appear. (figure 3.62)

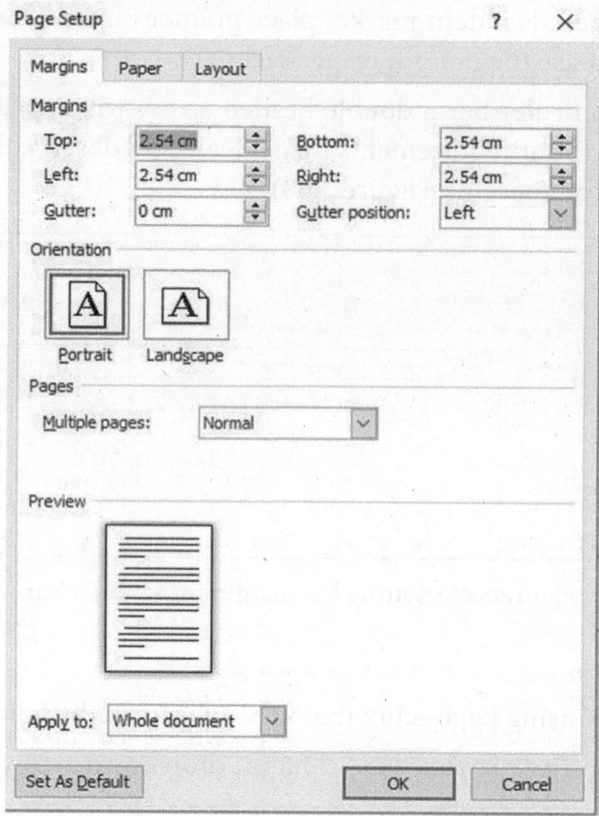

Figure 3.62: Page setup dialog box

In Page setup dialog box, you can specify left, right, top, and bottom field margin by either directly putting values in their box or by clicking on increment or decrement arrows. Once you are done with it, click on Ok button given in the right bottom of dialog box.

Page Orientation

In the above section we have learnt to set a margin of a page now we will learn to set or apply the page orientation. By default, there is Portrait orientation of page in word 2010 but you can switch to Landscape orientation when require. The page is taller than wider in case of Portrait orientation on other hand page become more wider and less taller in case of landscape orientation.

Steps to apply the page orientation are:

Open a document > click on Page Layout tab > Drop down arrow of orientation > Select orientation of your style. (figure 3.63)

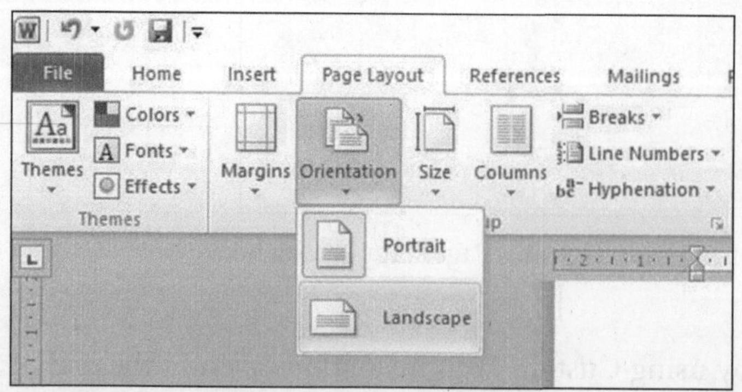

Figure 3.63: Page orientation

LETS KNOW MORE

By default, size of page is 8.5” x 11”.

Ctrl + M key is used to indent a paragraph from left side.

Summary

- To print a document in desired manner a page orientation and margins are used.
- Around the edges of a document there is blank space that is known as margins.
- To set page margin by using Page setup dialog box, Open the document > click on Page Layout tab > Margin drop down arrow > Select the required margin option.
- Portrait is a default orientation of Word.
- The page is taller than wider in case of Portrait orientation on other hand page become more wider and less taller in case of landscape orientation.
- To apply page orientation, open a document > click on Page Layout tab > Drop down arrow of orientation > Select orientation of your style.
- Ctrl + M is the shortcut key to indent a paragraph from left side.

Keywords: Page Margins, Ruler Bars, Page Setup dialog box, Orientation, Portrait, Landscape.

Self-Assessment

A. MULTIPLE CHOICE QUESTIONS

1. What is the shortcut key to indent a paragraph from left side:

   a. Ctrl + L b. Ctrl + M c. Ctrl + A d. Ctrl + T

2. Margins command comes under which group:

   a. Paragraph b. Editing c. Page setup d. Page background

3. Which of the following is not a type of orientation in word:

   a. Portrait b. Landscape c. Widescale d. None

B. FILL IN THE BLANKS

1. __________ is the default orientation of page in Word.
2. Orientation command is present in ________Tab

C. STATE WHETHER THE FOLLOWING STATEMENTS ARE TRUE OR FALSE

1. You can only set margin of left side of document. (T/F)
2. You can set page margin using Ruler Bars and Page setup dialog box. (T/F)
3. The landscape orientation are more wider than taller. (T/F)

D. ANSWER THE FOLLOWING QUESTIONS

1. Explain portrait orientation.
2. What are the two methods to set a page margin?
3. How the orientation of page can be change in Word 2010?

E. PRACTICAL WORK

Open a word document, create multiple page document, set half of them in portrait mode and rest in Landscape, set margins using custom option

ANSWERS

Multiple choice question:

1. b 2. c 3. c

Fill in the blanks:

1. Portrait
2. Page Layout

State whether the following statements are True or False:

1. False
2. True
3. True

SESSION 15: PRINT THE LETTER USING MAIL MERGE

Through Mail Merge feature a piece of text can be sent to multiple addresses. Example: Mail merge feature will change the invited guest names and address and send the same document to multiple guests. This results in time and effort saving.

Mail Merge

As mentioned above the mail merge feature is used for creating a series of same documents and sent it to multiple addresses. With this feature we can merge the main document that can be certificates or letter with mailing address of various persons. Its name is mal merge because in this main document is merged with mailing address that helps in sending letters, invitations, common document or certificates for number of peoples.

In such kind of cases the mail merge feature save time and resources. One of the way is creating a letter in Writer and copy the address from the address list for changing the address or first and last name of each employee. This procedure of copying and changing the name of employee is very time consuming and tedious. This approach is good when we have to send the letter to limited number of person but it is not possible in case of hundreds or thousands of addresses. In those cases use of mail merge feature is prove to be efficient through this the task can be accomplish in one stroke.

Let the common contents is the main document that you want to send to all of your employee or students and other will be the data source that holds the address list of all employee or students. The actual information is kept in form letter along with the variable names that will be different in every document.

LETS KNOW MORE

For example, if you are a manager and want to inform your customers of a meeting, then the meeting purpose is the same in all the documents, but there are changes in the recipient's information such as their first name, last name, and many more.

Definition Box

Mail merge is a feature within most data processing applications that enables users to send a similar letter or document to multiple recipients. It enables connecting a single form template with a data source that contains information about the recipient's name, address and other predefined and supported data.

Creating the data source:

Corresponding values are kept in data source that is a set of mailing address in multiple rows and columns that is also known as database. In this each row contain the record of each person that have other fields such as name, address, roll no., etc. Best way to create a database is use of spreadsheet as table format is used in this for storing the data. Other option is use of mail wizard for creating an address book during mail merge.

Steps to use Mail Merge are:

Create a new document and add data to be sent to multiple people: To create a new document, perform the following steps:

- Click on Tool

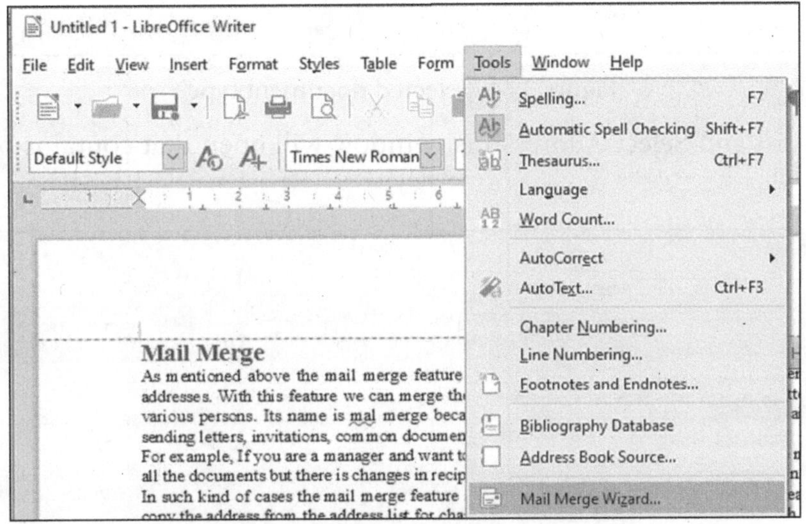

Figure 3.64: Mail Merge Wizard option

- Mail Merge Wizard and a new window will appear

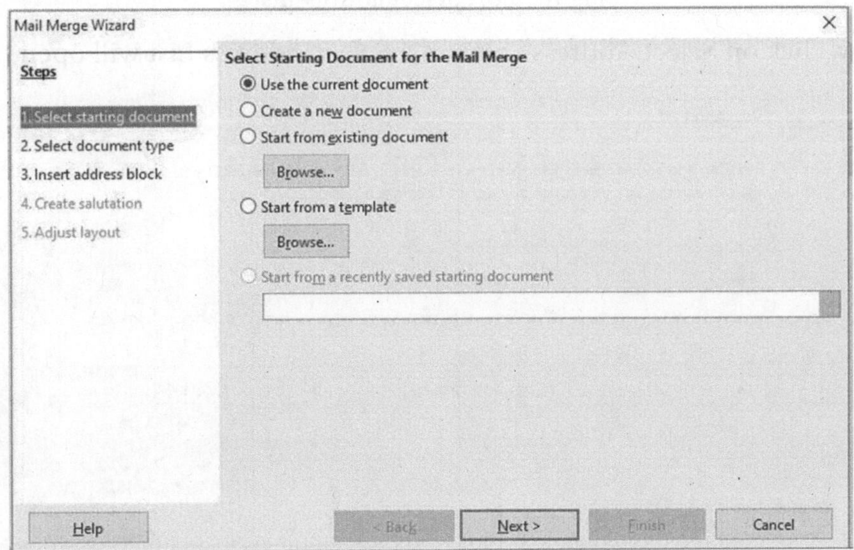

Figure 3.65: Mail Merge Wizard dialog box

- Select Starting document from Mail Merge Wizard dialog box > Use the current document > click on Next button given in the bottom of dialog box

✦ Then Click on Document type > E-mail message > Next button

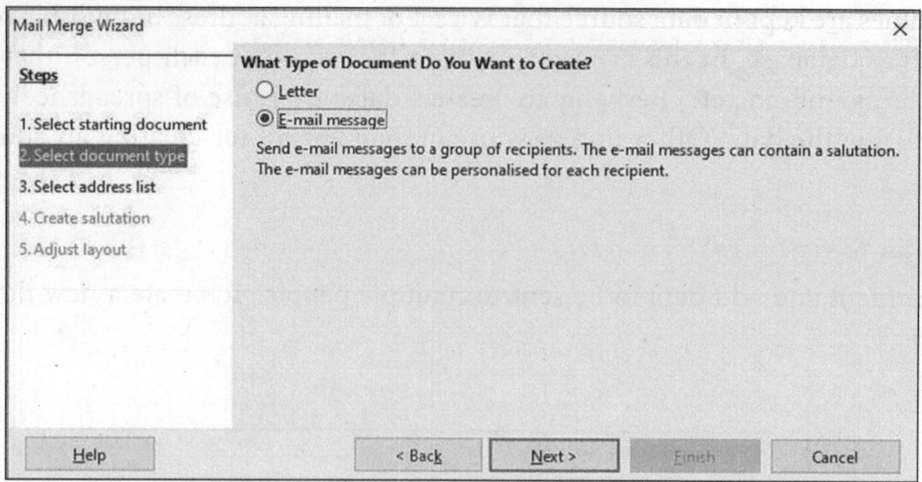

Figure 3.66: Selected document type

✦ Click on Address List and Select Address List window will open that contains option for creating the recipient list

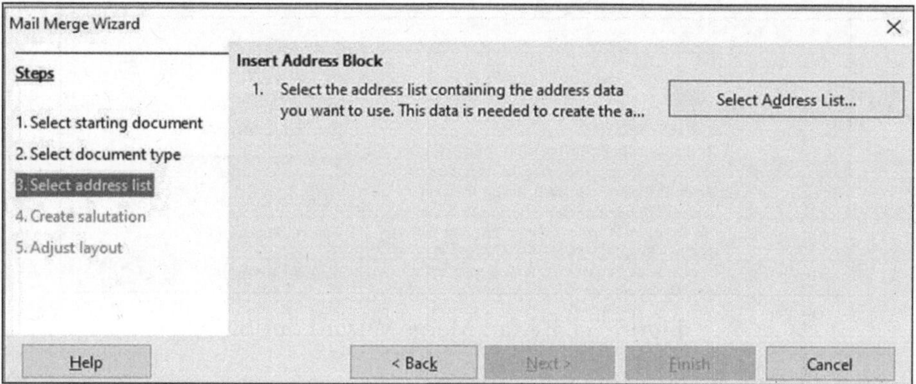

Figure 3.67: Select address list

✦ In above window, click on Select Address List and a Select Address List will open

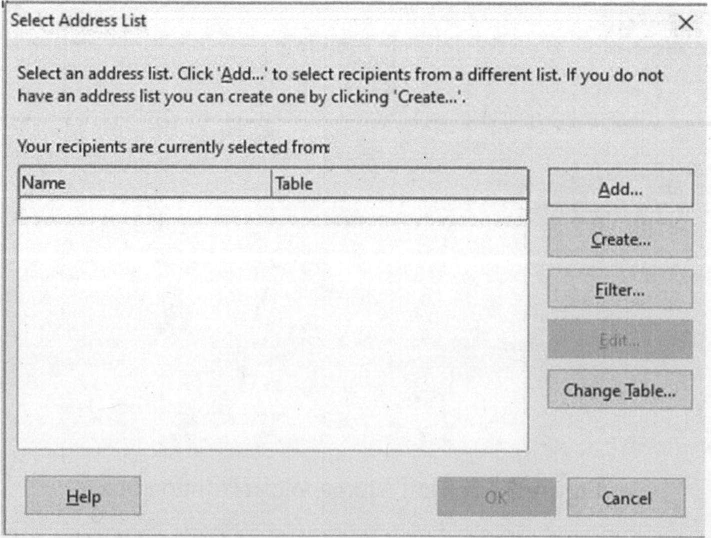

Figure 3.68: Select Address List dialog box

+ In above given dialog box, click on Add to add various members address > Click on Create button, this will open a New Address List window

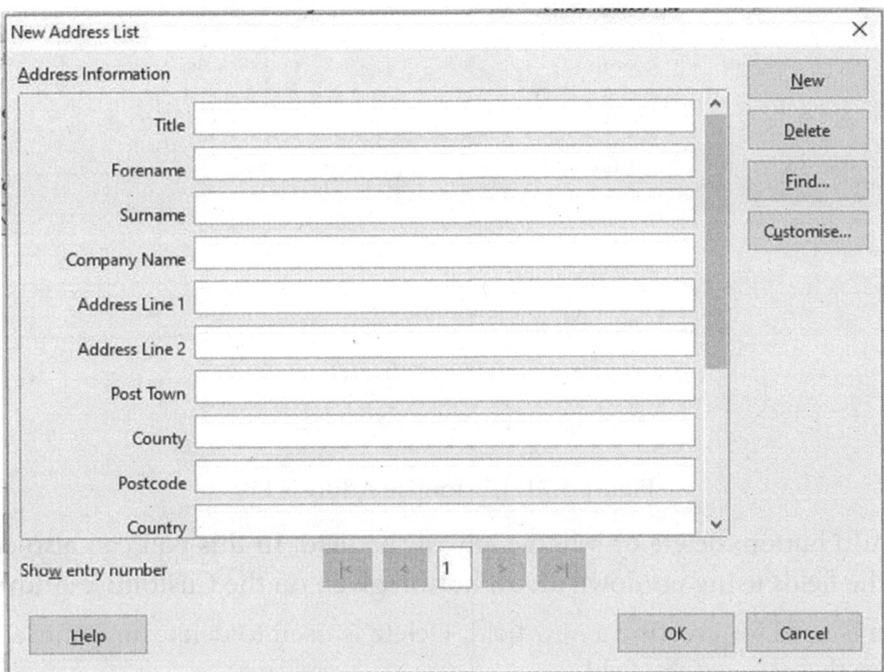

Figure 3.69: New Address list window

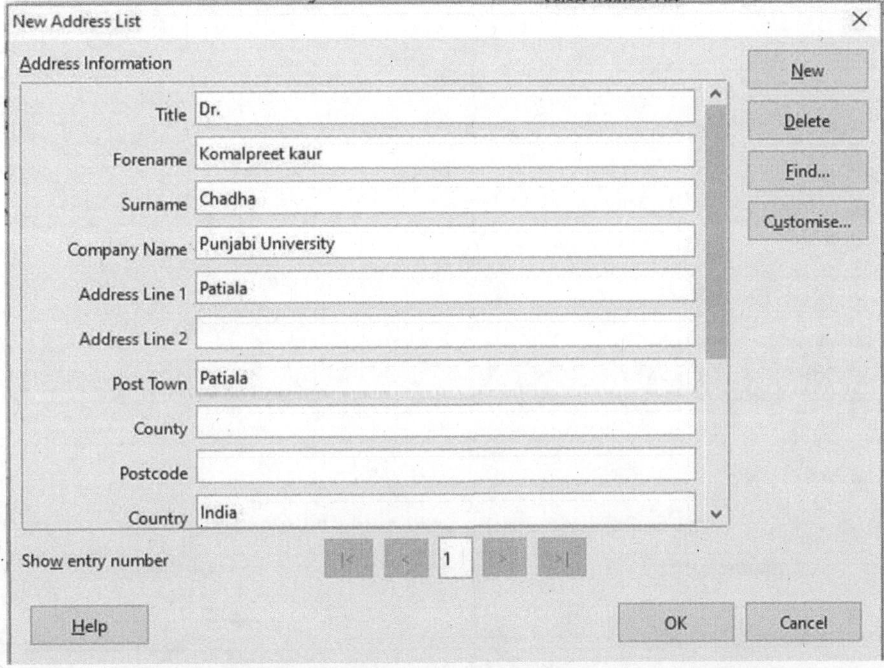

Figure 3.70: Adding data in New Address list window

+ If you want to Customise the fields of recipient information > Click on Customize button and Customise Address List window will appear as given in below figure 3.71.

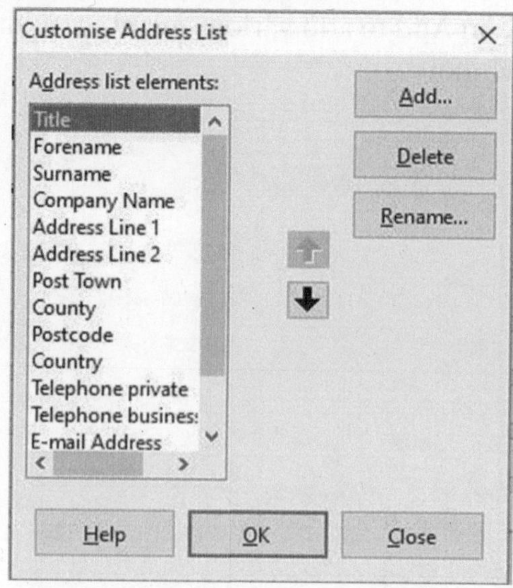

Figure 3.71: Customise Address List

- Now click on Add button, delete or rename any of the field. In this you can also change the order of appearance of the fields using up/down arrow button given on the Customise Address List window.

  The Add option is used for creating a new field, Delete is used to delete an unnecessary field, Rename is used to change the name of the field.
- Then click on Ok button to close the list and this will open a Save As dialog box.

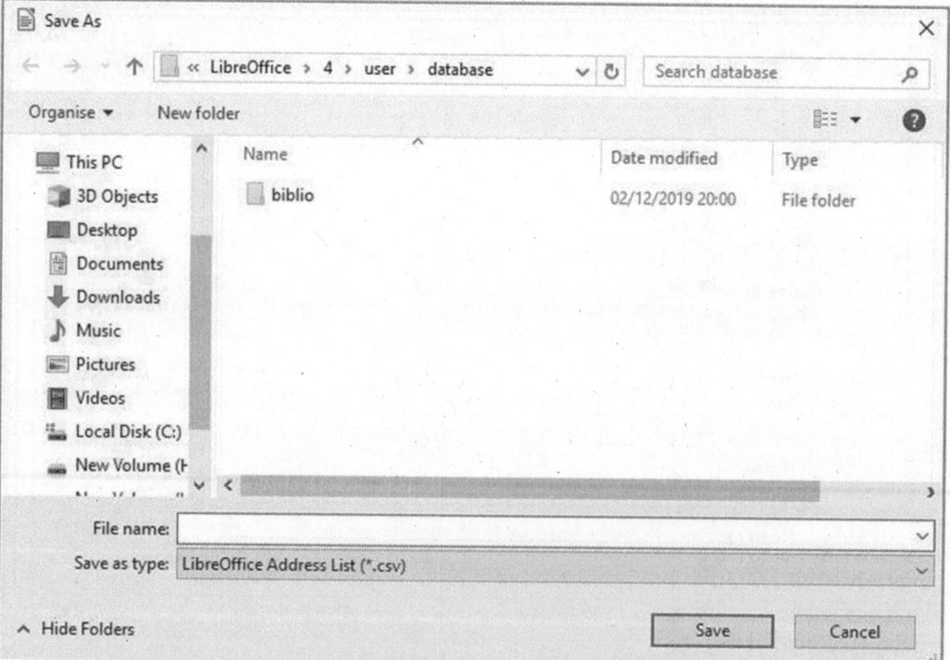

Figure 3.72: Save As dialog box

- In Save As dialog box, add the name in File name text box > Click on Save if you want to save the document in the opened location otherwise Change the location and Save it.
- A list window will appear after saving the list that will display all the recipient list created by you.
- From list you can select any of the created list > Click on Ok button to send the mail to selected list.

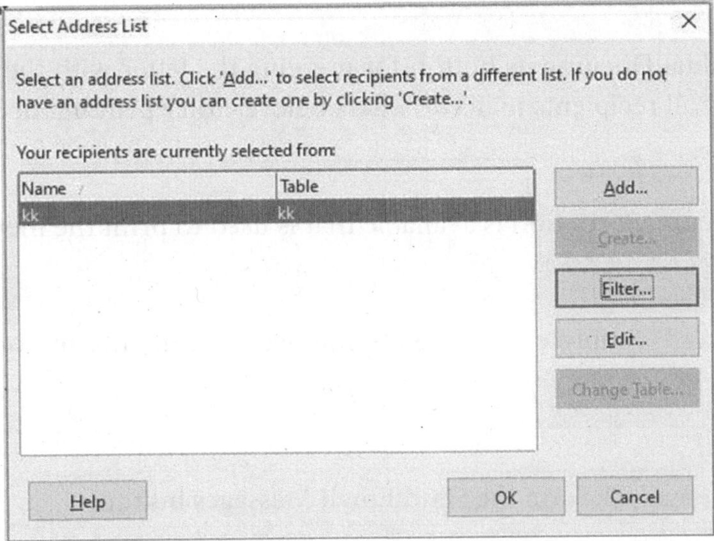

Figure 3.73: Selected Address List dialog box

- After selected the address from list, next step is to click on Create salutation > Add the required information > Click on Next button

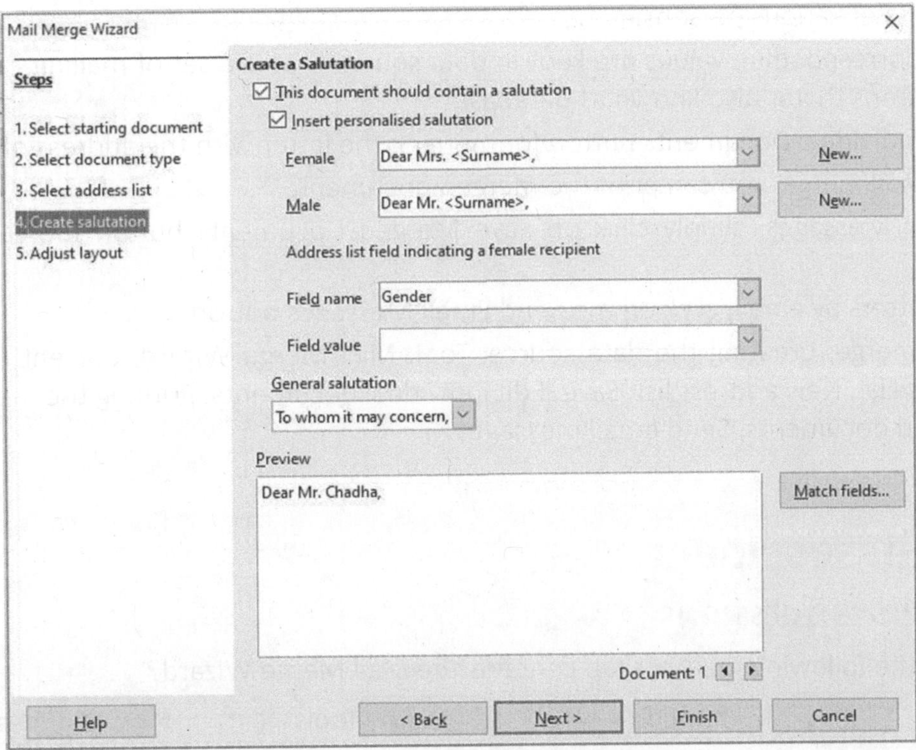

Figure 3.74: Create salutation window

- In the next step, a Writer will display the document with Mail Merge Toolbar

Skill Test Box

Enter the correct answer in the blanks given below:

1. ____________ Menu contain the Mail Merge Wizard option.
2. Corresponding values are kept in the ____________ that is a set of a mailing address in multiple rows and columns that is also known as a database.

Edit individual documents:

Now click on Edit individual Documents button for merging the letter with the address of the recipients. In this part you can verify all recipients mails or letters before either printing or sending it

Printing the Merged document:

- The Print Merged Documents option is available that is used to print the merged document

Saving the Merged document:

- To save Email Messages, simply click on Save Merged Documents button foe saving the merged document.

Send Email Messages:

- To send the letters by email, click on the Send Email Messages button.

Summary

- Through Mail Merge feature a piece of text can be sent to multiple addresses.
- With the feature of mail merge we can merge the main document that can be certificates or letter with mailing address of various persons.
- In MS Word Corresponding values are kept in data source that is a set of mailing address in multiple rows and columns that is also known as database.
- Click on Edit individual Documents button for merging the letter with the address of the recipients.
- In MS Word Mail merge, you can print the merged document.
- To save Email Messages, simply click on Save Merged Documents button foe saving the merged document.
- To send the letters by email, click on the Send Email Messages button.

Keywords: Mail merge, Creating the data source, Tool, Mail Merge Wizard, Current document, E-mail message, Address List, New address list, Save, Edit individual documents, Printing the merged documents, Saving the merged documents, Send email messages.

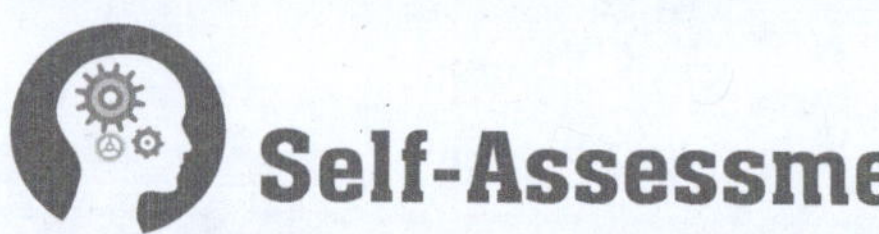

Self-Assessment

A. MULTIPLE CHOICE QUESTIONS

1. Which of the following menu or tab contains the Mail Merge Wizard?

   a. File　　b. Edit　　c. Tools　　d. Insert

2. Mail Merge is the process of combining document design with a list to create multiple copies of document for each entry in the list. The list is called______________.

   a. Main Document　　b. Data Source　　c. Form Label　　d. Database

Answer

1. c　　2. b

B. QUESTIONS

1. Define Mail Merge?

2. What is data source?
3. Write down the steps to create the data source?
4. How to add data in the field?
5. Is it possible to save the merged letter in MS Word? If yes, What is the process to save it.

C. PROJECT WORK

1. Demonstrate to print the letter or any document using Mail Merge.
2. Send your birthday invitation to your friends in one go through mail.

Exercise for Assessment

A. MULTIPLE CHOICE QUESTIONS

1. Which of the following is not the word processing application?
   a. WordPad b. Google Docs c. Notepad d. Sticky notes
2. ______________ is the shortcut key to open an existing file or document.
   a. Ctrl + C b. Ctrl + V c. Ctrl + O d. Ctrl + P
3. Copy, Cut, Paste and undo commands are available in which of the following tab.
   a. File Tab b. Edit Tab c. View Tab d. Insert Tab
4. The ______________ pointer is used in graphical based text processing applications.
   a. Grabber pointer b. Selection Pointer c. H-Beam d. I-Beam
5. Which of the following is the shortcut key to Redo the operation?
   a. Ctrl + X b. Ctrl + Y c. Ctrl + Z d. Ctrl + V
6. You can select all text in the document by pressing __________ keys of keyboard
   a. Ctrl + C b. Ctrl + V c. Ctrl + A d. Ctrl + X
7. Blue wavy line under the word or sentence represents:
   a. Spelling mistake b. Grammar mistake c. Word formation mistake d. All
8. Shortcut key to select the Clear Direct Formatting is:
   a. Ctrl + C b. Shift + C c. Ctrl + M d. Shift + M
9. The paragraphs are evenly aligned between the left and right side in case of which of the following paragraph alignment styles?
   a. Align Paragraph Left b. Center
   c. Align Paragraph Right d. Justify
10. The change in background colour of paragraph comes under ___________ tab
    a. Page b. Borders c. Alignment d. Area
11. You can insert column in a table either:
    a. Above b. Before c. After d. Both b. and c.

12. Which of the following menu or tab contains the Mail Merge Wizard?

a. File b. Edit c. Tools d. Insert

Answer

1. d	2. c	3. b	4. d	5. b	6. c
7. b	8. c	9. d	10. d	11. c	12. c

B. VERY SHORT QUESTIONS:

1. Give some of the formatting features comes under Word Processor.
2. Name any three word processing applications.
3. In Word processor you can save existing file with another? Justify the answer in one line.
4. Define Floating Toolbar?
5. Is it possible to remove the new addition in the document using single command? If, yes then name that command.
6. Name common text formatting features in Word processor.
7. What is Page Break?
8. How to copy a table in Word processor?
9. What is Mail Merge?

C. SHORT QUESTIONS:

1. Define Word Processor?
2. Write down the steps to start Word processor in Window?
3. What is display under Status Bar of Word processor?
4. What is mouse pointer? Name various cursor and mouse pointers.
5. Give various techniques of selecting text.
6. How to Find and replace the text in existing document.
7. How to check spelling and grammar mistakes using Synonyms and Thesaurus?
8. What do you mean by Superscript and Subscript?
9. Give a brief about various paragraph alignment styles in Word processor.
10. Use both the methods of inserting the table in the document. Write a short note on both methods.
11. What is the usage of print preview in Word processor?

D. LONG QUESTIONS:

1. What is Word processor? Give various advantages of Word processor?
2. Write a short note on various parts of Word processor window.
3. Write down the steps and options of moving and copying the text in Word processor?
4. How to check spelling and grammar mistakes in Word processor window? Give colours that indicate different mistakes in the document.
5. What is the purpose of using bullets and numbering in the document? Write the steps to create a list using bullets and numbering.

6. Write the steps to insert images, shapes and special characters in a document.
7. In Word processor is there any option of splitting and merging the table? If yes, then write down the steps to create two tables then merge it after that again split into same proportions.
8. Write down the steps to create a data source in mail merge?

E. APPLICATION BASED QUESTIONS:

1. Jasspreet wants to start Word processor in Ubuntu Linux, Help him in opening it in his system.
2. Komal is new to Word processor, tell her various parts of Writer Window that help her in working on MS Word Writer.
3. Rahul is working on making an assignment. He wants to copy data from one existing document but he don't need complete text, he just need non-consecutive text. Help him in copying non-consecutive text using both keyboard and mouse.
4. Simran wants to create a ordered list of Candle items he want to buy. Suggest him which option should he used to create an ordered list.
5. Gurutek wants to make an assignment in Word processor in which he have to write some equations using special characters, add pictures or images to make his document more attractive. Tell him about various ways to add images in the document and use of special character for writing the equations.

GROUP DISCUSSION:

1. Conduct a group discussion pros and cons of Word Processor.
2. Divide class into two parts and tell them to do a group discussion on various parts of a Word processor window and how it is useful.
3. Arrange a group discussion on various functions one can perform in editing the document.

F. PROJECT WORK

Apply or use change document views, Start a new document and save it, then open that saved existing document, close the document

Start a new document and type one paragraph in it then edit it, Use both option of mouse and keyboard for selecting, cut, copy, paste and moving text from one page to another page.

Use find and replace option to replace any of the existing word with new one.

Demonstrate how to insert non-printing characters in a document. How to check spelling and grammar mistakes in the document then apply changes in to correct it.

Demonstrate and format the paragraphs by indent it, assigning font colour, highlight it by adding background colour. Insert images, shapes, special characters in new document by dividing the page into columns and save it

Create a table, split and merge tables and copy an existing table and move it from one location to another location.

Use the option of Preview page before printing and demonstrate to print the letters using mail merge after creating a data source then save the merged letter for later use.

TEACHER NOTES:

1. Install or check for MS Word 2010 in the system of every students so that they can practically work on it.
2. Practically show class to step by step use of Mail merge for merging the main document with mailing address of various students.

EXAM TIPS:

1. Do all the things practically on computer to know exactly about various parts of Word Processor.
2. Send invitation to 2-3 Ids using mail merge in one go to keep the steps of it in mind for long time.
3. Make a document and apply all the formatting functions on it such as adding border, inserting image, adding color, etc.
4. Make list in a table then add more row and column. After that try splitting and merging function.

4 Spreadsheet

Learning Outcomes

After this chapter, you will have the knowledge of:

- Introduction to Spreadsheet Application
- How to start MS Excel Spreadsheet
- Various Parts of MS Excel Spreadsheet
- Worksheet and Range of cell
- How to enter data in Worksheet
- Mathematical Operators used in Formulae
- Simple calculations using values and operators
- How to enter Formulae with cell addresses and operators
- Commonly used Basic functions in Excel like Sum, Average, Max, Count, Today
- Formatting Tool in Excel
- Use of dialog boxes to format values
- How to speed up the data entry using fill handle
- What is Referencing in Excel and Various types of referencing.
- Importance and various types of charts in Spreadsheet

INTRODUCTION

In 15th century people use ledgers or oversized sheets of papers. The economic transactions of a company are recorded and calculated using these ledgers. You must have seen that your grandparents used to write their daily expenditure is dairy or sheet and calculate the total amount by categorizing the items. The spreadsheet is an electronic way of doing the same work which your grandparents used to do in dairy.

Definition Box

A spreadsheet or worksheet is a file made of numerical data. What makes a spreadsheet software program unique is its ability to calculate values using mathematical cells.

The varies task in which spreadsheet are used for arranging the data in tabular form, analysis and maintaining the data, graph generations, to manage inventory, performing various mathematical operations on new or existing data, creation of MIS records, financial calculations, etc. Microsoft Excel, LibreOffice Calc, Google sheets, Lotus 1-2-3 and Apache OpenOffice Calc are some of the existing popular spreadsheet software. In this session we will work on MS Excel-2010.

Resource Requirements:

A multimedia computer system is used as Hardware

A word processing application MS Excel-2010 Software is required

LETS KNOW MORE

In case of maintaining the long list of budgets, data, sales figures and other data, spreadsheets are used and Microsoft Excel is considered as one of the very useful spreadsheet.

SESSION 1: CREATE A SPREADSHEET

Introduction to Spreadsheet Application

In case of maintaining the long list of budgets, data, sales figures and other data, spreadsheets and Calc in LibreOffice is considered as one of the very useful spreadsheet. In the field of business and accounting part spreadsheets are used that is derived from the word 'Spread'. The bills you get from shopkeepers can be in handwritten form or printed from computer that contains the list and total amount of things you have buy from them including all taxes, discount, Vat part in it. These all tasks can be done using spreadsheet that organise the data in the form of rows and columns.

The steps need to follow for launching the spreadsheet program is:

Click on Start > Click on all programs > Microsoft Office > Microsoft Excel 2010

Or

Choose Start > Type Excel in search programs and files box > Click on the application to start it

In some system you will see the shortcut key of Excel on desktop. The Excel can start by clicking on shortcut key.

Parts of Spreadsheet

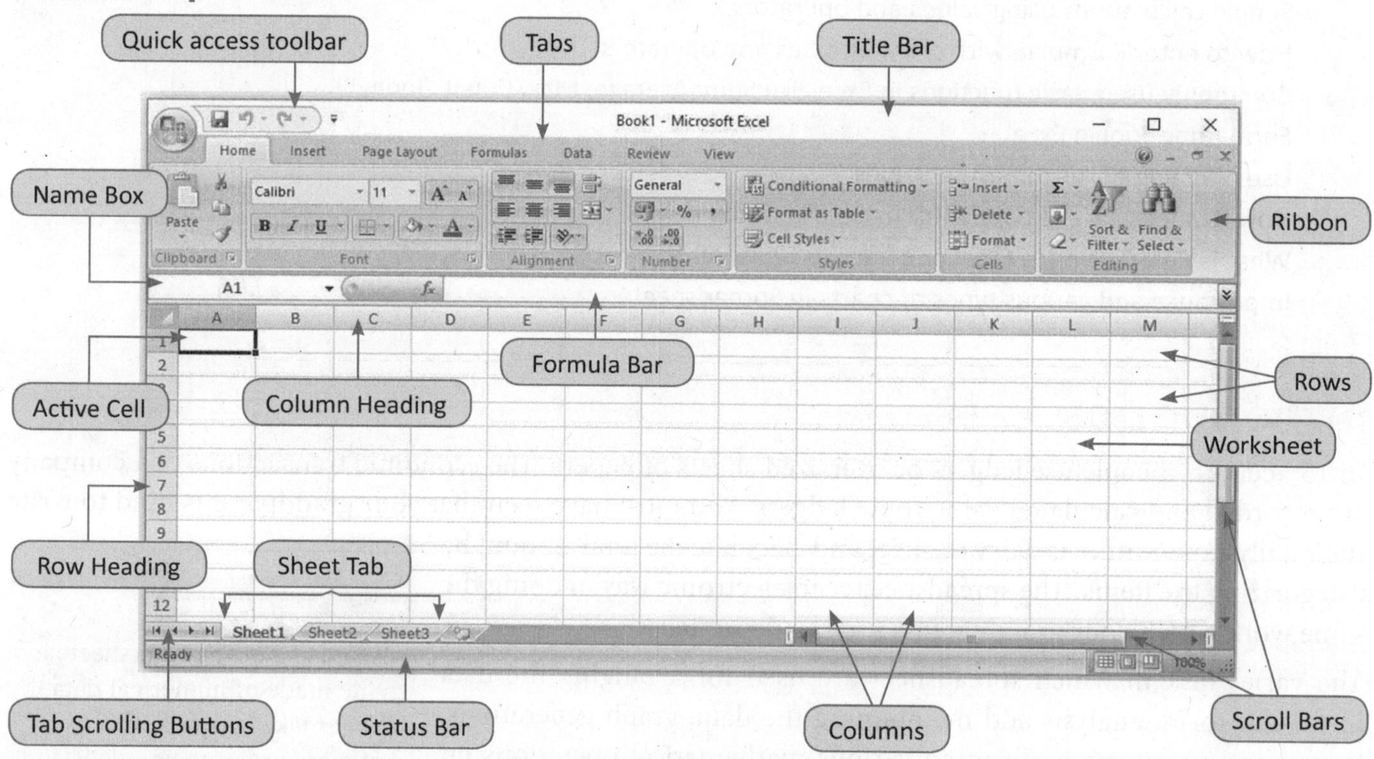

Figure 4.1: MS Excel 2010 File

Other name of MS excel file is Workbook in which user will write or store their data. There are by default three worksheet in each workbook whose count can be increased. The workbook is like a notebook and worksheet are like pages in it. At one time only one sheet can be made as Active worksheet and its name is appear in bottom left side with bold. There are number of rows and columns that make a worksheet. Various other components of Excel application window are:

Title Bar: On top and middle of excel window there is title bar. Both the name of program and its currently used document name is display on it. It also contains minimize, maximize and Close buttons.

Quick access toolbar: It is located in the top left side of title bar. The frequently used common buttons are present on it. Redo, Undo and save are three buttons that are present by default on it. We can remove or add other button through the drop down arrow present on it

Tabs: Below the title bar there is tabs that contains various group of command used to work in word. Some of the tabs in excel are home, insert, page layout, formulas, Data, review, view.

Ribbon: On clicking of any tab a ribbon appears. It contains tab, groups and commands. On top of ribbon button there are 7 tabs that contains groups of related commands. All related commands are organized in groups. As shown the figure the font contains its group of commands, clipboard contains commands related to it, etc. Within each group there are commands. By default the home tab appears after launching the word.

Name Box: Active cell name is present in Name box that is located on left side before the Formula box in top of worksheet.

Formula Bar: In formula bar user can directly enter the formulae or data or click on cell that contains formula then it will start appearing on formula bar. It is located in right side of Name box.

Scrollbar: It helps in page down or up and left or right the work window by which we can check the not visible part on the window. There are two types of scrollbars name as horizontal and vertical. The horizontal bar helps in navigating from left to right and it is present in bottom above the status bar. Other type is vertical bar that is present in right and used to navigate the document from top to bottom.

Status Bar: Below the horizontal scrollbar there is status bar that gives working worksheet status like sheet number, active working mode, zoom functioning along with other spreadsheet related important information.

Sheet Tabs: The sheet tabs are available on left bottom side of excel file. By defaults there are three sheets name as Sheet1, Sheet2 and Sheet3. The particular worksheet become active by clicking on it from bottom sheet tabs. More sheets can be added in it by clicking on inserting worksheet given next to Sheet3. The name of these sheets can be changed by right click on name of particular sheet and selecting rename option or by double clicking on name and entering the required name in it.

Quick access toolbar: It is located on the top left side of the title bar. The frequently used common buttons are present on it. We can remove or add another button through the drop-down arrow present on it.

Toolbars: There are by default two toolbars in Excel that provide a wide range of common commands and functions. A tooltip or small box is displayed by placing the mouse cursor over any icon.

- **Standard toolbar:** It shows the icons for most common operations such as editing, arranging, filtering, and more.
- **Formatting toolbar:** It consists of most common operations related to datasheet formatting such as font selection, size of text, alignment, cell value formatting and indentation, and more.

Control buttons: On the top right side of the Title bar, there are control buttons such as minimize, maximize, and close.

Column and row heading: The column and row heading are the names of rows and columns.

Active cell: A thick black color boundary appears on the cell when we click on it that makes it different from non-active cells. Users can enter or edit data only inactive cells. The name given to this highlighted box is the cell pointer.

Definition Box

The toolbar, also called bar or standard toolbar, is a row of boxes, often at the top of an application window, that control various functions of the software. The boxes often contain images that correspond with the function they control.

Skill Test Box

1. ____________ is located below the title bar.
2. The content of the selected cell is display on __________.
3. ____________ help in page down or up and left or right the work window by which we can check the not visible part on the window.
4. ______________ consists of commands to manipulate data such as define range, sort, calculate, data provider, and more.

Worksheet: Worksheet is a grid that consists of number of rows and columns in which data is enter by user. By default there are three worksheet in Excel, name as Sheet 1, Sheet2 and Sheet3 displayed at bottom left side. In case of working with huge data further sheets can be added in it by clicking on insert worksheet button given in figure 4.2. Rows run from left to right or horizontally and columns run from up to down or vertically.

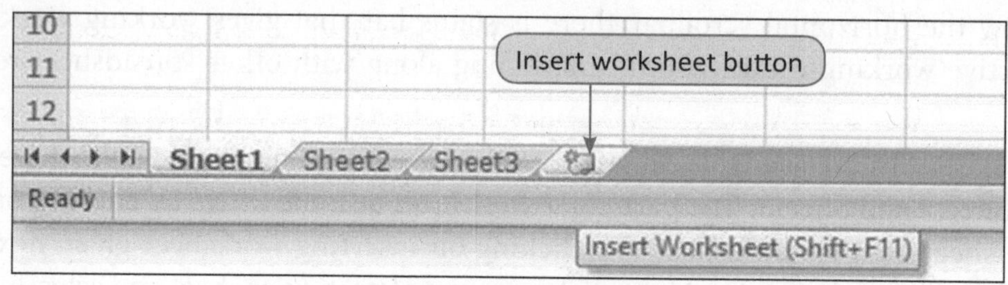

Figure 4.2: Insert worksheet button

Cell: Cell is a intersection of row and column. Number of cells makes a worksheet. Each row is identified by row number and column number that is known as address of cell. For e.g., A1, B2, N6, etc. User can enter data, text, formulas and number in each cell and upto 32767 characters can be come single cells.

Row: In excel rows are horizontal arrangement of cells and it is numbered in numerical digit start from 1, 2, 3, 4, 5 and so on.

Column: In excel columns are align vertically and alphabets are assigned to it start from A, B, C, so on.

Row header: On left hand side of sheet there is numeric number starts from 1 known as row header. It ranges from 1 to 1048576.

Column header: On top border of sheet there is alphabets starts from A and go first go from A to Z, AA… AZ, BA, BB, BC…..BZ, CA,. There are 16384 columns in every worksheet in Excel.

Active Cell: A thick black color boundary appears on cell when we click on it that makes it different from non-active cells. User can enter or edit data only in active cell. The name given to this highlighted box is Cell pointer.

Definition Box

A Worksheet is a collection of cells organized in rows and columns. It is the working surface you interact with to enter data. Each worksheet contains 1048576 rows and 16384 columns and serves as a giant table that allows you to organize information. Typically, a workbook contains several worksheets with related content and only one of the worksheets is active at a time.

LETS KNOW MORE

Users can enter data, text, formulas, and numbers in each cell, and up to 32767 characters can become single cells.

Skill Test Box

1. What is the Range of column header?
2. What is the Range of Row header?
3. Define the cell address?

Range of cells

It is the block of adjacent cells in a worksheet that is highlight.

- **Column Range:** It is the number of cells selected or spread across the column. In this case the cell address is represented by single column letter and multiple row number in a sequence. In below figure the column letter C is constant with rows varying from 5 to 13. In this case the range of cells starts with C4 and ends in C13 that consists of cells C5, C6, C7, C8, C9, C10, C11, C12, and C13. The range of cell can also be represented by C5:C13.

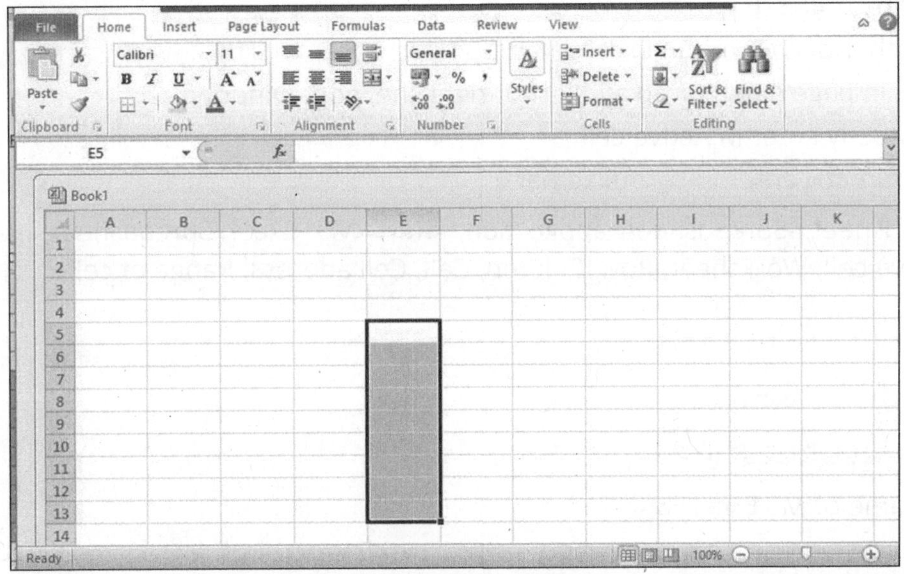

Figure 4.3: Column range

- **Row Range:** It is the number of cells selected or spread across the row. In this case the row address is represented by single row number and multiple columns in a sequence. In below figure the row number 11 is constant with columns varying from B to E. In this case the range of cells starts with B11 and ends in E11 that consists of cells B11, C11, D11 and E11. The range of cell can also be represented by B11:E11.

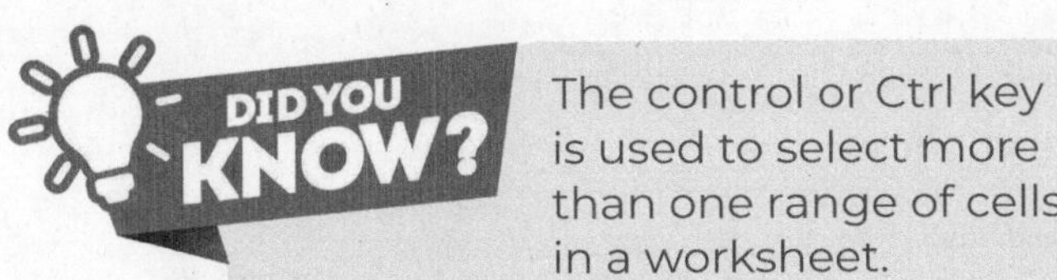

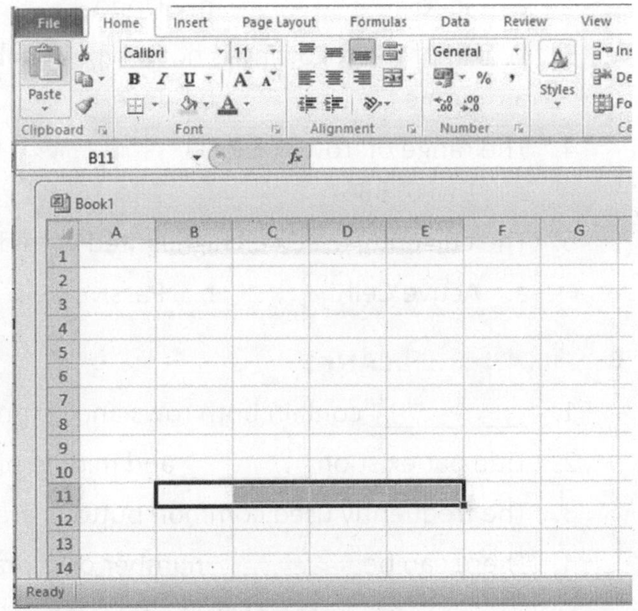

Figure 4.4: Row range

Summary

- To launch the spreadsheet program, Click on Start > Click on all programs > Microsoft Office > Microsoft Excel 2010
- Workbook is the another name of MS excel file used by users to write and store their data
- On top and middle of word window there is title bar.
- Quick access toolbar is located in the top left side of title bar.
- There are eight Tabs in MS excel
- Ribbon appears on clicking of any tab and it contains various tabs, groups and commands
- Worksheet is a grid consist of rows and columns in which data is enter
- Cell is a intersection of rows and column
- Rows are horizontal arrangement of Cells
- Column is the vertical arrangement of cells
- Limits of row are 1048576
- Maximum number of columns in Excel are 16384
- Scrollbar helps in page down or up and left or right the work window
- Data can be directly enter in Active cell
- Formulae can directly enter in Formulae bar

Keywords: Spreadsheet, Spreadsheet application, Start MS Excel Spreadsheet, Parts of MS Excel Spreadsheet, Active cell, Worksheet, Row, Column, Cell, Cell address, Range of cells.

Self-Assessment

A. MULTIPLE CHOICE QUESTIONS.

1. Another name of MS Excel is:
   a. MS Word b. Worksheet c. Workbook d. Table sheet
2. Which of the following is not a default commands of Quick access toolbar:
   a. Redo b. Undo c. Quick print d. Save
3. Which of the following is not a type of tab available on ribbon?
   a. Home b. Insert c. Editing d. Formulas
4. The range of row in Excel?
   a. 1 to 65536 b. 1 to 16384 c. 1 to 32767 d. 1 to 1048576
5. The currently used cell highlighted with dark boundary is known as?
   a. Active Cell b. Passive Cell c. New Cell d. Current cell

B. FILL IN THE BLANKS

1. ___________ contain both rows and column.
2. Title bar exist on _________ and middle of excel window
3. The frequently used common buttons are present on ___________
4. There can be _________ number of characters in single cells
5. ___________ is the default name of workbook in MS Excel.

C. TRUE FALSE

1. Theme is a Tab in Excel (T/F)
2. A cell consists of single row and multiple columns (T/F)
3. By default there are three number of worksheets available in MS Excel 2010 (T/F)
4. Cell can be identified with unique row number and column number (T/F)

D. ANSWER THE FOLLOWING QUESTIONS:

1. Explain Spreadsheet in detail along with count of default number of sheets.
2. What is Microsoft Excel?
3. Name four existing popular spreadsheet software?
4. Write down the steps to launch a workbook?
5. What is cell and its range?
6. Differentiate row and a column?
7. What is the functioning of scrollbar
8. Explain the status bar?

E. PRACTICAL WORK

1. Open a MS Excel, Identify all the components and use some of the commands of four groups in each tab, Write text in active cell and observe it
2. Make a spreadsheet or copy it from any source that contain huge database. Check the range of cell and column in it.

ANSWER:

A. Multiple choice question answers:

1. c   2. c   3. c   4. d   5. a

B. Fill in the blanks answers:

1. Worksheet
2. lop
3. Quick access toolbar
4. 32767
5. Book1

C. True False answers:

1. False   2. False   3. True   4. True

SESSION 2: MANAGING A WORKBOOK

This session help reader to open, save and close the worksheet along with deleting the existing worksheet.

Creating A New Workbook

A blank spreadsheet or workbook is appears on starting the MS Excel that contains by default three worksheets. But sometimes there is requirement of creating a new workbook for this follow the steps:

Click on File tab > New > Blank Workbook > Create

Or

Click on drop down arrow of Customize quick access Toolbars > New

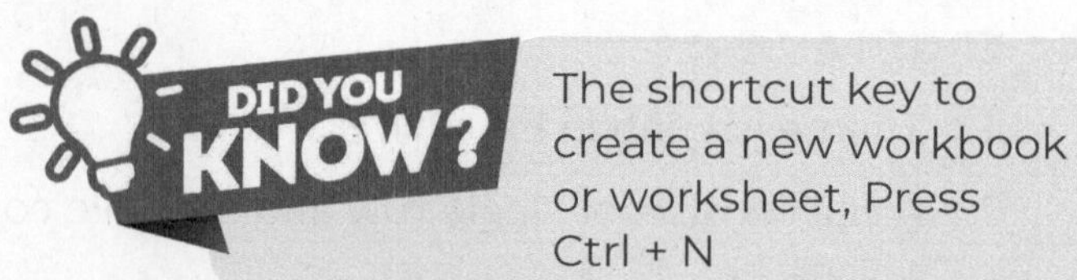

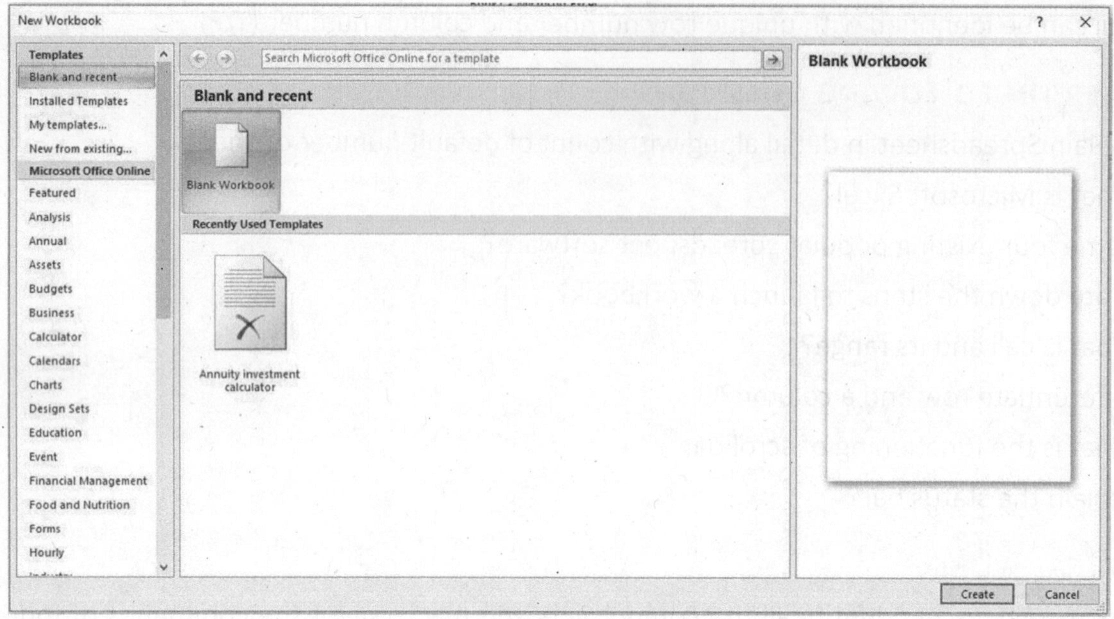

Figure 4.5: Opening new Blank workbook

The default name of workbook will be Book1 in case if name of previous workbook has been changed from book1 otherwise the name of new workbook will be Book2.

Inserting A Worksheet

As mentioned above by default there is only three worksheets in workbook. In case of entering a large amount of data there is need of more sheets. In Excel 2010 we can add number of worksheets according to our requirements. To insert a worksheet follow the steps:

Right click on Sheet3 > select Insert option > Worksheet > OK

When we right click on sheet3 then various options come from which select the Insert option. After clicking on Insert, a insert dialog box will appear select worksheet and then click on OK button given in the right bottom.

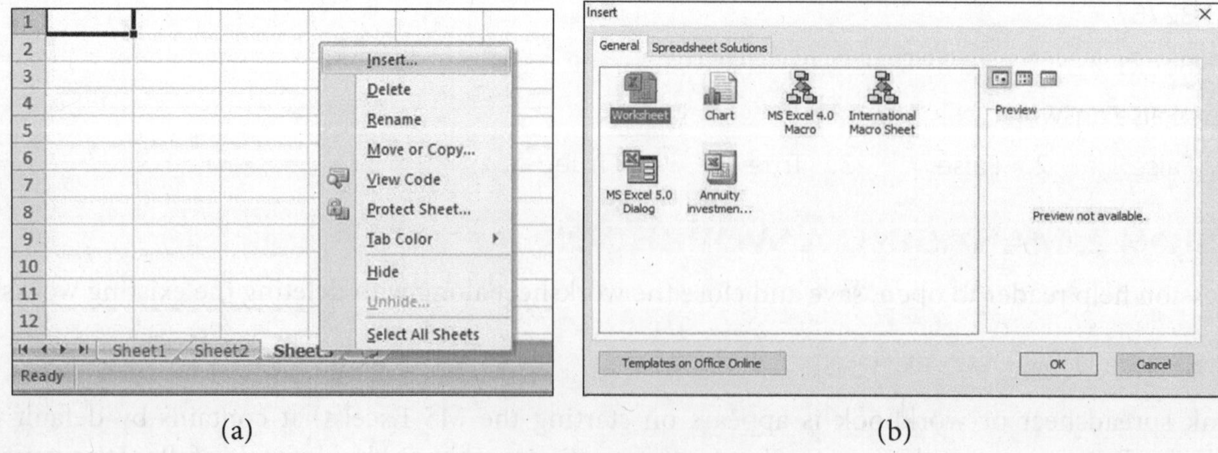

Figure 4.6: Insertion of New Worksheet

Or

Click on Insert worksheet button present next to Sheet3 tab

Saving A Worksheet

We have created a workbook or worksheet in previous section now next part is to save it. To save a worksheet or workbook follows the steps:

Click on File > Save > Select the location from given list in the left of Save As dialog box > Enter name in file name text box

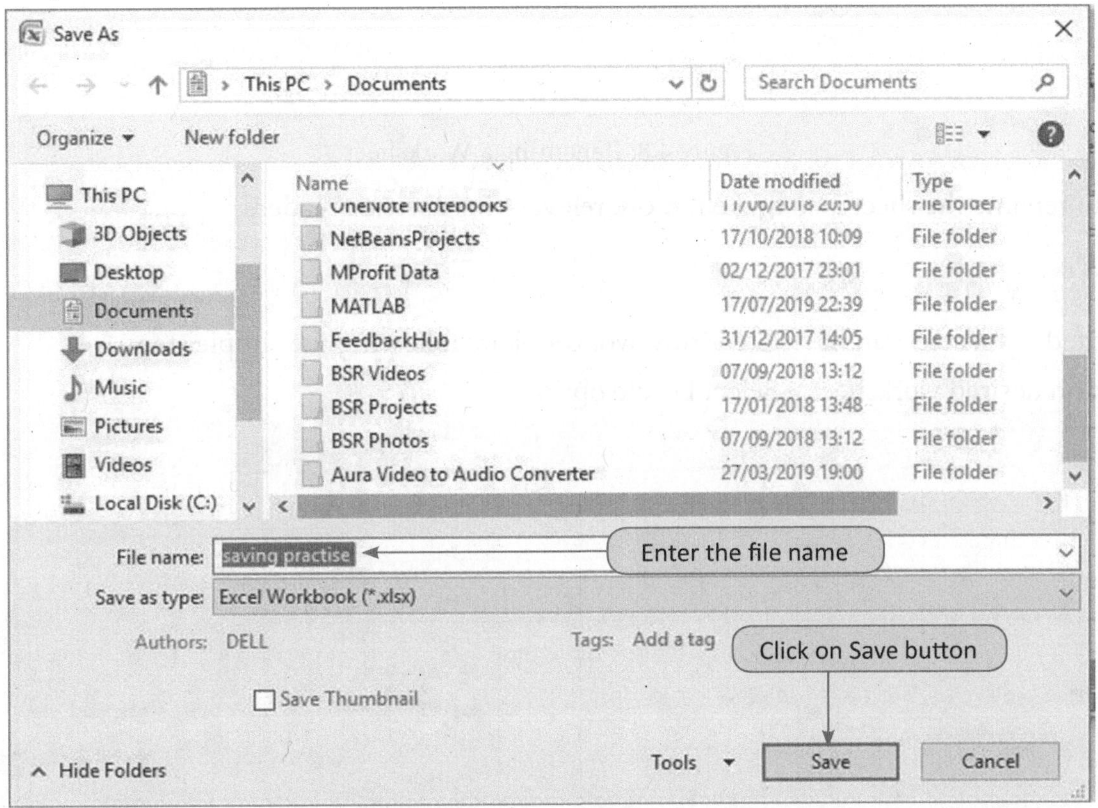

Figure 4.7: Saving a Workbook or Worksheet

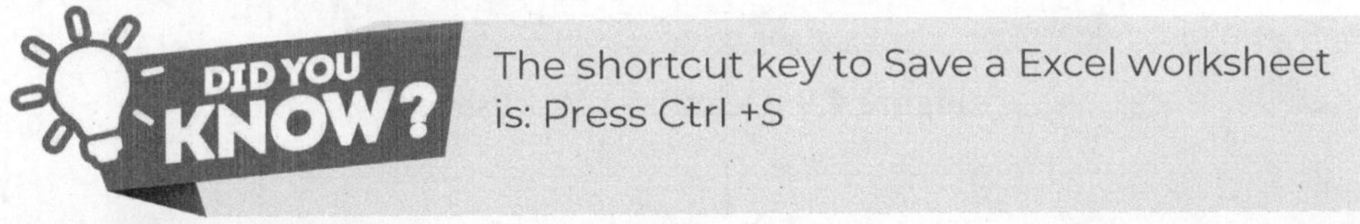

Renaming A Worksheet

In last section we have learned to save a workbook or worksheet and renaming it while saving. In Excel 2010 we can also rename the worksheet by simply following the steps:

Double click on the sheet tab given in bottom left side > Type a name > Press Enter button given on keyboard

Or

Right click on sheet tab > select rename option > Assign new name by typing on it

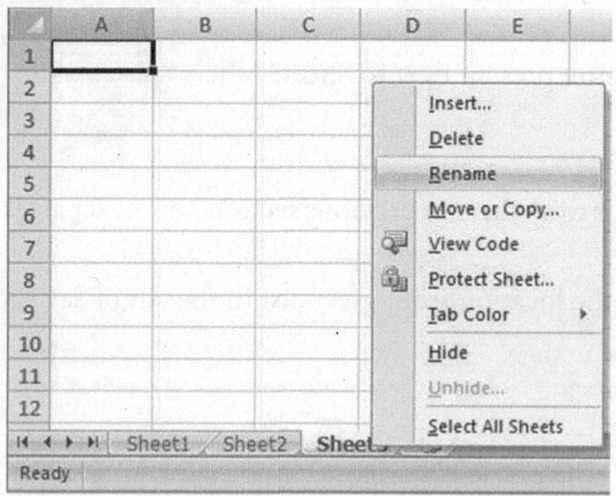

Figure 4.8: Renaming a Worksheet

The need to rename the sheet is to make it more relevant for users or readers.

Deleting A Worksheet

The unwanted worksheet can be deleted from workbook by following the simple steps:

Right click on desired worksheet > Select Delete option

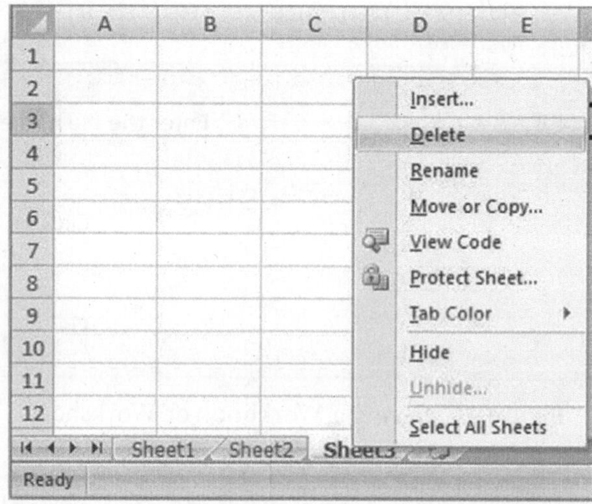

Figure 4.9: Deleting a Worksheet

Or

Select the sheet tab given below in left side of worksheet > Click on delete option given in Cells group of Home tab

Once you have followed any of the above given step a sheet will get deleted from your workbook.

Move A Worksheet

The worksheet can be copy or move within a workbook or between workbooks. To copy or move a worksheet performs the following steps:

Right click on desired sheet tab > Select Move or Copy option

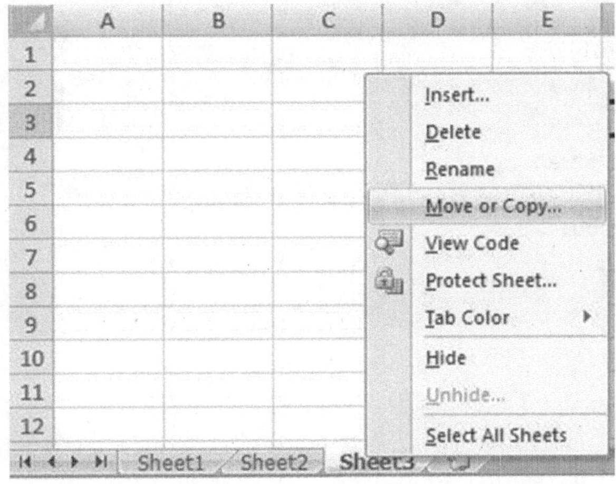

Figure 4.10: Move or Copy a Worksheet

Once you have selected the Move and copy option its dialog box will come and further there are two approaches that can be used one is to move worksheet within a workbook and other is between workbook.

To move worksheet within the same workbook

To perform the task of moving worksheet within the same workbook:

Select the worksheet from the list before which you want to move the worksheet > click OK

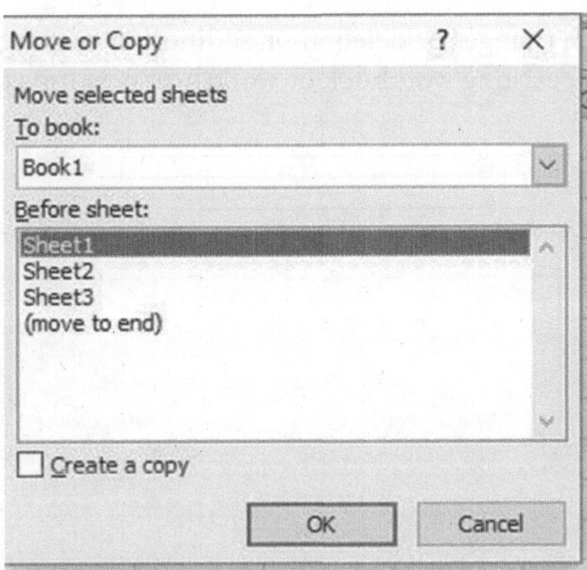

Figure 4.11: Move or Copy dialog box

This will move the worksheet is desired place. Another option to perform the same task is by simply dragging sheet tab and drop it into a desired place.

To move worksheet Between two workbook

To perform the task of moving worksheet from one workbook to another, perform the following steps:

Click on To book drop down list > Choose new book option > Click on OK

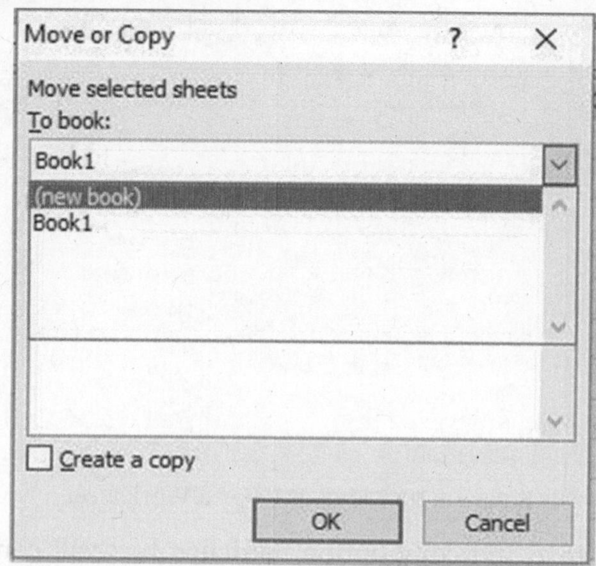

Figure 4.12: Move or Copy to another workbook

Once you will done with performing the above given steps and press Ok in last then you will see a new workbook with the name of book2 that contains the worksheet selected to move.

Opening Of Existing Workbook Or Worksheet

When there is need to do some changes or deletion or addition in existing workbook or worksheet then you have to open it. To open an existing workbook or worksheet performs the following steps:

Click on File > Open

Or

Click on Open button from drop down arrow of Customize quick access Toolbar

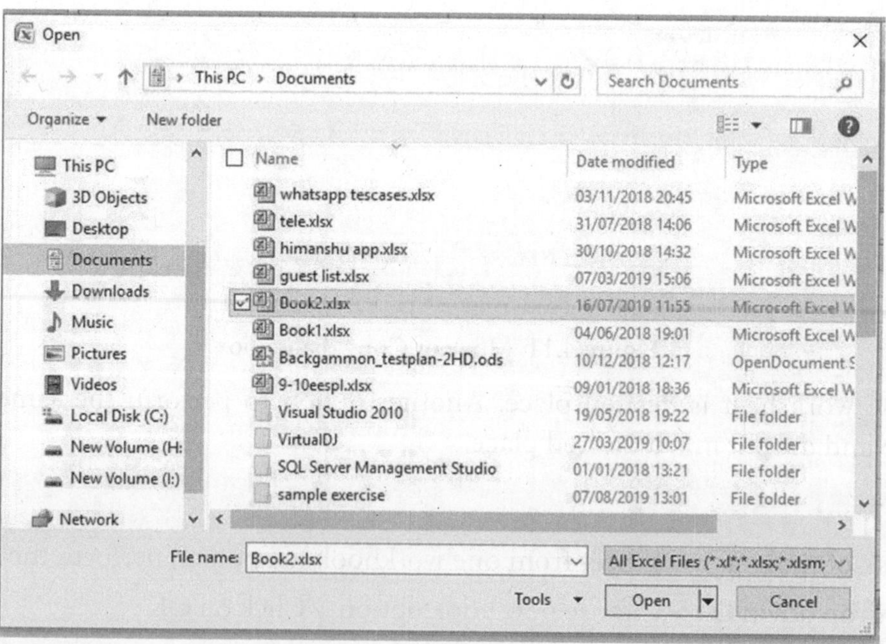

Figure 4.13: Open dialog box

In all the cases user have to select their file by opening the location from directories given in left side of dialog box. The select the file and click on Open button given in the right bottom of Open dialog box.

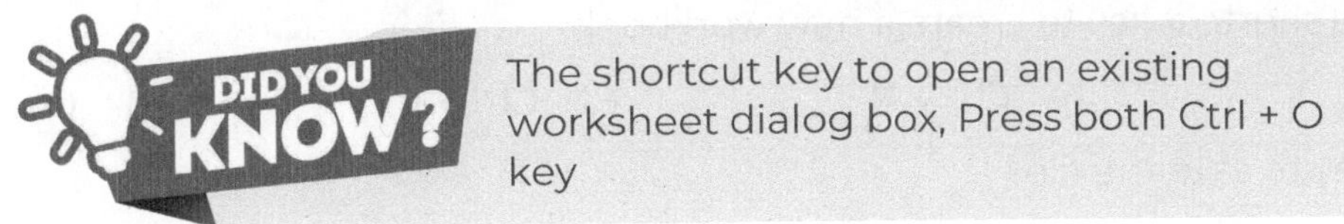

The shortcut key to open an existing worksheet dialog box, Press both Ctrl + O key

Closing Of Opened Workbook Or Worksheet

When user is done with the entire task on worksheet or workbook and saved all data then next step will be close the workbook. In order to close the workbook performs the following steps:

Click on File Tab > Close

Or

Click on cross button given on the right upper corner of title bar. This will exist the MS Excel 2010.

In case if that file is not saved previously then a dialog box will pop-out that gives option of yes, no and cancel button to save, don't save and cancel the task respectively.

The shortcut key to Close an existing worksheet, Press both Ctrl + W

Summary

- Extension of MS excel file is .xlsx.
- To create a new workbook, Click on File tab > New > Blank Workbook > Create
- Ctrl + N is the shortcut key to create new workbook
- By default sheet1 is the active worksheet
- To insert a worksheet, Right click on Sheet3 > select Insert option > Worksheet > OK or click on Insert worksheet button present next to Sheet3 tab or Press Shift + F11
- To save a workbook or worksheet, Click on File > Save > Select the location from given list in the left of Save As dialog box > Enter name in file name text box
- To rename a worksheet, Double click on the sheet tab given in bottom left side > Type a name > Press Enter button given on keyboard or Right click on sheet tab > select rename option > Assign new name by typing on it
- To delete a worksheet, Right click on desired worksheet > Select Delete option
- To move a worksheet, Right click on desired sheet tab > Select Move or Copy option
- To move worksheet between two workbook, Click on To book drop down list > Choose new book option > Click on OK
- To open existing workbook or Worksheet, Click on File > Open or Click on Open button from drop down arrow of Customize quick access Toolbar Or press CTRL + O key
- To close a workbook, Click on File Tab > Close Or Press both Ctrl + W

Keywords: Creating a new workbook, Inserting a worksheet, Saving a worksheet, Renaming a worksheet, Deleting a worksheet, Moving a worksheet, Opening an existing worksheet, Closing an opened worksheet.

Self-Assessment

A. MULTIPLE CHOICE QUESTIONS

1. Extension of MS Excel file is:

   a. .xcl b. .doc c. .xlxs d. .xlsx

2. What is the shortcut key to create a new workbook:

   a. Ctrl + C b. Ctrl + N c. Ctrl + P d. Ctrl + W

3. Shortcut key to save the file?

   a. Ctrl + A b. Ctrl + C c. Ctrl + S d. Ctrl + N

B. FILL IN THE BLANKS

1. A cell can be activate by ___________.
2. _________ is the shortcut key to open a workbook
3. You can close the file by clicking on File > ________ option

C. TRUE FALSE

1. Theme is a Tab in Excel (T/F)
2. A cell consists of single row and multiple columns (T/F)
3. By default there are three number of worksheets available in MS Excel 2010 (T/F)
4. Cell can be identified with unique row number and column number (T/F)
5. A new worksheet can be added in the workbook (T/F)

D. ANSWER THE FOLLOWING QUESTIONS:

1. How to create a new workbook and add worksheet in it.
2. How formula bar can be used to enter the data in Active cell?
3. Write down the steps of various methods to add a worksheet in workbook?
4. Gives the various option of renaming the worksheet?
5. Describe the process of saving a workbook and what happen when user close the workbook without saving it?
6. Write down the steps of deleting a worksheet?

E. PRACTICAL WORK

Open a MS Excel, Insert new worksheet, add data given below in table, Save it with your name, Close it, Reopen it, delete the worksheet then again close it using shortcut key

Student name	Roll No.	Age
Komal	12	13
Simran	13	12
Gurutek	14	13
Harshan	15	13

ANSWER:

A. Multiple choice question answers:

   1. d 2. b 3. c

B. Fill in the blanks answers:

   1. Clicking on Cell

2. Ctrl + O
3. Close

C. True False answers:

1. False 2. False 3. True 4. True 5. True

SESSION 3: ENTER AND EDIT THE TEXT IN SPREADSHEET

Entering Data in Worksheet

In MS Excel spreadsheet or worksheet, there is need to select the cell before entering data in worksheet or cell. To select a cell simply position the pointer in that particular cell. You can enter label, values or formula data in the cell.

- **Label:** It is any text that can be letters, numbers and special symbols that entered using keyboard. By default labels are aligned in left side.

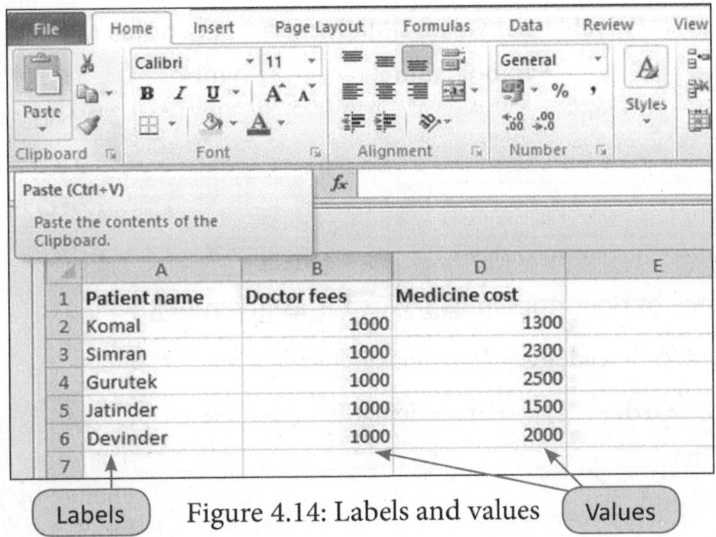

	A	B	D	E
1	Patient name	Doctor fees	Medicine cost	
2	Komal	1000	1300	
3	Simran	1000	2300	
4	Gurutek	1000	2500	
5	Jatinder	1000	1500	
6	Devinder	1000	2000	
7				

Figure 4.14: Labels and values

- **Values:** It is the numeric data consists of only numbers. By defaults they are aligned on right side. Various forms of values are integer, decimal, etc.
- **Formulae:** It is the expression that begins with an equals "=" sign. Formula is always start by "=" and followed by values, cell address and functions. After entering the formula in a cell, then the value of the equation is displayed in the cell and formulas bar contains the formula.

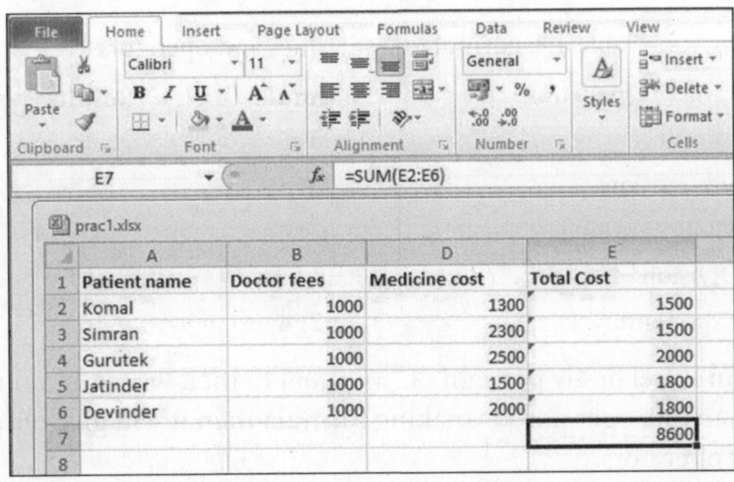

	A	B	D	E
1	Patient name	Doctor fees	Medicine cost	Total Cost
2	Komal	1000	1300	1500
3	Simran	1000	2300	1500
4	Gurutek	1000	2500	2000
5	Jatinder	1000	1500	1800
6	Devinder	1000	2000	1800
7				8600
8				

Figure 4.15: Expressions as Formula

LETS KNOW MORE

The preceding zero is not displayed in values. To display preceding "0" or zero, there is a need to specify the data type as Text.

Skill Test Box

Fill the correct answer in the blanks given below:

1. _______________ are aligned on the right side.
2. _______________ are aligned on the left side.
3. _____________ is the expression that begins with an equals (=) sign.

Mathematical operators used in Formulae

In Excel or spreadsheet software there is most powerful features by which user can calculate numerical data by applying various formulae. Formulas are simply equations that perform calculations on values in our sheet. This can include numbers, parenthesis, cell address and arithmetic operators and result will be displayed on the cell where user has entered the formula. In this section we deal with performing various operations using formulas.

Table 4.1: Various Mathematical operation

Operation	Symbol Name	Symbol	Example
Addition	Plus sign	+	B2+C2, B3+6
Subtraction	Minus sign	-	B2-C2
Multiplication	Asterisk	*	C2*D2
Division	Forward slash	/	C2/D2

Precedence: The precedence of operators in MS Word is as given below:

Table 4.2: Precedence of various operation

Order	Precedence
First	( )
Second	^
Third	/, *
Fourth	+, -

LETS KNOW MORE

The order of evaluation can be change by putting that expression in brackets. As the expressions within the brackets will be evaluated first.

Simple calculations using values and operators

In above section we have given few operations along with examples. Formula can include one or more than one mathematical operator.

Table 4.3: Formula using values and operators

Operation	Formula	Results
Addition	=3+5	8
Subtraction	=13 – 5	8
Multiplication	=5*7	35
Division	=8 / 2	4
Exponential	=2^4	16

To evaluate any formula in Excel firstly put sign of "=" equal to then write the values along with operators. You can also use more than one operator for making formula then it will give output by doing calculation according to the order of operators.

Table 4.4: Changes in results after addition of bracket

Formula	Evaluation	Results
=3+5*6	=3+30	33
=(3+5)*6	=8*6	48
=5*7^2	=5*14	70
=(5*7)^2	35^2	1225

Skill Test Box

What is the output of given equation:

1. 4 + 6*7
2. (5*7)^2
3. 3 + 6

Formulae with cell addresses and operators

In Excel or spreadsheet you can also enter formulae with cell addresses and operators as like values and operators. The main advantage of using cell addresses instead of values is that the results obtained by the formulae will gets updated by change in the values of concerned cells.

MEMORY BOX

For example to perform addition between two cells B1 and B2 and result of addition in B3, if you use 5+6 where 5 is the value of cell B1 and 6 is the value of cell B2 then addition in B3 will be 11 but if you put 7 in cell B2 instead of 6 then you have to again change the values in cell B3 but in case of using cell address the formula in cell B3 = B1+ B2. Now if you change the value of either cell B1 and B2 then the result in B3 cell will be updated automatically.

Addition:

There is only operator involve in basic formula. The steps need to perform for addition in Excel is:

Open the spreadsheet > Enter the required data > Enter the cell name in the cell where you want the answer with + sign in between and = in starting

Below figures show the data of patient in hospital that includes the column of patient name, doctor fee, nurse fee, medicine cost and total amount. In the end we have to put the sum of total cost for each patient in column E. To perform addition write the formula in column E2, =B2+C2+D2. Or another option is typing the formula in formula box given below the ribbon.

There are two figures name as a and b. The figure 4.16 a part shows the data enter by user and figure b part shows the data along with formula use to add all the data in row 2. Same formula by change in cell name can be used to perform addition on rest of the rows. Once you have typed the formula in cell press enter and addition answer will be displayed on that cell.

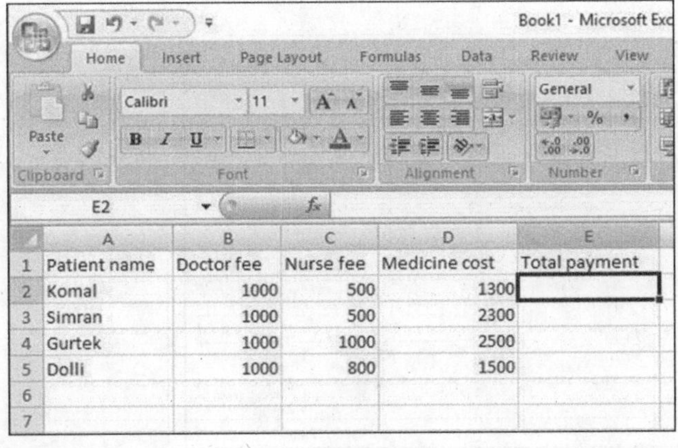

(a)

(b)

Figure 4.16: Basic addition formula

User don't have to write formula again and again for every row, simply copy the formula written for one row into another row and it will change the row number by itself to give addition. Same like this way addition of all the rows and columns can be obtain.

Subtraction:

In this section we will learn to perform subtraction on data. The steps need to perform the subtraction in worksheet are:

Open the spreadsheet program > Enter the required data > Enter the cell name in the cell where you want the answer with - sign in between and = in starting

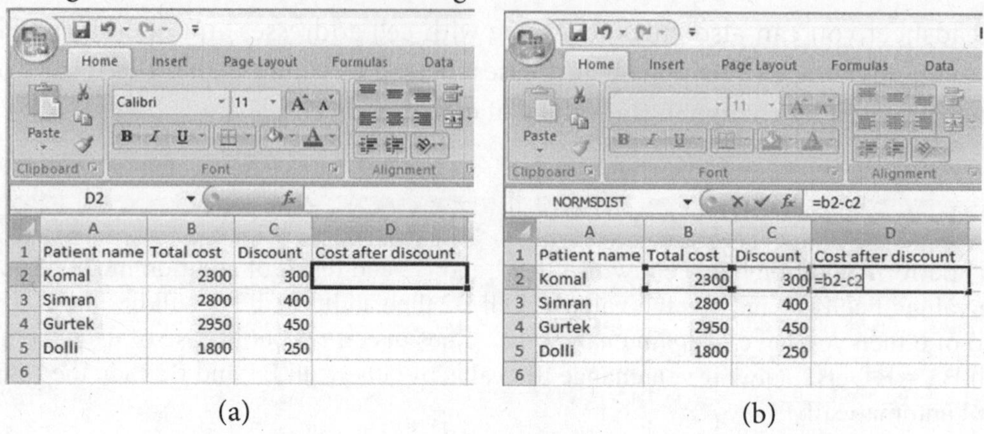

(a) (b)

Figure 4.17: Basic Subtraction formula

First enter the data in worksheet as given in figure 4.17 a part then to get the final cost after discount enter the formula by typing cell name separated by – sign. This will give the difference of cells. Like in case of addition, a subtraction can be perform by copying the formula written in particular cell to another cell.

Or

Another option simply type = sign in required cell then click on cell on which you want to perform the calculation this will add that cell name after the = sign in particular cell where user want the answer. After that add the – sign to perform subtraction and select another cell on which you want to perform subtraction.

Multiplication:

The (*) sign is used to perform the multiplication on data given in the worksheet. To perform multiplication on required data in excel sheet perform the following steps:

Open the spreadsheet program > Enter the required data > Go to the cell in which you want the answer > Type the cell name separated with * sign

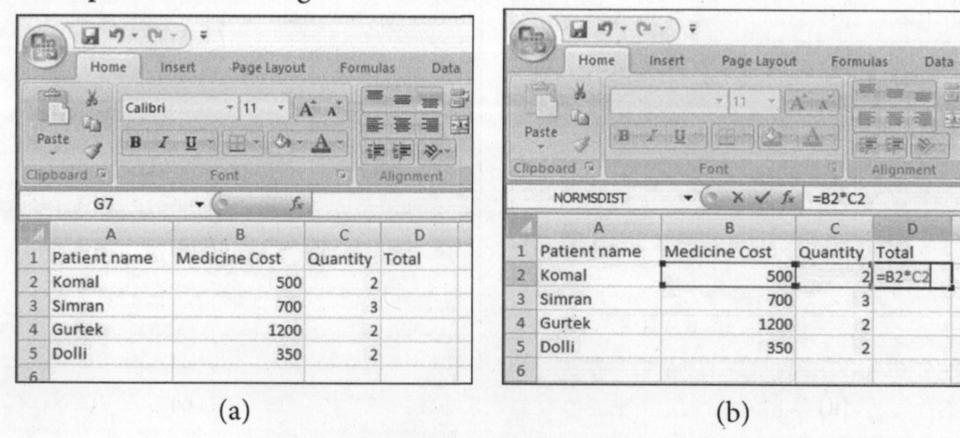

(a) (b)

Figure 4.18: Basic Multiplication formula

Enter the required cell name in cell D2 separated with * sign. For example to get the total medicine cost of patient komal, enter = B2 * C2 in cell D2. Same will be repeated for rest of the cells.

Division:

The same above given steps will be followed for division except the * sign will be replaced with (/) sign.

Same like this way compound formula can be used to perform calculation. In order to perform the simple interest user need to perform both multiplication and division. In these kind of cases both are combined to get the final result.

USING SIMPLE FUNCTIONS

In Excel there are predefined formulas that can be used to perform the required calculations. In above method where we type formulas to perform the various calculations there will be more chances of error. Arguments are accepted by it and in return it will give values. Arguments and Structure are two parts that make a complete function.

The input values to function is known as arguments that can be a text, numbers, logical values, formulas or range of a cell written in between the parenthesis.

On other hand basic skeleton is defined by structure part that makes the basis of writing a general function or its syntax. The syntax is:

=FUNCTION NAME(argument1, argument2, ...)

SUM( )

Just like + sign in basic formulas a SUM() function will add all the numbers given in the arguments between the parenthesis of sum function. Basic steps need to perform are:

Click on cell where you want to enter the result > Type =SUM(B2:B6) or =SUM(B2,B6)

These both function will give you the sum of data in cell B2 to B6. User can also enter the direct value in parenthesis instead of entering the cell name. For example =SUM(2,4,6)

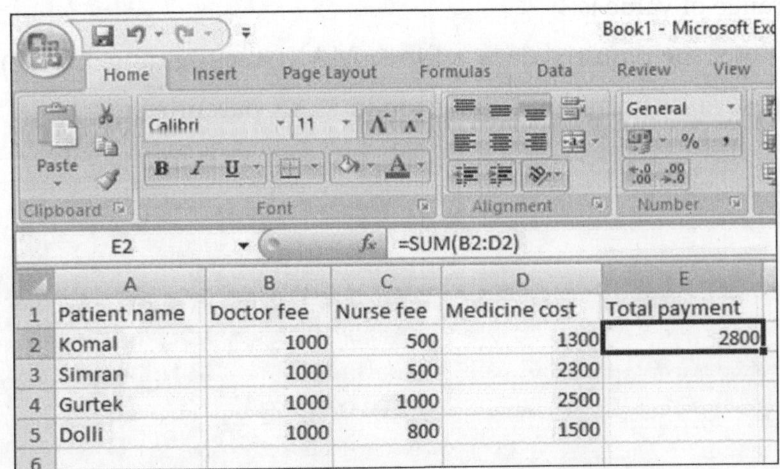

	A	B	C	D	E
1	Patient name	Doctor fee	Nurse fee	Medicine cost	Total payment
2	Komal	1000	500	1300	2800
3	Simran	1000	500	2300	
4	Gurtek	1000	1000	2500	
5	Dolli	1000	800	1500	
6					

Figure 4.19: Addition using SUM function

AVERAGE( )

The arithmetic mean and average of the arguments is return by AVERAGE function. In arguments user can enter the range of cells, direct numbers, both numbers and cell reference. For example:

AVERAGE(B2:B6)

Or

AVERGAE(B2,B6)

Or

AVERAGE(1,4,3)

Or

AVERAGE(B2:D2,B3:D3) : In this we have given two ranges of cells. It will return the average for cell B2 to D2 and B3 to D3 as given in below figure 13.

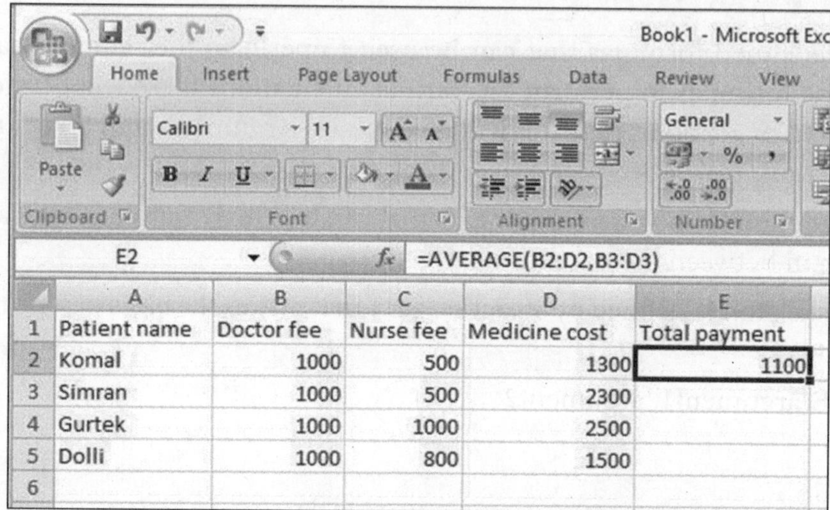

E2 =AVERAGE(B2:D2,B3:D3)

	A	B	C	D	E
1	Patient name	Doctor fee	Nurse fee	Medicine cost	Total payment
2	Komal	1000	500	1300	1100
3	Simran	1000	500	2300	
4	Gurtek	1000	1000	2500	
5	Dolli	1000	800	1500	
6					

Figure 4.20: Average using AVERAGE function

MAX( )

The MAX function will return the largest value from specified arguments in parenthesis of MAX function. It accept only numeric data and logical values as arguments and return zero 0 in other cases. Steps to find the largest value from range of value is:

Open the document > Enter the required data > Type –MAX(starting range: Ending range)

This will return the largest value from the range given in MAX parenthesis.

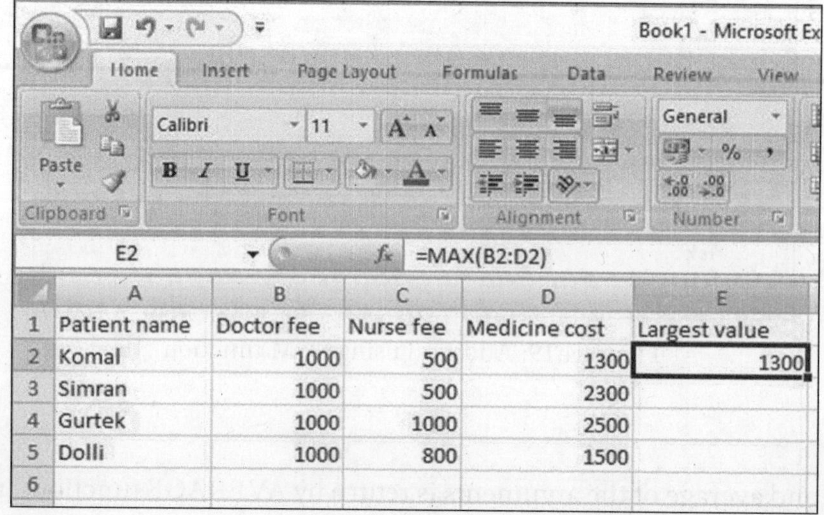

E2 =MAX(B2:D2)

	A	B	C	D	E
1	Patient name	Doctor fee	Nurse fee	Medicine cost	Largest value
2	Komal	1000	500	1300	1300
3	Simran	1000	500	2300	
4	Gurtek	1000	1000	2500	
5	Dolli	1000	800	1500	
6					

Figure 4.21: Largest value using MAX function

Same like MAX function a lowest value in the cell can be obtained using MIN function.

TODAY( )

The current date of particular cell can be display using the function TODAY( ).

Example type =TODAY() function in cell E3 it will display the date of E3 cell.

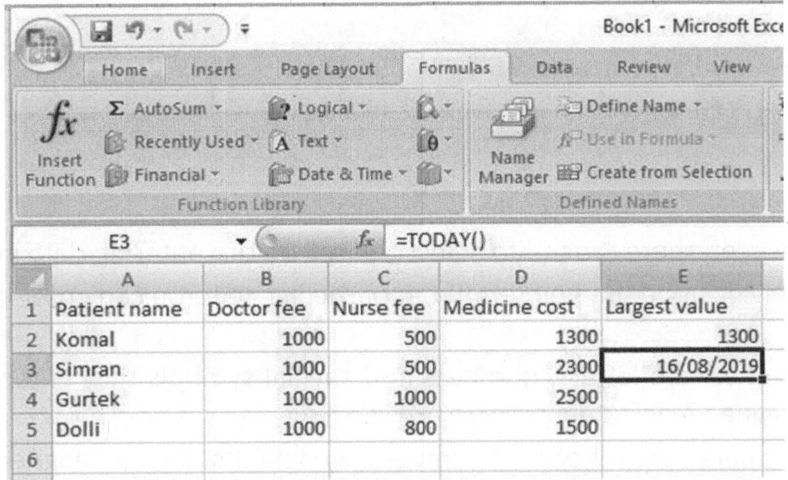

Figure 4.22: Current date of cell using TODAY function

This today function can also be using with other functions to get the current month, day and year. For example:

=DAY(TODAY()) function will return the current date in number form. To get the result in text form write =TEXT(TODAY(), "DDDD").

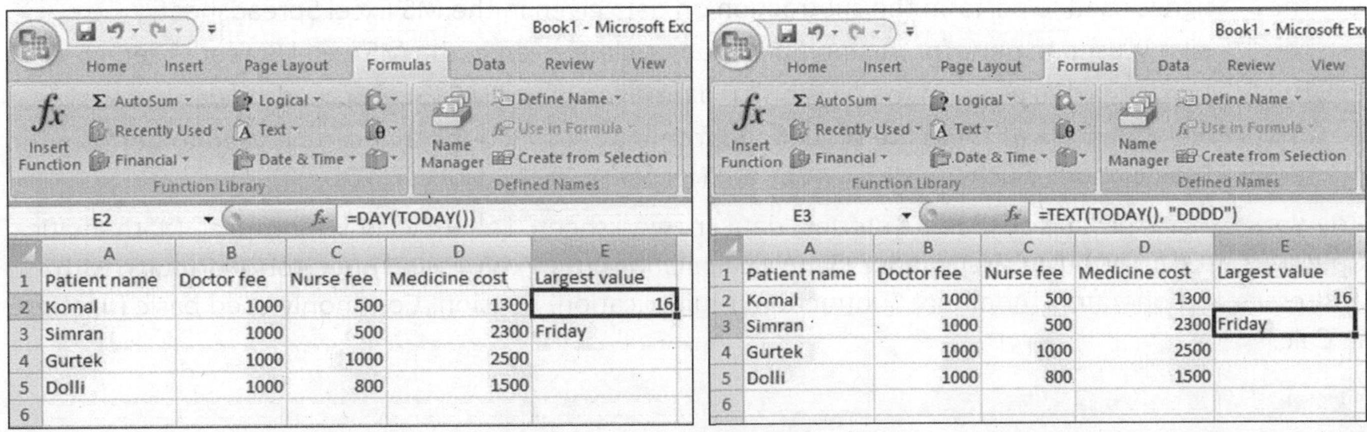

Figure 4.23: Current date and day

There is function library group in Formulas tab through which various operations can be performed.

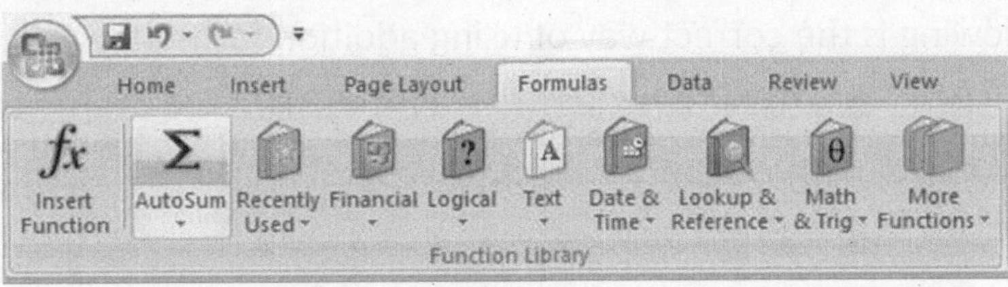

Figure 4.24: Function Library group

Skill Test Box

Choose the correct option from following options given under questions:

1. The Sum ( ) function and addition gives the same.
   a. True b. False
2. The Average ( ) function do the same operation as Division.
   a. True b. False
3. The Today( ) function will give the current date.
   a. True b. False

Summary

- In MS Excel Spreadsheet, there is need to select the cell before entering data in worksheet or cell.
- To select a cell simply position the pointer in that particular cell. You can enter label, values or formula data in the cell.
- Label is any text that can be letters, numbers and special symbols that entered using keyboard. By default labels are aligned in left side.
- Value is the numeric data consists of only numbers. By defaults they are aligned on right side. Various forms of values are integer, decimal, etc.
- Formula is the expression that begins with an equals "=" sign. Formula is always start by "=" and followed by values, cell address and functions.
- In MS Excel Spreadsheet or spreadsheet you can also enter formulae with cell addresses and operators as like values and operators.
- The "+" sign is used to perform the addition on data given in the MS Excel Spreadsheet.
- The "-" sign is used to perform the subtraction on data given in the MS Excel Spreadsheet.
- The "*" sign is used to perform the multiplication on data given in the MS Excel Spreadsheet.
- The "/" sign is used to perform the division on data given in the MS Excel Spreadsheet.
- In MS Excel Spreadsheet there are predefined formulas or functions that can be used to perform the required calculations. Such as SUM(), AVERAGE(), MAX(), MIN(), COUNT, TODAY().

Keywords: Edit the spreadsheet, Entering data in worksheet, Label, Values, Formula, Mathematical operators used in formulae, Precedence, Simple calculations using values and operators, Formulae with cell addresses and operators, Addition, Subtraction, Multiplication, Division, Commonly used basic functions in Calc.

Self-Assessment

A. MULTIPLE CHOICE QUESTIONS

1. Which of the following is the correct way of using addition formula:
   a. B2+C2 b. (B2+C2) c. =B2+C2 d. £B2+C2
2. The output of MAX(3, 2, 4, 8) will be:
   a. 3 b. 2 c. 4 d. 8
3. Which of the following is the correct way of using addition formula:
   a. B2+C2 b. (B2+C2) c. =B2+C2 d. £B2+C2

4. The Autosum command available in which group of Home tab:

   a. Clipboard b. Data c. Styles d. Editing

5. The name given to predefined formulas to Excel is ?

   a. Basic formula b. Formulas c. Formulae d. None

6. The output of MAX(3, 2, 4, 8) will be:

   a. 3 b. 2 c. 4 d. 8

B. FILL IN THE BLANKS

1. In Excel every formula begins with ________ sign.
2. ________ pair of brackets are used to denote a negative value in MS Excel
3. To perform calculations ________ expression cam be enter in the cell.
4. Output of A2-B2-C2, where A2= 7, B2=2 and C2=1 will be ________
5. The output of SUM(A1:A3),Where A1, A2 and A3 is 2, 3 and 5 respectively.
6. The formula to find the largest value for range of value between A2 to D2.
7. The AVERAGE(1,2,3) function will give________ of three numbers in parenthesis.
8. In Excel user can measure the day, ________ and date of particular cell

C. TRUE FALSE

1. The default position of number in cell is right (T/F)
2. Colons are used to separate seconds or hors in Excel (T/F)
3. Colons are used to separate seconds or hors in Excel (T/F)
4. The calculation can be perform on any type of data in Excel (T/F)
5. In Excel we can perform calculation on data given in range of cells using single instruction (T/F)
6. The output of C2/D2 is 2.5. Where C2 is 4 and D2 is 2
7. TODAY() function written in particular cell will give the time of it

D. QUESTIONS:

1. What is Label?
2. Define Values in Spreadsheet?
3. How to enter formula in Worksheet?
4. Write a short note on various mathematical operators used in Formulae?
5. How to perform simple calculations using Values and operators?
6. Give various commonly used Basic functions in Spreadsheet along with example of each.
7. Gives the name of type of data can enter in cells.
8. How negative number are define in excel?
9. What is a Formulae and its use?
10. What are the formats of writing date in cell? Give examples of each format.
11. Name the four basic mathematical operations supported by Excel.

12. Give example of using SUM function for addition of range of values.
13. Write down the steps to perform addition, subtraction, multiplication and division in Excel using formulas.
14. How average can be calculated in Excel using their functions.
15. Explain the usage of DAY(TODAY()) function in MS excel 2010.
16. How result of current day or month can be obtained in text form.
17. Explain the functioning of AutoSum command given in editing group of Home tab?

E. PROJECT WORK

Demonstrate to enter the text, numeric data in a cell, identify the label, values and formula in the cell.

Open a MS Excel, and type the given data in it, Calculate sum using addition formula and SUM function and subtraction and put result of subtraction in output after discount column

Student name	Fees	Discount	Output after discount
Komal	5500	500	
Simran	5000	450	
Gurutek	5500	500	
Harshan	5500	500	
Total			

ANSWER:

A. Multiple choice question answers:

1. c   2. d   3. c   4. d   5. c   6. d

B. Fill in the blanks answers:

1. Equal to or =   2. Parenthesis   3. Numeric   4. 4
5. 10   6. MAX(A2:D2)   7. Average   8. Time

C. True False answers:

1. True   2. True   3. True   4. False   5. True   6. False   7. False

SESSION 4: FORMATTING CELLS AND ITS CONTENTS

To make data or information attractive for users there are various formatting features in Excel. User can change Font, its size, color or merge text, Create border, make text bold or italic, etc in Excel 2010. This section will help reader in learning the various formatting options available in Excel.

Worksheet Formatting

To make the worksheet looks presentable and make it attractive for reader MS Excel formatting features can be used that improves the overall look of the workbook. Before using formatting features user have to select the number of cells. The steps need to follow for formatting are:

Open the workbook program > Select the number of cells > Select formatting features given in Cells group of Home tab

Or

Open the workbook program > Select the number of Cells > Right click on it > Select the Format Cells option

This will open a new dialog box where you can select the desired function for formatting.

Formatting tool

To make the worksheet looks presentable and make it attractive for reader MS Excel spreadsheet, formatting features can be used that improves the overall look of the spreadsheet. In a spreadsheet, any type of data can be held by cell, and there is a formatting toolbar or cell formatting window that makes it possible to format the cell. You can also format cells using formal cells dialog.

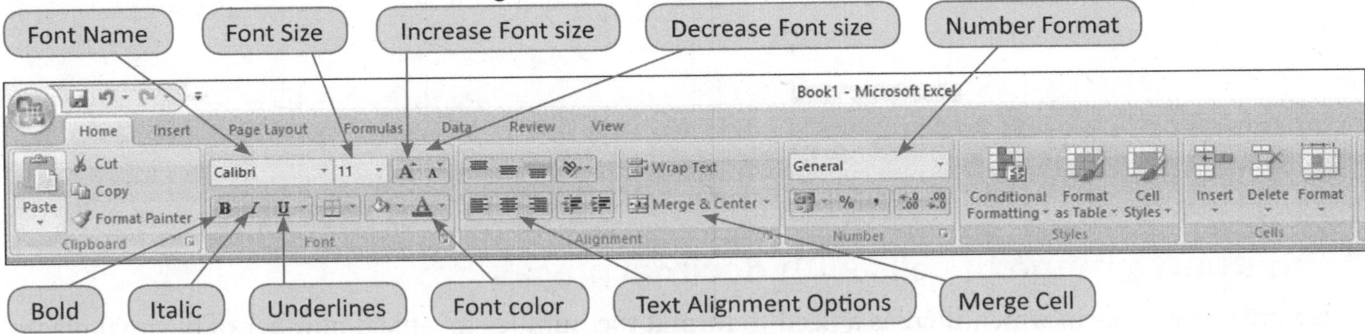

Figure 4.25: Formatting toolbar

Various formatting option available on formatting toolbar are:

- **Font Name:** Through it, you can apply different font types on a worksheet.
- **Font size:** Through it, you can change the font size on a worksheet.
- **Bold:** Through it, you can make the selected text bold.
- **Italic:** Through it, you can make the selected text italicize or tilted.
- **Underline:** Through it, you can make the selected text underlined.
- **Left alignment:** Through it, you can align the text in the cell to the left.
- **Center alignment:** Through it, you can align the text in the cell to the center.
- **Right alignment:** Through it, you can align the text in the cell to the right.
- **Justify:** Through it, you can align the text in the cell to equal from left and right.
- **Increase decimal places:** It shows more precise value by showing more decimal places.
- **Decreased decimal places:** It shows less precise decimal places.
- **Merge cell:** It will merge two or more cells together.

Use of dialog boxes to format values

As mentioned above, the format cells dialog box can be used to format the cells in the spreadsheet. The format cells dialog box can be used to find more about formatting cells or a range of cells.

To open the format dialog box, perform the following steps:

1. Select the cells and click on the **Format command** given in Cell group of Home tab and then select the **Format Cells** and a dialog box will open.

LETS KNOW MORE

The shortcut key to open Format cells dialog box: Press Ctrl + 1.

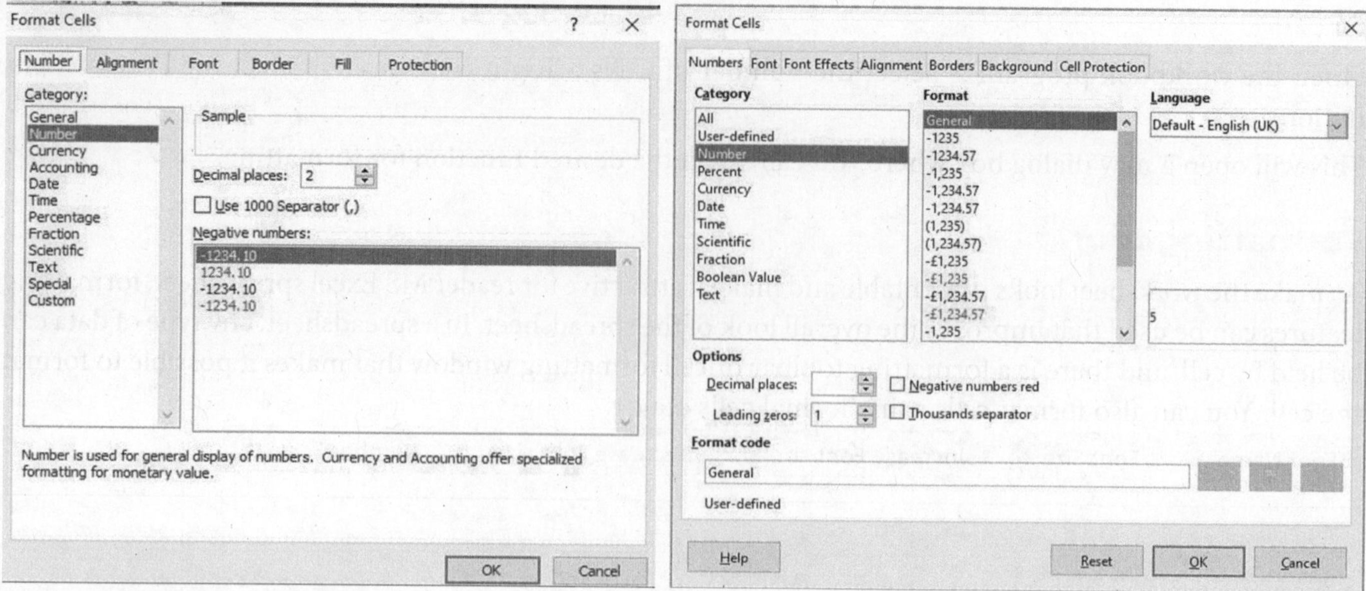

Figure 4.26: Format cells dialog box

Formatting a range of cells with decimal places

There are some cases in which there is a need to format the number to a fixed number of decimal places. These cases can come when the division of different numbers results in varied decimal places in the quotient. To format the cell to the required number of decimal places, perform the following steps:

1. Select the range of cells and click on the Format command in Cell group of Home tab. Click on **Cell and Format Cells** dialog box will open as given in Figure 4.27:

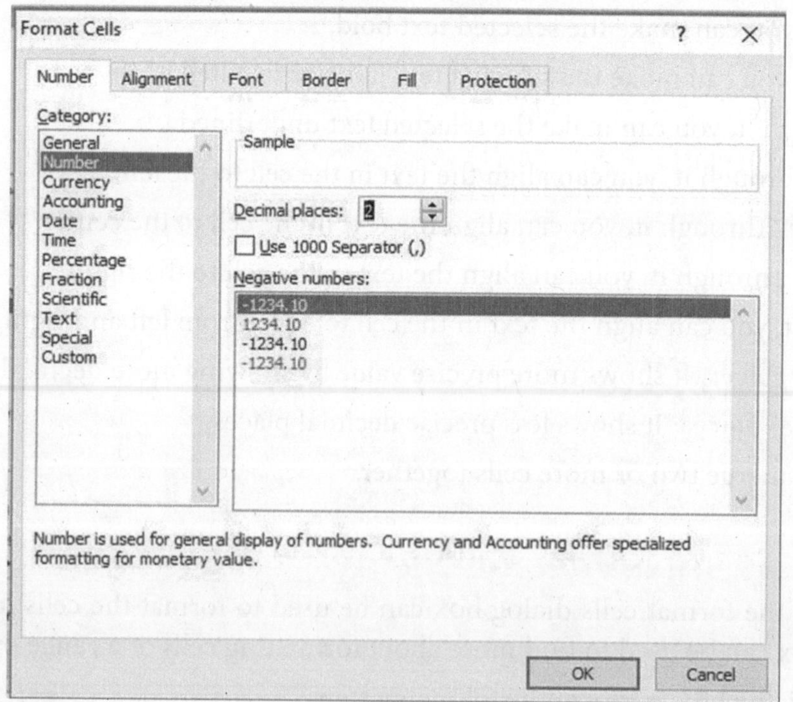

Figure 4.27: Formatting numbers tab for setting the decimal places

2. After that, click on the **Number** tab on **Format Cells** dialog box and select number and change the decimal places as required. Click on the **OK** button.

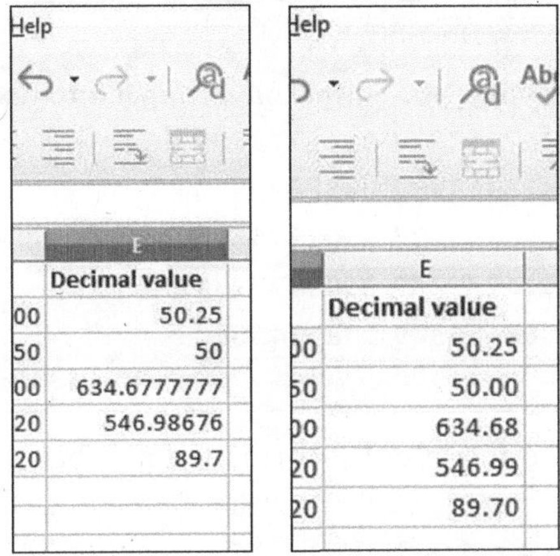

Figure 4.28: Before and after formatted to two decimal places

Formatting a range of cells to be seen as labels

There are some cases in which there is a need to format a range of cells to be seen as labels. These cases can come in telephone numbers in which every country STD code starts with 0. But when you enter the telephone number in a spreadsheet with prefix as 0, then the "0" will disappears from the telephone number because, in a spreadsheet, it stores as a numeric value that does not have a preceding 0 or zero.

But to take 0 as a prefix in the spreadsheet, we take numeric values as text. To format the selected range of cells that consist of a telephone number as text, perform the following steps:

1. Select the range of cells and click on the **Format** command in Cell group of Home tab. Click on the cell, and **Format Cells** dialog box will open as given in Figure 4.29.
2. Click on **Numbers** tab and select **Text** and click **OK** button.

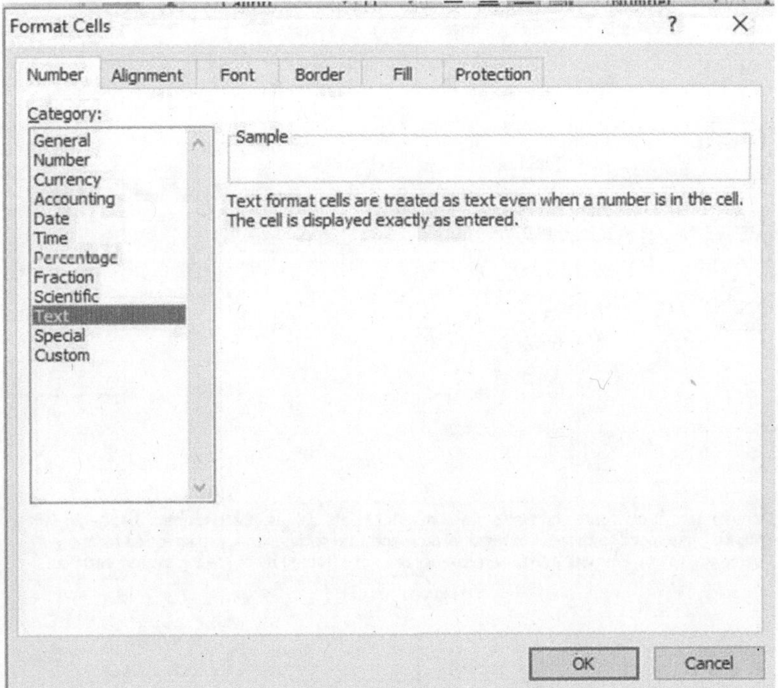

Figure 4.29: Selecting text

3. Now you can enter the numbers in a spreadsheet with prefix 0.

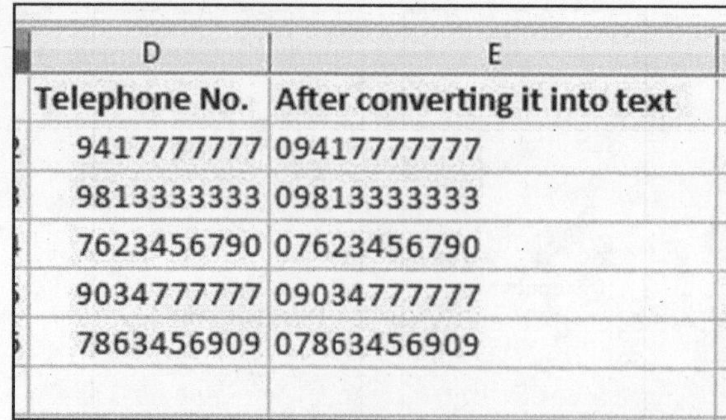

D	E
Telephone No.	After converting it into text
9417777777	09417777777
9813333333	09813333333
7623456790	07623456790
9034777777	09034777777
7863456909	07863456909

Figure 4.30: Before and after the formatted number to text or as labels

Formatting a range of cells as scientific

There are some cases in which there is a need to format a range of cells as scientific. These cases can come into entering the date. As the default date format in the spreadsheet is American format:

(mm/dd/yyyy): mm means month, dd means date and yyyy means year

Example: 12/07/2018: This means the date is 7th December 2018.

In the spreadsheet, we have a number of Date formats. To change the date format, perform the following steps:

1. Select the range of cells and click on the **Format** command in Cell group of Home tab. Click on the Format and cell, and **Format Cells** dialog box will open as given in Figure 4.31.
2. Click on **Numbers** tab and select **Date** category, select the required date format, and then click on the **OK** button.

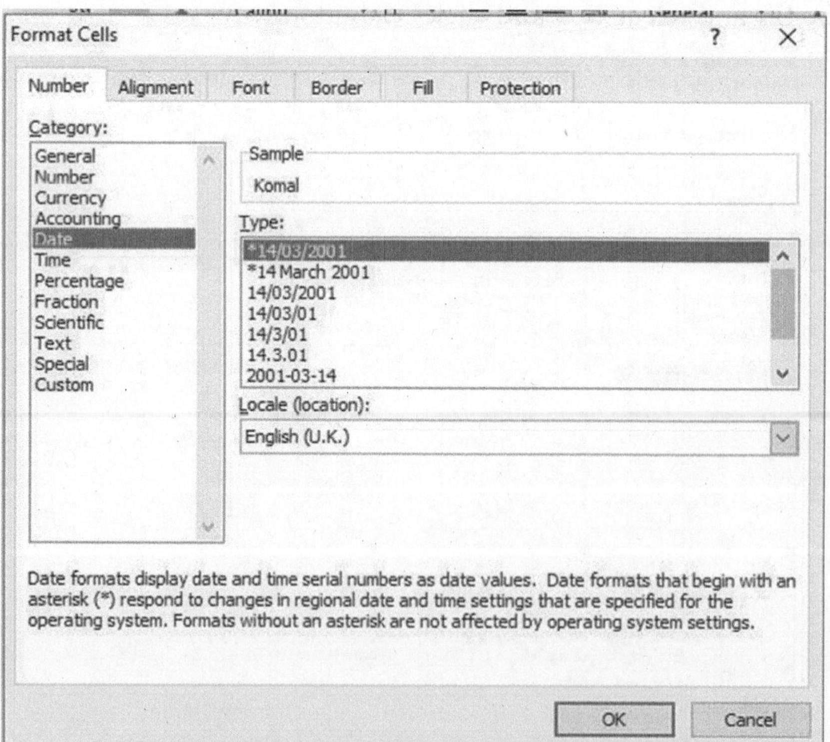

Figure 4.31: Various date format options

Observe some of the various types of data formats available in the MS Excel spreadsheet spreadsheet (Figure 4.32).

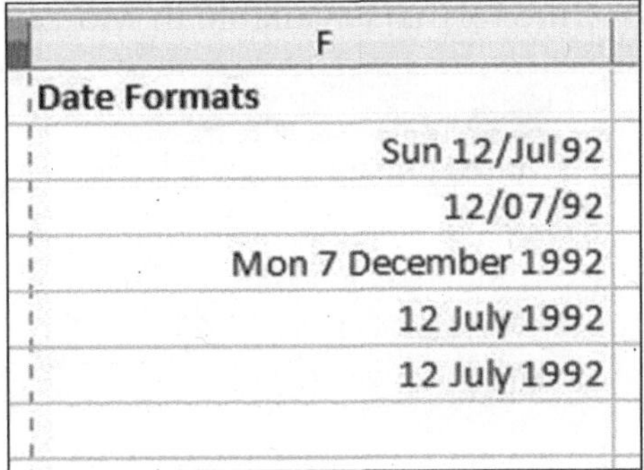

Figure 4.32: Various date formats

Formatting a range of cells to display time

There are some cases in which there is a need to format a range of cells to display time. These cases can come in the time indicated on a computer. In the computer, the common format of the time is hh:mm:ss AM/PM.

In the above-given format, the *hh* means hours, *mm* means minutes, and *ss* means second.

To format a range of cells to display the time, perform the following steps:

1. Select the range of cells, click on the **Format** command in Cell group of Home tab, and then click on the Format cells. A **Format Cells** dialog box will open, as given in Figure 4.33
2. Click on the **Numbers** tab, select the **Time** category, and then select the format of time. Click on the **OK** button.

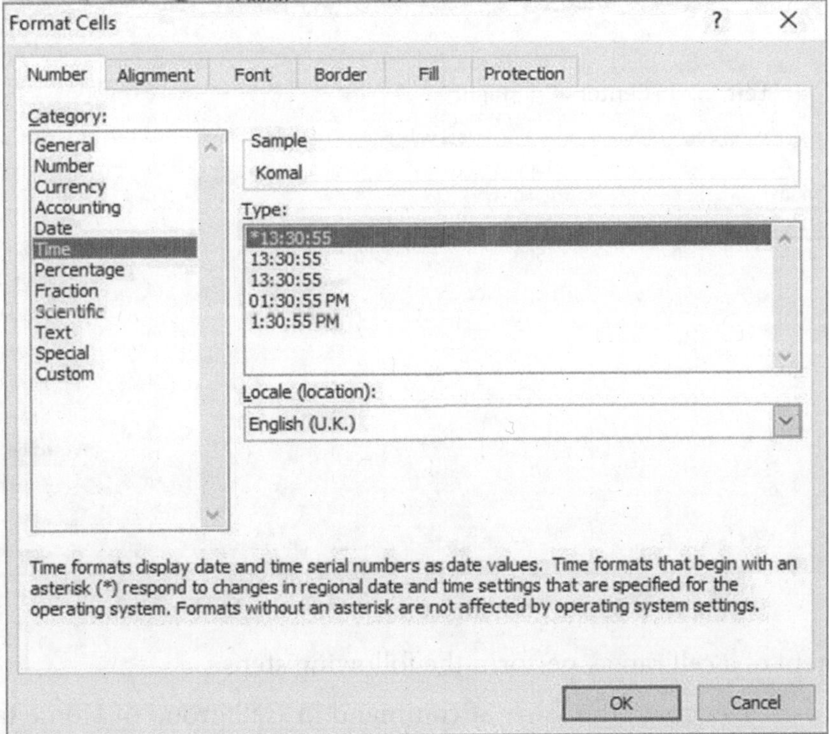

Figure 4.33: Various time format options

Observe some of the various types of time formats available in MS Excel spreadsheet (Figure 4.34).

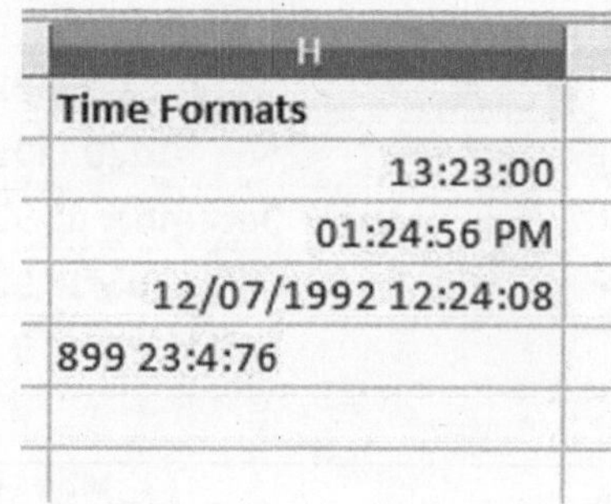

H
Time Formats
13:23:00
01:24:56 PM
12/07/1992 12:24:08
899 23:4:76

Figure 4.34: Various time formats

Formatting alignment of a cell range

There are some cases in which there is a need to format the alignment of a cell range. These cases can come when we enter values and labels as by default, and labels are aligned to the left side, and values are aligned by the right side. By choosing formatting alignment icons (left, right, and center) on the standard toolbar, you can align labels or values to the left, center, or right of a cell range.

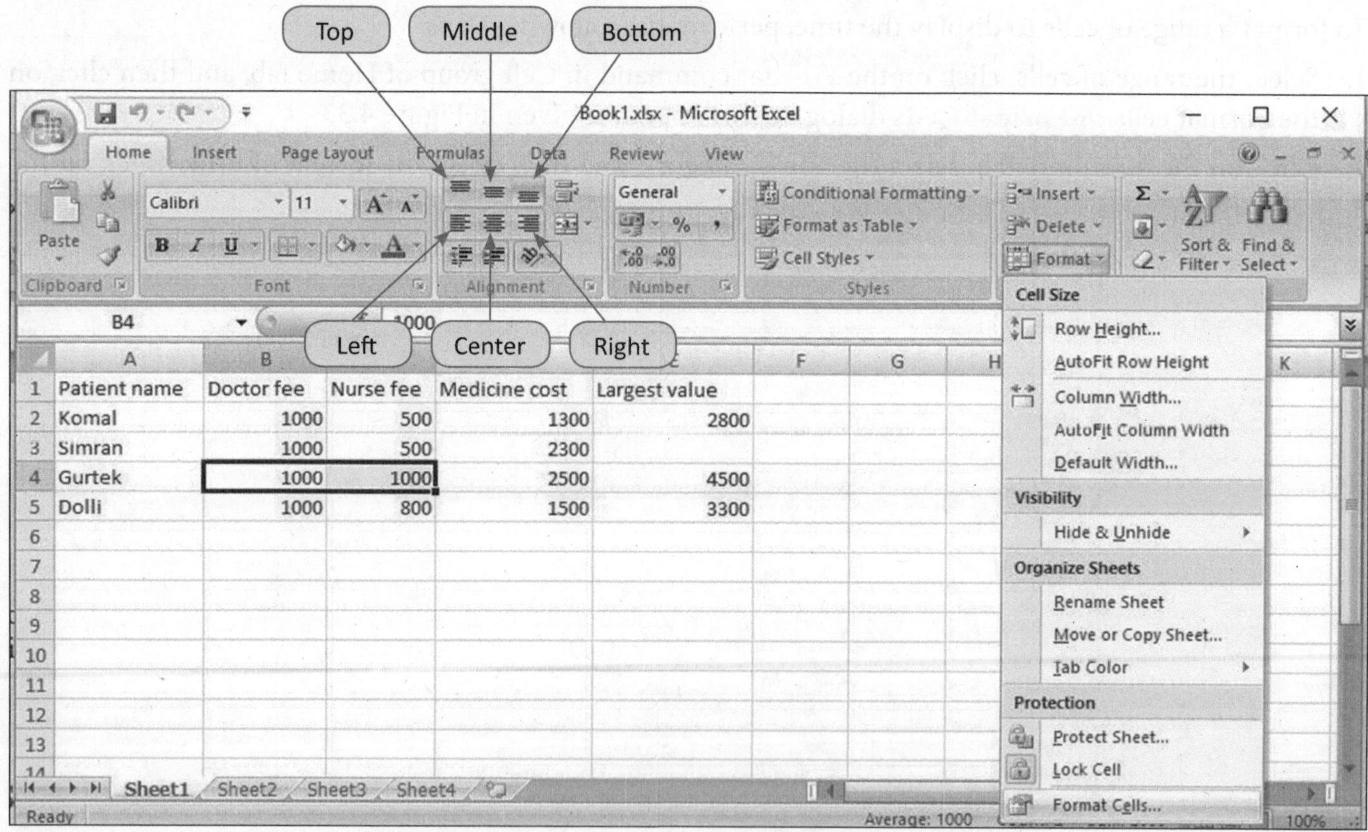

Figure 4.35: Alignment icons on the standard toolbar

To change the alignment of a cell range, perform the following steps:

1. Select the range of cells, click on the **Format** command in Cell group of Home tab, and then click on the cell. A **Format Cells** dialog box will open:

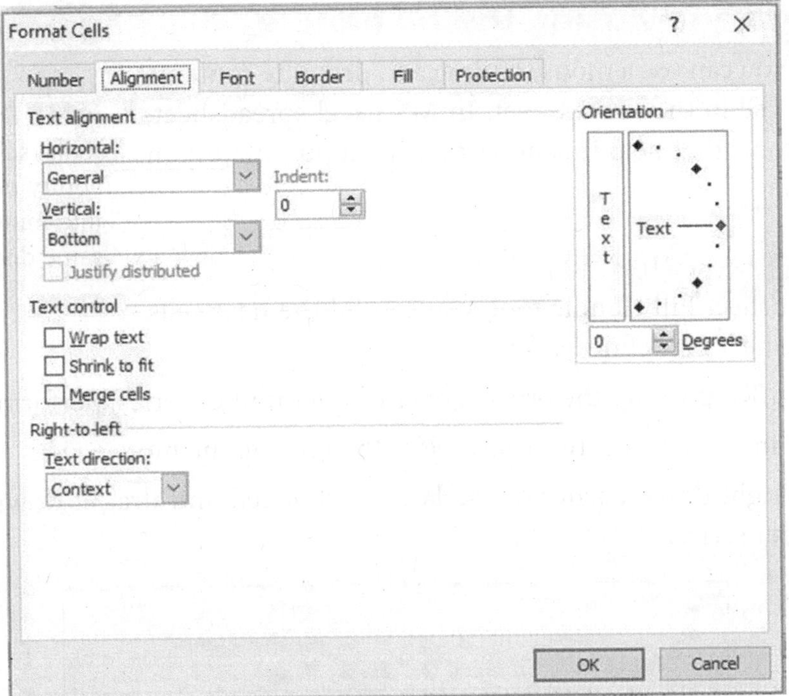

Figure 4.36: Alignment tab

2. Now you can select the left, right, or center alignment is given in the horizontal drop down, and you can also format the alignment vertically by top, middle, bottom, justify, and more.

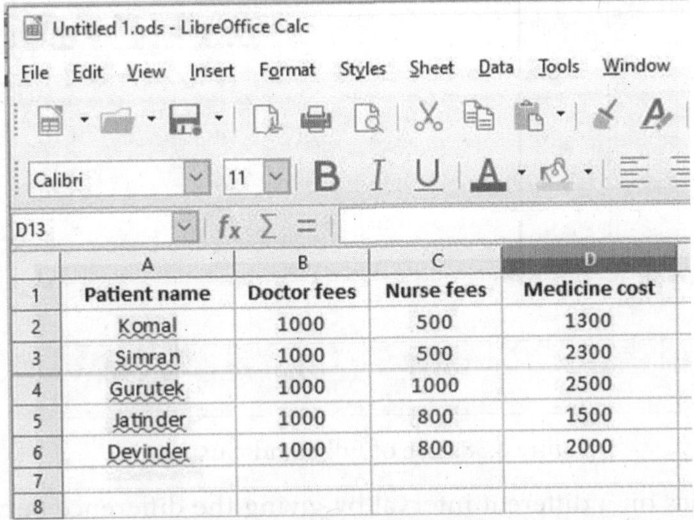

	A	B	C	D
1	Patient name	Doctor fees	Nurse fees	Medicine cost
2	Komal	1000	500	1300
3	Simran	1000	500	2300
4	Gurutek	1000	1000	2500
5	Jatinder	1000	800	1500
6	Devinder	1000	800	2000
7				
8				

Figure 4.37: Center align data

The above Figure 4.37 shows the center align data.

Skill Test Box

1. What is the correct format to display time:

   a. mm:hh:yy b. hh:mm:ss c. mm:hh:ss

2. What is the default alignment of Values:

   a. Left side b. Right side c. Center

Speeding up data entry using the fill handle

To speed up the work, you can use a mouse to drag and drop the contents of one cell to another cell in the spreadsheet. In MS Excel spreadsheet, there are some other tools that help in automating the input, mainly in case of repetitive tasks.

> **LETS KNOW MORE**
>
> To speeding up the data entry in MS Excel, it includes filling tools, selection lists, and the ability to input the information into multiple sheets of the same document.

Uses of fill handle for copying formulae

In the MS Excel spreadsheet Fill Handle tool, you can fill the next cells by dragging it with the next predefined value.

- **For number series:** To speed up the process of entering number series, perform the following steps:

1. Type numbers 1, 2 in two consecutive cells, select them using the mouse.
2. Now, click on the right down corner of the last selected cell and drag it down till that you want to continue the number series.

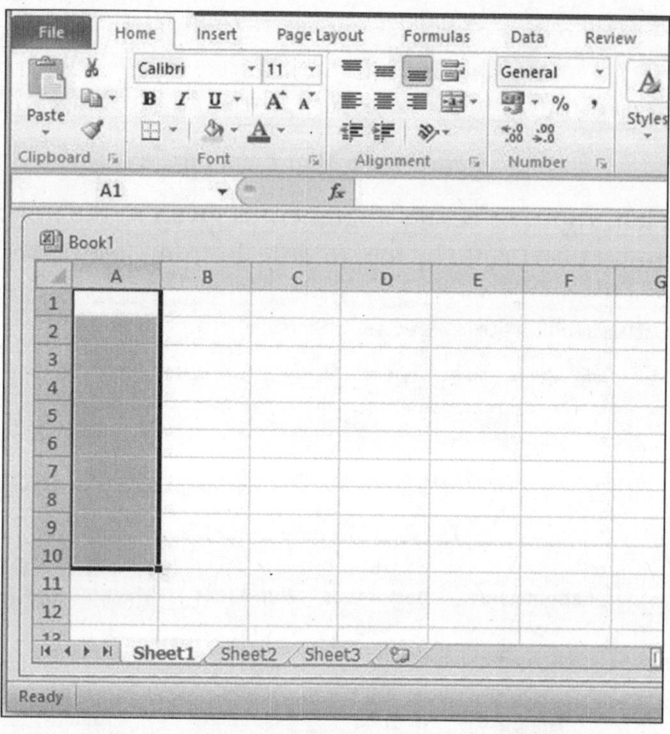

Figure 4.38: Use of Fill Handle using Cell

3. You can also get a series on a different interval by giving the difference between two consecutive cell values then drag them downward.

- **Copying formula:** To speed up the process of entering the same formula to the number of cells in the rows or columns, one can do it by entering it again and again in each cell rows or columns. Another option is copying the formula and paste it in cells that results in save of time and effort when you have to enter the same long and complex formulae.

  Various options to copying a formula and using it are:

  - **Use of copy and paste commands:** In this, you just have to select the cell contain formula then select the cell on which you want to enter that same formula. Now press **Paste** command to paste that same formula in the selected cell.

MEMORY BOX

For example, you want to fill the roll numbers, month, week, days, and many more, then you can input one or two in sequence, then select them and drag it to the next cell or till that you want to continue that series of sequence.

Shortcut key to copy press Ctrl + C and paste press Ctrl + V.

Fill handle of a cell

The fill handle of a cell is the small black square in the bottom of the right corner of the last selected cell. You can also use Fill handle for copying a formula by performing the following steps:

1. Select the cell that contains the formula and click on a small black square or fill the handle of the selected cell.
2. Now, drag it down up to the required cell.

MEMORY BOX

value. For example, you want to fill the roll numbers, month, week, days, and many more, then you can input one or two in sequence, then select them and drag it to the next cell or till that you want to continue that series of sequence.

Summary

- To change the format of number, Select the Cells > Click on Format button drop down arrow given in the Cells group of Home tab
- There are various options to format the text like text alignment, color, style, size, font, Wrap text, etc.
- Various formatting options available on the formatting toolbar are the font, font size, bold, italic, underline, left alignment, center alignment, right alignment, increase decimal places, and decrease decimal places.
- To open the Format dialog box, select the cells, and click on the Format command in Cells group of Home tab drop-down menu. Select the cell, and Format Cells dialog box will open.
- The shortcut key to open Format cells dialog box: press Ctrl + 1.
- There are some cases in which there is a need to format the number to a fixed number of decimal places. These cases can come when the division of different numbers results in varied decimal places in the quotient.
- There are some cases in which there is a need to format a range of cells to be seen as labels. These cases can come in telephone numbers in which every country STD code starts with 0.
- There are some cases in which there is a need to format a range of cells as scientific. These cases can come into entering the date.
- There are some cases in which there is a need to format a range of cells to display time. These cases can come in the time indicated on a computer.
- There are some cases in which there is a need to format the alignment of a cell range. These cases can come when we enter values and labels as by default, and labels are aligned to the left side, and values are aligned by the right side.
- To speed up the work, you can use a mouse to drag and drop the contents of one cell to another cell in the spreadsheet. In MS Excel spreadsheet, there are some other tools that help in automating the input, mainly in case of repetitive tasks.
- In the MS Excel spreadsheet Fill Handle tool, you can fill the next cells by dragging it with the next predefined value. For example, you want to fill the roll numbers, month, week, days, and many more, then you can input one or two in sequence, then select them and drag it to the next cell.
- Fill handle of a cell is the small black square in the bottom of the right corner of the last selected cell.

Self-Assessment

A. MULTIPLE CHOICE QUESTIONS

1. The Vertical and Horizontal Text alignment commands are available in which Group:
   a. Clipboard b. Alignment c. Font d. Number
2. The Top Align command aligns the data in a cell to which side:
   a. Left b. Right c. Down d. Up
3. Which of the following not comes under the Text formatting commands?
   a. Increase Font size b. Number Format c. Text Alignment d. Cell Style

B. FILL IN THE BLANKS

1. To change the Font user have to click on__________ command.
2. __________ command or feature is used to fix text in single cell.
3. _________ is the default font size in Excel 2010.

C. TRUE FALSE

1. You cannot change the Font size of the already written Text in the cell (T/F)
2. Only horizontal alignment can be perform in Excel using Alignment group (T/F)
3. Times New Roman is the default Font in Excel 2010 (T/F)

D. ANSWER THE FOLLOWING QUESTIONS:

1. Write down the steps of formatting number in Excel.
2. Name and explain the Formatting Text options available in Home Tab of Excel.
3. How user can change the Font and Font size?
4. Write down the mechanism of changing Text Color.
5. Significance of Bold, Italic and Underline features on Hoome tab?
6. Give both the methods of changing the width of Column and Row.
7. What are the options comes under vertical and horizontal text alignment.
8. Give the process and purpose of Text wrapping in Excel.
9. Give the significance of Merge and Center command in Excel.

E. PRACTICAL WORK

Open a MS Excel, and type the given data in it, Change the Font and its size, Merge the top row of table given below, Put Blue color in top row, Reduce the column width of Roll No. section, Increase the width of Name column, Give pink color to text present in Name section or first column, Align all text in left side except the top row or heading put it in middle

Attendance Sheet of 6th class students				
Name	Roll No.	Age	12/07/1992	13/07/1992
Komalpreet Kaur				
Simran				
Gurutek				
Harsh				
Simar				

ANSWER:

A. Multiple choice question answers:

1. b   2. d   3. d

B. Fill in the blanks answers:

1. Font
2. Wrap Text
3. 11

C. True False answers:

1. False
2. False
3. False

SESSION 5: USE REFERENCING

In MS Excel spreadsheet there is feature of referencing which is the way to refer any formula or function of one cell to the next cell along the row or column. In MS Excel spreadsheet there are mainly three types of referencing such as:

- Relative Referencing
- Absolute Referencing
- Mixed Referencing

Relative Referencing: By default all the cell references are relative references in which the formula gets copied in the new cell when you select any formula and drag it to new cell. There is changes in formula on the basis of relative position of rows and columns.

When you select the cell contain formula and drag it downwards in columns then the row number of the cell address gets one added in it. On other hand the column name of the cell address gets one added by dragging the cell contain formula in right.

For Example: The formula is B2+C2+D2 and you copy it and drag it to lower cell then it will become B3+C3+D3.

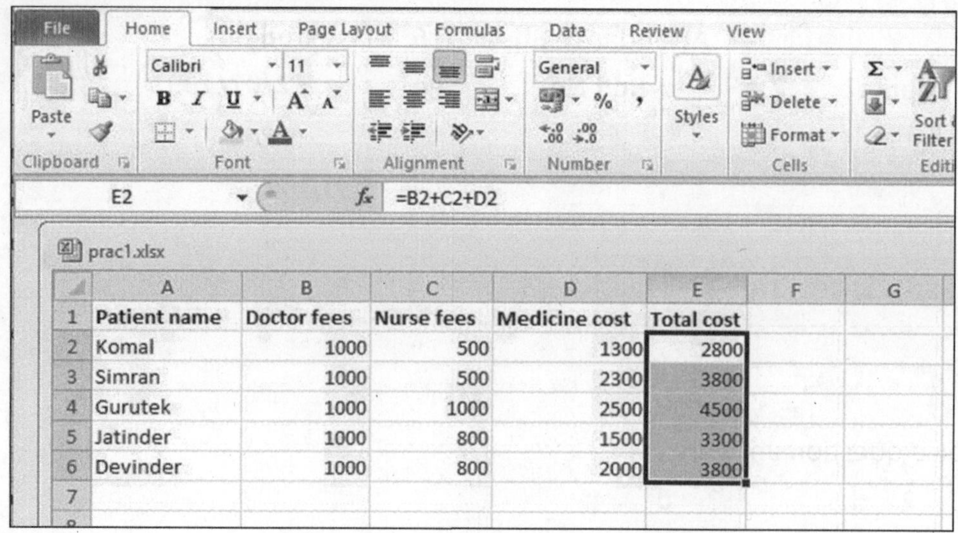

	A	B	C	D	E
1	Patient name	Doctor fees	Nurse fees	Medicine cost	Total cost
2	Komal	1000	500	1300	2800
3	Simran	1000	500	2300	3800
4	Gurutek	1000	1000	2500	4500
5	Jatinder	1000	800	1500	3300
6	Devinder	1000	800	2000	3800

Figure 4.39: Relative Referencing

Absolute Referencing: There are cases when you don't want a cell reference to change when copied to other cells as happen in relative referencing. In those cases absolute referencing is used as it will not change when copied and filled in another cell. To use Absolute referencing a $ symbol is used before the column name and row number that make it constant for any formula.

For example: B3, C7. In this case the cell name remain constant when the formula is copied and drag it in any direction. It is mainly used in higher classes.

Mixed Referencing: It is the combination of relative and absolute referencing. It is used when we have to make some row number and column name constant and some has to vary accordingly. To make the row number and column name constant a $ sign is used before it.

For Example: In below figure 4.40 we have entered the number of class 9th students in English, =hindi, maths and IT subject. In Total marks we have taken the sum in which the relative referencing is used as arguments cell name is varying according to their position. Same is for average but in GR total column you can observe that the Sum column is varying and grace marks column name is constant and $ sign is added before the row number. This shows the mixed referencing.

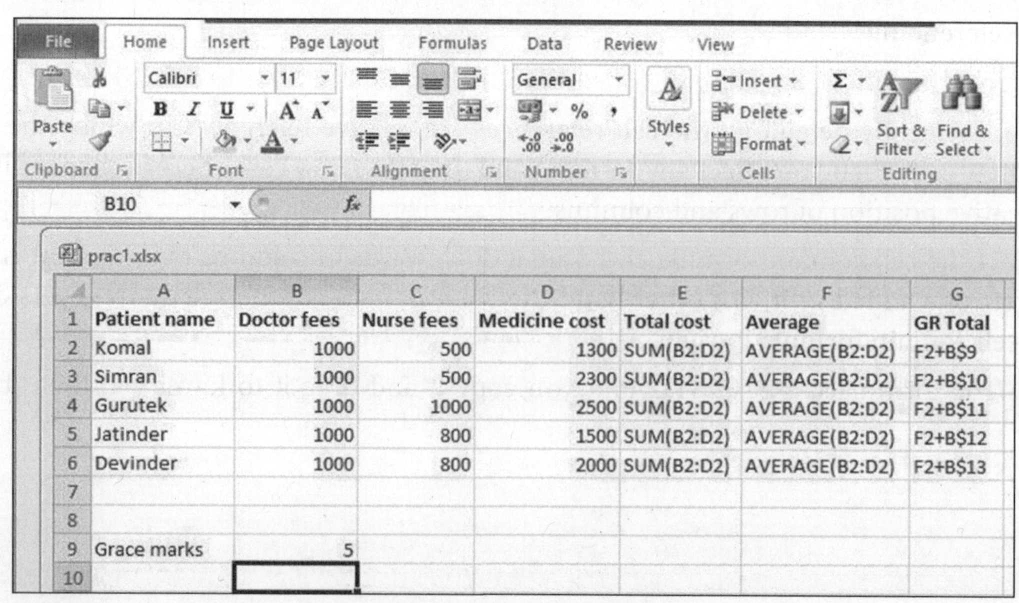

	A	B	C	D	E	F	G
1	Patient name	Doctor fees	Nurse fees	Medicine cost	Total cost	Average	GR Total
2	Komal	1000	500	1300	SUM(B2:D2)	AVERAGE(B2:D2)	F2+B$9
3	Simran	1000	500	2300	SUM(B2:D2)	AVERAGE(B2:D2)	F2+B$10
4	Gurutek	1000	1000	2500	SUM(B2:D2)	AVERAGE(B2:D2)	F2+B$11
5	Jatinder	1000	800	1500	SUM(B2:D2)	AVERAGE(B2:D2)	F2+B$12
6	Devinder	1000	800	2000	SUM(B2:D2)	AVERAGE(B2:D2)	F2+B$13
7							
8							
9	Grace marks	5					
10							

Figure 4.40: Mixed Referencing

Summary

- In MS Word there is feature of referencing which is the way to refer any formula or function of one cell to the next cell along the row or column.
- By default all the cell references are relative references in which the formula gets copied in the new cell when you select any formula and drag it to new cell.
- There are cases when you don't want a cell reference to change when copied to other cells as happen in relative referencing. In those cases absolute referencing is used as it will not change when copied and filled in another cell.
- To use Absolute referencing a $ symbol is used before the column name and row number that make it constant for any formula.
- It is the combination of relative and absolute referencing. It is used when we have to make some row number and column name constant and some has to vary accordingly.

Self-Assessment

A. MULTIPLE CHOICE QUESTIONS

1. Which of the following shows Absolute referencing?

   a. B2+C2   b. B2*C2   c. B$2+C$2   d. B2*C$2

2. B2+C$9 is comes under which type of referencing?

   a. Relative referencing   b. Absolute Referencing

   c. Mixed Referencing   d. Both (b) and (c)

Answer:

1. b   2. c

B. QUESTIONS:

1. Define Referencing?
2. Name various types of Referencing in Excel?
3. Explain Relative, Absolute and Mixed referencing in Excel along with example of each.

C. PROJECT WORK

Demonstrate to use Relative, absolute and mixed referencing in spreadsheet.

SESSION 5: INTRODUCE THE TYPES OF CHARTS IN A SPREADSHEET

In case of representation of large amount of data a visual representation is always preferred. That is the reason there is Charts feature in every spreadsheet so that data can be visually represented in different ways.

A chart is a graphical representation of data in which the data is represented by symbols like bars in a bar chart, lines in a line chart and slices in a pie chart. You can also create charts in a tabular numeric data, function or some kind of qualitative structures. An easier way to read and data understanding is provided by charts. In MS Excel spreadsheet you can create, modify and format charts on the basis of data given in spreadsheet.

Importance of Charts in Spreadsheets

- As mentioned above the visual representation of data is preferred in case of large amount of data. That's why a charts are introduced in every spreadsheet.
- It is not easy to compare and analyse data when they are represented as numbers in large quantity
- The data in the form of charts are more effective in communication and understanding
- You can create charts in tabular numeric data, function or some kind of qualitative structure

Types of Charts in Spreadsheets

As we know charts are the pictorial representations of worksheet data that present it in graphical or pictorial form that is easier to read and understand. Excel provides various types of charts that let you to represent your data in different ways with different looks. Some of the existing types of charts are:

Type of chart	Explanation
Column Chart	Column charts are used for comparing several items in a specific range of values. Column charts are ideal in case of comparing a single category of data between individual sub-items such as when comparing revenue between regions. It depicts data as vertical bars.
Line Chart	Line chart is one of the most frequently used chart types that is used to show trends over a period of time. It depicts data as a series of line. Mostly people consider line chart when there is need to changes chart over time.
Pie Chart	Pie chart represents the distribution or proportion of each data item over a total value. It is most effective to use pie chart in plotting no more than three categories of data. It depicts data as series of slices. It is used in portray different items percentage of a store.
Bar Chart	Bar charts are used for comparing several categories of data. It is ideal to be used for visualizing the distribution or proportion of data items when there are more than three categories. For instance a bar chart can be used for comparing the overall revenue distribution for a given set of products.
Area Chart	Area charts are ideal for clearly illustrating the magnitude of change between two or more data points. For example you can give your audience a visual feel for the degree of variance between the high and low price of each month. It depicts a line chart whose data files in the areas between the lines and x-axis. It is mainly used in conveying the relative depth of data.
Scatter Chart	Scatter charts are also known as XY scatter plot charts that are very good for showing the correlations between two sets of values. It can be used to illustrate the correlation between employee performance and competency, demonstrating that employee performance rises as competency improves. The x and y axes work together for representing data plots on the chart on the basis of intersection of x values and y values.
Bubble Chart	Bubble chart is like a scatter chart with an additional third column that specify the size of the bubbles.

Creation of Charts using Spreadsheets

To create a chart in Spreadsheet, perform the following steps:

Select the range of data > Click on Insert menu bar > Click on Chart and Chart Wizard dialog box will open

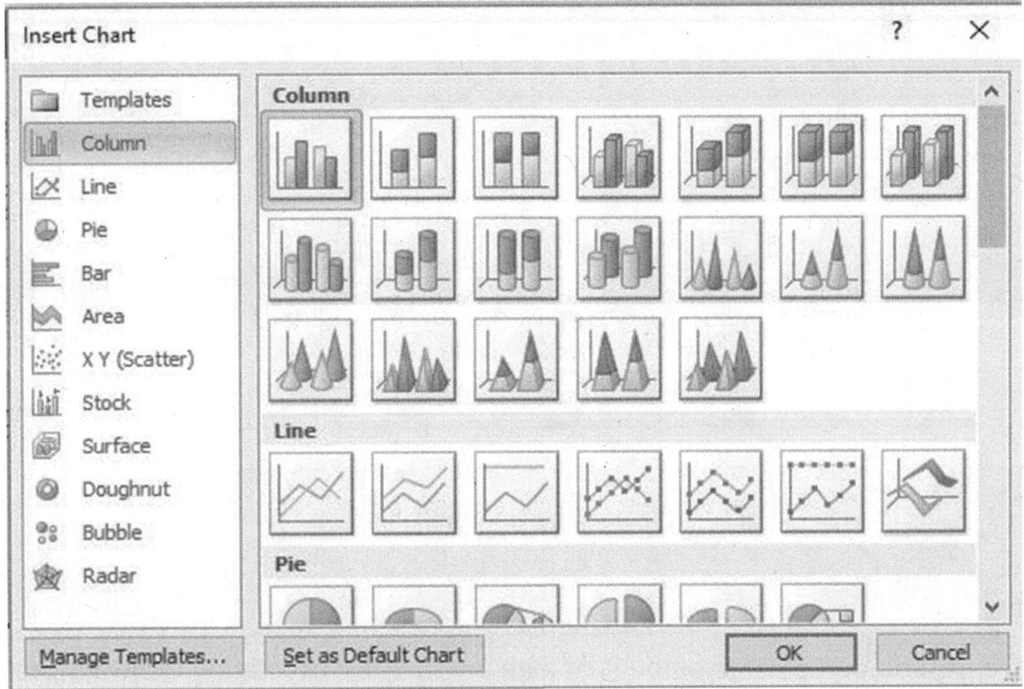

Figure 4.41: Insert Chart dialog box

From Insert Chart dialog box you can choose the required type of chart given under Choose a Chart Type > Click on Finish button.

Example: Let we want to create a Column chart of students for comparing their results.

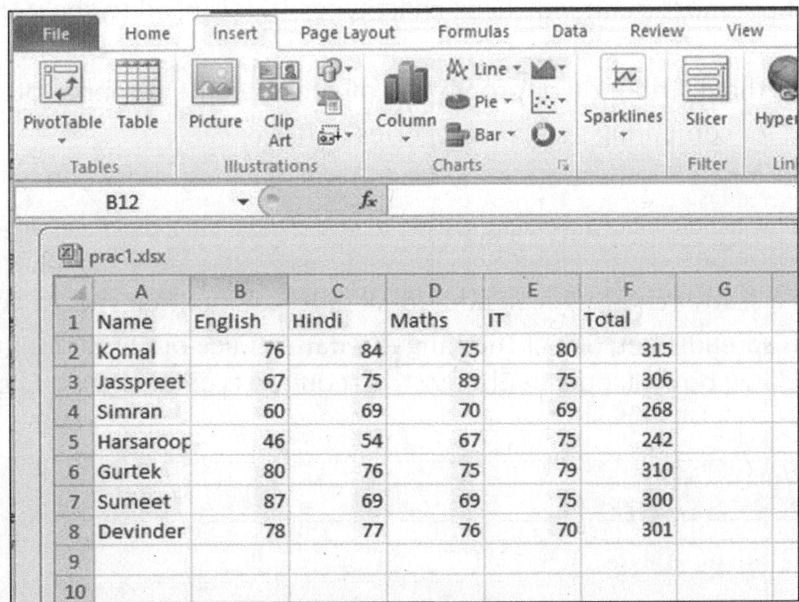

	A	B	C	D	E	F	G
1	Name	English	Hindi	Maths	IT	Total	
2	Komal	76	84	75	80	315	
3	Jasspreet	67	75	89	75	306	
4	Simran	60	69	70	69	268	
5	Harsaroop	46	54	67	75	242	
6	Gurtek	80	76	75	79	310	
7	Sumeet	87	69	69	75	300	
8	Devinder	78	77	76	70	301	
9							
10							

Figure 4.42: Class 9th student marks data

In the above figure given in figure 4.42, we have entered the 9th class student marks data and taken there total. The below figure 4.43 shows the Column chart of student marks that make it easy to compare the performance of each individual.

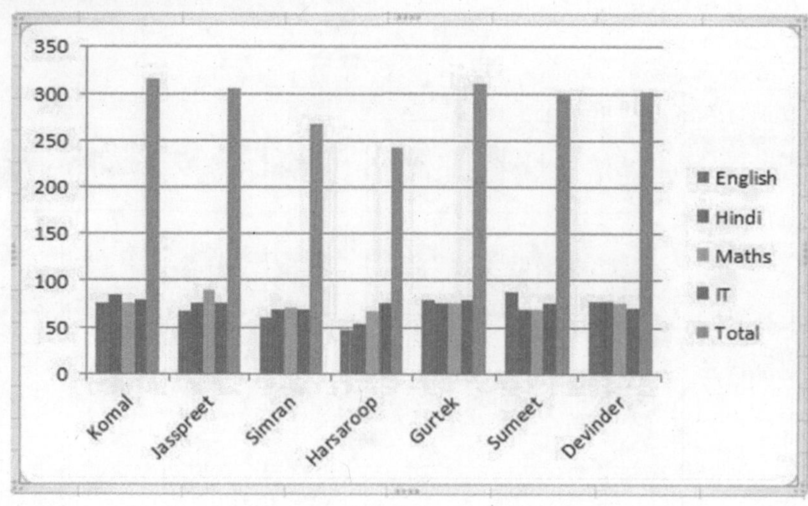

Figure 4.43: Column Chart

Summary

- In case of representation of large amount of data a visual representation is always preferred. That is the reason there is Charts feature in every spreadsheet so that data can be visually represented in different ways.
- A chart is a graphical representation of data in which the data is represented by symbols like bars in a bar chart, lines in a line chart and slices in a pie chart.
- Column charts are used for comparing several items in a specific range of values.
- Line chart is one of the most frequently used chart types that is used to show trends over a period of time.
- Pie chart represents the distribution or proportion of each data item over a total value.
- Bar charts are used for comparing several categories of data.
- Area charts are ideal for clearly illustrating the magnitude of change between two or more data points.
- Scatter charts are also known as XY scatter plot charts that are very good for showing the correlations between two sets of values.
- Bubble chart is like a scatter chart with an additional third column that specify the size of the bubbles.
- To create a chart in spreadsheet, Select the range of data > Click on Insert menu bar > Click on Chart and Chart Wizard dialog box will open > Choose the required type of chart > Click on Finish button

Self-Assessment

A. MULTIPLE CHOICE QUESTIONS

1. Which tab contain chart?

   a. Home tab b. Insert tab c. View tab d. Edit tab

2. __________ chats are used for comparing several items in a specific range of values.

   a. Column b. Line c. Pie d. Area

Answer

1. b 2. a

B. QUESTIONS:

1. What is a chart?
2. State any five types of charts.
3. Write down the steps of creating a chart.

C. PROJECT WORK

Open Excel and create a sheet that contains product details with their costs, create a pie chart to display the differences among various years.

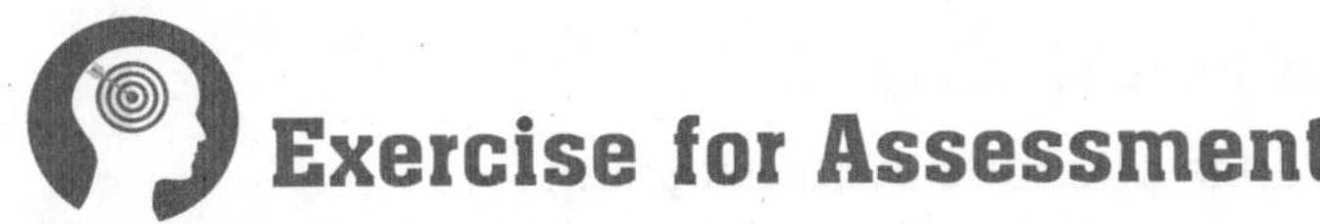

Exercise for Assessment

A. MULTIPLE CHOICE QUESTIONS

1. _______________ consists of items for inserting elements into a spreadsheet, such as Toolbars, Column, Row, Headers, Full Screen, Zoom, etc.

   a. File b. Edit c. Insert d. Styles

2. The currently used cell highlighted with dark boundary is known as?

   a. Active Cell b. Passive Cell c. New Cell d. Current cell

3. Which of the following is not a part of MS Excel?

   a. Title Bar b. Insert Function c. Status bar d. Word count

4. The range of Column in MS Excel?

   a. 1 to 124 b. 1 to 1048576 c. 1 to 1024 d. 1 to 1023

5. The default position of Value in MS Excel spreadsheet is?

   a. Left b. Right c. Center d. Justify

6. C2/D2 is which of the following mathematical operator?

   a. Addition b. Subtraction c. Multiplication d. Division

7. What will be the output of (2+7)*6

   a. 44 b. 42 c. 54 d. 56

8. The TODAY( ) function in spreadsheet display _____________.

   a. Current time b. Current month c. Current Date d. Current Day

9. The output of 634.8877777 after selecting two decimal places from Format Cells dialog box will be:

   a. 6.3488 b. 634.8877 c. 63.488 d. 634.88

10. You can enter number with preceding 0 after converting numeric value as:

    a. Data b. Label c. Text d. Character

11. Which of the following shows Relative referencing?

    a. B2+C2 b. B2*C2 c. B$2+C$2 d. B2*C$2

Answer

1. c 2. a 3. d 4. c 5. a 6. d
7. c 8. c 9. d 10. c 11. a or b

B. VERY SHORT QUESTIONS:

1. Name any five parts of MS Excel.
2. What is cell in Worksheet?
3. What is the default position of Label in MS Excel spreadsheet?
4. Write a formula for multiplication with cell address and operators?
5. Write down the steps to open Formal Cells dialog box?
6. Define Fill handle of a cell?
7. Name various types of Referencing in MS Excel?
8. Give example of absolute referencing.
9. What are the importance of Charts in Spreadsheet?
10. What is the another name of Scatter Chart?

C. SHORT QUESTIONS:

1. What is the purpose of Help tab in MS Excel main Window?
2. What is Toolbar? What is the purpose of Formatting toolbar in MS Excel?
3. What is Worksheet?
4. Give various mathematical operators used in Formulae with example.
5. How to format a range of cells with decimal places?
6. Give various formatting alignment of a cell range?
7. What do you mean by Referencing in MS Excel?
8. What is Mixed Referencing?
9. Write down the steps to create charts using spreadsheets?
10. Where Line chart is used?

D. LONG QUESTIONS:

1. Write down the steps to start MS Excel?
2. What do you mean by range of cells: Column range and Row range?
3. Name the commonly used used basic functions in MS Excel. Give example of each basic function?
4. How to format a range of cells to be seen as labels, values, as scientific and to display time?
5. Write a short note of speeding up data entry using Fill handle?
6. What is Referencing? Explain with example various types of referencing in MS Excel?
7. Explain briefly the types of charts in spreadsheet?

E. APPLICATION BASED QUESTIONS:

1. Jasspreet was unable to complete the assignment given in holiday homework, Help him to compete the assignment given below:

Name	English	Hindi	Maths	IT	Total	Percentage
Komal	76	84	75	80		
Jasspreet	67	75	89	75		
Simran	60	69	70	69		
Gurutek	46	54	67	75		
Harshan	80	76	75	79		
Samarbir	87	69	69	75		

2. Komal was assigned a task to enter the data of 70 students. The roll number of students is in continuous. Help him to speed up the entering Roll No. in the spreadsheet.
3. Simran has used drag fill handle to use the formula. Every time he drag the formula its row number gets changed. Help him to do copy the formula and its row number must remain constant.
4. The class teacher asked Harshan to observe the following worksheet carefully and answer the questions:

Name	English	Hindi	Maths	IT	Total	Average	GR Total
Komal	76	84	75	80	315		
Jasspreet	67	75	89	75	306		
Simran	60	69	70	69	268		
Gurutek	46	54	67	75	242		
Harshan	80	76	75	79	310		
Samarbir	87	69	69	75	300		
Grace marks	5						

a. Enter the data in MS Excel spreadsheet.

b. Calculate the Average using Drag and drop the fill handle.

c. Help him to copy the grace marks in every cells of GR Total.

F. PROJECT WORK

Demonstrate to enter the text, numeric data in a cell, identify the label, values and formula in the cell.

Work on calculating the formula using mathematical operators, identify formulae with cell addresses and operators.

Use basic functions to perform calculations on data.

Demonstrate to format a arrange of cells to labels, as scientific and to display time.

Demonstrate to align the cell data range, create number series using handle, copy formula by dragging the formula using fill handle.

Practically use the relative, absolute and mixed referencing in MS Excel spreadsheet.

Illustrate the example of chart in MS Excel.

TEACHER NOTES:

1. Arrange a practical class to start MS Excel and performing various basic functions in it that help students to understand it more thoroughly.
2. Prepare a presentation on various types of charts in MS Excel spreadsheet with example of each type.

EXAM TIPS:

1. Do all the things practically on computer to know exactly about various parts of MS Excel spreadsheet.
2. Check each parts and its further commands of MS Excel spreadsheet
3. Make a worksheet on any topic that includes label, values and formula and check everything in it like range of column, row, etc.
4. Perform different calculations both using formula and inbuilt functions.
5. Format any existing file.

5 Digital Presentation

Learning Outcomes

After this chapter, you will have the knowledge of:

- Concept of Presentation
- Elements of Presentation
- Characteristics of good quality Presentation
- How to Start PowerPoint
- Various parts of PowerPoint Window
- Closing PowerPoint
- Create a Presentation using Template
- Selecting a Slide Layout
- Saving a Presentation
- Running a Slide Show
- Saving a Presentation in PDF
- Closing a Presentation
- Using Help
- How to insert duplicate slide
- How to insert a new slide
- Various slide layout
- Steps to copy and move slide
- Deleting and Renaming the slide
- View a Presentation: How to control the size of view
- Various workspace view,
- Format toolbar of PowerPoint
- Working on Tables in PowerPoint presentation
- Entering data in Table
- Selecting cell, row, column and table: adjusting column width and ow height
- Inserting Table borders and background
- Inserting images from file, gallery
- Formatting Images
- Drawing Graphics
- Working with Slide Master and Adding Transitions

INTRODUCTION

The process of providing information to audience using audio, graphics, video and text is the process comes under digital presentation. The projectors and transparencies overhead are replaced by graphic software by the advent of advanced presentation. This digital or data presentation are becomes more comprehensive, appealing and colourful. The digital boards have taken the place of blackboard for teaching. As it provides easy understanding and represent information that makes a better impact on audience.

LETS KNOW MORE

The multimedia presentation is created in the form of slides arranged in a sequential manner to motivate, convey, entertain, and persuade information. Various software is available to create a presentation like Microsoft PowerPoint, Impress Presentation, Adobe Connect, and Google Slides.

SESSION 1: DESCRIBE THE QUALITY OF GOOD PRESENTATION

Concept of Presentation

Presentation software is used to display information in a sequence of slides or slide show that is used in colleges, schools, organizations, etc for various purpose. MS PowerPoint is one of the presentation software that allow to make dynamic slide presentations that can include images, videos, animation and text. It is a part of Microsoft Office that provides various templates, layouts, wizards, themes and tools.

Definition Box

A presentation is a means of communication that can be adapted to various speaking situations, such as talking to a group, addressing a meeting or briefing a team.

LETS KNOW MORE

Presentation skills include the content and flow of the presentation. There are number of advantages to using a presentation prepared by computer. Such as organization, educational field, entertainment, conferences, and seminars.

Elements of Presentation

Various Elements of presentation that makes it effective are:

- **Be Prepared:** This depends on how many times you practice your speed that must be 30 hours of rehearsal time for every hour you will be speaking.
- **Give of Yourself:** While giving presentation try to use personal examples but make sure it support your point and message you want to convey through presentation.
- **Stay Relaxed:** You will be relaxed if you have prepared for your presentation.
- **It has a clear objective:** Define your goals clearly, right at the outside. The objective of your presentation will drive everything from your script to your slide deck.
- **It's useful to your audience:** Make sure your presentation should genuinely and meaningfully offer value to its audience. That means sharing key strategies that have worked for you, offering up enlightening data or insights or telling story that may be able to learn from.
- **Use little text in your presentation desk:** Don't give audience a reading assignment. As it will make overall experience of your presentation less enjoyable. Your audience is liable to feel distracted and even a little stressed.

A good presentation may also include Regular text, lists items, Table, Graphics elements, Sound and Video and Animation, etc.

LETS KNOW MORE

Also, focus on your message instead of an audience and use gestures like walking patterns, and many more.

Being prepared is one of the most important elements of the presentation.

Skill Test Box

Select the correct option:

1. Which of the following is not an element of presentation?

   a. Be prepared   b. Give of yourself   c. Stay relaxed   d. Make it before time

Characteristics of good quality Presentation

A good presentation must convey an exact message clearly to the audience. Various points or characteristics of good presentation are:

- **Opening and Closing phrases:** The opening and closing of presentation must be carefully framed by keeping in view the situation, subject and audience. The opening should attract listeners attention and their interest using some relevant statements related to your subject.

- **Number of lines:** Try to limit the number of lines, it should be between 5 to 8 lines in one slide. As adding paragraph or more number of lines takes more time to read a single slide due to use of small font size to add more data.
- **Font size:** The Font size of Text on presentation is also one of the important thing to be consider. Font size is set according to the distance between the screen and the audience.
- **Use of Quotations:** The speaker should be very cautious in using quotations. He should avoid the use of large number of quotations as well as long.
- **Correctly use grammar and language:** The use of language and grammar in the presentation should be correct because the mistakes in it will replicate the number of persons in the audience.
- **Insert Images, clips, tables or graphs:** Use images, clips, tables or graphs in the presentation make it more attractive to audience.
- **Simplicity:** The speaker must deliver the speech in simple words and sentences as it make speech more effective.
- **Use Colours:** Try to use dark colours, bold letters with different fonts for highlighting certain points. For fonts try to use fair or silent background and dark colours.
- **Animation, sounds and Videos:** Make sure you don't insert or include more than one animation or video in one slide as it will overlap the sounds and can also results in confusion to the audience.
- **Availability of Voice and Words:** The very first requirement of good presentation in any given circumstances the voice and words should be audible.

- Mainly the font size must be at 32 points or more so that it is easily read by the audience.
- To make the presentation of good quality, avoid inserting more than two images, drawing, tables or charts in any slide.
- Make sure the colors used in the presentation for background and foreground must be readable to the audience.

Skill Test Box

Fill the correct blank in the blanks given below:

1. For easily readability by audience, the font size must be __________.
2. The use of language and grammar in the presentation should be _______.
3. In one slide the number of lines should be _____________ for making a good presentation.

Summary

- Presentation software is used to display information in a sequence of slides or slide show that is used in colleges, schools, organizations, etc., for various purpose.
- MS PowerPoint is one of the presentation software that allow to make dynamic slide presentations that can include images, videos, animation and text.
- Elements if Presentation are: Be prepared, Give of yourself, It has a clear objective, Its useful to your audience and Use little text in your presentation desk.
- You will be relaxed if you have prepared for your presentation.

- While giving presentation try to use personal examples but make sure it support your point and message you want to convey through presentation.
- Characteristics of good presentation are: Opening and Closing phrases, Number of lines, Font size, Use of Quotations, Correctly use grammar and language, Insert Images, clips, tables or graphs, Simplicity, Use of colours, Animation, sounds and videos, Availability of Voice and words.
- Try to limit the number of lines, it should be between 5 to 8 lines in one slide.

Keywords: Presentation, MS PowerPoint, Elements of presentation, Characteristics of good quality presentation.

Self-Assessment

A. MULTIPLE CHOICE QUESTIONS

1. Which of the following is not the element of presentation?

   a. Be Prepared b. Stay Relaxed c. Motivate others d. It has clear objective

2. The most preferred Font size for presentation is:

   a. 12 b. 20 c. 28 d. 32

Answer

1. c 2. d

B. QUESTIONS:

1. Define Presentation Software?
2. Give various elements of Presentation?
3. What need to be there in good quality presentation?

C. PROJECT WORK

1. Make an assignment on various elements of a presentation and its usage.
2. Create a presentation on study of Microsoft Office and apply all the characteristics in it that makes your presentation of good quality. Then observe the differences.

SESSION 2: CREATE A PRESENTATION

Presentation software is used to display information in a sequence of slides or slide show that is used in colleges, schools, organizations, etc for various purpose. Microsoft PowerPoint 2010 is one of the presentation software that allow to make dynamic slide presentations that can include images, videos, animation and text. It is a part of Microsoft Office 2010 that provides various templates, layouts, wizards, themes and tools.

To enhance the presentation both 2D and 3D clipart can be used along with animations, special effects and translation styles and high impact drawing tools. Its use has been found in organization, educational field, entertainment, conferences and seminars. The data written in word can also be used in powerPoint presentation very easily.

Definition Box

PowerPoint is a Microsoft presentation program that creates a slide show of important information, charts, and images to display during a presentation. It is most often used for business and school presentations.

Start Powerpoint

To start or launch PowerPoint perform the following steps:

Click on Start > All Programs > Microsoft Office > Microsoft PowerPoint 2010

Or

Choose Start > Type PowerPoint in search programs and files box > Click on the application to start it

Or simply double click on PowerPoint icon if it is present on the desktop as shortcut

When you done with any of the above given steps a blank presentation with name Presentation1 will appears on the screen

PowerPoint Window

Below figure 5.1 gives the interface of MS PowerPoint 2010. This section will give the brief detail about all the components of PowerPoint 2010.

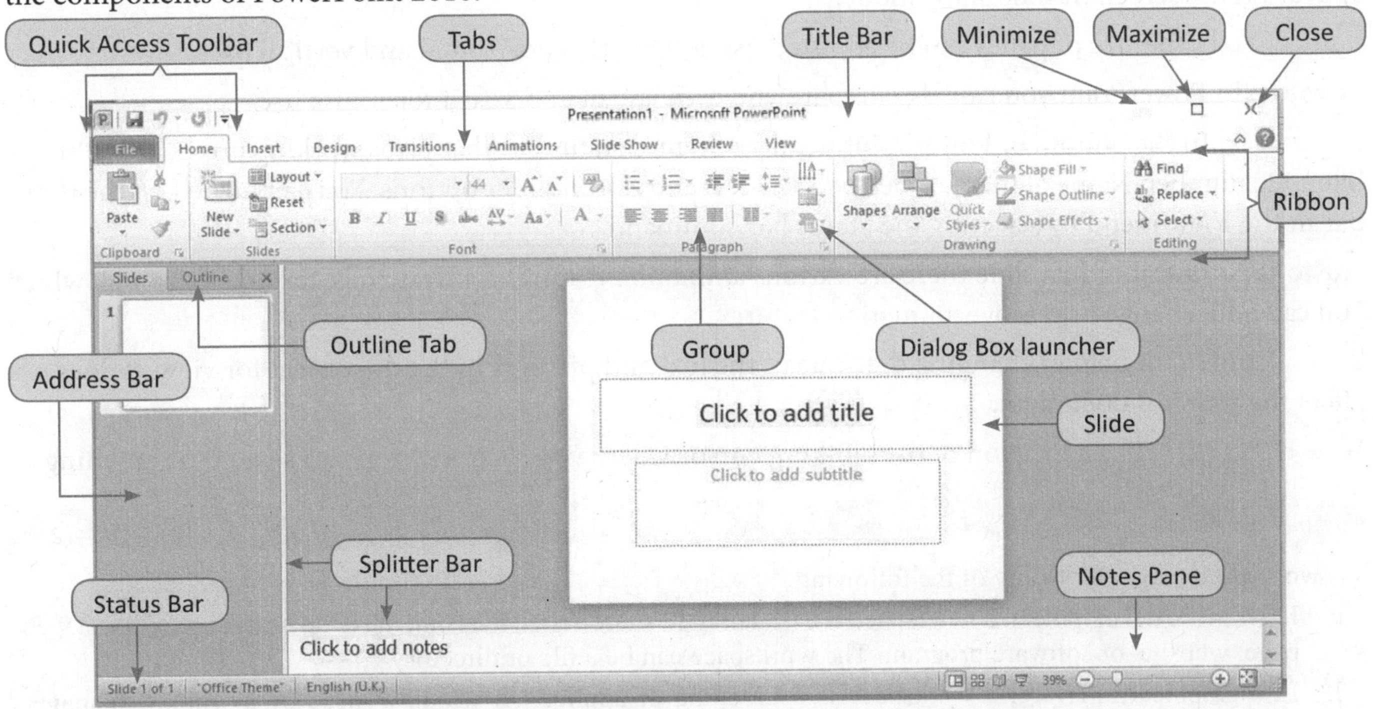

Figure 5.1: Interface of Microsoft PowerPoint 2010

Title Bar: On top and middle of word window there is title bar. Both the name of program and its currently used presentation is display on it. The default name of presentation is Presentation1 and name of application is Microsoft PowerPoint.

Quick access toolbar: It is located in the top left side of title bar. The frequently used common buttons are present on it. Redo, Undo and save are three buttons that are present by default on it. We can remove or add other button through the drop down arrow present on it.

Ribbon: On clicking of any tab a ribbon appears. It contains tab, groups and commands. On top of ribbon button there are 9 tabs that contains groups of related commands. All related commands are organized in groups. The name of Tabs are File, Home, Insert, Design, Translations, Animations, Slide Show, Review and View. By default the home tab appears after launching the word.

Window Management Buttons: In PowerPoint there are Minimizer, Maximize or restore and Close window management buttons. Each have their own functioning as to hide buttons from desktop screen a minimize button is used and to enlarge window back to its standard size a maximize button is used and to close application a Close button is used.

Slides Pane: The thumbnail of slides is display in slides pane or a place where user can design the slides. It allow user to add new slides, remove or rearrange slides.

Slides: On slide user can add text, image, video and audio.

Outline Tab: It displays the outline of text present in each slide and in this view user can directly edit their text.

Status Bar: In the bottom of PowerPoint window there is status bar that gives working document status like slide number, Name of theme, Spell check, View and Zoom slider options. View button consists of Normal view, Slide sorter view, Reading view and Slide show view and the zoom slider in right side helps to zoom in and out the slide.

Notes Pane: Users can type the personal notes about the current slide in notes pane and these notes do not appear on the screen in slide show mode.

Splitter Bar: The size of panes can be adjusted using these two horizontal and vertical bars.

Layouts: In PowerPoint you can also prepare ypu own layput and safe it for future use.

Status Bar: In the bottom of PowerPoint window there is status bar that gives working presentation status like slide number, Name of theme, Spell check, View and Zoom slider options. You can turned off the status bar in the View menu by selecting the Status bar command.

Custom Animation: In a slide there are various animation features for drawings, text, etc., through which you can add, change or remove animation features.

Zoom Control: It help in changing the scale of the text and pictures in the document for view. It does not affect the physical document.

Insertion Point: It is a location of the blinking cursor where your text will appear as you type anything.

LETS KNOW MORE

A workspace may refer to any of the following:

1. In software development, a workspace is a grouping of source code files that make up a larger unit, like a web page, website, or software program. The workspace can be a file or directory.
2. In a graphical interface, a workspace is a grouping of application windows used by a window manager applications to help reduce clutter on the desktop screen. Workspaces are commonly found on Unix operating systems.
3. For software as a service, a workspace is used to describe online applications that allow users to organize and exchange files with other users over the Internet.

On the title bar right corner, there are three window manipulation buttons that are minimized, maximize, and close buttons.

Closing a Presentation:

Till now we have learnt to create and save a presentation with or without password. Now, next step is to close the presentation. To close presentation performs the following steps:

Click on File tab > Select Close option from drop down menu

When user will click on close option a presentation will be closes. But in case user have not saved the last changes done in presentation then a message box will appear that contains three options Save, Don't Save and Cancel.

Save: On clicking on this option a changes will be saved and presentation will be close

Don't Save: On clicking on this option the last changes done in presentation will not save and presentation will be close

Cancel: In this case the process of closing presentation will be stop and user will return to presentation

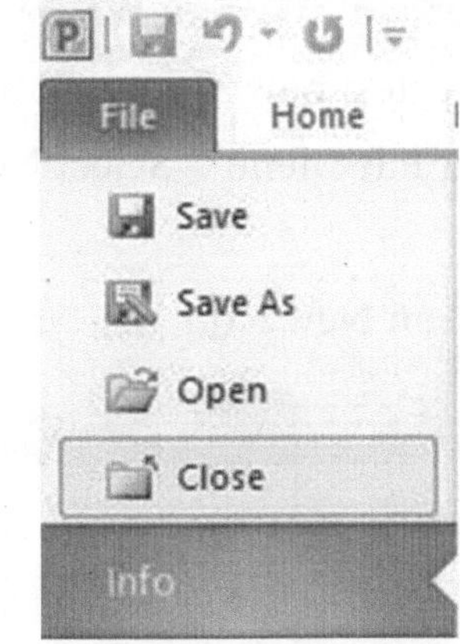

Figure 5.2: Closing a presentation

Creating a Presentation:

When user launch the MS PowerPoint 2010 a blank presentation with default name of Presentation1 is appear on screen. In this you can either start working on that presentation or create new presentation. The steps need to follow to create a new presentation are:

Click on File tab > Select New option > Select template or blank presentation as per your requirements > Click on create button

LETS KNOW MORE

Shortcut to close PowerPoint is: Press Alt + F4 keys

Press Ctrl + Q

On clicking on file tab a drop down menu will appear from it select the New option then select blank presentation an empty presentation will be created. User can also select from the inbult templates given in the software. Once user is done with template selection part, click on Create button given in the right side of the window. After clicking on create button a blank or template presentation will start appearing on the window. The created presentation contains dotted rectangular boxes or placeholders where user can enter the text.

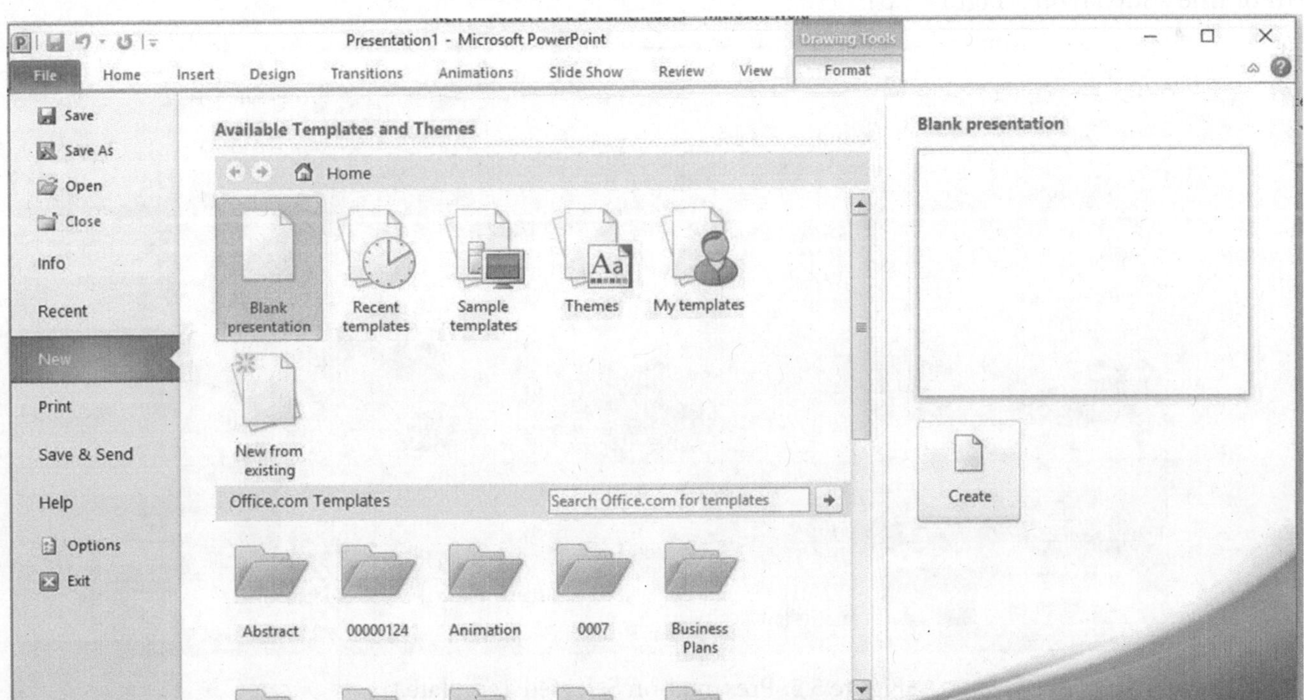

Figure 5.3: Creating presentation

Creating a Presentation using Template

To create a new presentation, perform the following steps:

Select File Menu > Select New

OR

Click on New icon

> **LETS KNOW MORE**
>
> Shortcut to create a presentation is: Press Ctrl + N keys

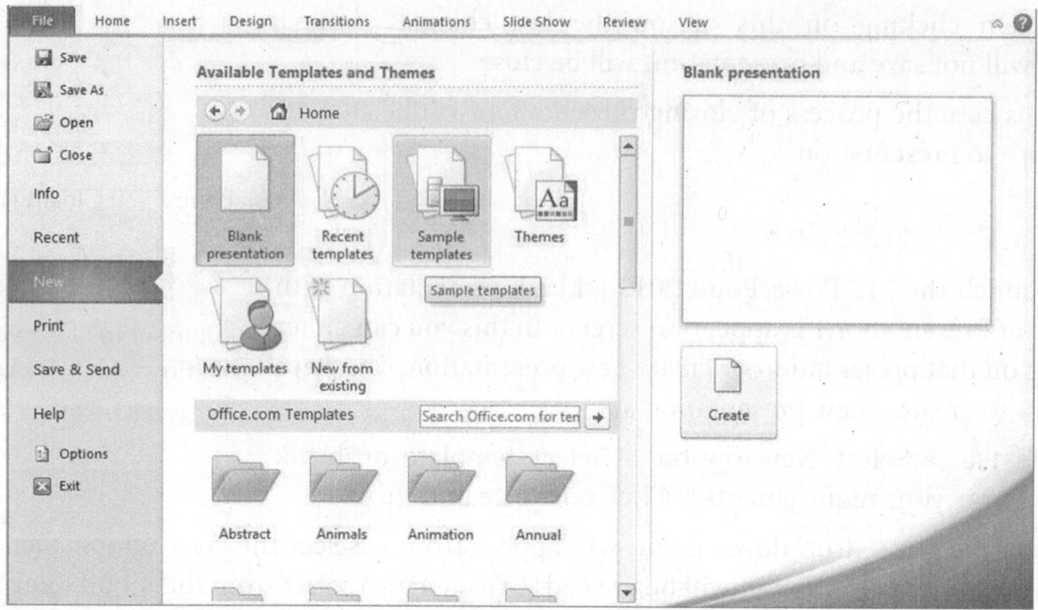

Figure 5.4: Select a Template Window

After selecting the New icon a "Select a Template" window will appear (Figure 5.4). From this window you can double click on the template to select it as per your choice. Then a selected template will appears in the form of title slide layout (Figure 5.5).

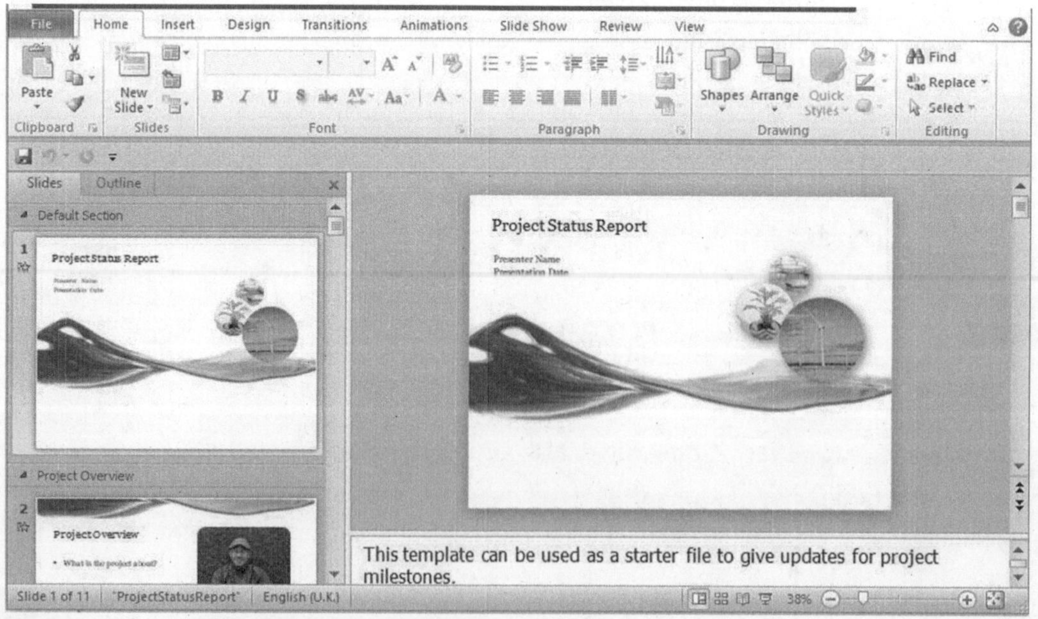

Figure 5.5: Presentation Selected Template

In this the first slide is title slide. You can observe that the first slide for creating a presentation is the title slide. Then as per your title slide, you can use either a blank layout or one of the title layouts.

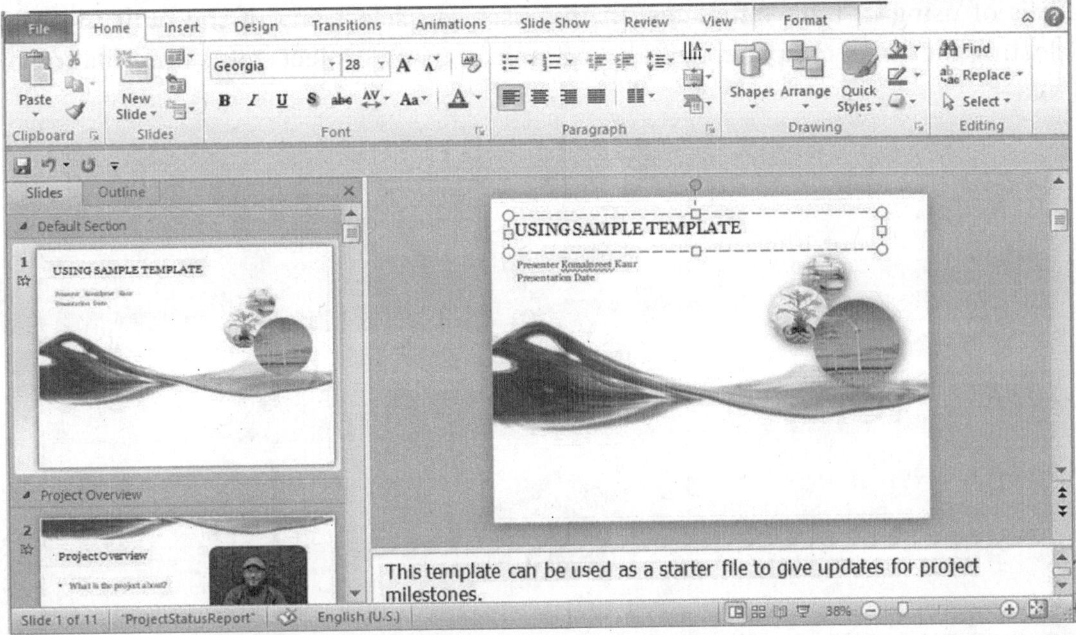

Figure 5.6: Entering data on the Slide

Now enter the title text in the selected template (*Figure 5.6)*

Selecting a Slide Layout

In case of blank presentation there is title slide as the first slide and for rest of the created slides there will be title and content in default layout. The default layout of the slide can be change by clicking on layout command given in the Slides Menu. From this display list user can select the desired layout.

In case of blank presentation there is title slide as the first slide and for rest of the created slides there will be title and content in default layout. The default layout of the slide can be change by clicking on layout command given in the Slides group of home tab. From this display list user can select the desired layout.

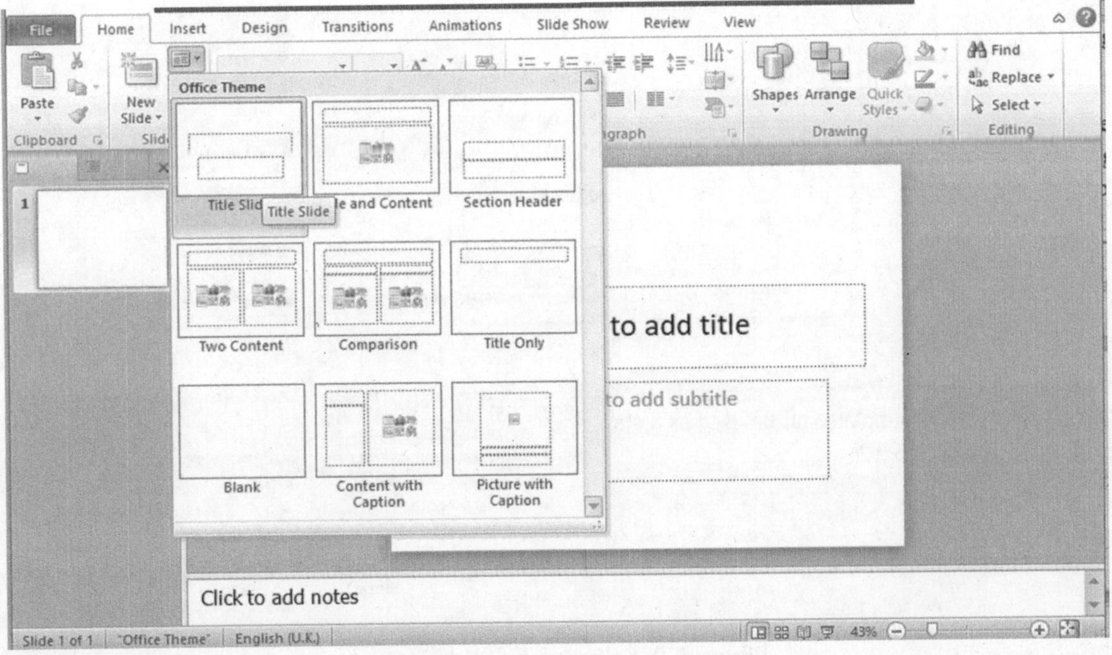

Figure 5.7: Layout options

Another case is of using in-built templates. In this user can select any of the built in sample template instead of selecting the blank template. Let take example of using project status presentation template that contains 11 slides.

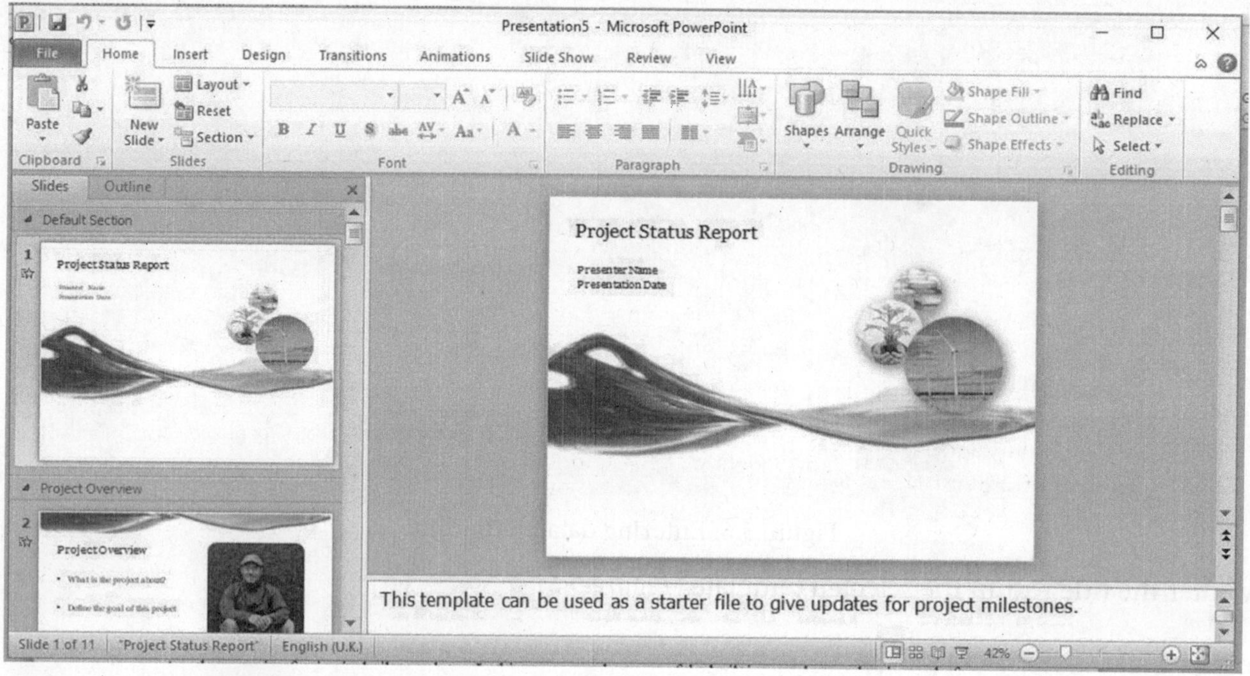

Figure 5.8: Project status sample template

You can see (Figure 5.9) there are layouts from a blank slide to slide with six context box given in the end. To select a Slide layout, perform the following steps:

- Select Slide Menu > Slide Layout > Title slide.

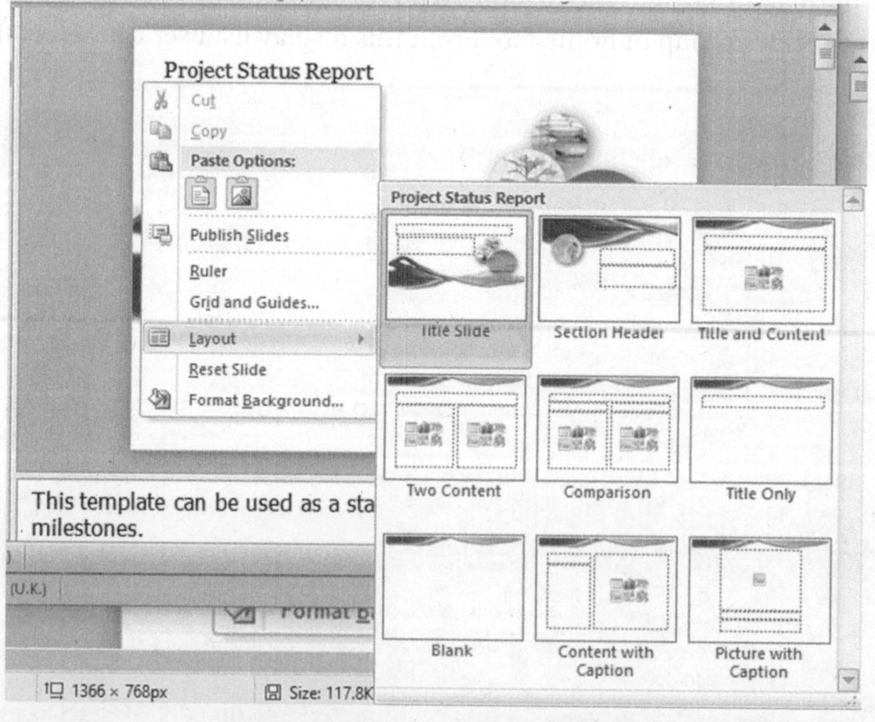

Figure 5.9: Selection of Slide Layout

You can select any of the layout. For example, we have selected the Layout: Title and 2 Content and it will be applicable in the right side of the window.

OR

You can also select the layout from Layouts section given in the right side of presentation.

Now to further add text to slide, simply click on Click add text in the text frame and type the text.

LETS KNOW MORE

In MS PowerPoint, slide layout refers to design and placement of different elements on a slide. The default slide layout is a title at the top of the slide, and text underneath the title. However, this default can be modified to include alternate text, images, and even video. The slide layout can be considered an overview of the information being presented by the user.

Saving a Presentation

Once you are done with creating a presentation either using blank presentation or in built presentation, the next step is to save it. This step is done to avoid the loss of data. The steps need to follow to save the presentation are:

Click on File tab > Select Save option given in the drop down menu > Save As dialog box appears > Specify the name in File name Text box > Click on Save button given in the bottom right side of dialog box

Or

Click on Save given in the Quick Access Toolbar then rest of the steps will be same

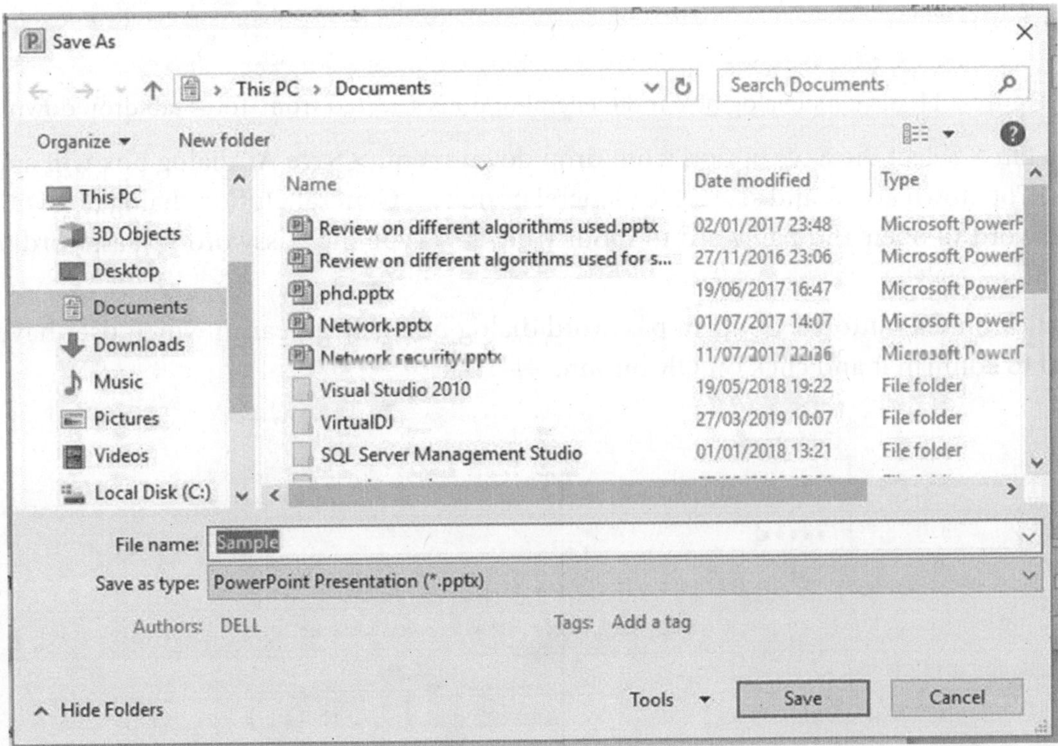

Figure 5.10: Save As Dialog box for saving a presentation

The extension of presentation file is .pptx

Saving a presentation using password protection:

Sometimes we make presentation on confidential data that we need to protect from others. In those cases the saving presentation using password protection of PowerPoint 2010 is used. To add password perform the following steps:

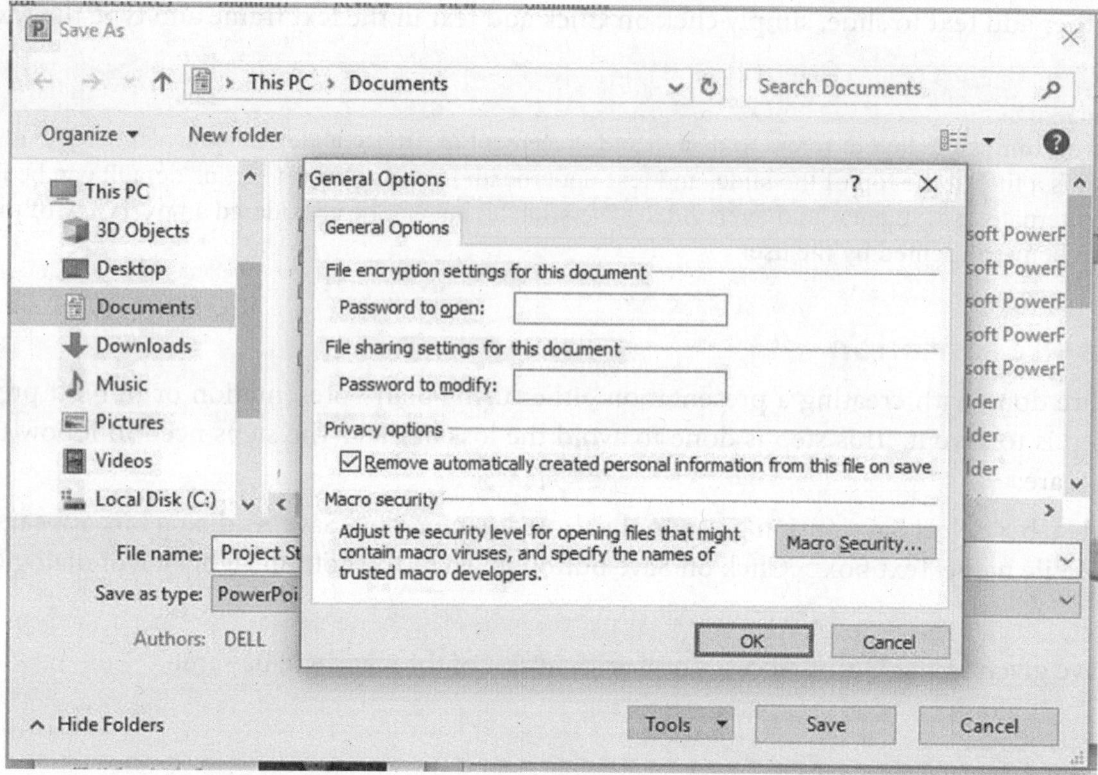

Figure 5.11: Save As Dialog box and General options selected from Tools tab drop down

Click on File tab > Select the Save option from drop down menu > Save As dialog box will appear > Click on Tools tab drop down arrow and select the General options > General Option dialog box will appear that contains password to open and password to modify fields > Type the password in Password to open field > Click on OK

When user click on Ok button a Confirm password dialog box will appear in which user have to re-enter the password to confirm it and click on OK button.

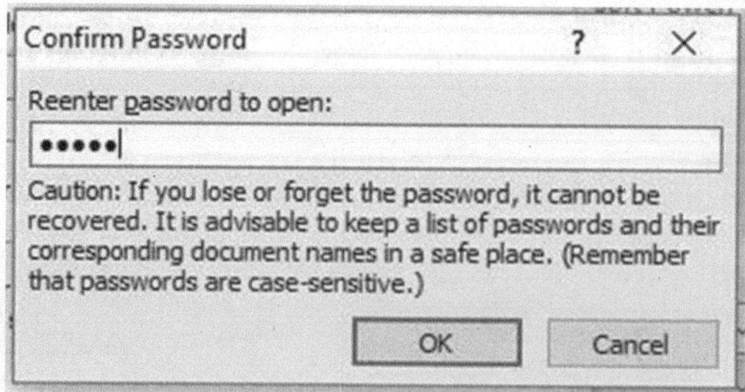

Figure 5.12: Confirm password dialog box

In this section we did a setting of password for opening a presentation further password can be set to modify a presentation. To do it user have to set the password for password to modify text box rest things will remain same as for setting the password for opening the presentation.

Saving a Presentation with different Name

You can also save the existing presentation with different name. To save the presentation with different name, perform the following steps:

Select File > Save As

This will open a Save As dialog box.

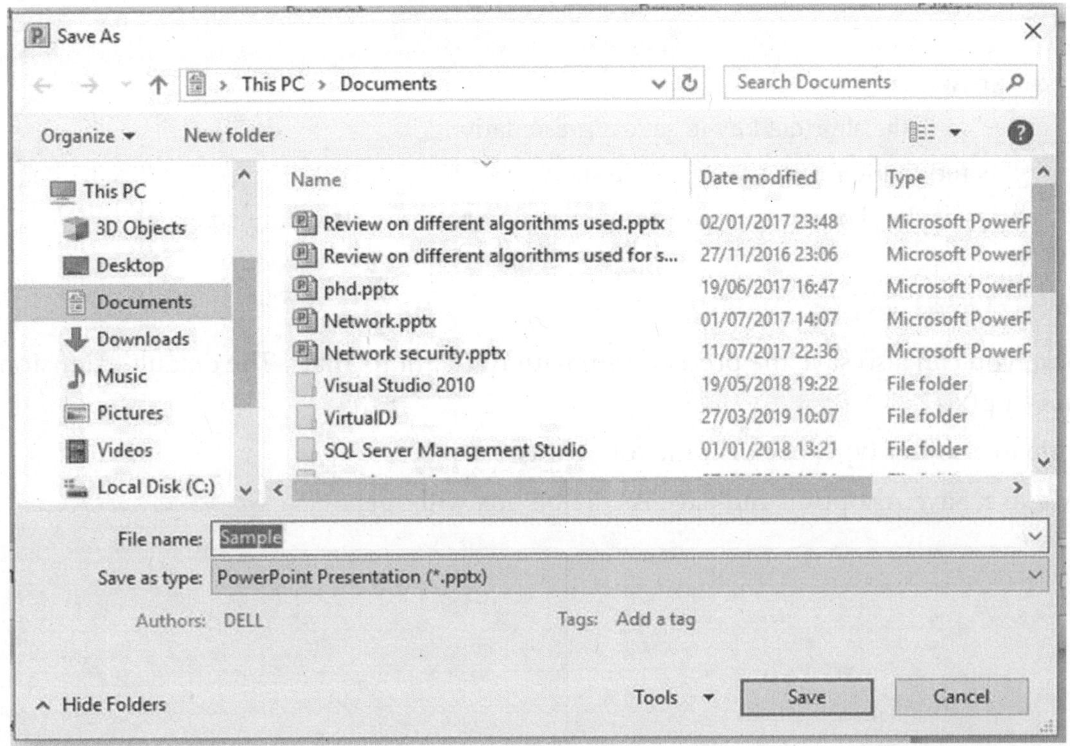

Figure 5.13: Save As dialog box

In Save As dialog box, you can enter the new presentation in File name text box > Click on Save button

> **LETS KNOW MORE**
>
> Shortcut to Save As a presentation is:
> Press Shift + Ctrl +S keys

Running a Slide Show

Till above we have learnt to create and save a presentation. Now we will lean to run a slide show. To run the slide show, perform the following steps:

- Click on Slide Show > Select from Beginning on the Start slide show menu bar

  OR

- Click on Slide Show icon on the presentation toolbar

  OR

  Select Slide Sorter toolbar.

> **LETS KNOW MORE**
>
> Shortcut to run a Slide show a presentation is: Press F5 key

By starting Slide show by any of the option a slide show starts to run. Now further to move to next slide, click the mouse button.

- Use the arrow keys on the keyboard

  OR

- Use the spacebar key on the keyboard

In order to navigate the slide and set other options, right click anywhere in the screen and it will open a menu for navigating the slides.

- To Exit the presentation in between, click on Esc button on the keyboard.

  OR

- Click to exit presentation when you will reach on the last slide.

Skill Test Box

Fill the correct answer:

1. ______________ is the shortcut key to save a presentation.
2. __________ is the shortcut key to run a slide show.
3. _____________ is the shortcut key to save a presentation with a different name.

Save a Presentation in PDF

In PowerPoint, you can also save the presentation with different formats. The default extension of saving a presentation is .pptx.

To save the file in another type, perform the following steps:

Select File Menu > Save As option and Save As dialog box will open

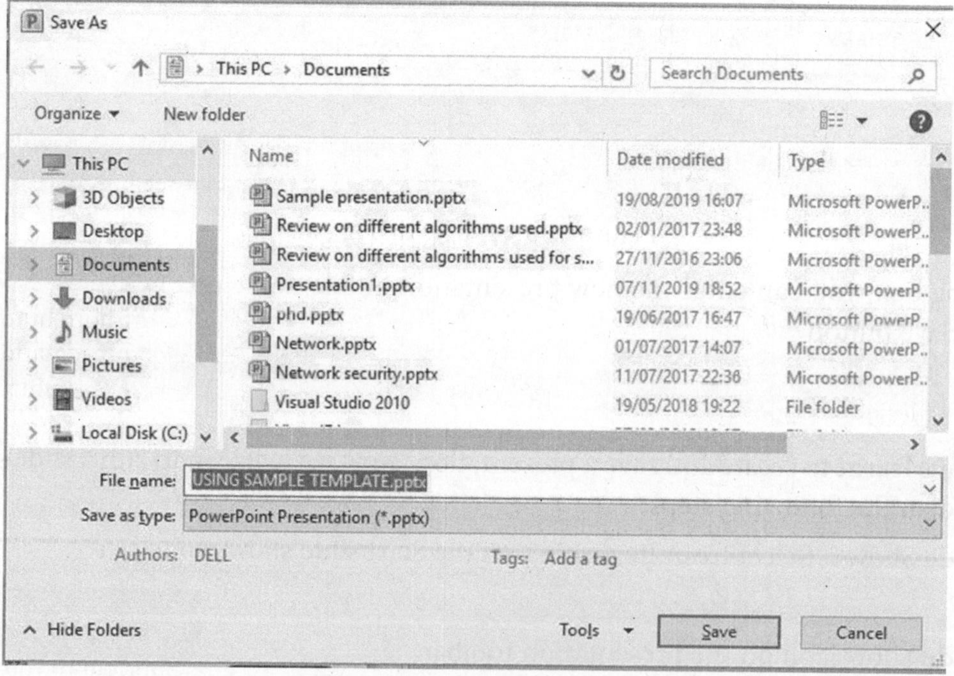

Figure 5.14: Save As .pptx format

In Save As dialog box, you can select the required format type from Save as type drop-down menu. In figure 5.14 we have used PowerPont 2007-2019 (*.pptx).

OR

To save a presentation file in Portable document format (PDF) format, perform the following steps:

Click on File Menu > Export as PDF

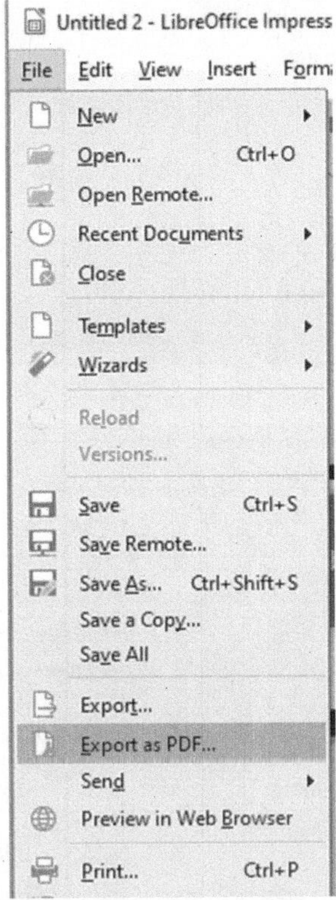

Figure 5.15: Export as PDF option

This will open a PDF Options dialog box > Click on Export button and Export window will open

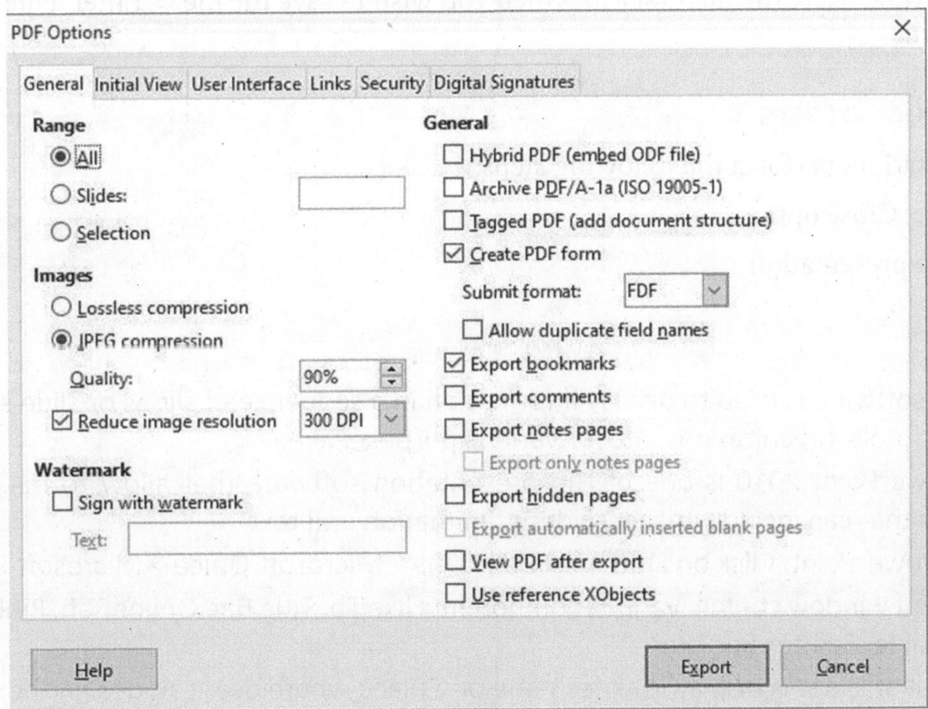

Figure 5.16: PDF Options dialog box

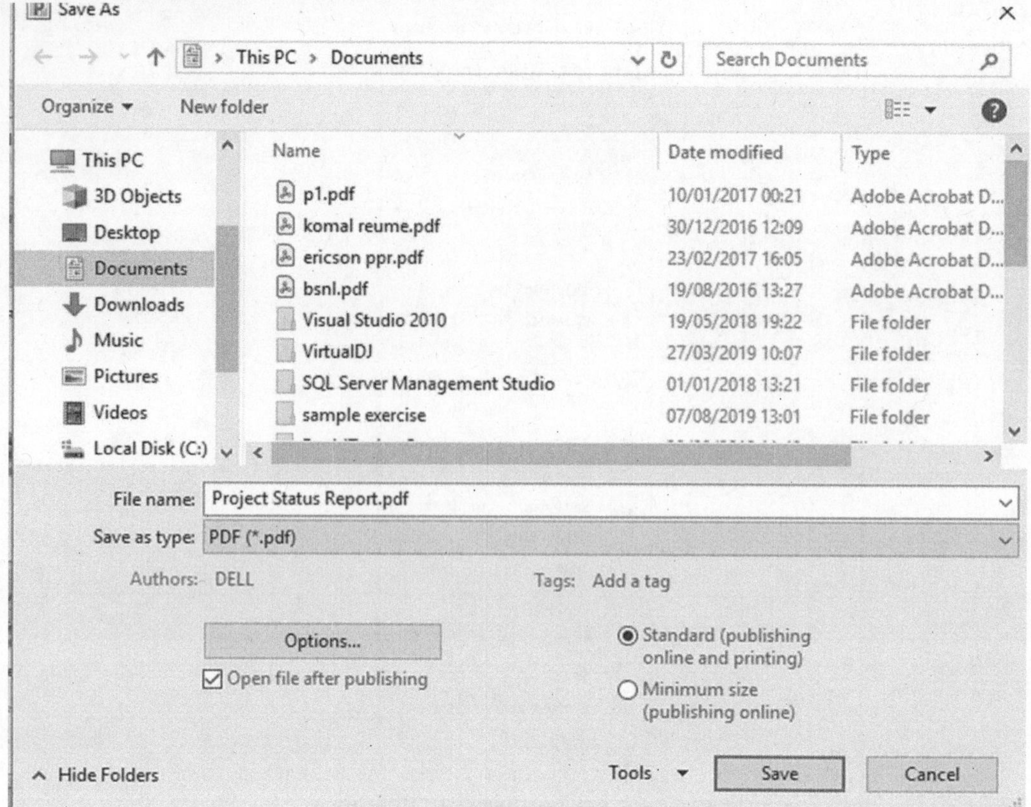

Figure 5.17: Export Window

From Export window select the directory in which you wish to save the file. > Enter a file name > Click on Save button

Closing a Presentation

To close a presentation, perform the following steps:

Select File Menu > Close option

This will close the presentation

LETS KNOW MORE

Shortcut to close a presentation is: Press Ctrl + W key

Summary

- Presentation software is used to display information in a sequence of slides or slide show that is used in colleges, schools, organizations, etc for various purpose.
- Microsoft PowerPoint 2010 is one of the presentation software that allow to make dynamic slide presentations that can include images, videos, animation and text.
- To Launch a PowerPoint, Click on Start > All Programs > Microsoft Office > Microsoft PowerPoint 2010
- The PowerPoint window contain various components like Tb, Title Bar, Online Tab, Ribbon, Slides pane, Notes pane, Slide, Splitter Bar, etc.
- The thumbnail of slides is display in slides pane or a place where user can design the slides.
- Slide is just like a paper in notebook where user can add text, image, video and audio.
- Outline tab displays the outline of text present in each slide
- Users can type the personal notes about the current slide in notes pane
- The thumbnail of slides is display in slides pane or a place where user can design the slides.

- The slides are present in the left part of the window. On slide user can add text, image, video and audio.
- It is the area in the central part of the window that is reserved for typing and adding pictures or clipart.
- To Close PowerPoint, Select the File Menu > Exit option.
- To select a slide layout, Select Slide Menu > Slide Layout > Title slide.
- To Save a Presentation, Select File Menu > Save option
- To Save a presentation with different name, Select File > Save As
- To run a Slide Show, Click on Slide Show > Select Start from Fist Slide on the main menu bar
- To Close a Presentation, Select File Menu > Close option

Keywords: Starting PowerPoint, Steps to start presentation, Parts of PowerPoint window, Closing PowerPoint, Creating a presentation using a template, Selecting a slide layout, Saving a presentation, Saving it with different name, Running a slide show, Save a presentation in PDF, Closing a presentation, Using Help.

Self-Assessment

A. MULTIPLE CHOICE QUESTIONS

1. Which of the following component gives Name of theme?

   a. Outline Tab b. Home Tab c. Status Bar d. Notes pane

2. Which of the following is not the Tab of PowerPoint:

   a. File tab b. Page Layout tab c. Insert tab d. Design tab

3. _______________ is not a display on Status bar.

   a. Slide number b. Name of theme c. Slide Style d. Spell check

4. What is the shortcut key to save a presentation?

   a. Ctrl + A Keys b. Ctrl + S Keys c. Shift + A Keys d. Shift + S Keys

B. FILL IN THE BLANKS

1. ___________ is the process of displaying information in a sequence of slides.
2. Thumbnail of slides is display in ___________
3. In PowerPoint ribbon there are ___________ number of tabs
4. _______________ is the default name of presentation

C. TRUE FALSE

1. Notes pane allow to enter the important notes related to current slide (T/F)
2. Open is a window management button (T/F)
3. The title bar in PowerPoint contains Presentation name and name of application (T/F)

D. ANSWER THE FOLLOWING QUESTIONS:

1. What is presentation and name the software that can be used to make a presentation?
2. What do you mean by slide in PowerPoint?

3. What is the difference between slide and slide show?
4. What is a Ribbon and name components available in it.
5. What is the use of Notes pane?
6. Write down the steps to launch a PowerPoint 2010.

E. PRACTICAL WORK

1. Start PowerPoint, demonstrate the various components of PowerPoint main Window and also observe the various workspace views in it.
2. Create a presentation of 2-3 slides for inviting your friends on event organize by you. These slides will include all the details of event held by you then save it in PDF format and send to your friend through mail.

ANSWER:

A. Multiple choice question answers:

1. c 2. b 3. c 4. b

B. Fill in the blanks answers:

1. Slide show
2. Slides Pane
3. Nine
4. Presentation1

B. True False answers:

1. True
2. False
3. True

SESSION 3: WORK WITH SLIDES

In MS PowerPoint, you can insert a new slide into the presentation and duplicate slide. A copy of existing or selected slide will be inserted in the presentation by inserting a duplicate slide.

Inserting a Duplicate Slide

Sometimes there are requirement to insert the same slide as the previous ones. In those cases you can copy the slide to next slide. To insert a duplicate slide, perform the following steps and using the options given below:

Select the slide from Slide Pane > Select New Slide drop down from slides group from Home tab> Duplicate selected Slides

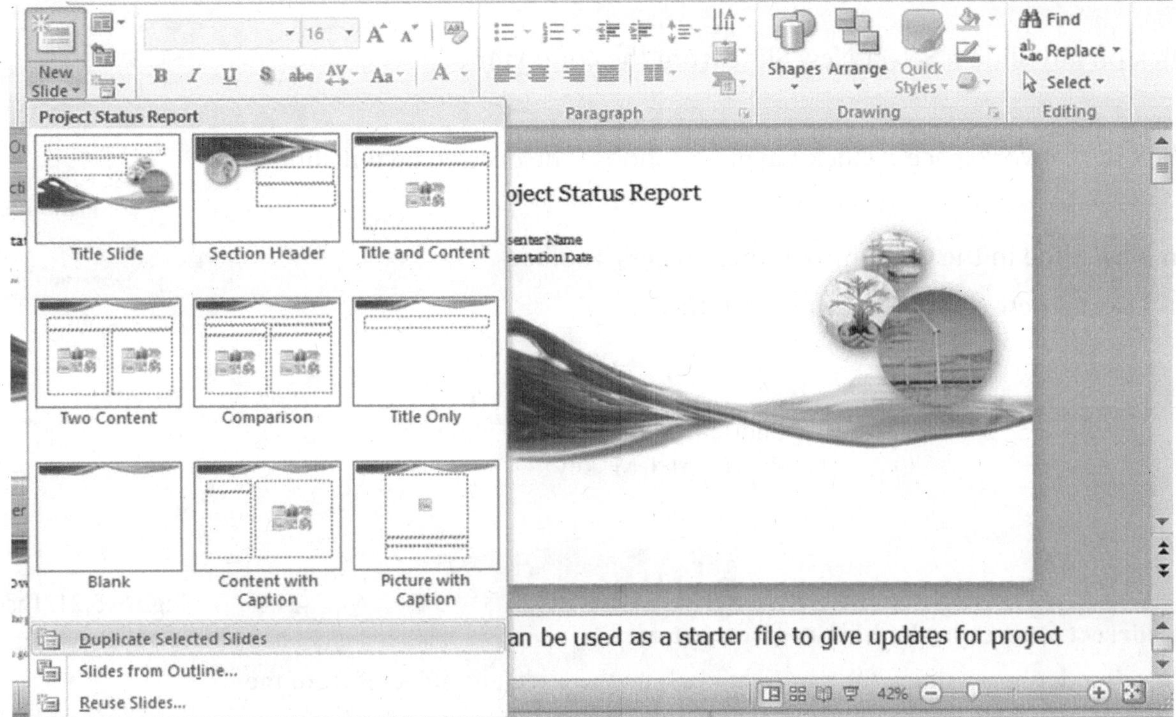

Figure 5.19: Inserting Duplicate Slide

Another option is: Right click on the slide > Select Duplicate Slide from the menu

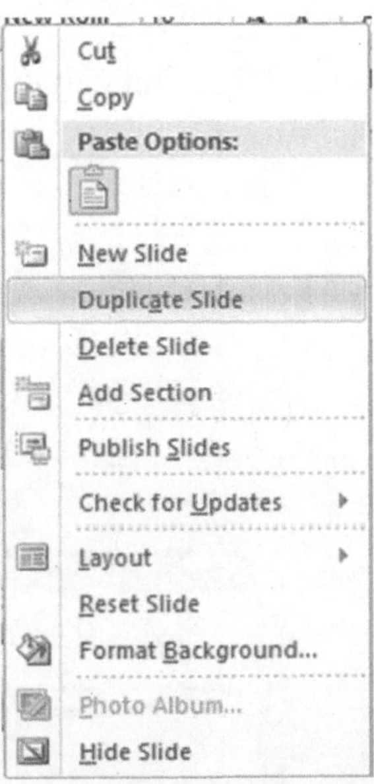

Figure 5.20: Inserting Duplicate Slide

Click on Duplicate Slide icon given in the presentation toolbar.

Inserting new Slide

Like duplicate slide, you can also insert a new slide of different layout. To insert a new slide, perform the following steps:

Click on drop down menu of New Slide given in Slides group of Home tab > Select the layout as per your requirements

OR

Right click on any slide > Select New Slide from the context menu

OR

Right click in the workspace > Click Layout > Choose the desired layout slide

OR

Click on New Slide in the Customize Quick Access Toolbar

This will insert a new slide into the presentation.

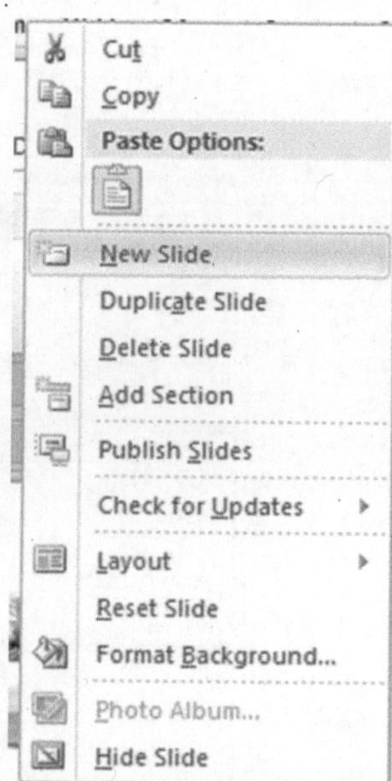

Figure 5.21: Inserting New Slide

LETS KNOW MORE

Shortcut to Insert a new slide is:
Press Ctrl + M key

Skill Test Box

Fill the correct answer in the blanks given below:

1. To insert a duplicate slide, one can right click on the slide and select it from the ____________.
2. ____________ is the shortcut key to insert a new slide.

Slide Layout

There are number of layouts available in PowerPoint that can contains one or more content boxes. In these content boxes you can insert images, charts, movies, tables, sound, text, etc. On the basis of content you want to add, you can select the icon.

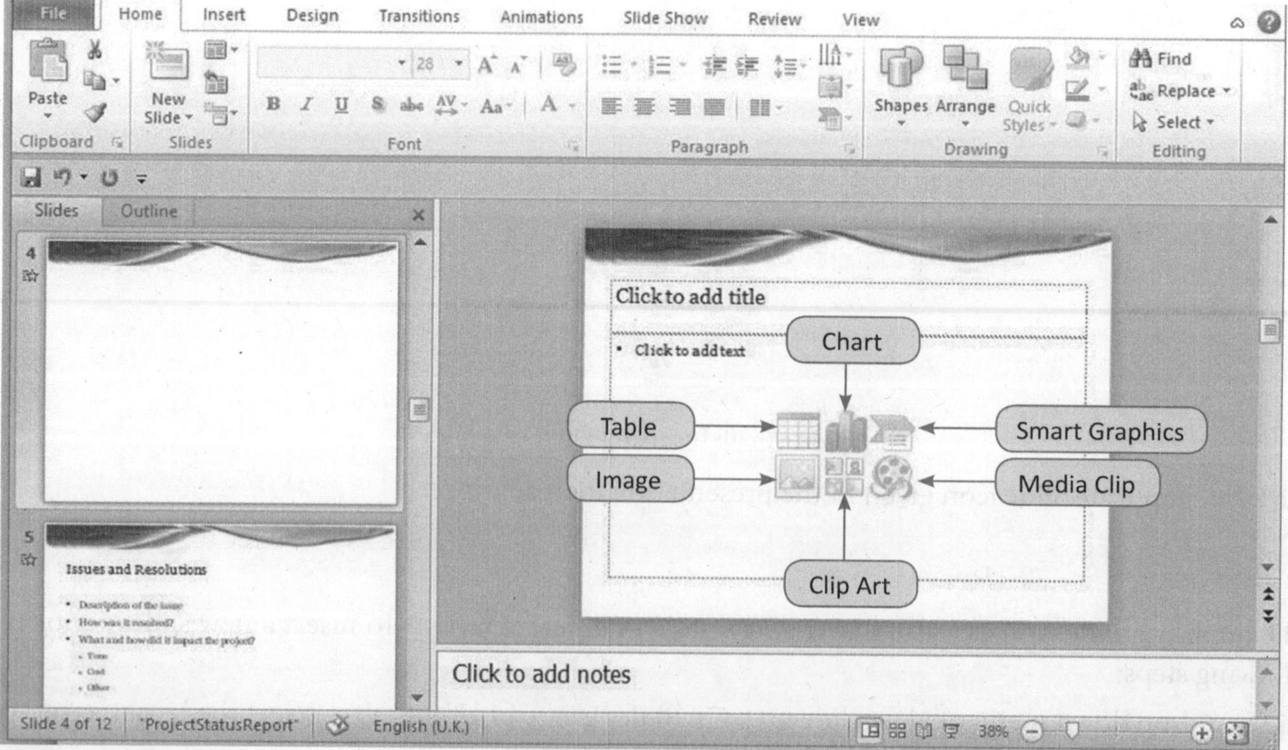

Figure 5.22: Various Content type

The default layout of the slide can be change by clicking on layout command given in the Slides Menu. From this display list user can select the desired layout.

OR

Select Home Tab > Slide Layout > Select the slide

OR

Select the slide from the Slides Pane

By choosing layout from any of the above given options a slide with that layout starts appearing in the workspace . Some layout contains one content boxes, two or more content boxes.

In case you want to add text in content box, perform the following steps:

Click to add text > Enter the text

Copying and Moving Slides

It is very time consuming to create the same slide again and again. In PowerPoint there is option to reuse the existing slide within the presentation or in any other presentation. To move the slide to another location or to reuse it use the cut and paste and copy and paste process respectively.

To Cut and Paste or Move the Slide, perform the following steps:

- Select the slide > Right click on mouse button > Select the Cut option from context menu

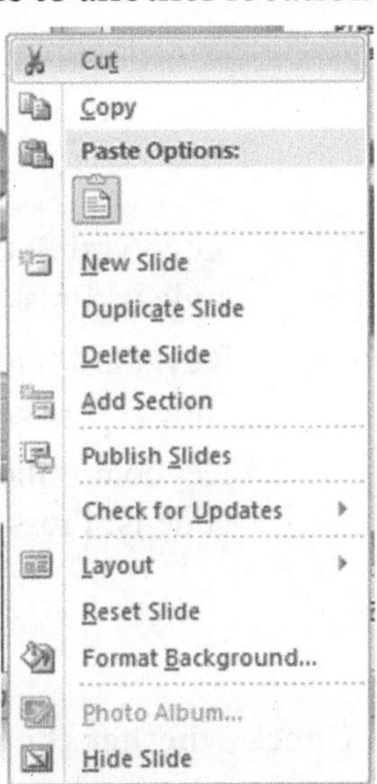

Figure 5.23: Cut Slide

Now mark the place in the presentation where you want to move the slide > Right click the mouse button > Select the Paste option from the context menu

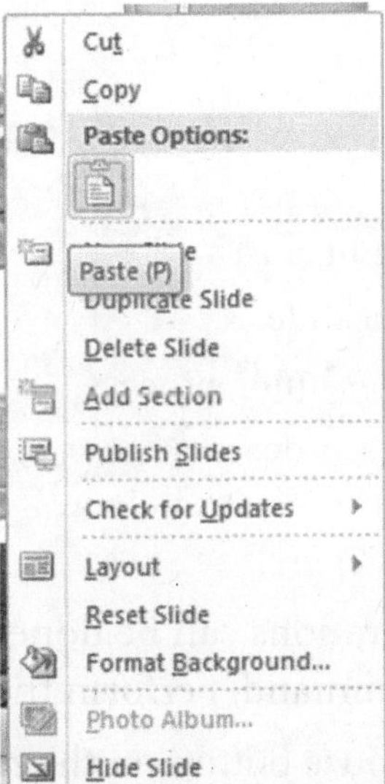

Figure 5.24: Paste Slide

To Copy and Paste or Reuse the Slide, perform the following steps:

- Select the slide > Right click on mouse button > Select the Copy option from context menu

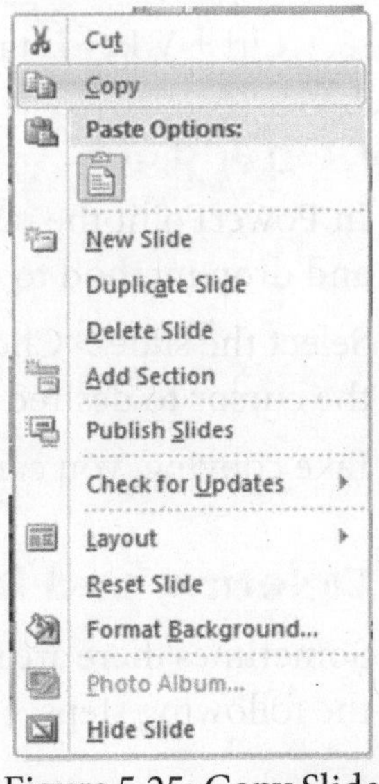

Figure 5.25: Copy Slide

Now mark the place in the presentation where you want to reuse the slide > Right click the mouse button > Select the Paste option from the context menu

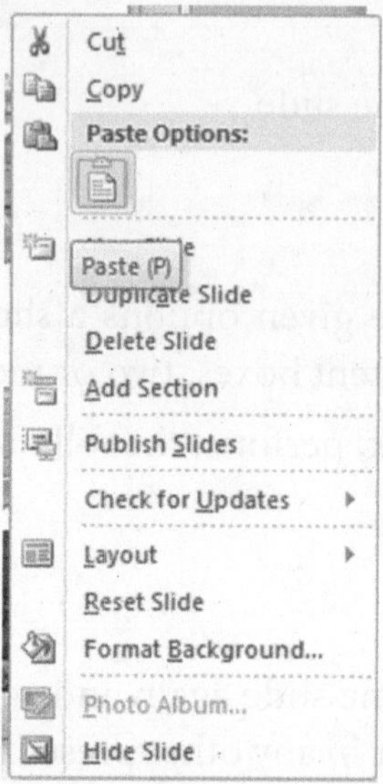

Figure 5.26: Paste Slide

LETS KNOW MORE

Keyboard Shortcut to Cut a slide is: Press Ctrl + X key

Keyboard Shortcut to Copy a slide is: Press Ctrl + C key

Keyboard Shortcut to Paste a slide is: Press Ctrl + V key

Copying and moving commands in MS PowerPoint will save your time while making big projects.

Skill Test Box

Check whether the given statement is true or not:

1. Ctrl + X key is the shortcut key to copy a slide.
2. Copying and moving a slide is a time consuming process.
3. Ctrl + V key is the shortcut key to paste a slide.

Drag and drop Copying and Moving method:

In PowerPoint the cut, copy and paste operations can be done using Drag and drop method. To use drag and drop method to copy and paste the command, perform the following steps:

Select the slide > Click and hold the left mouse button on the marked slide along with Ctrl button > Move the cursor to desired location > Release the left mouse button

Like copying, you can also move the text using drag and drop method.

Deleting and Renaming a Slides

Sometimes there are requirement to delete or rename the slide. **To delete any slide in PowerPoint,** perform the following steps:

Select the slide > Right click the mouse on the selected slide > Select the Delete slide option from the context menu

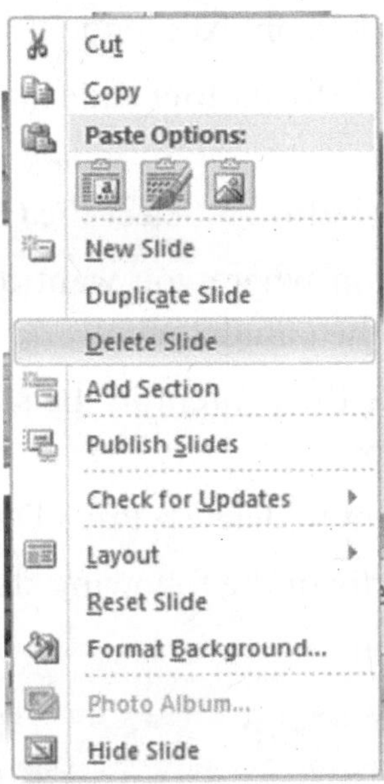

Figure 5.27: Delete Slide

OR

Select the slide > Press the Delete button given on the keyboard

The default name of slides are slide1, slide2, etc. **To rename any slide in PowerPoint**, perform the following steps:

Select the slide > Click on drop down menu of Section command in Slides group > Select the Rename slide option from the context menu

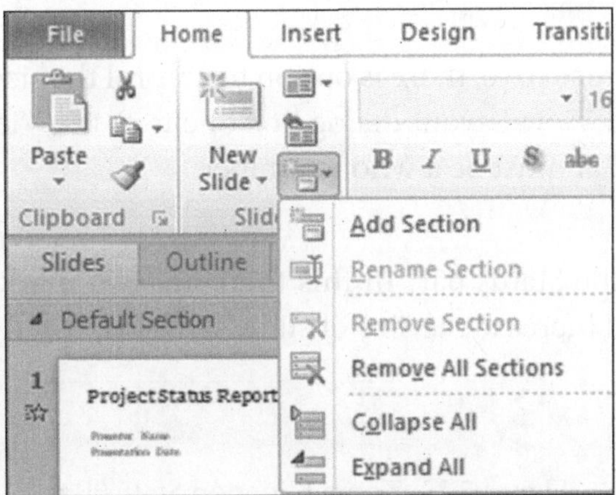

Figure 5.28: Rename Slide

Copying, Moving and deleting content

Sometimes there is requirement of using same data as used in existing slide. In those cases we can copy, move and also delete the content in MS PowerPoint as we do in MS Word. This will save time and efforts that user have to put in writing the same data again in different location.

To **Copy and Paste the content** from one slide to another slide in same or another presentation, perform the following steps:

- Select the slide > Right click on mouse button > Select the Copy option from context menu
- Now mark the place in the presentation where you want to reuse the slide > Right click the mouse button > Select the Paste option from the context menu

To **Cut and Paste the content** from one slide to another slide in same or another presentation, perform the following steps:

- Select the slide > Right click on mouse button > Select the Cut option from context menu
- Now mark the place in the presentation where you want to reuse the slide > Right click the mouse button > Select the Paste option from the context menu

Sometimes there are requirement to delete the content in the slide. **To delete any content from the slide in PowerPoint**, perform the following steps:

- Put the cursor after the content you want to delete > Press Delete or Backspace button on the keyboard.

To delete the line or paragraph or text, perform the following steps:

- Select the Content > Press delete button

LETS KNOW MORE

There is a difference in the *Delete* and *Backspace* button. As the delete button will delete the content from the right of the corner, on the other hand, the *Backspace* key or button will delete from the left of the corner. Pressing any of the Delete or *Backspace* key will delete one character at a time.

View a Presentation

In PowerPoint there are number of ways to view the created presentation. One can view the presentation in larger size, some in smaller size and medium size. So, as per user requirements one can view the presentation in different sizes.

Controlling the size of the view

To view the presentation in different sizes, there is option to control the size of the view. You can control the size of the view using Zoom and View Layout dialog box opens in the View tab. Using it you can increase zoom or enter your own value that must be a whole number.

OR

Use the Zoom Slider given on the Status bar: In this there are two marked sections one is –ve sign that reduce the size and +ve Sign will increase the size of slide.

Figure 5.29: Zoom Slider on Status Bar

OR

Use of the Zoom button on the Standard toolbar

OR

Use the menu option: Click on View tab > Select the appropriate option from it.

Workspace Views

In MS PowerPoint we can view a presentation with different views like Normal, Slide Sorter, Notes Page and Slide show. The default view of PowerPoint 2010 is Normal view. Various view options are given in bottom right side that can be change by simply clicking on desired option or you can also select it from Presentation view group of View tab. This session will give brief details about various types of views available in PowerPoint 2010.

Normal View:

This is the default type of view and in this view images, text, animation, video and audio can be added on slide. User can see Slide pane, Notes pane and left pane that have Outline and Slide tab. The outline structure of presentation can easily view in outline tab and in this text can be easily edited. To open Normal view of presentation performs the following steps:

Click on Normal view icon present on the bottom right side in status bar

Or

Click on View tab > Select Normal view command from Presentation views group

These both ways will open a Normal view of presentation.

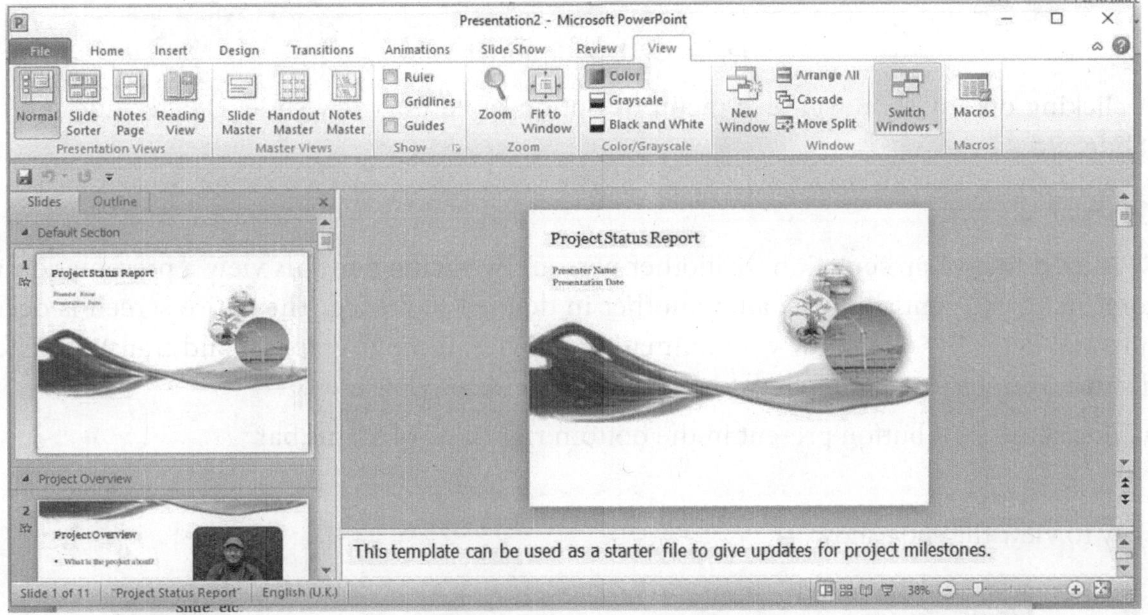

Figure 5.30: Normal View

In this view a large view of current slide appears in the center section of the PowerPoint window. In this section user can enter text, image, animation, graphics, charts, text boxes, hyperlinks, audio and video. Here user can also easily add, arrange or delete slides. The Notes pane is present at the bottom of the MS PowerPoint screen. The space to write speaker notes or information about particular slide in the presentation is provided by it that can be helpful for speaker at the time of giving presentation.

Slide Sorter View:

In Slide sorter view user will get the miniature view of all the slides that is mainly helpful in rearranging, deleting, changing order of slides, adding translation, setting the timings for the slide show and adding a new slide, etc. To select the Slider sorter view perform the following steps:

Click on Slide Sorter view button given in the right bottom side of status bar next to Normal view button

Or

Click on View Tab > Select Slide Sorter view command given in the Presentation views group

Figure 5.31: Slide Sorter View

On right clicking on any slide will give menu or option of adding new slide, Delete slide, Add section, Publish Slide, etc.

Slide Show View:

This view is used to give presentation to another person. By clicking on this view a presentation will start either from first or current slide one after another in defined sequence. The entire screen is occupied by single slide that helps in seeing how your animation, movies, timings graphics and transition effects look in actual show. The steps need to follow to select the Slide show view are:

Click on Slide show view button present in the bottom right side of Status bar

Or

User F5 key to view the slide show

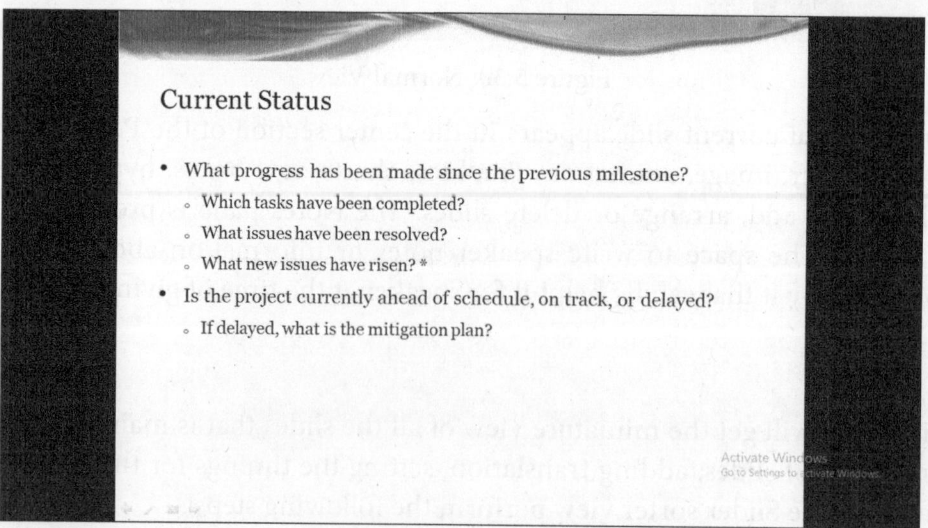

Figure 5.32: Slide Show View

Once you have selected the Slide show view then to move to next slide click on Mouse button or use space/ enter key present on keyboard. User has to click on Esc to quit the Slide show view.

Notes Page view:

This will give the Note page for particular slide to edit the speaker notes information which is not visible to other person while giving presentation. This will help speaker in remembering the important points to discuss and giving to audience.

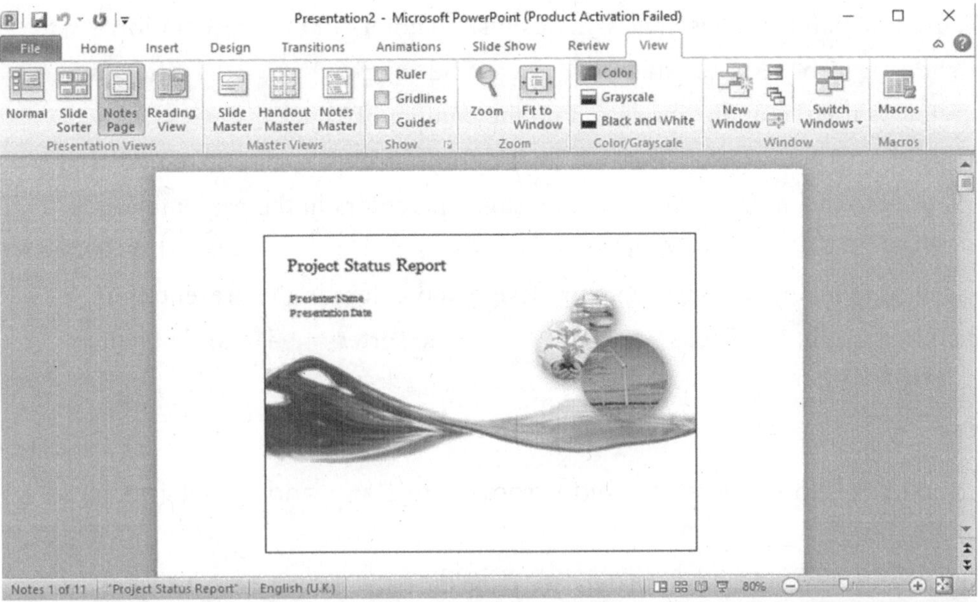

Figure 5.33: Notes Page

If section part is not present then user can get it by right clicking on slide to add new section.

Reading View:

It is similar to slide show view as in both slide is shown in full screen mode. The only difference in reading view is that title bar and status bar is displayed in it. This view helps in easily navigate during slide show as in slide show view along with that it provides an easy access to window task bar to switch to other open window or programs.

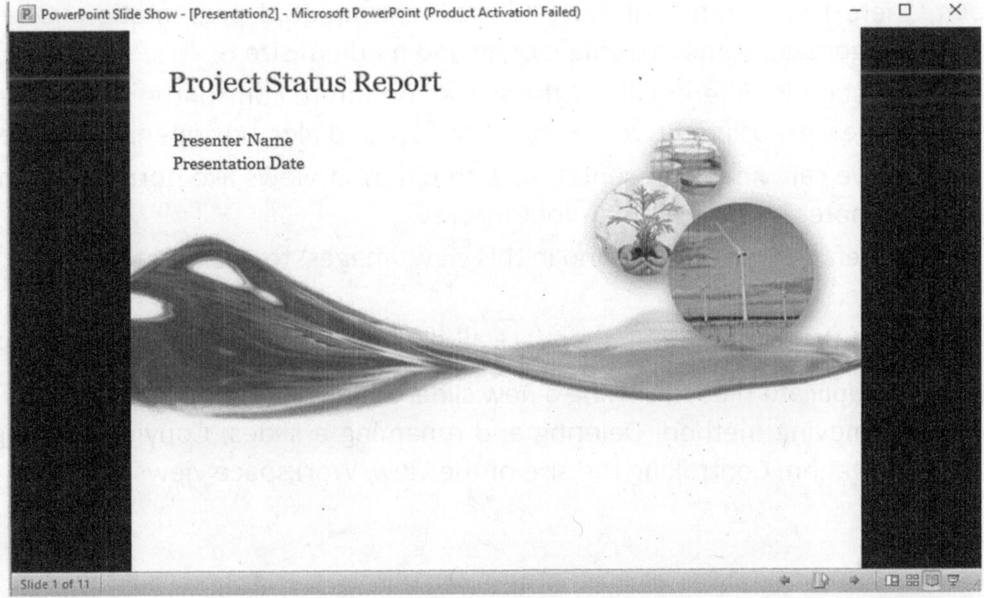

Figure 5.34: Reading View

Skill Test Box

Choose the correct option:

1. Which view is generally used for creating, formatting and designing slides?
   a. Outline view b. Notes c. Slide Sorter view d. Normal view
2. ________ is used to maintain consistency in design and colors in the presentation.
   a. Normal slide b. Master slide c. Slide sorter d. Slide layout
3. Which slide view is used to apply animation on the content of slide?
   a. Normal slide b. Master slide c. Slide sorter d. Slide layout
4. _________ is used to maintain consistency in design and colors in the presentation.
   a. Normal slide b. Master slide c. Slide sorter d. Slide layout
5. _________ is used to maintain consistency in design and colors in the presentation.
   a. Normal slide b. Master slide c. Slide sorter d. Slide layout

Summary

- To insert a duplicate slide, select the slide from **Slide Pane** and select the **Slide | Duplicate Slide** option.
- To insert a new slide, select **Slide | New Slide** option.
- There is a number of layouts available in PowerPoint that can contain one or more content boxes.
- It is very time-consuming to create the same slide again and again. In PowerPoint, there is an option to reuse the existing slide within the presentation or in any other presentation.
- In PowerPoint, the cut, copy, and paste operations can be done using the drag and drop method.
- To use the drag and drop method, select the slide and click and hold the left mouse button on the marked slide along with the Ctrl button, move the cursor to the desired location and then release the left mouse button.
- To delete the content from the slide, put the cursor after the content you want to delete and press Delete or Backspace button on the keyboard.
- In PowerPoint, there is a number of ways to view the created presentation. One can view the presentation in a larger size, some in a smaller size and medium size.
- To view the presentation in different sizes, there is an option to control the size of the view. You can control the size of the view using the zoom, and view layout dialog box opens in the view tab.
- In MS PowerPoint, we can view a presentation with different views like normal, outline, slide sorter, notes, slide master, notes master, and handout master.
- Normal view is the default type of view, and in this view, images, text, animation, video, and audio can be added on the slide.
- In the outline view of the presentation, there are all slides of the presentation in a sequence.

Keywords: Inserting a duplicate slide, Inserting a new slide, Slide layout, Copying and moving slides, Drag and drop copying and moving method, Deleting and renaming a slides, Copying, moving and deleting content, , View a presentation, Controlling the size of the view, Workspace views.

Self-Assessment

A. MULTIPLE CHOICE QUESTIONS

1. What is the shortcut to insert a new slide in presentation?

   a. Ctrl + C Keys b. Shift + C Keys c. Ctrl + M Keys d. Shift + M Keys

2. Which of the following command is used to rollback your undo command?

   a. Undo b. Ctrl + X c. Ctrl + V d. Redo

3. Presentation is created in which view of PowerPoint?

   a. Normal view b. Outline view c. Slide sorter view d. Notes view

Answer:

1. c 2. d 3. a

B. QUESTIONS:

1. Is it possible to insert a duplicate slide in PowerPoint? If yes, then write down the steps to insert a duplicate slide.
2. What do you mean by Slide layout in PowerPoint?
3. How to copy and move slides using drag and drop method?
4. Write down the steps to rename the existing slide?
5. What is the way to control the size of the view of slide in Presentation?
6. Name various view option in PowerPoint?

C. PROJECT WORK

1. Create a presentation the to save time insert a duplicate and new slide in a presentation and also change the layout of existing presentation.
2. Open a Microsoft PowerPoint 2010, Create a new presentation and add slides and type data in Normal view, Organize the slides by deleting, adding and changing position of slides in slide sorter view, Add notes in Notes Page view, Review contents of your presentation in reading view
3. Make a presentation in which you have to add 2-3 slides and add the same slides twice then delete 2 of them just to review these features of PowePoint.

SESSION 4: FORMAT THE TEXT IN PRESENTATION

Formatting is the change of appearance of text by changing font color, size and style. This helps in enhancing the appearance of presentation and attracts readers by simply changing the font size, color, style, alignment, spacing and inserting bullets or numbers. The formatting can be applied to complete slide or limited text present on it.

Adding Text:

The text can be added in slide by simply clicking on it and start typing. In case to add more text than the area provided for entering text user can insert a text box. To add a text box in a slide perform the following steps:

Create a new presentation > Write text in given space > Click on Insert Tab > Select Text Box command from Text group > Create a text box by dragging the mouse on the slide then release it > Now simply take mouse and click in it to start typing a text

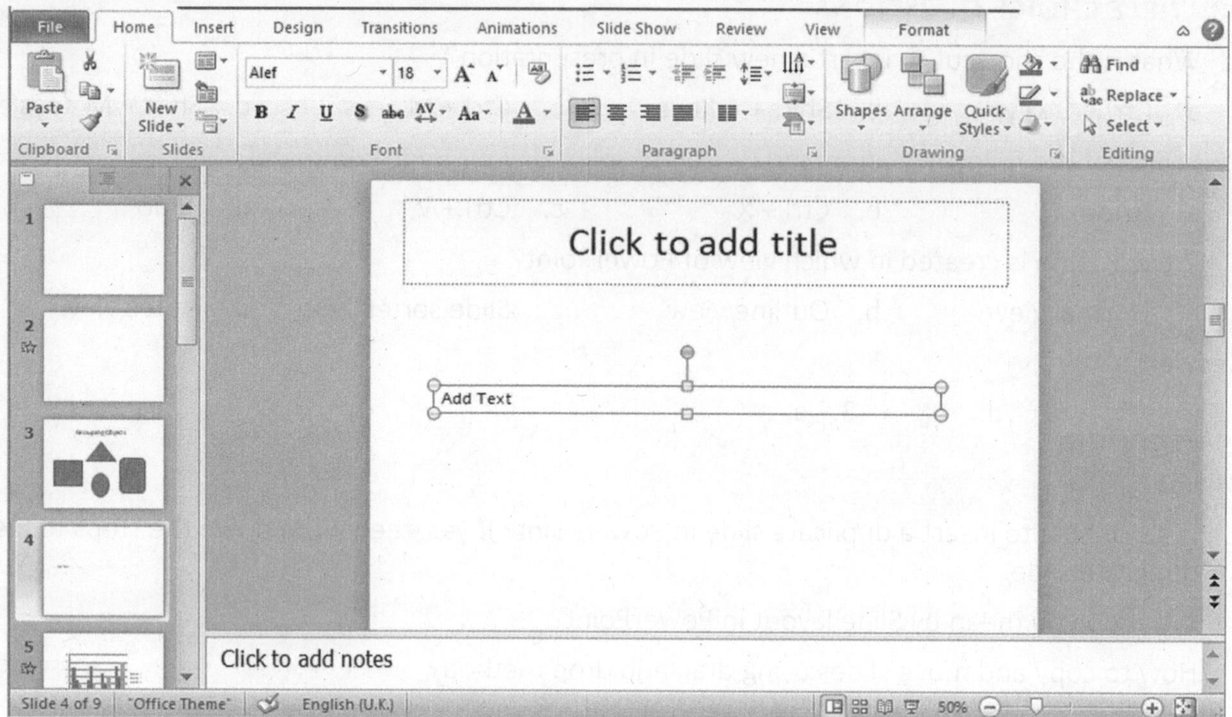

Figure 5.35: Inserting Text Box

In case of text larger than the size specified by user, it will adjust itself and move text in next line rather than to going out from user view.

Formatting Text:

User can also edit text in presentation like changing the alignment, highlighting the text by making it bold, italic and underline and changing the color of textbox.

Align Text

It is related to the position of text in the slide. There can be four ways or option to align a text.

Align Text left: The left text alignment is a default type of alignment. In this case there is little space in the right side. Click on Align Text left command given in Paragraph group of Home tab or Shortcut key (Ctrl + L)

Center: This will align the text in the center of document and leave little space from both the ends. Mainly its use has been found in writing the title. Click on Center command given in Paragraph group of Home tab or Shortcut key (Ctrl + E)

Align Text Right: This is the opposite case of left text alignment as in this the text is align towards right side and leave little space in the left. Mainly used to put sign and date option or sometimes giving the chapter heading. Click on Align Text right command given in Paragraph group of Home tab or Shortcut key (Ctrl + R)

Justify: In this case text is evenly aligned between the left and right side. Click on Justify command given in Paragraph group of Home tab or Shortcut key (Ctrl + J)

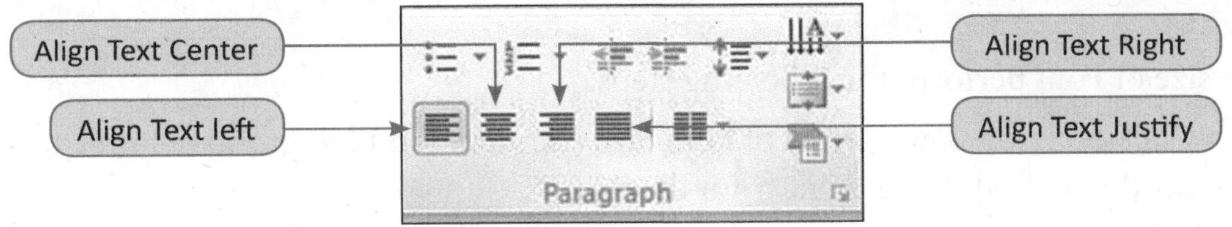

Figure 5.36: Text Alignment

Skill Test Box

Select the option from following options:

1. To make the text center align one can use ____________ as shortcut key.
2. ______________ shortcut key to align the text left.
3. ______________ is the shortcut key to align the text in right.

Make Text Bold, Italic and Underline

This section will help user to decorate their text by using bold, italic and underline commands of font group. In Font group of home tab there is command written as B in capital. To highlight the text using Bold command: Select the text > Click on Bold 'B' command from Font group of Home tab > then write the text. Or Press key Ctrl + B

Or you can also first write the text then select it before selecting the Bold command.

To perform italic or tilt on text press italic command from Font group and write the text or select the text which you want to tilt then click on Italic command. Or Press key Ctrl + I

Another command is underline that will highlight the text by putting underline below the text. In MS PowerPoint 2010 we have different style options of underlying the text. Or Press key Ctrl + U

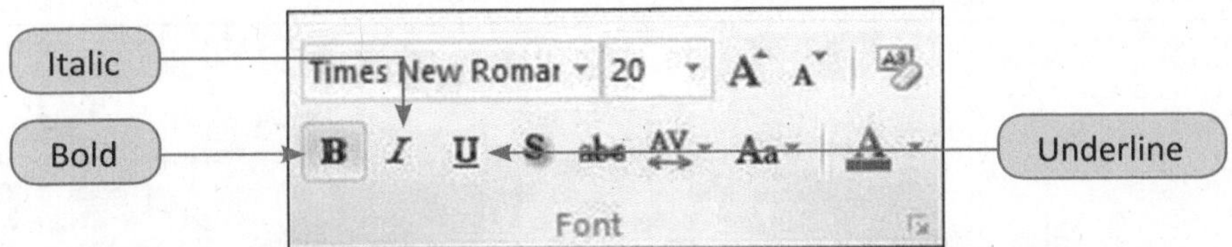

Figure 5.37: Bold, Italic and Underline Commands

Change Font

To change the font of Text performs the following steps:

Select the text > Click on Drop down arrow of Font command in Font group of home tab > Select the desired type of Font from the list

After selecting the desired font from the list it starts appearing on the selecting text

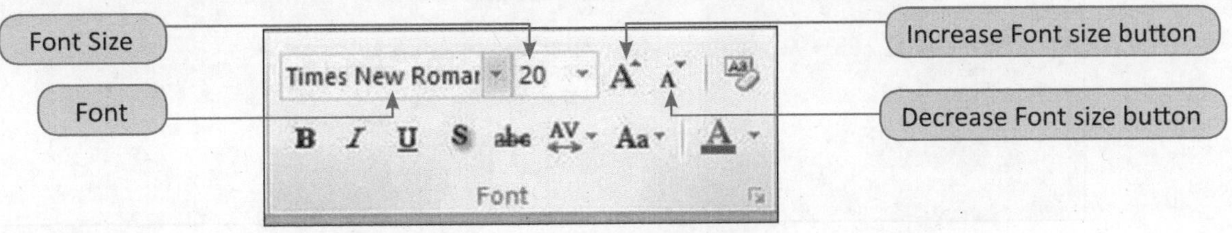

Figure 5.38: Change type and size of Font

Change Font Size

To Change the size of Font perform the following steps:

Select the text > Click on Drop down arrow of Font Size command in Font group of home tab Or press Ctrl + Shift + P > Select the desired size of Font from the list

Or

Click on Shrink font or press Ctrl + < keys to decrease the font size of text after selecting it

And Click on Grow font or press Ctrl + > keys to increase the font size of text after selected it

Superscript and Subscript: After selecting subscript whatever user type will come below the baseline and it will look smaller than other normal text in the document.

- **To perform subscript:** Select the text > Select the Format > Text > Subscript Or Press Shift + Ctrl + B

  On other hand the superscript will place the text above the baseline.

- **To perform subscript:** Select the text > Select the Format > Text > Superscript Or Press Shift + Ctrl + P

Skill Test Box

Check whether the given statement is true and false:

1. By selecting subscript, whatever user type will come below the baseline.
2. Shift + Ctrl + B is the shortcut key to subscript the text.
3. The superscript will place the text above the baseline.

Change Font Color

The color of text can be change by using Font Color command of PowerPoint. To change the color of text select the required text and select the color from drop down menu.

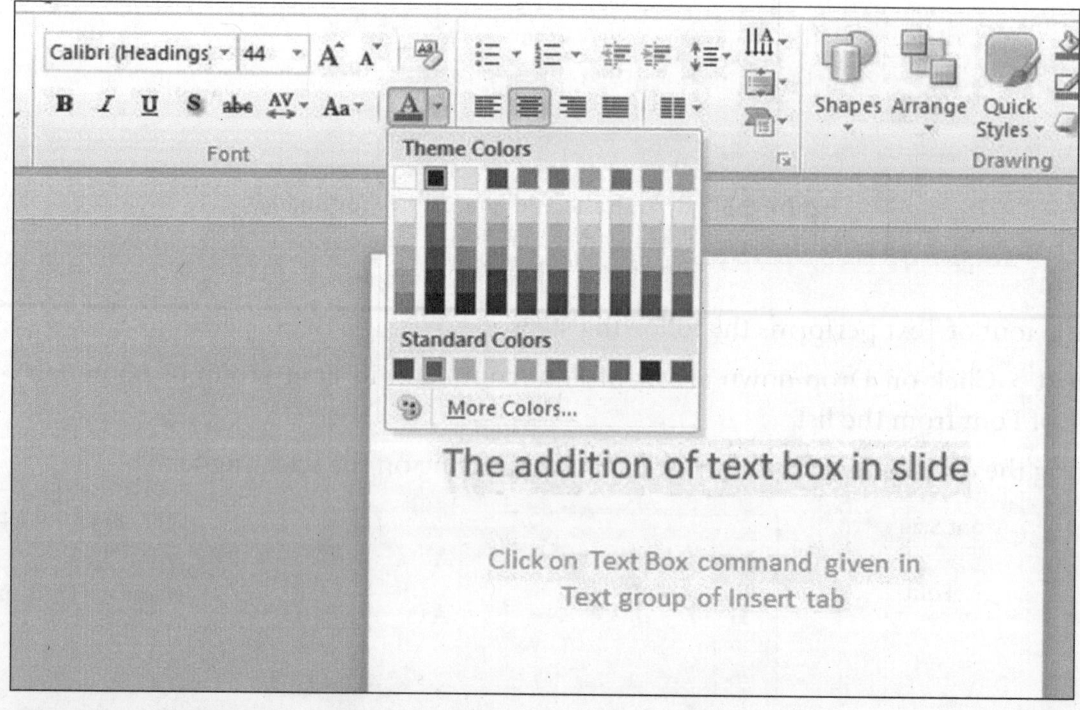

Figure 5.39: Font Color command

Changing background color of Text Box

In last section we have learnt to change the color of text, in this session will learn to change the background color of text box. The steps need to follow to change the background color of text box are:

Select the required text box > Click on Shape fill command drop down arrow > Select the required color and observe it

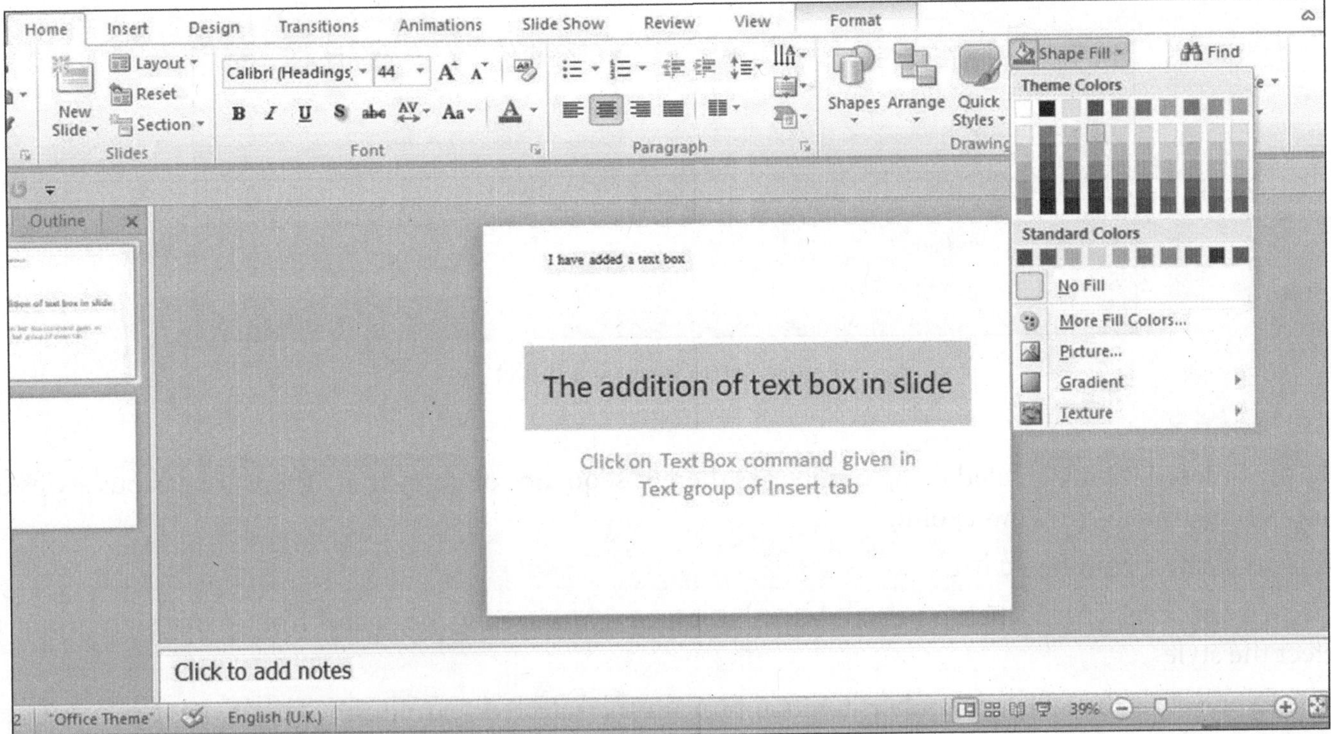

Figure 5.40: Use of Shape fill command from Drawing group

Apply Bullets and Number list

To put list of items in a well manner format there is option of bullet and numbering in PowerPoint. These both will arrange the content in the form of lists. These both options are there in paragraph group of Home tab. There are various style of bullet and number available in PowerPoint 2010.

Bullets

Mainly unordered list are created using bullet as there is no sequence of items in it. There are various styles of bullets available in Powerpoint.

Steps to create a bullet list:

Create a list > select it > click on drop down button on Bullets command from paragraph group > select the style

When you select the style of bullet it will start appearing on the selected text in the slide. Now if you want to use bullet on other typed document then simply take cursor on last text with bullet, press enter and write the text or list.

To stop bullet option simply again click on it and start typing.

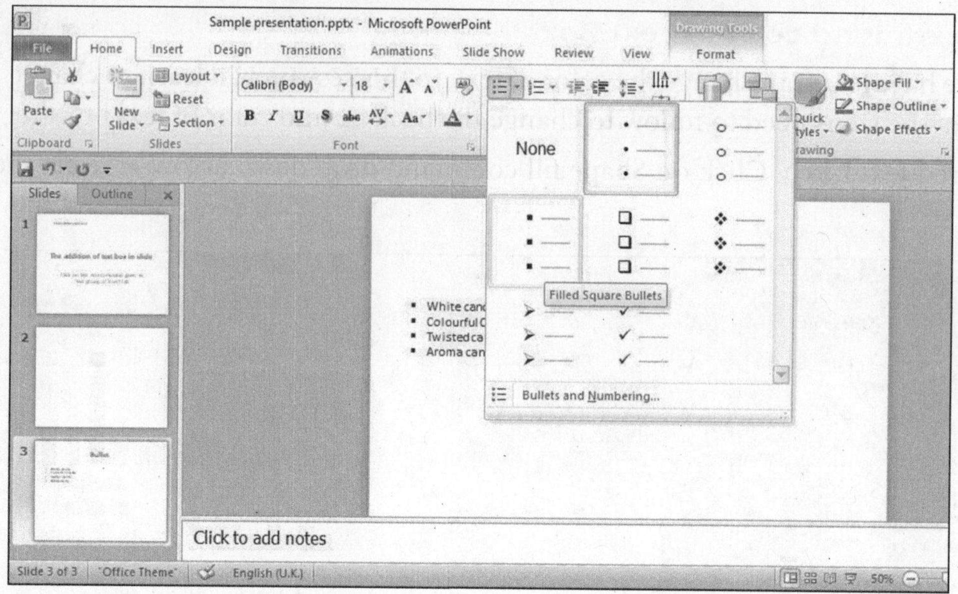

Figure 3.41: Creating a Bullet

Numbering

Mainly ordered list are created using number as there is sequence of items in it. There are various styles of numbering available in PowerPoint.

Steps to create a Numbered list:

Create a list > select it > click on drop down button on Numbering command from paragraph group > select the style

When you select the style of number it will appear on the selected text on the Slide. Now if you want to continue with count on other typed document then simply take cursor on last numbered text, press enter and write the text or list.

To stop Numbering option simply again click on it and start typing.

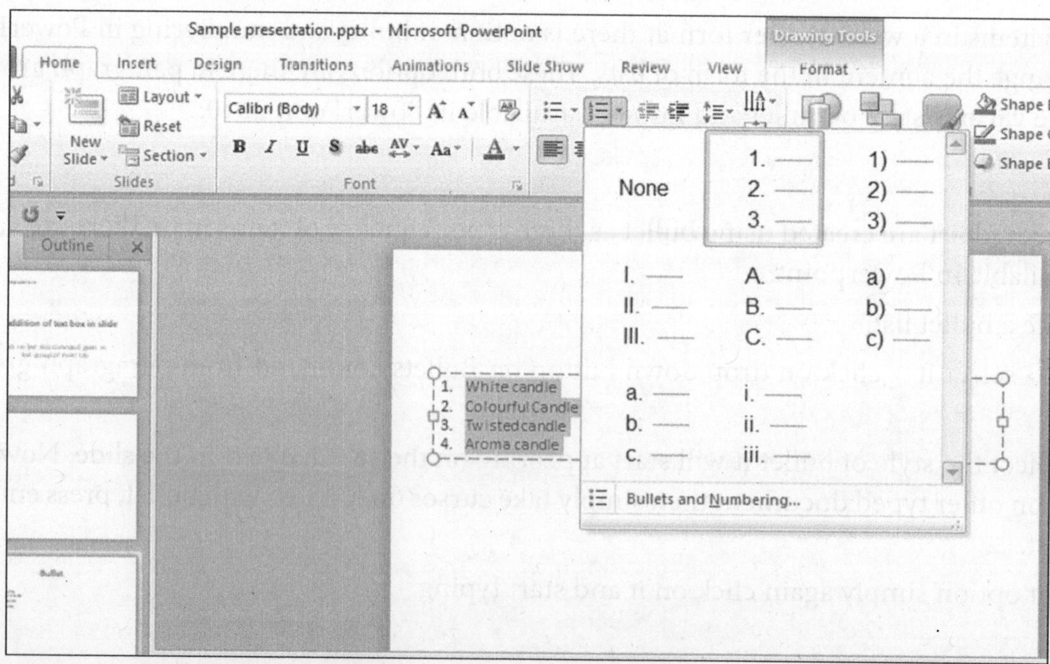

Figure 3.42: Creating a Number

To Apply Shadow Effect

We can also use shadow feature on Text. To apply shadow perform the following steps:

Select the Text > Click on Text Shadow button given in Font group of Home tab

The shadow effect start appearing on the selected text. To remove it double click on it.

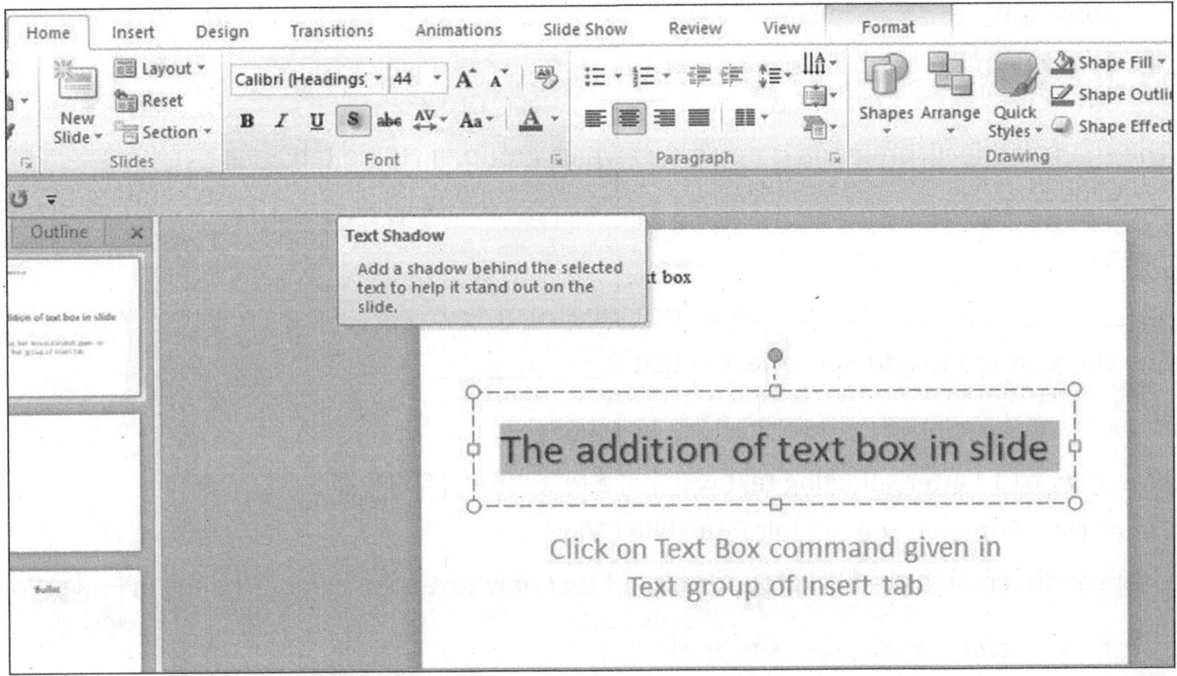

Figure 3.43: Shadow Effect

Summary

- Formatting is the change of appearance of text by changing font color, size and style.
- To add text in slide, Create a new presentation > Write text in given space > Click on Insert Tab > Select Text Box command from Text group > Create a text box by dragging the mouse on the slide then release it > Now simply take mouse and click in it to start typing a text
- Formatting Text include changing the alignment, highlighting the text by making it bold, italic and underline and changing the color of textbox
- The bold, italic and underline commands of font group can be added in slide. To change fonrt of Text, Select the text > Click on Drop down arrow of Font command in Font group of home tab > Select the desired type of Font from the list Or click
- Select the text > Click on Drop down arrow of Font Size command in Font group of home tab Or press Ctrl + Shift + P > Select the desired size of Font from the list
- Ctrl + > key is used to increase the font size of text and Ctrl + < keys are used to decrease size of text
- To add Bullets in text, Create a list > select it > click on drop down button on Bullets command from paragraph group > select the style
- To create a number list, Create a list > select it > click on drop down button on Numbering command from paragraph group > select the style
- To apply shadow effect, Select the Text > Click on Text Shadow button given in Font group of Home tab

Keywords: Format toolbar, Align text, Make text bold, italic and underline, Change font size, Change font name, Superscript and subscript, Change font color, Highlight color, Bullets and number list.

Self-Assessment

A. MULTIPLE CHOICE QUESTIONS

1. Which tab contain the command of Text box?
   a. Home tab b. Insert tab c. Design tab d. View tab
2. Shortcut key to increase the size of text?
   a. Ctrl + I b. Ctrl + < c. Ctrl + > d. Ctrl + +
3. The shadow effect command is present in which group of Home tab
   a. Clipboard b. Slides c. Font d. Editing

B. FILL IN THE BLANKS

1. __________ is the shortcut key to reduce the size of text.
2. The shortcut key to add Bold effect in text is __________

C. TRUE FALSE

1. Pressing Ctrl + I after selecting text will make text tilted (T/F)
2. Times New Roman is the default font style (T/F)
3. User cannot change the background color of text only text color can be change in PowerPoint (T/F)

D. ANSWER THE FOLLOWING QUESTIONS:

1. How extra text can be added in slide?
2. Name the group of Text box command and explain its usage.
3. What do you mean by formatting text? Name four ways to align text.
4. Give the steps to change Font Face in PowerPoint.
5. What are the shortcut key to make text Bold, Italic and Underline?
6. Write down the steps to change Font size and Color of Text?
7. Can we change the background color of text? If yes, then give steps to change it.
8. What is the use of Bullets and Numbering command in PowerPoint and how it can be apply to text.

E. PRACTICAL WORK

1. Open a Microsoft PowerPoint 2010, Create a new presentation, Add new blank slide then add text box to write text of 5 lines in it, Align top line in Center and Bold and rest of line are align as justify, Use Times New Roman font style, Give 16 font size top line and 12 to rest of the text in box, Change the background color of text box to light pink.
2. Make a things to be cover slide of your presentation in which you have to add the numbered list.
3. Make a slide with given instructions on the slide example given in below figure.

ANSWER:

A. Multiple choice question answers:

1. b 2. c 3. c

B. Fill in the blanks answers:

1. Ctrl + <
2. Ctrl + B

C. True False answers:

1. True
2. False

SESSION 5: CREATE AND USE TABLE IN PRESENTATION

MS PowerPoint enables the user to add tables in the slides for representation of statistical data meaningfully. Table is a grid of cells arranged in rows and columns format. Cell is each type in a table that is independent of all other entries that can contain graphics, text, numeric data, etc.

Tables are proving to be useful in various tasks, like presenting text information and numerical data.

Inserting Tables in Presentation

To insert a table in presentation, perform the following steps:

Select the Insert menu bar or Tab > Table

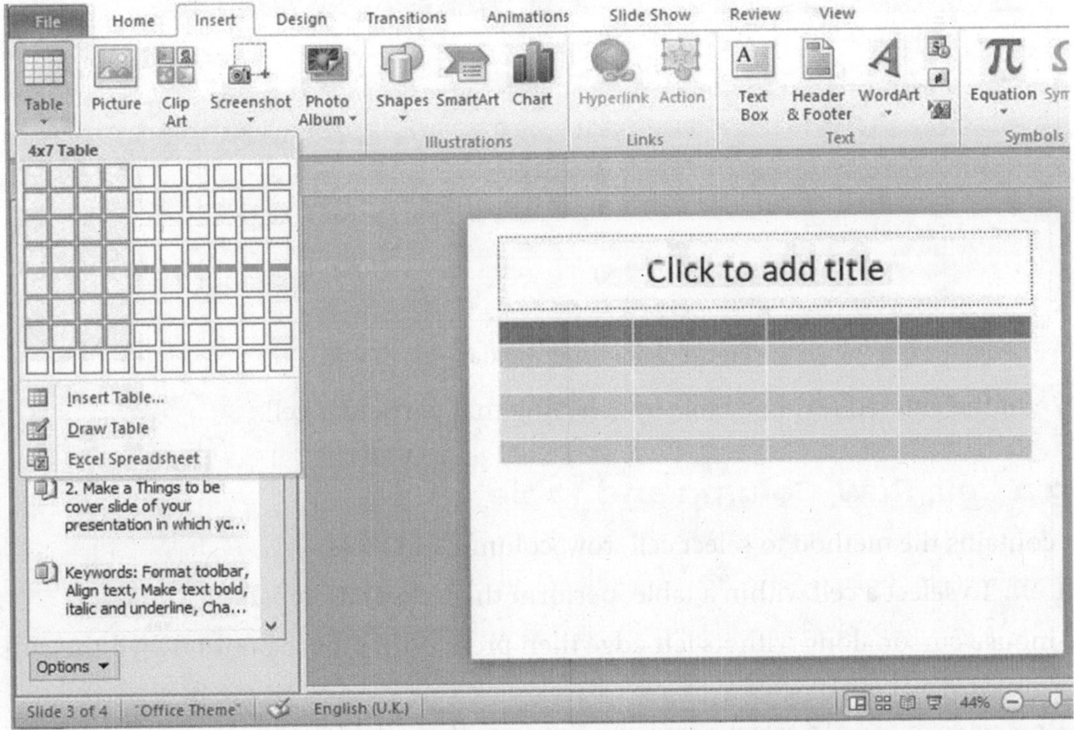

Figure 5.44: Table command from Insert Menu bar

After clicking on Table command a Insert Table dialog box will open.

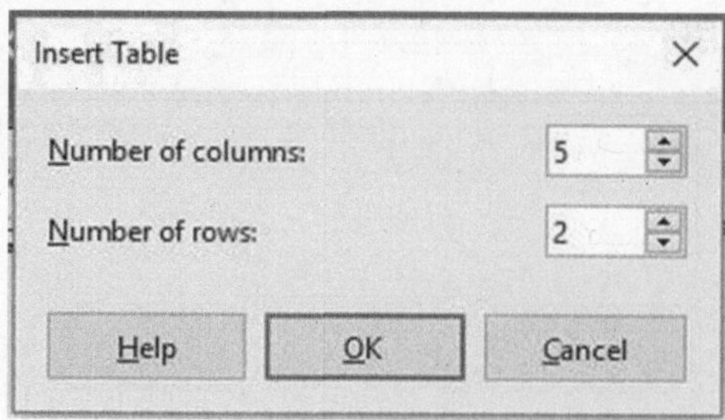

Figure 5.45: Insert Table dialog box

Mention the number of columns and Number of rows > Click on OK button

This will insert the table with mention number of columns and rows in the slide.

Entering and editing data in a Tables

To enter the data in a table, place the insertion point in a required cell then start typing text or data you want to enter in it. To move the insertion point in a table, use any of the following ways:

- Press the left mouse button
- Press the Tab key on a keyboard
- Press arrow keys on the keyboard.

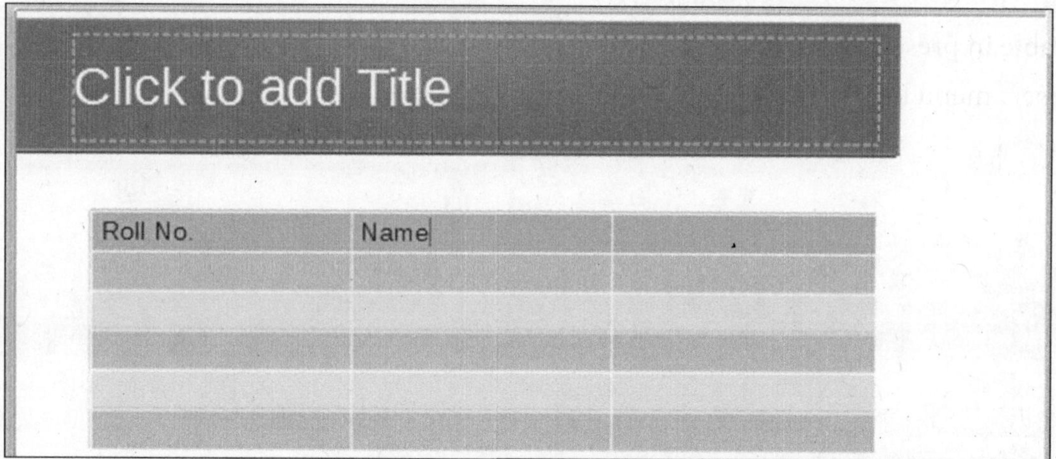

Figure 5.46: Entering data in a Table

You can also edit the entered text in a table by selecting that particular cell.

Selecting a Cell, Row, Column and Table

This section contains the method to select cell, row, column and table.

Selecting a Cell: To select a cell within a table, perform the following steps:

Position the mouse cursor along with its left edge then press right mouse button when the cursor changes to a sloped white arrow (Figure 5.46).

Selecting a Row or Column: To select a row or column within a table, perform the following steps:

Position the mouse arrow to row and column then press the left button and drag it to the end of the row or column when the mouse cursor changes to a sloped arrow.

OR

Press right mouse button on the row or column you want to select > Select option from the context menu

Selecting a Table: To select an entire table, perform the following steps:

Click on the edge of table > Click on the left mouse button when the mouse cursor changes to a slopped arrow

To move the Table: Position on the edge of Table > Drag the table to a specified location when the cursor changes to a sloped arrow.

Adjust Column width and Row height

To change the **width of the Column** using mouse, perform the following steps:

- Position on the border line between two columns > Press the left mouse button when the cursor position changes to both side arrow sign > Drag it until column comes to desired width.

To change the **height of the Row** using mouse, perform the following steps:

- Position on the border line between two rows > Press the left mouse button when the cursor position changes to both side arrow sign > Drag it until row comes to desired height.

Changing Background Color or Style of a Table

To change the default color of table in selected theme user has to perform the following steps:

Click on Background Styles command drop down arrow present in Background group of Design tab > Move mouse over various styles available in it and observe their effects on the slide > Click on Format Background option > Select Solid fill radio button from the Format Background dialog box > Click on Color button drop down arrow > Select color > Click on Close

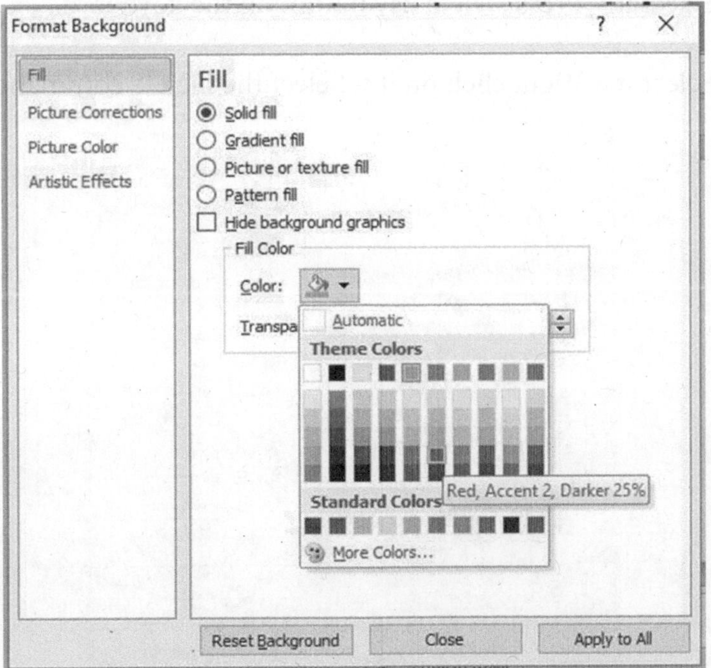

Figure 3.47: Format Background Dialog box

Select More colors option from Color button drop down menu in case to select colors apart from given list. A Colors dialog box will appear then click on standard option and choose the color you want. You can also create your own color by selecting custom option then click on Ok button given in the upper right side.

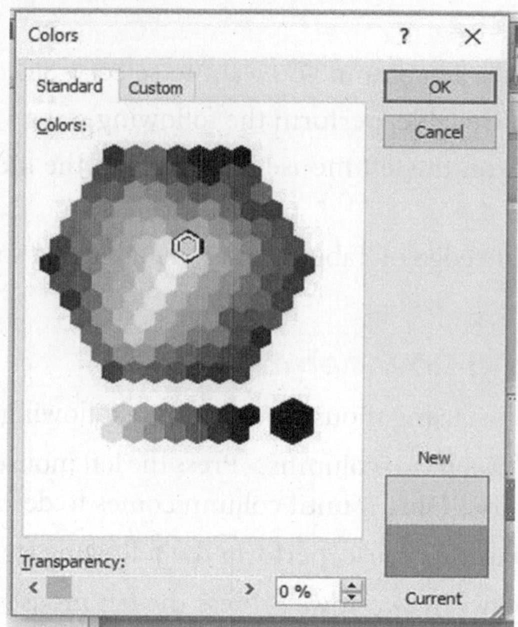

Figure 3.48: Standard Colors Dialog box

This will apply color to selected slide. In case to apply changes to all the slides present in presentation, click on Apply to All button present in Format Background dialog box then close the dialog box by clicking on Close button given in the bottom of Format Background dialog box.

Deleting a Table

To delete a Table, perform the following steps:

- Click on the Table > Select it > Press Delete key button on the keyboard
  OR
- Click on the Table > Select it > Right click on it > Select the Delete command from context menu

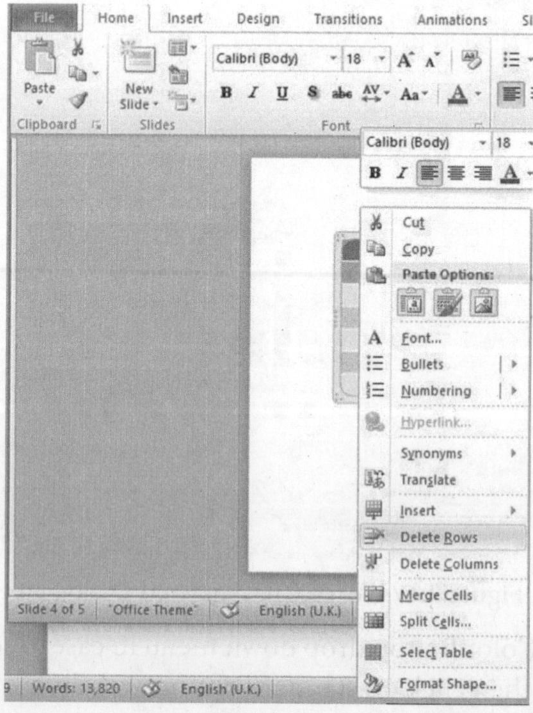

Figure 5.49: Delete command

Summary

- MS PowerPoint enables the user to add tables in the slides for representation of statistical data meaningfully.
- Table is a grid of cells arranged in rows and columns format.
- To enter the data in a table, place the insertion point in a required cell then start typing text or data you want to enter in it.
- To select a cell within a table, Position the mouse cursor along with its left edge then press right mouse button when the cursor changes to a sloped white arrow
- To select a row or column within a table, Press right mouse button on the row or column you want to select > Select option from the context menu
- To select an entire table, Click on the edge of table > Click on the left mouse button when the mouse cursor changes to a slopped arrow
- To adjust column width, Position on the border line between two columns > Press the left mouse button when the cursor position changes to both side arrow sign > Drag it until column comes to desired width.
- To adjust Row height, Position on the border line between two rows > Press the left mouse button when the cursor position changes to both side arrow sign > Drag it until row comes to desired height.
- To apply Border to the Table, Right click on the border of table > Click on Table Properties dialog box will open > Now click on Border tab > Do the needful changes in the borders.
- To delete a Table, Click on the Table > Select it > Press Delete key button on the keyboard

Keywords: Inserting tables in a presentation, Entering and editing data in a tables, Selecting a cell, row, column and table, Adjust column width and row height, Table borders and background, Deleting a table.

Self-Assessment

A. MULTIPLE CHOICE QUESTIONS

1. Which of the following is not the way to move the insertion point in a table?
   a. Press the left mouse button   b. Press the right mouse button
   c. Press the Tab key   d. Press the arrow keys
2. The Borders and Background tabs are available in which of the following tabs?
   a. Cell Properties   b. Row properties   c. Column properties   d. Table properties

Answer

1. b   2. d

B. QUESTIONS:

1. Define Table?
2. How to insert a table in Presentation?
3. What are the various ways to enter data in a table?
4. Is it possible to adjust the column width and row height of existing table in slide? If yes, then write down the steps to adjust it.
5. Write down the steps to delete table?

C. PROJECT WORK

1. Insert table in one of the Slide of presentation then enter and edit data in it. Also, try add more row and column feature of it.
2. Make a table in slide and fill the table by collecting data from your class friends.

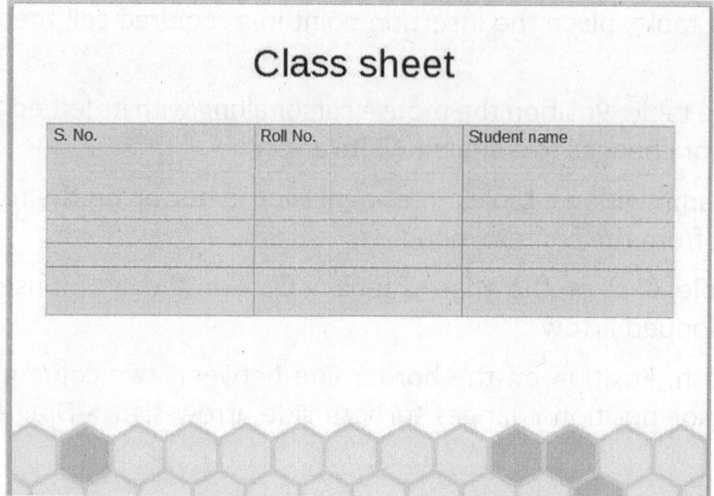

SESSION 6: INSERT AND FORMAT IMAGE IN PRESENTATION

It is said that Picture speaks louder than words. So, addition of images and pictures will enhance the presentation. In PowerPoint you can insert graphics or images from the gallery, files stored in the computer, etc.

Inserting pictures from files:

The pictures can be added in slide from saved pictures in your system of different formats. The pictures can be of JPG, BMP, PNG, JPEG and GIF format. The steps need to perform for inserting pictures from file:

Place the cursor on the location of adding picture > Click on Picture command from Images group of Insert tab or apply the slide layout that contains picture > Insert dialog box will appear, select the picture from the folder and double click on it or select picture and click on Insert button given in bottom right side

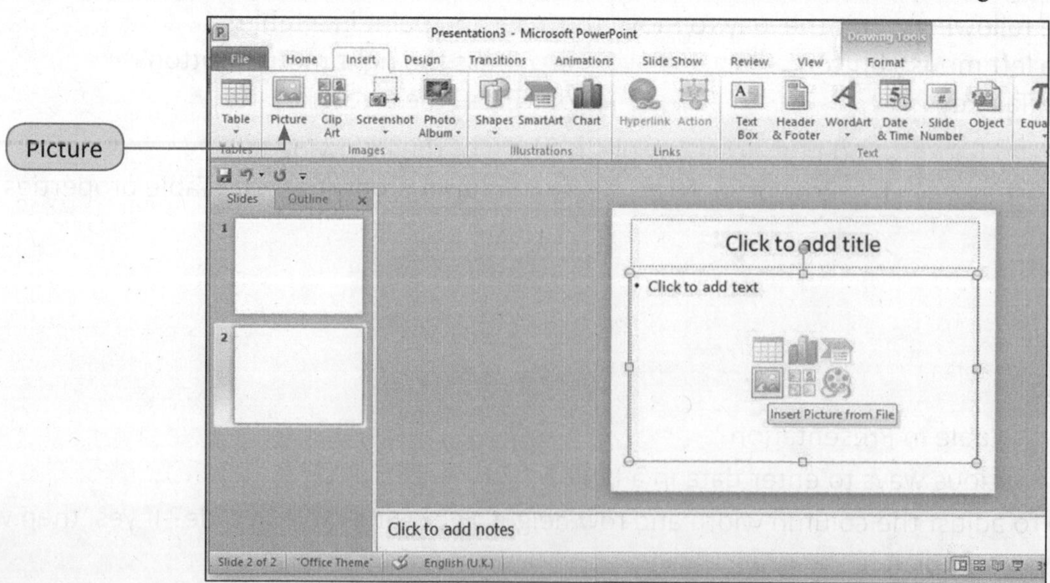

Figure 3.50: Inserting Picture

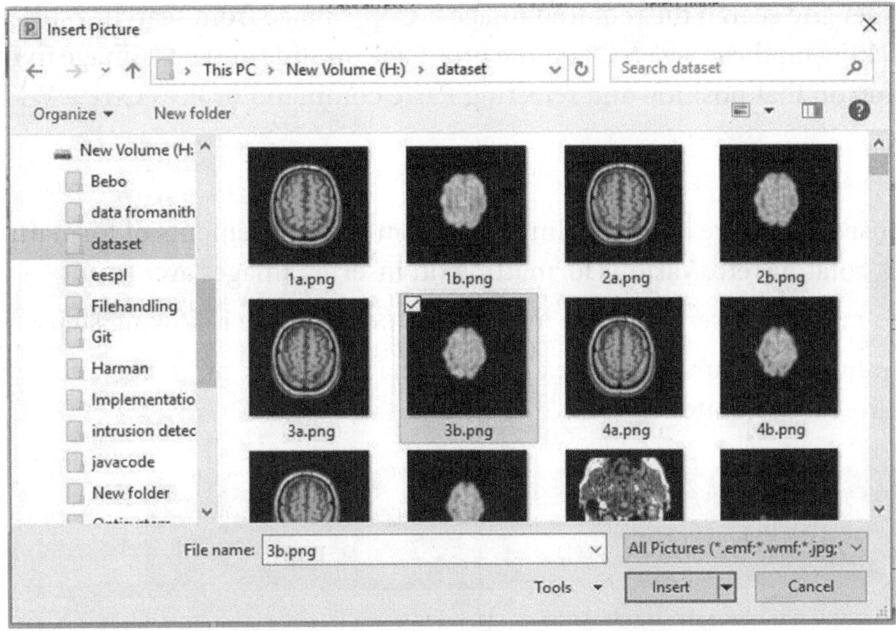

Figure 3.51: Inserting Picture Dialog Box

Inserting pictures from Clip Art:

Another option is adding pictures in slide from clip art. To add pictures in slide from clip art perform the following steps:

Click on Insert tab > Clip Art command present in Images group of Insert Tab > At right side of window a Clip Art task pane is displayed > Here you can enter the name of the required clip art in search text box > Click on Go button > Click on desired clip art

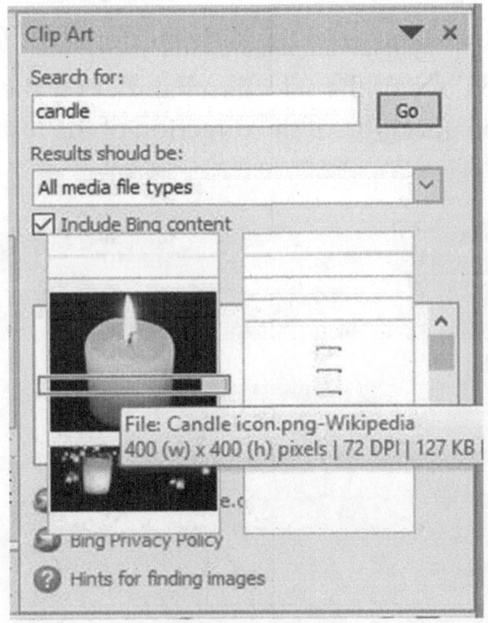

Figure 3.52: Inserting Clip Art Task Pane

Inserting Images from the Internet:

Sometimes there are cases when image is not present in system or you don't want to add clip art. In those cases images are taken from Internet. To insert specific image from Internet perform the following steps:

Open the web browser and search the required image > Copy image from search result images from option come after right clicking on the image > Open the presentation slide and past image in required position of slide by right clicking on that position and selecting Paste command or Pres Ctrl + V key.

Formatting Images

We have learnt to insert an image but sometimes there can be requirements of formatting that image such as moving, resizing, rotating, etc. Various formatting on inserted images are:

Moving Images: To move an inserted image in the slide, perform the following steps:

Click on Image > wait till the cursor changes to hand shape > Click on image and drag it to the desired position > Release the mouse button

Figure 5.53: Moving Image

Resizing Images: To resize an inserted image in the slide, perform the following steps:

Click on Image > Put the cursor on one of the selection handles on the image and the cursor will change the shape by giving a graphical representation of the direction of the resizing > Click and drag the image to resize it > Release the mouse button

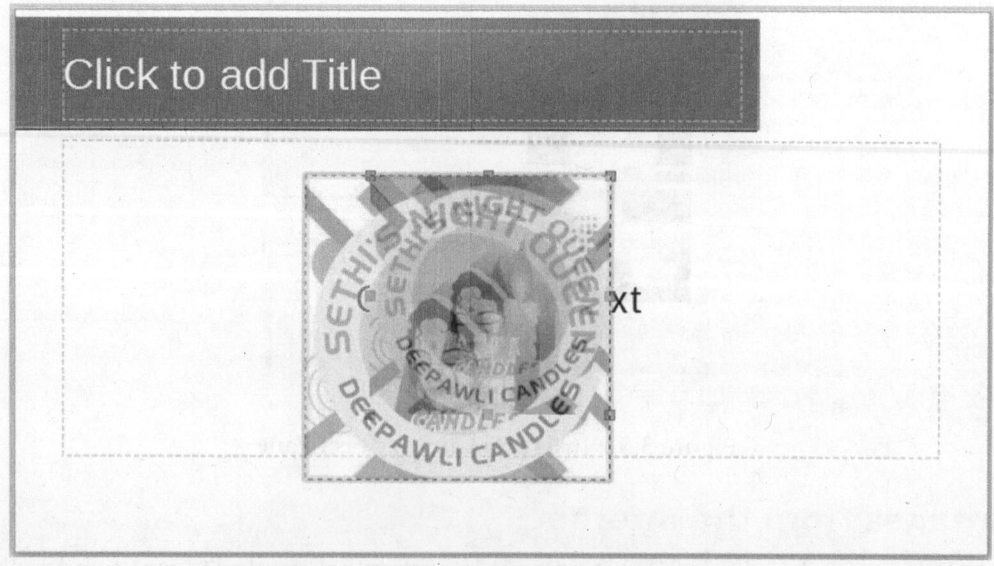

Figure 5.54: Resizing Image

Rotating Images: In PowerPoint you can also rotate the image in any direction using rotating icon or manually. To rotate an inserted image in the slide, perform the following steps:

Click on Image > Click on Rotate icon on the Arrange group > Click again on the selected image and shape and colour of selection handles get changed > Click the mouse and move it in the required direction > Release the mouse button

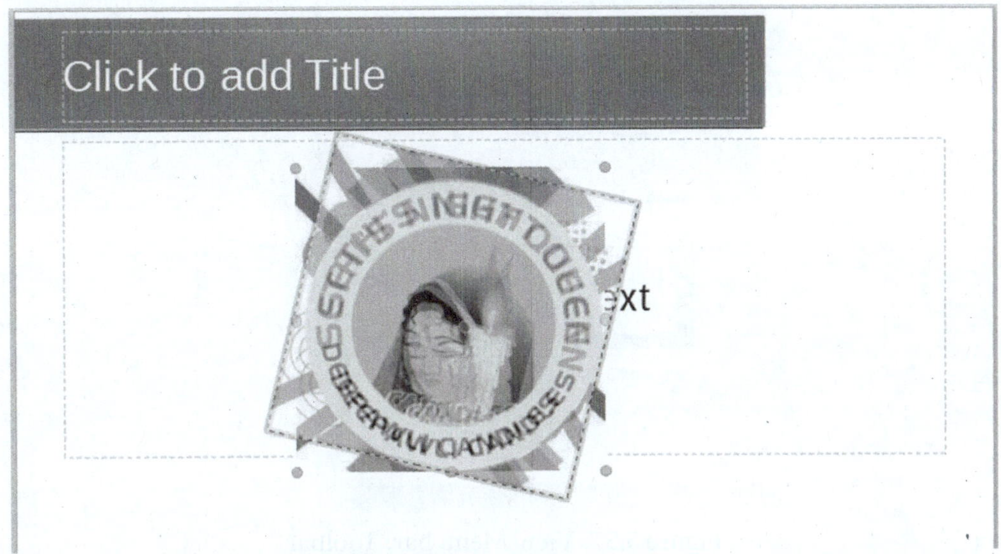

Figure 5.55: Resizing Image

Formatting using the Image toolbar:

Instead of formatting manually, you can also format the image using Image toolbar. It comes under properties window after selecting the image in the slide.

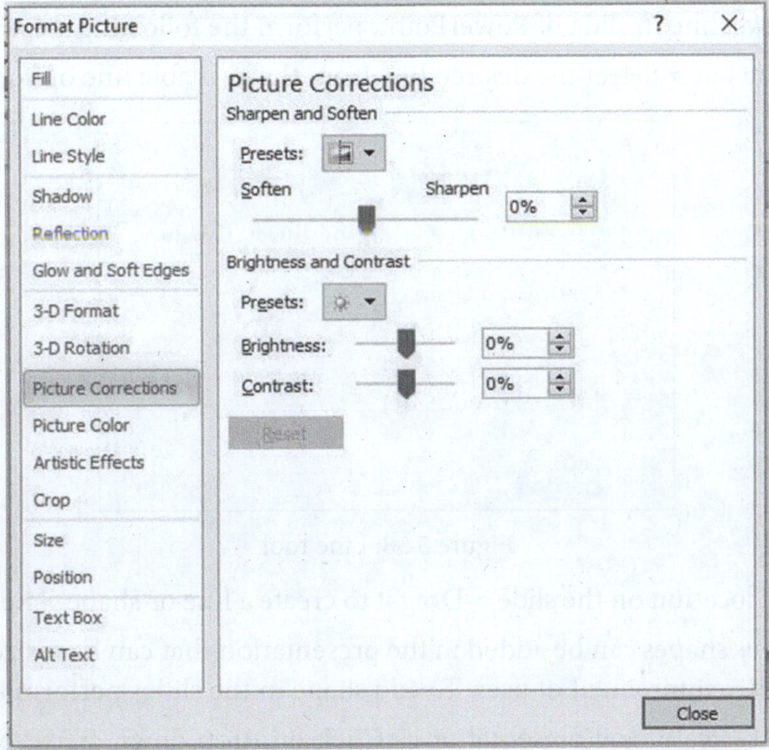

Figure 5.56: Image Toolbar

The toolbar contains number of formatting options. Other option to display Image toolbar is:

Right click on the image > Format Picture option

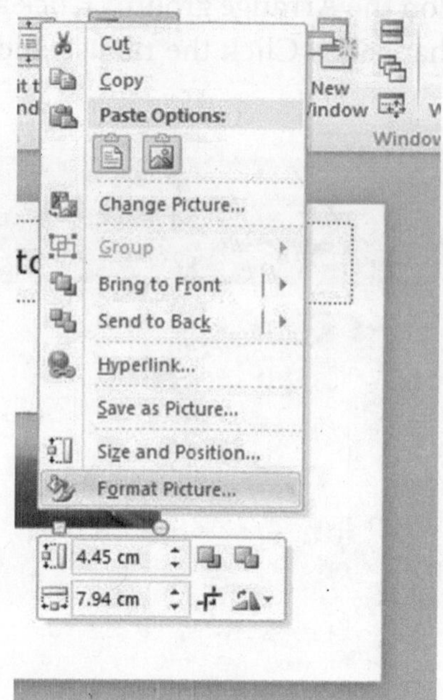

Figure 5.57: View Menu bar: Toolbar

Drawing graphic objects

In PowerPoint there are number of drawing tools that have various tools for creating graphical objects. In case the drawing tools are not activated the perform the following steps to activate it:

- Select Insert Menu bar > Shapes

Drawing Lines: To draw a line in slide of PowerPoint, perform the following steps:

- Click on Insert Menu bar > Select the desired line from the available line option.

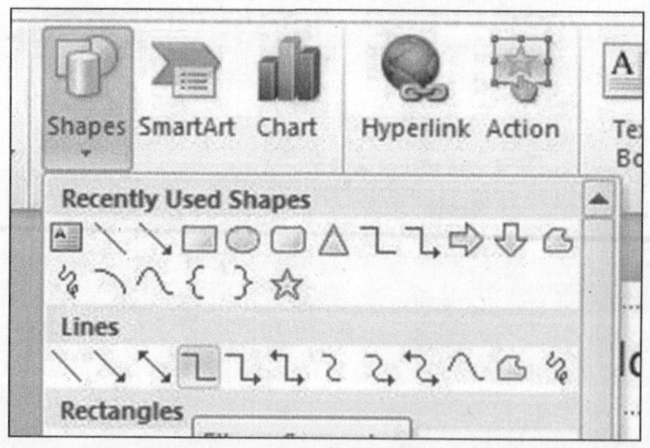

Figure 5.58: Line tool

- Click on the desired location on the slide > Drag it to create a line or shape > Release the mouse button

Drawing Shapes: Various shapes can be added in the presentation that can be resized, flipped, rotated and coloured according to the requirement of user. To add shape in the slides perform the following steps:

Launch a PowerPoint > Create new presentation > Click on drop down arrow of Shapes command or button given in the Illustrations group of Insert tab > Click on the shape given in menu

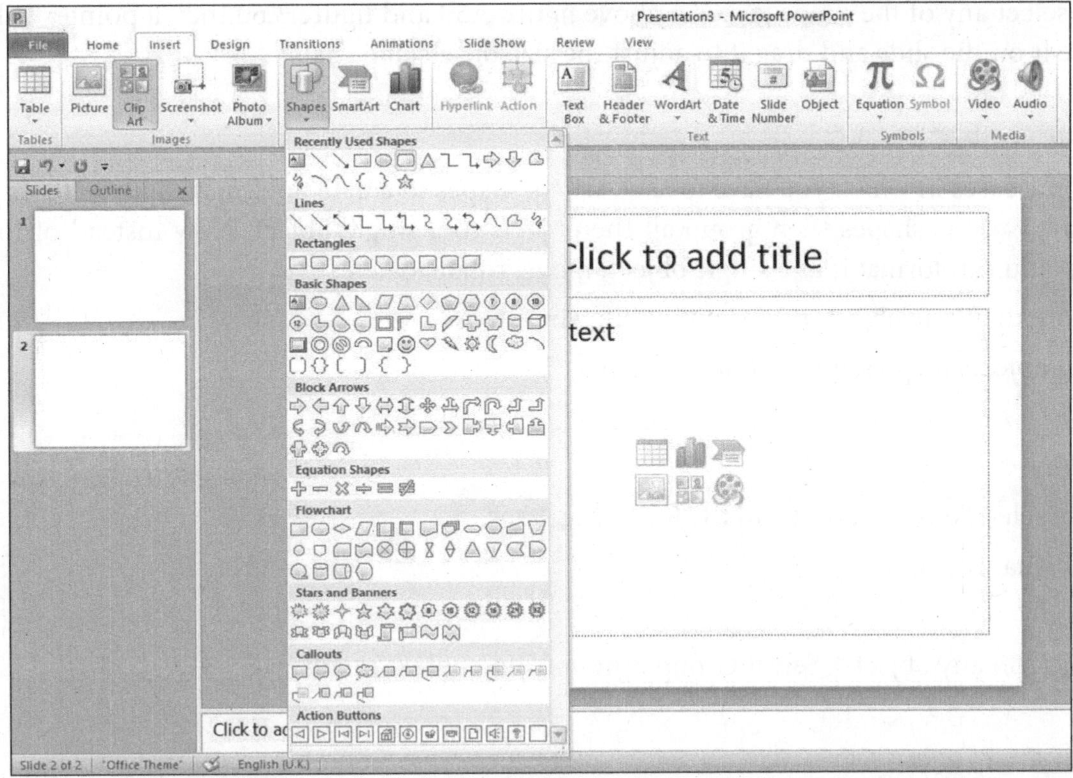

Figure 3.59: Using Shapes command of Images group of Insert Tab

Or

Click on shapes given Shapes drop down arrow given in the Drawing group of Home tab > Select the required shape > Click on desired location of slide and then drag to the place of shape

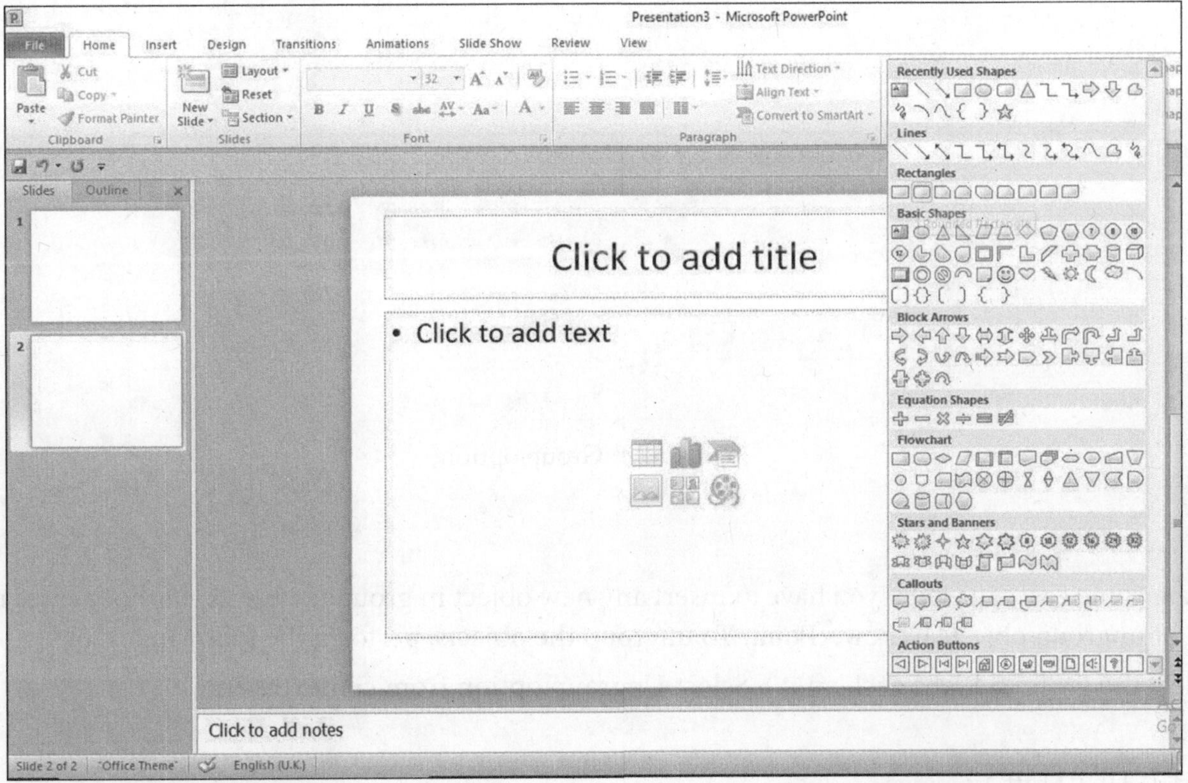

Figure 3.60: Using Shapes given in Drawing group of Home tab

When user select any of the shape given in above figure 3.59 and figure 3.60 then a pointer will change to + sign, place it on the slide and drag it to adjust the size of selected shape.

Grouping Objects

There are some cases in which you have to use various shapes to create flowchart, figure, etc. In those cases you can draw various shapes then group all the objects to a single object. Now instead of formatting it individually, you can format it as a single object, move, rotate, delete, etc.

To select more than one object, perform the following steps:

- Select all objects by pressing Ctrl or Shift key

  OR

  Ctrl + A

To group the selected object, perform the following steps:

- Select Format > Group

  OR

- Right click on any object > Select Group option from context menu

  OR

- Ctrl + Shift + G keys

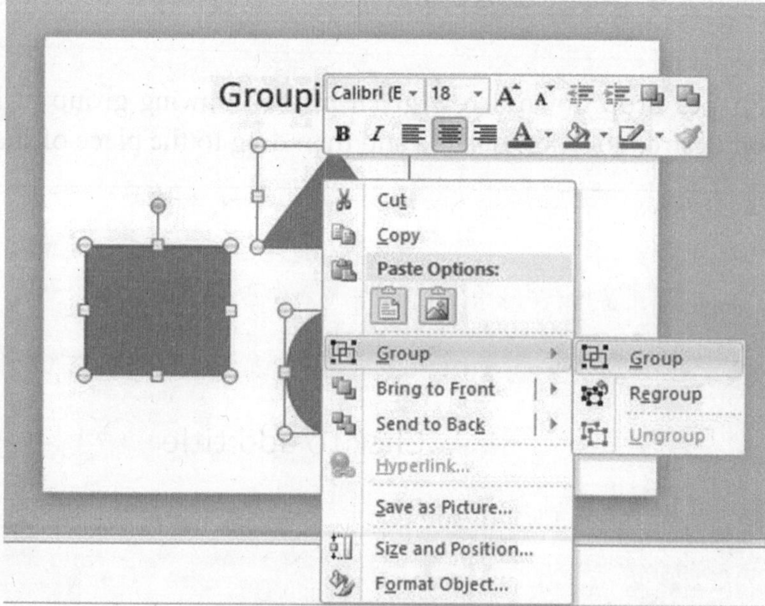

Figure 5.61: Group option

Ungrouping Objects

There are some cases in which you have to insert any new object in grouped objects. In those cases there is option of ungroup objects in PowerPoint. To ungroup the objects, perform the following steps:

- Select the group > Right click on it > Select Ungroup option from context menu

  OR

  Ctrl + Alt + Shift + G keys

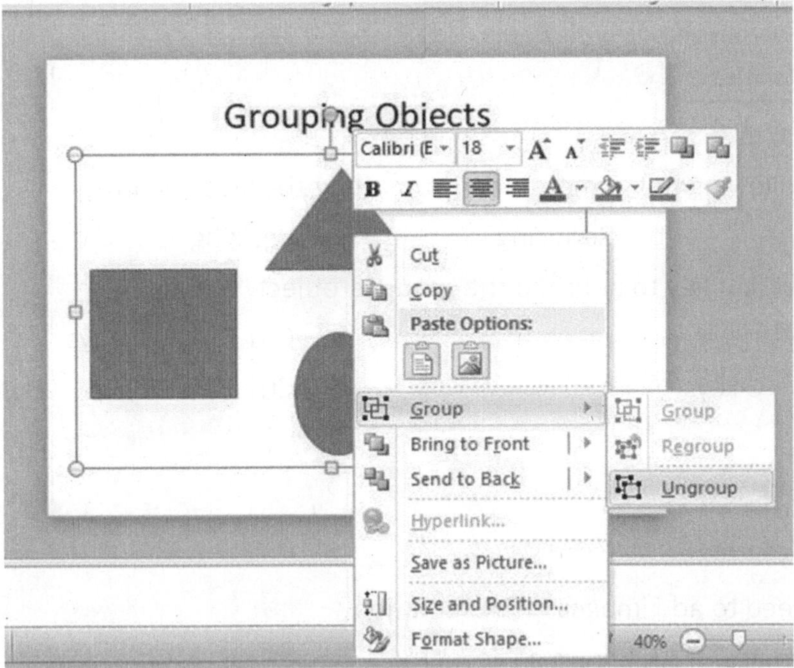

Figure 5.62: Ungroup option

Summary

- In PowerPoint you can insert graphics or images from the gallery, files stored in the computer, etc.
- The pictures can be added in slide from saved pictures in your system of different formats.
- To move the inserted image, Click on Image > wait till the cursor changes to hand shape > Click on image and drag it to the desired position > Release the mouse button
- To resize the image, Click on Image > Put the cursor on one of the selection handles on the image and the cursor will change the shape by giving a graphical representation of the direction of the resizing > Click and drag the image to resize it > Release the mouse button
- To rotate the Image, Click on Image > Click on Rotate icon on the Line and Filling toolbar > Click again on the selected image and shape and colour of selection handles get changed > Click the mouse and move it in the required direction > Release the mouse button
- Instead of formatting manually, you can also format the image using Image toolbar. It comes under properties window after selecting the image in the slide.
- In PowerPoint there are number of drawing tools that have various tools for creating graphical objects.
- To draw a line in a slide of PowerPoint, Click on Insert Menu bar > Click on shapes command > Select the desired from the available line option.
- To draw a shape in slide of PowerPoint, Click on Insert Menu bar > Click on shapes command > Select the desired from the available shape option.
- In PowerPoint you can draw various shapes then group all the objects to a single object.
- To ungroup the object, Select the group > Right click on it > Select Ungroup option from context menu

Keywords: Inserting an image from a file, Formatting images, Resizing images, Rotating images, Formatting using the image toolbar, Drawing graphic objects, Drawing lines, Drawing shapes, Grouping objects, Ungrouping objects.

A. MULTIPLE CHOICE QUESTIONS

1. Which of the following not comes under formatting the inserted images?
   a. Moving b. Reducing c. Resizing d. Rotating
2. What is the shortcut key to ungroup the grouped object:
   a. Ctrl + G keys b. Ctrl + Alt + G keys
   c. Ctrl + Shift + G keys d. Ctrl + Alt + Shift + G keys

Answer:

1. b 2. d

B. QUESTIONS:

1. Why there is need to add images in Presentation?
2. How to insert image in Slide from a File?
3. Write down the steps to insert an image from the gallery?
4. What is the way to move, resize and rotate the image in slide?
5. How to format the image using Image toolbar?
6. How to group and ungroup the objects in Slide?

C. PROJECT WORK

1. Demonstrate and practically insert an image from file and gallery in presentation then apply formatting options to it.
2. Insert any image from your gallery, if there is no image in it then first downloads one from Internet then insert it in the slide.
3. Use Shapes given in PowerPoint to make a figure and elaborate it in your words on the same slide corresponding to shape.

SESSION 7: WORK WITH SLIDE MASTER

A slide master controls the overall appearance, such as formatting and design, of each slide layout, and therefore each slide in your presentation. When you modify the slide master within your presentation, the changes will be applied to every slide layout. All templates contain at least one slide master.

Working with Slide Masters

Customising a theme is a quick way to change some elements of a presentation. The slide master, however, controls everything about its appearance, including the position and layout of placeholders as well as fonts, colours and backgrounds, and allows you to make much more extensive changes. If you want to change the layout of your slides, for example, the font size, the colour of the bullet points, or the alignment of the text in the titles, you should do this on the slide master, not on the slides themselves.

Adding Transitions

You can also create your own slide master like modifying the default slide master. To enable editing of a slide masters, perform the following steps:

- Select View menu bar > Master Slide

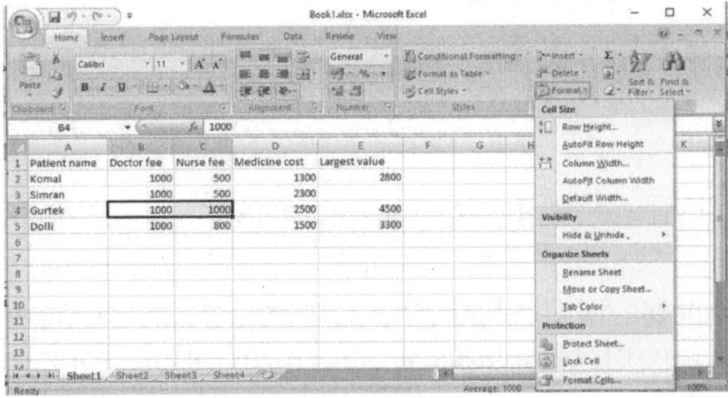

Figure 5.63: Master Slide to edit

In last close the Master view by clicking on Close Master View icon.

Adding Transitions

There are various transition you can apply on the slide in PowerPoint such as:

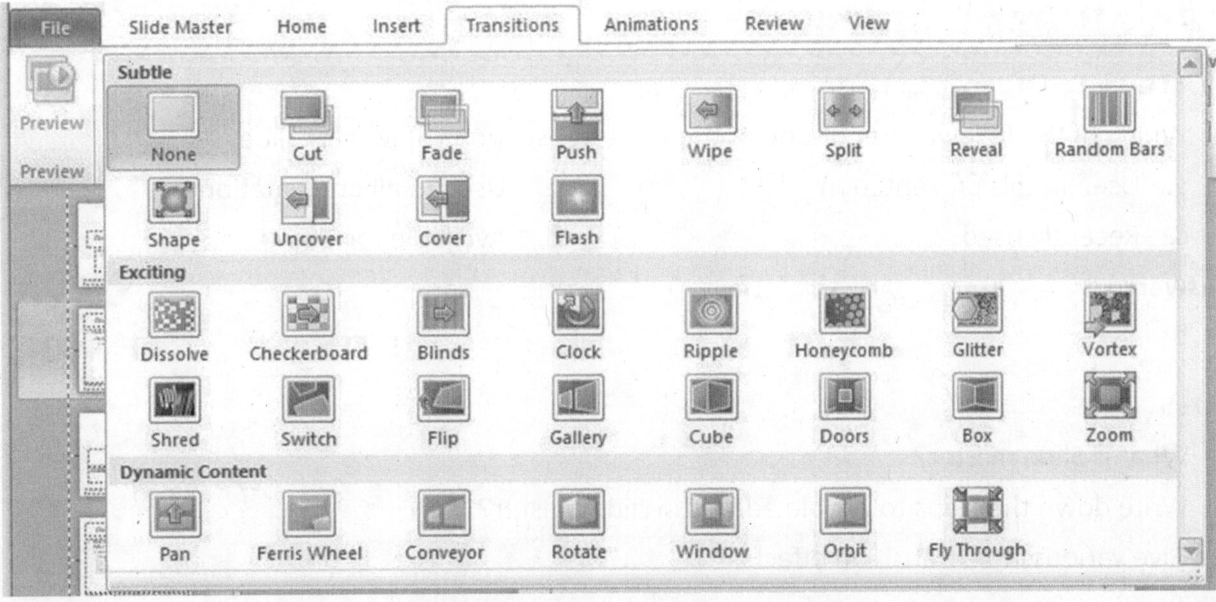

Figure 5.64: Slide Transition effects

- **To open the slide Transition section:** Click on the Slide Transition drop down arrow available in Transition Tab
- **To apply transition to all the slides:** Select the slides from Slides pane or Slide Sorter view to apply the transition to all the slides.
- **To select a transition:** Select a transition in the Apply to selected slides list.

- **To play the sound during transitions:** Select a sound from Sound list.
- **To change the speed of transition:** Select the speed from Modify transition section.
- **To advance to the next slide (manually):** Use mouse click
- **To advance to the next slide (automatically):** Specify how long the slide should remain visible then automatically advances it to the next slide.
- **To start the slide show from the current slide:** Click on Slide show

Summary

- PowerPoint comes with five prepacked slide masters. These are shown in the Master Pages section of the Tasks Pane or Sidebar.
- All the slide masters in Available for Use list is from a template of the same name. This list also contains your own created templates or templates added from other sources, slide masters from those templates.
- You can also create your own slide master like modifying the default slide master.
- To enable editing of a slide master, Select View menu bar > Master Slide
- To open the slide Transition section, Click on the Slide Transition icon available in Sidebar
- To apply transition to all the slides, Select the slides from Slides pane or Slide Sorter view to apply the transition to all the slides.
- To select a transition, Select a transition in the Apply to selected slides list.
- To play the sound during transitions, Select a sound from Sound list.

Self-Assessment

A. MULTIPLE CHOICE QUESTIONS

1. Which of the following is not one of the three subsections of Master slides?

   a. Used in this presentation b. Used in all presentation

   c. Recently used d. Available for Use

Answer:

1. b

B. QUESTIONS:

1. What is Slide master?
2. Write down the steps to enable editing in slide master?
3. Give various Slide transition effects

C. PROJECT WORK

Create a slide and apply the slide master view option to the presentation.

Create a presentation on new topic that you think your friends should know about it, To make it effective insert the slide transition effects on different slides.

Exercise for Assessment

A. MULTIPLE CHOICE QUESTIONS

1. Which of the following is not the element of presentation?
   a. Be Prepared b. Stay Relaxed c. Motivate others d. It has clear objective
2. Which of the following is the shortcut key to close PowerPoint?
   a. Ctrl + Q b. Alt + Q c. Shift + Q d. Ctrl + N
3. _______________ is not a display on Status bar.
   a. Slide number b. Name of theme c. Slide Style d. Spell check
4. _____________ is the undo command?
   a. Ctrl + X b. Ctrl +Z c. Ctrl + Y d. Inverse redo
5. What is the short form of performing superscript on the text?
   a. Ctrl + P b. Shift + Ctrl + B c. Ctrl + B d. Shift + Ctrl + P
6. Which of the following is an unordered way of making list?
   a. Table. b. Numbering. c. Bullets d. All
7. Which of the following is not the way to move the insertion point in a table?
   a. Press the left mouse button b. Press the right mouse button
   c. Press the Tab key d. Press the arrow keys
8. The Borders and Background tabs are available in which of the following tabs?
   a. Cell Properties. b. Row properties
   c. Column properties d. Table properties
9. Which of the following not comes under formatting the inserted images?
   a. Moving b. Reducing c. Resizing d. Rotating
10. What is the shortcut key to group the grouped object:
    a. Ctrl + G keys b. Ctrl + Alt + G keys
    c. Ctrl + Shift + G keys d. Ctrl + Alt + Shift + G keys

Answer:

1. c	2. a	3. c	4. b	5. d
6. c	7. b	8. d	9. b	10. c

B. VERY SHORT QUESTIONS:

1. How many numbers of lines should be there in single slide in case of good quality presentation?
2. What is the operation of Slide Pane in Presentation?
3. What is the short form of closing PowerPoint?
4. Give the shortcut key to run a slide show in PowerPoint?
5. Is it possible to save a presentation in pdf format?
6. Name various View option in PowerPoint?

7. What is the purpose of Redo button in PowerPoint window?
8. How to Bold the text in Slide?
9. How to control the size of the view in presentation?
10. Give various ways to enter data in a table?
11. Why there is need to add or insert image in Presentation?

C. SHORT QUESTIONS:

1. Name any five main elements of good presentation?
2. Define Presentation software?
3. What items or commands come under Insert menu bar in PowerPoint?
4. What do you mean by Slide Layout?
5. Is it possible to insert a duplicate slide in PowerPoint? If Yes, then write down the steps to insert a duplicate slide in it.
6. Write down the steps to rename the existing slide?
7. What is subscript and superscript in PowerPoint? How it affects the data.
8. Define Table?
9. How to insert a table in Presentation?
10. How to group and ungroup the objects in Slide?
11. What is Slide Master?

D. LONG QUESTIONS:

1. What are various characteristics of good quality presentation?
2. Name various parts of PowerPoint Window. Explain any five.
3. Explain any three view option of PowerPoint?
4. Is it possible to copy and move the existing slide in presentation? If yes, explain the drag and drop method for performing copying and moving operation.
5. Can we change the font colour of content in slide? If yes, then write down various ways to change it.
6. What do you mean by aligning the text? Name and explain various alignment types in PowerPoint.
7. Write down the steps to insert and delete table from Slide?
8. Write down the steps to insert an image from file and gallery? What are the ways to move, resize and rotate the image.
9. Write down the steps to enable editing in slide master? Also give various Slide transition effects in PowerPoint?

E. APPLICATION BASED QUESTIONS:

1. Komal got a Homework of making presentation on BPS Publication. She has created the presentation but forget to insert the two slides in the end for Thank you and Questions. Help her to add two slides into the presentation.

2. You have to make a presentation that contains repetitive slides of same data. Instead of wasting time to create a new slide what else you will do to save the time and make presentation on time.
3. Simran has downloaded the assignment that he has to present in the school. The problem is the name given in the first slide, suggest him what to do for changing the name and deleting the extra slides from it.
4. Jasspreet has to create a presentation on his ideal in life. He wants to add the pictures of his parents as they are his ideal. Suggest him, how he can insert an image of her parents in it.
5. You have create a presentation but you have found that the slides in the presentation are not in perfect order. How you can change the order of slides in the presentation.

GROUP DISCUSSION:

1. Make a group discussion on various characteristics of good quality presentation.
2. Conduct a group discussion on the pros and cons of PowerPoint and PowerPoint Presentation software. Which is better than other?
3. Arrange a group discussion of features of PowerPoint that make it prior to PowerPoint and vice a versa.

F. PROJECT WORK

Identify and list all the characteristics of good quality presentation and prepare for your presentation by considering these characteristics.

Create a new presentation using Wizard, try Run, Save and close option of presentation using keyboard.

Make a presentation on any topic and take data from different presentation available on internet Work using copying and moving slides and content in presentation.

Set the presentation on different view options, Observe the difference.

Make a Presentation in which align the heading in middle with big font size. Also make two list and apply bullets on first one and numbering on second list.

Make a table and assign borders and background to it, also adjust the column width and row height of the table.

Add any image in a presentation then set it according to your requirements by using resize, rotate and other related features.

Make a presentation and draw line, shapes using graphic objects. Also demonstrate to group and un-group objects.

TEACHER NOTES:

1. Tell students to make presentation in the class on particular topic in which they have to make table and insert images.
2. Arrange a Presentation competition in the class after completion of the chapter and tell them to consider the characteristics and elements of quality of good presentation.

Worksheet - 1 (Solved)

MULTIPLE CHOICE QUESTIONS

1. ____________ is not a display on Status bar.

   a. Slide number b. Name of theme c. Slide Style d. Spell check

2. What is the shortcut key to group the grouped object:

   a. Ctrl + G keys b. Ctrl + Alt + G keys

   c. Ctrl + Shift + G keys d. Ctrl + Alt + Shift + G keys

3. Which of the following is not a punctuation key?

   a. Comma (,) b. Semicolon (;) c. Parenthesis ({}) d. Equal sign (=)

4. A number of keys on Window keyboard are:

   a. 98 b. 110 c. 104 d. 106

5. __________ is a form of BPM that is a cost-saving technique which involves contracting business tasks to a third party.

   a. IT b. BPO c. ITeS d. None

6. The output of MAX(3, 2, 4, 1) will be:

   a. 3 b. 2 c. 4 d. 8

7. What is the full form of EEG?

   a. Electricagram b. Electroencepalogy

   c. Electroencephalography d. Electrocardiogram

8. __________ Technique selects a sentence in Word.

   a. Single-click b. Double click c. Triple-click d. Click four times

9. Which of the following shows absolute referencing?

   a. B2+C2 b. B2*C2 c. B$2+C$2 d. B2*C$2

10. Which of the following is not the common action performed using the mouse?

    a. Left-click b. Pick and drop c. Scroll d. Double click

Answers:

1. c 2. c 3. d 4. c 5. b

6. c 7. c 8. c 9. b 10. b

VERY SHORT TYPE QUESTIONS AND ANSWERS

1. Name the home row keys.
2. Define BPO services.
3. Name various types of referencing in Excel?

4. What is a mail merge?
5. 5. What is the operation of slide pane in the presentation?
6. 6. Define the I-Beam mouse pointer on the document.

Answers:

1. The home keys are the row of keys on the computer keyboard your fingers rest on when not typing. The Alphabets ASDF are home keys for left hand and LKJ along with semi-colon (;) are for the right hand. For both hands, the thumb rests on the spacebar.
2. In India, various kinds of jobs are outsourced by a highly organized industry of BPO. Some of the BPO services included are:
   - Taxation and insurance services
   - Software testing services
   - Financial and accounting services
   - Health care services
   - Web promotion and e-publishing
   - Document management services
   - Multimedia and design services
3. In Microsoft Excel, there are mainly three types of references, such as:
   - Relative referencing
   - Absolute referencing
   - Mixed referencing
4. The mail merge feature is used for creating a series of same documents and sent it to multiple addresses. With this feature, we can merge the main document that can be certificates or letters with a mailing address of various persons. Its name is mal merge because in this main document is merged with a mailing address that helps in sending letters, invitations, common documents or certificates for a number of peoples.
5. The thumbnail of slides is displayed in slides pane or a place where the user can design the slides. It allows users to add new slides, remove or rearrange slides.
6. The I-beam pointer is used in graphical-based text processing applications. This is used in word processors or various desktop publishing systems for marking the blocks of text and moves the insertion point.

SHORT TYPE QUESTIONS AND ANSWERS

1. What is mixed referencing?
2. Define Rapid Touch Typing?
3. What is the structure of the IT-BPM industry? Give three parameters of the IT-BPM Industry.
4. What is the usage of print preview in MS Word?
5. Name any five main elements of a good presentation?
6. What is the toolbar? What is the purpose of the Formatting toolbar in Excel?

Answers:

1. Mixed is a combination of relative and absolute referencing. It is used when we have to make some row number and column name constant, and some have to vary accordingly. The $ sign is added before the row number and column name to make it constant.

   For example, We have entered the number of class 9th students in English, Hindi, Maths, and IT subject. In total marks, we have taken the sum in which the relative reference is used as arguments cell name is varying according to their position. The same is for average, but in GR total column, you can observe that the sum column is varying, and grace marks column name is constant, and $ sign is added before the row number. This shows the mixed referencing.

2. Rapid Typing Tutor is a free and open-source software that is designed for learning typing skills on the computer. Learning to type with a Rapid typing tutor is a fun and typing game. Rapid touch typing tutor is used for making the use of computer more efficient for kids and adults. There is a number of games, exercises, and training sessions that sharpen the skills of users and help them to work efficiently in a short time.

3. BPM stands for Business Process Management that defines how a company creates, edits, and analyses the predictable processes that make up the core of its business. BPM is considered as the bridge between information technology (IT) and business due to its focus and control over complex IT processes.

   The three parameters of the IT-BPM industry are:

   - The geographic spread of operations
   - Sectoring serve by organization
   - Revenues and size of operations

4. In MS Word, there is the option of a print preview that helps in checking the document before printing it. This helps in checking whether the document is as per our needs like the borders or content or margins set in it.

5. The five main elements of the presentation that makes it effective are:

   - Be prepared: Being prepared is one of the most important elements of the presentation. This depends on how many times you practice your speed that must be 30 hours of rehearsal time for every hour you will be speaking.
   - Give of yourself: While giving the presentation tries to use personal examples, but make sure it supports your point and message you want to convey through the presentation.
   - Stay relaxed: You will be relaxed if you have prepared for your presentation. Also, focus on your message instead of an audience and use gestures like walking patterns, and more.
   - It has a clear objective: Define your goals clearly, right at the outside. The objective of your presentation will drive everything from your script to your slide deck.
   - It's useful to your audience: Make sure your presentation should genuinely and meaningfully offer value to its audience. That means sharing key strategies that have worked for you, offering up enlightening data or insights, or telling a story that may be able to learn from.

6. There are, by default, two toolbars in Excel that provide a wide range of common commands and functions. A tooltip or small box is displayed by placing the mouse cursor over any icon.

7. The formatting toolbar consists of the most common operation related to datasheet formattings such as font selection, size of text, alignment, cell value formatting and indentation, and more.

LONG TYPE QUESTIONS AND ANSWERS

1. Is it possible to copy and move the existing slide in a presentation? If yes, explain the drag and drop method for performing copying and moving operations.
2. How to check spelling and grammar mistakes in the MS Word window? Give colors that indicate different mistakes in the document.

Answers:

1. It is very time-consuming to create the same slide again and again. In PowerPoint, there is an option to reuse the existing slide within the presentation or in any other presentation. To move the slide to another location or to reuse it, use the cut and paste and copy and paste process, respectively. In PowerPoint, we can copy and move the existing slide in the presentation. One of its methods is drag and drop. To use drag and drop method to copy and paste the command, perform the following steps:

   Select the slide and click and hold the left mouse button on the marked slide along with the Ctrl button and then move the cursor to the desired location. Then, release the left mouse button.

   Like copying, you can also move the text using the drag and drop method.

2. Errors are related to spelling and grammar mistakes. In MS Word, there is a built-in feature of checking and correcting the errors. It helps in correcting the spelling as well as grammar. You can use both separately or in combination with each other. You will observe the different colors of the line for a different type of mistake in your text.
   - The blue line will come under the word or sentence if there are grammatical errors in the text. These types of errors can be removed by right-clicking on it and selecting the right option. In the context menu that comes after right-clicking on the blue wavy line, the first entry gives the name of suspected grammatical error, and in the second entry, it gives suggestions for correction.
   - The spelling checker checks for spelling mistakes in the typed text or words that are not present in the installed dictionary list.
   - The red wavy line highlights the errors related to spelling mistakes. In case, if you found a red line under your text, then: Right-click on the text that has a red wavy line and selects the matching word.

Worksheet - 2 (Solved)

MULTIPLE-CHOICE QUESTIONS

1. ____________ is a study, design, development, implementation, storing, support and management of all computer-based information system
   a. Communication b. Information Technology
   c. Process d. Technology
2. You can select all text in the document by pressing ____________ keys of the keyboard.
   a. Ctrl + C b. Ctrl + V c. Ctrl + A d. Ctrl + X
3. The output of 634.8877777 after selecting two decimal places from the Format Cells dialog box will be:
   a. 6.3488 b. 634.8877 c. 63.488 d. 634.88
4. Selection pointer in word processors represents:
   a. Typing text b. Make blocks of text
   c. Moving over the page d. Moving the insertion point
5. The change in background color of paragraph comes under ____________ tab
   a. Page b. Borders c. Alignment d. Area
6. ____________ is the undo command?
   a. Ctrl + X b. Ctrl +Z c. Ctrl + Y d. Inverse redo
7. Caps lock key is used to ____________
   a. Type text in uppercase b. Type text in lower case
   c. Type numeric data d. All
8. What will be the output of (2+7)*6
   a. 44 b. 42 c. 54 d. 56
9. Which of the following is not a part of the MS Excel window?
   a. Title Bar b. Menu Bar c. File Bar d. Standard Tool Bar
10. The range of row in Excel?
    a. 1 to 65536 b. 1 to 16384 c. 1 to 32767 d. 1 to 1048576

Answers:

1. B 2. C 3. D 4. A 5. D
6. B 7. A 8. C 9. D 10. D

VERY SHORT TYPE QUESTIONS AND ANSWERS

1. Name common text formatting features in MS Excel.
2. What is the full form of ITeS?

3. What is the purpose of undo and redo in MS PowerPoint?
4. What is the purpose of the redo button in the Powerpoint window?
5. Define the floating toolbar?
6. What is the function of the Backspace key in the keyboard?

Answers:

1. The common text formatting features in Microsoft PowerPoint are:
    - Change of font-size: You can change the font size by selecting the font size.
    - Change of font style: You can change the font style by either making it bold, italic or underline.
    - Change of font type: You can change the font type by selecting font dropdown.
    - Change of font color: You can change the font color by selecting the font color icon.
2. ITeS is an abbreviation for Information technology-enabled services and also known as web-enabled services or Teleworking that defined as outsourcing of processes that enabled with information technology and covered diverse areas like HR, healthcare, finance, administration, manufacturing, telecommunication, and many more.
3. If you have done some changes in the existing document or in a new document that is not required, then you can use undo to remove it from your document. On the flip side, If by mistake you have deleted some data but want to add it again then click on Redo option
4. If, by mistake, you have deleted some data but want to add it again or you want to rollback your undo command, then use the Redo option.
5. The floating toolbar is just below the Standard Toolbar. It is context-sensitive that shows the tools relevant to the current position of the cursor or the selected object.
6. The backspace key is similar to the delete key that removes texts in a word. It deletes the text in the left of the cursor and moves the cursor to that position.

SHORT TYPE QUESTIONS AND ANSWERS

1. What are the various actions performed by the mouse?
2. What is the purpose of the error window in Rapid Touch Typing?
3. How is IT used in home computing?
4. What is display under the status bar of Microsoft office?
5. What is a slide master?
6. What do you mean by referencing in Excel?

Answers:

1. A mouse is a pointing device that consists of two or three buttons. One button is present on the left side, one on the right side and one in the middle. It can be used to perform more than one actions like:
    - Selecting menu commands
    - Resize windows
    - Selecting actions from screen icons and more

The left side button is used most commonly to select or activate the application. In order to check the list of commands on the screen, a right button of the mouse is used. Its use has been found in various applications like designing to drag the pictures, etc. Through mouse, one is able to delete, copy, cut, and move files on the screen. The middle scroll wheels or button is used to scroll down the page, folders, documents, and more.

2. The detailed statistics for the current lesson can be seen on the Error tab that shows your errors and delays percentage both in the table and graphical view. This helps in understanding the hard letters to type for you. You can switch between Errors in percent chart and delay in percent chart. In bar charts, the letters used in the lesson are given on X-axis, and delays or errors related to each letter are shown on Y-axis. The chart will not be shown for no errors and delays for a certain character.

3. For working at homes, a personal computer or PC is used for performing household work. It is used for surfing the web, creating and listening to music, playing games, doing household account, playing puzzles, and more.

   The aim of personal computers at home is to help families in need to use the internet and developing basic computer skills in their everyday lives that result in an increase in children's literacy rate.

4. The status bar is on the left bottom of the writer window that displays the number of pages, word count, language used and zooming function, and more.

   PowerPoint comes with five prepacked slide masters. These are shown in the master pages section of the tasks pane or sidebar. This section has three subsections:

   - Used in this presentation
   - Recently used
   - Available for use

   You can also expand it by clicking upward arrow marker available next to the name of a subsection

5. In master pages, you can modify the existing architecture of slides and also can set the common style for all slides. In PowerPoint, there are some default slide master pages. PowerPoint comes with five prepacked slide masters. These are shown in the master pages section of the tasks pane or sidebar. This section has three subsections:

   - Used in this presentation
   - Recently used
   - Available for use

   You can also expand it by clicking the upward arrow marker available next to the name of a subsection.

6. In Microsoft Office, there is a feature of referencing, which is the way to refer any formula or function of one cell to the next cell along the row or column. In MS Office, there are mainly three types of references, such as:

   - Relative referencing: By default, all the cell references are relative references in which the formula gets copied in the new cell when you select any formula and drag it to a new cell. There are changes in the formula on the basis of the relative position of rows and columns.
   - Absolute referencing: There are cases when you don't want a cell reference to change when copied to other cells, as happens in relative referencing. In those cases, absolute referencing is

used as it will not change when copied and filled in another cell. To use Absolute referencing a $ symbol is used before the column name and row number that make it constant for any formula.

- Mixed referencing: It is the combination of relative and absolute referencing. It is used when we have to make some row number and column name constant, and some have to vary accordingly. The $ sign is added before the row number and coumn name to make it constant.

LONG TYPE QUESTIONS AND ANSWERS

1. How to format a range of cells to be seen as labels, values, as scientific and to display time?
2. What is the purpose of using bullets and numbering in the document? Write the steps to create a list using bullets and numbering.

Answers:

1. To format a range of cells to be seen as labels, values, scientific and display time, perform the following steps:
   - Formatting a range of cells to be seen as labels: There are some cases in which there is a need to format a range of cells to be seen as labels. These cases can come in telephone numbers in which every country STD code starts with 0. But when you enter the telephone number in a spreadsheet with prefix as 0, then the "0" will disappears from the telephone number because in a spreadsheet it stores as a numeric value that does not have a preceding 0 or zero.

     But to take 0 as a prefix in the spreadsheet we take numeric values as text. To format the selected range of cells that consist of a telephone number as text, perform the following steps:

     Select the range of cells and click on the Format tab menu bar and click on the cell, and Format Cells dialog box will open. Click on Number tab | Text | OK.
   - Formatting a range of cells as scientific: There are some cases in which there is a need to format a range of cells as scientific. These cases can come into entering the date. As the default date format in the spreadsheet is American Format:

     (mm/dd/yyyy): mm means month, dd means to date and yyyy means year

     Example: 12/07/2018 : This means the date is 7th December 2018.

     In the spreadsheet, we have a number of Date formats. To change the date format, perform the following steps:

     Select the range of cells and click on the Format tab menu bar and click on the cell, and Format Cells dialog box will open Click on Number tab and select Date category. Select the required date format and click on the OK button.
   - Formatting a range of cells to display time: There are some cases in which there is a need to format a range of cells to display time. These cases can come in the time indicated on a computer. In Computer, the common format of the time is hh:mm:ss AM/PM.

     In the above-given format, the hh means hours, mm means minutes, and ss means second.

     To format a range of cells to display the time, perform the following steps:

     Select the range of cells > Click on Format Tab menu bar > Click on Cell and format cells dialog box will open > Click on Number tab > Select Time category > Select Format of Time > Click on Ok button

2. To put a list of items in a good format, there is an option of bullet and numbering in MS office. These both will arrange the content in the form of lists. Both options are available in Formatting Toolbar.

   A mainly unordered list is created using bullet as there is no sequence of items in it. You can also create a nested list by using the customize option on Bullets and Numbering toolbar

   To apply either Bullet or Numbering for making a list, perform the following steps:

   Select the text on which you want to apply bullets or Numbering > Click on Bullet option drop down and select the required style of a bullet from it.

   The same can be done for numbering the document by selecting the option from the numbering list.

Model Test Paper-1 (Solved)

Time = 2 Hours **Maximum Marks are 50**

General Instructions:

i. Read the question paper carefully

ii. Question Paper is divided into four sections

Attempt any of 10 questions from this section:

Section A: Multiple choice questions (1 marks each)

Attempt any of 6 questions from this section:

Section B: Very short Answer (2 marks each)

All questions are compulsory in these sections:

Section C: Short Answer (3 marks each)

Section D: Long Answer (5 marks each)

SECTION – A

1. Verbal communication involves:
   a. Any message that uses words of different languages
   b. A written message
   c. A Spoken message
   d. Both (b) and (c)
2. R in SMART strategy stands for_________?
   a. Real b. Rate c. Realistic d. Required
3. Which of the following component of the Internet is the interface between the World wide web and the user.
   a. Internal b. Internet Browser c. Web pages d. Web portal
4. Rainwater harvesting is the example of ___________-
   a. Social job b. Green job c. Hydel work d. Traffic job
5. Which of the following is the Non-cooperate type of business enterprise?
   a. Joint-stock company b. Cooperative society
   c. Sole Proprietorship d. None
6. Which of the following is the shortcut key to close PowerPoint?
   a. Ctrl + Q b. Alt + Q c. Shift + Q d. Ctrl + N
7. _______________ are Home row keys for left hand.
   a. SDFG b. LKJ c. ASDF d. HJK
8. BPO stands for:
   a. Business portal organization b. Business Process Outsourcing
   c. Business Process organization d. Business portal outsourcing

9. The ____________ pointer is used in graphical-based text processing applications.

   a. Grabber pointer b. Selection Pointer c. H-Beam d. I-Beam

10. Which of the following is the shortcut key to Redo the operation?

   a. Ctrl + X b. Ctrl + Y c. Ctrl + Z d. Ctrl + V

11. The range of Column in Excel spreadsheet?

   a. 1 to 124 b. 1 to 1048576 c. 1 to 1024 d. 1 to 1023

12. The default position of Value in the spreadsheet is?

   a. Left b. Right c. Center d. Justify

Answers:

1. d	2. c	3. b	4. c	5. c	6. a
7. c	8. b	9. d	10. b	11. c	12. a

SECTION – B

1. Define Encoding and Decoding?
2. Write down the full form of SMART strategy.

   OR

   Give various characteristics of Entrepreneurship.
3. What is the use of the Cardiac Screening machine?
4. Name various View option in PowerPoint?
5. Define the Fill handle of a cell?
6. Name any three-word processing applications.
7. Name common text formatting features in MS Word.
8. What is the short form of closing PowerPoint?

Answers:

1. Encoding or converting data or information into the coded language that is not understood by any other person.

   The encoded information is decoded at the receiver side to understand the sent message or information. The messages should be decoded according to the pattern used by the receiver while encoding it that helps in having correct information.
2. In SMART Strategy,
   - S stands for specific,
   - M stands for Measurable like divide your tasks whose completion gives measurable outcome,
   - A stands for Achievable that means set a task that can be achieved,
   - R stands for Realistic,
   - T stands for Time-bound

   OR

Various characteristics of Entrepreneurship are:

- It is a function of Innovation
- It is a function of leadership
- It is an Organization building function
- It involves the operation and creation of an enterprise
- It is concerned with managing, developing and employing the factors of production

3. The Cardiac Screening Machine is used to displays the physiology of the heart and its inside movements. This machine is mainly used for diagnosis the problems related to heart like thinning of veins.
4. In MS PowerPoint, we can view a presentation with different views like Normal, Outline, Slide Sorter, Notes, Slide Master, Notes Master, and Handout Master.
5. In the MS Excel Fill Handle tool, you can fill the next cells by dragging it with the next predefined value. For example, you want to fill the Roll numbers, Month, Week, Days, etc., then you can input one or two in sequence, then select them and drag it to the next cell or till that you want to continue that series of sequence.
6. The three-word processing applications are:
   - WordPad
   - Microsoft Word
   - Google Docs
   - Notepad
   - OpenOffice Writer
   - LibreOffice Writer
7. The common Text formatting features in MS Word are:
   - Change of Font size: You can change the font size by selecting font size.
   - Change of Font Style: You can change the font style by either making it bold, italic or underline
   - Change of Font type: You can change the font type by selecting font dropdown
   - Change of Font Color: You can change the font color by selecting the font color icon
8. The short form of closing PowerPoint is:

   Press Alt +F4 or Press Ctrl + Q keys of the keyboard

SECTION – C

1. How is IT used in Home computing?
2. Define the EEG machine, and what is its purpose?
3. What are the various actions performed by the mouse?
4. Give a brief about various paragraph alignment styles in MS Word.
5. Is it possible to insert a duplicate slide in PowerPoint? If Yes, then write down the steps to insert a duplicate slide in it.
6. What is Mixed Referencing?

Answers:

1. The purpose of the use of IT in Home computing is for working at homes a personal computer or PC is used for performing household work. It is used for surfing the web, creating and listening to music, playing games, doing household account, playing puzzles, etc.

   The aim of personal computers at home is to:

   - Help families in need to use the internet and developing basic computer skills in their everyday lives that result in an increase in children's literacy rate.

2. EEG stands for Electroencephalography Machine that is a test used to evaluate the electrical activity in the brain. Brain cells communicate with each other through electrical impulses. The potential problems associated with this activity can be detected by this machine. It also records and tracks the patterns of brain waves. The small electrical probes are attached to the head for receiving the electrical impulses of the brain and send signals to a computer for recording the results.

3. The mouse is a pointing device that consists of two or three buttons. One button is present on the left side, one on the right side and one in the middle. It can be used to perform more than one actions like:

   - Selecting menu commands,
   - Resize windows,
   - Selecting actions from screen icons, etc.

     The left side button is used most commonly to select or activate the application. In order to check the list of commands on the screen, a right button of the mouse is used. Its use has been found in various applications like designing to drag the pictures, etc. Through mouse, one is able to delete, copy, cut, and move files on the screen. The middle scroll wheels or button is used to scroll down the page, folders, documents, etc.

4. The position of paragraph between the page margins is known as paragraph alignment. By default, the text is aligned on the left side of the document, and the right margins in the document are known as horizontal text alignment.

   There are mainly four-paragraph alignment styles comes under this category are:

   - **Align Paragraph left:** The left Paragraph alignment is a default type of alignment. In this case, there is little space on the right side.
   - **Center:** This will align the Paragraph in the center of the document and leave little space from both the ends. Mainly its use has been found in writing the title.
   - **Align Paragraph Right:** This is the opposite case of left Paragraph alignment as in this, the Paragraph is aligning towards the right side and leave little space in the left. They are mainly used to put sign and date options or sometimes giving the chapter heading.
   - **Justify:** In this case, Paragraph is evenly aligned between the left and right sides.

5. Yes, You can insert a duplicate slide in PowerPoint.

   To insert a duplicate slide, perform the following steps and using the options given below:

   Select the slide from Slide Pane > Select Slide menu bar > Duplicate Slide

   OR

   Another option is: Right-click on the slide > Select Duplicate Slide from the menu

6. Mixed is a combination of relative and absolute referencing. It is used when we have to make some row number and column name constant, and some have to vary accordingly. The $ sign isadded before the row number or column name to make it constant.

   For example, We have entered the number of class 9th students in English, =hindi, maths, and IT subjects. In Total marks, we have taken the sum in which the relative reference is used as arguments cell name is varying according to their position. The same is for average, but in GR total column, you can observe that the Sum column is varying, and the grace marks column name is constant, and $ sign is added before the row number. This shows the mixed referencing.

SECTION – D

1. Write down the steps to insert an image from the file and gallery? What are the ways to move, resize, and rotate the image?
2. Write a short note of speeding up data entry using Fill handle?

Answers:

1. To insert an image from the gallery, perform the following steps:

   Select Insert Menu bar > Media > Gallery and the available themes with images are displays in the gallery.

   Now from the gallery you can select the theme and find a suitable form by scrolling > Click on the image > Drag it onto the workspace > Release the mouse button and image will be observed on the slide.

   Formatting Images: We have learned to insert an image, but sometimes there can be requirements of formatting that image such as moving, resizing, rotating, etc. Various formatting on inserted images are:

   Moving Images: To move an inserted image in the slide, perform the following steps:

   Click on Image > wait till the cursor changes to hand shape > Click on the image and drag it to the desired position > Release the mouse button

   Resizing Images: To resize an inserted image in the slide, perform the following steps:

   Click on Image > Put the cursor on one of the selection handles on the image and the cursor will change the shape by giving a graphical representation of the direction of the resizing > Click and drag the image to resize it > Release the mouse button

   Rotating Images: In PowerPoint you can also rotate the image in any direction using the rotating icon or manually. To rotate an inserted image in the slide, perform the following steps:

   Click on Image > Click on Rotate icon on the Line and Filling toolbar > Click again on the selected image and shape, and color of selection handles get changed > Click the mouse and move it in the required direction > Release the mouse button

   Formatting using the Image toolbar:

   Instead of formatting manually, you can also format the image using the Image toolbar. It comes under the properties window after selecting the image in the slide.

   The toolbar contains a number of formatting options. Other option to display Image toolbar is:

   Select View menu bar > Toolbars > Image

2. In the MS Excel Fill Handle tool, you can fill the next cells by dragging it with the next predefined value. For example, you want to fill the Roll numbers, Month, Week, Days, etc., then you can input one or two in sequence, then select them and drag it to the next cell or till that you want to continue that series of sequence.

   - **For number series:** To speed up the process of entering number series, perform the following steps:

   - Type numbers 1, 2 in two consecutive cells > Select them using mouse > Click on the right down corner of the last selected cell and drag it down till that you want to continue the number series. You can also get a series on a different interval by giving the difference between two consecutive cell values then drag them downward.

   - **Copying Formula:** To speed up the process of entering the same formula to the number of cells in the rows or columns, one can enter it again and again in each cell rows or columns or copy the formula and paste it in cells that results in save of time and effort when you have to enter the same long and complex formulae.

   - **Various Options to Copying a Formula and using it are:** Use of copy and paste commands: In this, you just have to select the cell contain formula then select the cell on which you want to enter that same formula. Now Press Paste command to paste that same formula in the selected cell.

Model Test Paper-2 (Solved)

Time = 2 Hours **Maximum Marks are 50**

General Instructions:

i. Read the question paper carefully

ii. Question Paper is divided into four sections

Attempt any of 10 questions from this section:

Section A: Multiple choice questions (1 marks each)

Attempt any of 6 questions from this section:

Section B: Very short Answer (2 marks each)

All questions are compulsory in these sections:

Section C: Short Answer (3 marks each)

Section D: Long Answer (5 marks each)

SECTION – A

1. Which of the following is not a type of phrase?

a. Noun b. Adjective c. Adverbial d. Pronoun

2. O in SWOT stands for ___________

a. Operation b. Organization c. Opportunity d. Openly

3. Which of the following primary components of the ecosystem that are producers of energy.

a. Autotrophs b. Heterotrophs c. Non-living matter d. All

4. The maximum length of the tweet is:

a. 120 words b. No limit c. 140 words d. 280 words

5. Rainwater harvesting is the example of ___________-

a. Social job b. Green job c. Hydel work d. Traffic job

6. An Entrepreneur ______________

a. Sets the interest rates of banks b. manages financial investments

c. takes risks to earn profits d. enforces government regulations

7. Which of the following defines how a company creates, edits, and analyses the predictable processes that make up the core of its business.

a. Government b. BPO c. IT d. BPM

8. What is the shortcut key to group the grouped object:

a. Ctrl + G keys b. Ctrl + Alt + G keys

c. Ctrl + Shift + G keys d. Ctrl + Alt + Shift + G keys

9. What is the short form of performing superscript on the text?

a. Ctrl + P b. Shift + Ctrl + B c. Ctrl + B d. Shift + Ctrl + P

10. The blue wavy line under the word or sentence represents:

a. Spelling mistake b. Grammar mistake c. Word formation mistake d. All

11. Which of the following color display the percentage of completion of the lesson?

a. Red b. Green c. Blue d. Yellow

12. What will be the output of (2+7)*6

a. 44 b. 42 c. 54 d. 56

Answers:

1. d	2. c	3. a	4. d	5. b	6. c
7. d	8. c	9. d	10. b	11. b	12. c

SECTION - B

1. Give any two disadvantages of written communication.
2. What do you understand by overexploitation of Natural resources?
3. Define Mouse?

   OR

   What is Page Break?
4. What is the default position of Label in the spreadsheet?
5. Define BPO services.
6. Define the Floating Toolbar?
7. Name the Home row keys.
8. What is the importance of Charts in Spreadsheet?

Answers:

1. The disadvantages of Written communication are:
   - Written content has legal validity
   - It helps the user to draft comprehensive message
   - In case of lengthy messages, it is considered a suitable mode
2. This means overuse of natural resources to such extent that it almost reaches a stage off enervation. We can see this phenomenon in the exploitation of:
   - Forest and natural vegetation,
   - Grazing pastures,
   - Medical plants,
   - Wildlife,
   - Fossil fuels,
   - Fish stock and water aquifers.
3. The mouse is a pointing device that consists of two or three buttons. One button is present on the left side, one on the right side and one in the middle.

   OR

Page break is also known as a hard page break that is a code inserted by a software program like MS Word that tells the printing device were to end the current page and begin the next. It will move the text to a new page before reaching the end of the page.

4. The default position of Label in Excel is the Left side.
5. BPO is the abbreviation of Business Process Outsourcing services that are meant to perform business operations through an outside service provider. In the BPO, complete transfer of the business process or the function to an external service provider takes place.
6. The floating toolbar is just below the Standard Toolbar. It is context-sensitive that shows the tools relevant to the current position of the cursor or the selected object.
7. The home keys are the row of keys on the computer keyboard; your fingers rest on when not typing. The Alphabets ASDF are home keys for left hand and LKJ along with semi-colon ";" are for the right hand. For both hands, the thumb rests on the spacebar.
8. Importance of Charts in Spreadsheet are:
   - As mentioned above, the visual representation of data is preferred in case of a large amount of data. That's why charts are introduced in every spreadsheet.
   - It is not easy to compare and analyze data when they are represented as numbers in large quantity
   - The data in the form of charts are more effective in communication and understanding
   - You can create charts in tabular numeric data, function or some kind of qualitative structures

SECTION – C

1. How to check spelling and grammar mistakes using Synonyms and Thesaurus?
2. Give various processes of the workplace where IT is used.
3. Give various mathematical operators used in Formulae with example.
4. Define Rapid Touch Typing?
5. What is the purpose of the Error window in Rapid Touch Typing?
6. What is subscript and superscript in PowerPoint? How it affects the data.

Answers:

1. The synonyms, antonyms, word substitute, and alternative spelling comes in word through a thesaurus. Both the dictionary and thesaurus are different from each other as there are synonyms; antonyms in the thesaurus; on the other hand, the dictionary contains pronunciation and definitions. Synonyms are a word having a similar meaning to the word you have enter. On the other hand, antonyms are words option with the opposite meaning of the typed word. Thesaurus helps users while writing by giving suggestions to make them to better understand their words. To use a thesaurus, follow the steps:

   Select the word > to right-click on it > click on synonyms from the context menu

   The selected word or phrase will be highlighted in the document and will get the same meaning word for the selected word.
2. Technology is such an integral part of the 21-st century workplace that any business without some level of technical knowledge will fail. In workplaces or offices, computers and their applications

are used to perform work more effectively that makes computer use as prevalent. Some offices or companies may find functioning without them is virtually impossible.

3. In Excel or spreadsheet software, there are most powerful features by which the user can calculate numerical data by applying various formulae. Formulas are simple equations that perform calculations on values in our sheet. This can include numbers, parenthesis, cell address, and arithmetic operators, and the result will be displayed on the cell where the user has entered the formula.

Operation	Symbol Name	Symbol	Example
Addition	Plus sign	+	B2+C2, B3+6
Subtraction	Minus sign	-	B2-C2
Multiplication	Asterisk	*	C2*D2
Division	Forward slash	/	C2/D2

4. Rapid Typing Tutor is a free and open-source software that is designed for learning typing skills on the computer. Learning to type with a Rapid typing tutor is a fun and typing game. The rapid touch-typing tutor helps in using the computer more efficiently by kids and adults for typing purpose. There is a number of games, exercises, and training sessions that sharpen the skills of users and helps them to work efficiently in a short time.

5. The detailed statistics for the current lesson can be seen on the Error tab that shows your errors and delays percentage both in the table and graphical view. This helps in understanding the hard letters to type for you. You can switch between Errors in percent chart and delay in percent chart. In bar charts, the letters used in the lesson are given on X-axis, and delays or errors related to each letter are shown on Y-axis. The chart will not be shown for no errors and delays for a certain character.

6. After selecting subscript, whatever user type will come below the baseline, and it will look smaller than other normal text in the document.

   - To perform subscript: Select the text > Select the Format > Text > Subscript Or Press Shift + Ctrl + B

   On the other hand, the superscript will place the text above the baseline.

   - To perform subscript: Select the text > Select the Format > Text > Superscript Or Press Shift + Ctrl + P

SECTION - D

1. Write down the steps and options of moving and copying the text in MS Word?
2. Explain any three-view option of PowerPoint?

Answers:

1. If you want to create or use the same data, then the copy command of MS Word can be used. Either single or multiple copies of data can be created by using a single command without affecting the existing data. This will save time and effort that the user has to put in writing the same data again in different locations. The copy operation can be done by performing the following steps:

   Copy and Paste: It is used when you want the duplicate copy of the selected text. To perform copy and paste, perform the following steps:

Step 1: Select the text > Click on Edit menu > Click on Copy option

Or

Another option to Copy the text is to select the text > Right-click on it > Select the Copy option

Step 2: Put the cursor on the desired location > Click on Edit menu > Click on the Paste option

Another option to Paste the text is Right-click on the desired position > Select Paste option

Shortcut to Copy the text: Press Ctrl + C key

Shortcut to Paste the text: Press Ctrl + V key

Cut and Paste: In the case of copy command, we will get a copy of that data, which is further being pasted on different locations. On the other hand, the cut command will remove that data from a particular location, and it will paste the text in another location. To perform the cut and paste operation, perform the following steps:

Step 1: Select the text > Click on Edit menu > Click on Cut option

Or

Another option to Cut the text is to select the text > Right-click on it > Select cut option

Step 2: Put the cursor on the desired location > Click on Edit menu > Click on the Paste option

Another option to Paste the text is Right-click on the desired position > Select Paste option

Shortcut to Cut the text: Press Ctrl + X key

2. In MS PowerPoint, we can view a presentation with different views like Normal, Outline, Slide Sorter, Notes, Slide Master, Notes Master, and Handout Master. The default view of PowerPoint is the Normal view. Various view options can be selected from the View menu.

   Normal View: This is the default type of view, and in this view, images, text, animation, video, and audio can be added on the slide. This is also the main view for working with individual slides and format or design. In this view, the position of the slide will be in the middle, and on the left side, there is slide pane.

   To select the Normal view, Click on View Menu bar or tab > Select Normal view command

   Outline View: In Outline View of the presentation, there are all slides of the presentation in a sequence. In the Outline format, you can see each slide, and in the workspace, only the text is visible in each slide. It also displays the slide text in the form of a structure.

   To select the Outline view, Click on View Menu bar or tab > Select Outline view command

   Notes View: In Notes view, there is an option to add notes for each slide that contains the information for the presenter. This information is not visible to another person while giving a presentation. This will help the speaker in remembering the important points to discuss and giving to the audience.

   To select the Notes view, Click on View Menu bar or tab > Select Notes to view command

Model Test Paper-3 (Unsolved)

Time = 2 Hours **Maximum Marks are 50**

General Instructions:

i. Read the question paper carefully

ii. Question Paper is divided into four sections

Attempt any of 10 questions from this section:

Section A: Multiple choice questions (1 marks each)

Attempt any of 6 questions from this section:

Section B: Very short Answer (2 marks each)

All questions are compulsory in these sections:

Section C: Short Answer (3 marks each)

Section D: Long Answer (5 marks each)

SECTION – A

1. People with self-confidence have a___________ outlook:

   a. Negative b. Arrogant c. Outward d. Positive

2. Which of the following is not an example of written communication?

   a. Emails b. Reports c. body language d. Letters

3. Which of the following is not a type of speech?

   a. Noun b. Pronoun c. Adverb d. Adjective

4. _________ and _________ are two parts of an email address

   a. portal address and email address b. User name and domain name

   c. Portal address and domain name d. Email address and user name

5. Which of the following is not a pronged approach proposed by UNEP for attaining a green economy?

   a. Low Carbon growth b. Low oxygen growth

   c. Resource efficiency d. Social Inclusivity

6. ___________ is a study, design, development, implementation, storing, support and management of all computer-based information system

   a. Communication b. Information Technology

   c. Process d. Technology

7. You can select all text in the document by pressing ___________ keys of keyboard

   a. Ctrl + C b. Ctrl + V c. Ctrl + A d. Ctrl + X

8. The output of 634.8877777 after selecting two decimal places from the Format Cells dialog box will be:

   a. 6.3488 b. 634.8877 c. 63.488 d. 634.88

9. Selection pointer in word processors represents:

   a. Typing text
   b. Make blocks of text
   c. Moving over the page
   d. Moving the insertion point

10. The change in background colour of paragraph comes under __________ tab

   a. Page
   b. Borders
   c. Alignment
   d. Area

11. ______________ is the undo command?

   a. Ctrl + X
   b. Ctrl +Z
   c. Ctrl + Y
   d. Inverse redo

12. Caps lock key is used to ____________

   a. type text in uppercase
   b. Type text in lower case
   c. Type numeric data
   d. All

SECTION – B

1. Give full form of any two: MODEM, CPU, ALU, NIC and Wi-Fi
2. Define Habitat Distinction?
3. What is an MRI machine?

   OR

   Define the EEH machine, and what is its purpose?
4. Define the I-beam mouse pointer on the document.
5. What is the purpose of the Redo button in the PowerPoint window?
6. Write a formula for multiplication with cell addresses and operators?
7. What is Mail Merge?
8. What is the operation of Slide Pane in the Presentation?

SECTION – C

1. Gives the advantages and disadvantages of using ICT?
2. Use both the methods of inserting the table in the document. Write a short note on both methods.
3. Define the usage of Numeric keypad.
4. What is Toolbar? What is the purpose of the Formatting toolbar in Excel?
5. What do you mean by Slide Layout?
6. Give various techniques for selecting text?

SECTION – D

1. What is Referencing? Explain with example various types of referencing in Excel?
2. Is it possible to copy and move the existing slide in a presentation? If yes, explain the drag and drop method for performing copying and moving operations.

Model Test Paper-4 (Unsolved)

Time = 2 Hours **Maximum Marks are 50**

General Instructions:

i. Read the question paper carefully

ii. Question Paper is divided into four sections

Attempt any of 10 questions from this section:

Section A: Multiple choice questions (1 marks each)

Attempt any of 6 questions from this section:

Section B: Very short Answer (2 marks each)

All questions are compulsory in these sections:

Section C: Short Answer (3 marks each)

Section D: Long Answer (5 marks each)

SECTION – A

1. Group of words that make complete sense are

   a. Phrase b. Sentence c. Both (a) and (b) d. None

2. _________ is your ability to participate as a team member.

   a. Rational Abilities b. Personal qualities c. Interpersonal skill d. Communication skill

3. What are the three aspects of humanity in relation to the environment?

   a. Economic, social, chemical b. Physical, chemical, mental

   c. Physical, Economical, Social d. None

4. _________ is a process of improving skills and knowledge of entrepreneurs through various training and classroom programs

   a. Enterprise b. School

   c. Entrepreneurship development d. College

6. In Twitter _________ term is used to handle user account name

   a. Tweets b. Twitter feed c. Twitter handle d. Hashtags

7. The ______________ pointer is used in graphical-based text processing applications.

   a. Grabber pointer b. Selection Pointer c. H-Beam d. I-Beam

8. CPM stands for?

   a. Character per minute b. Component per minute

   c. Character cases per minute d. None

9. Which of the following is the benefits of the use of IT in business:

   a. Improve efficiency b. Minimise waste c. Increase profit d. All

10. The range of Column in Excel?

a. 1 to 124 b. 1 to 1048576 c. 1 to 1024 d. 1 to 1023

11. The TODAY( ) function in spreadsheet display ____________.

a. Current time b. Current month c. Current Date d. Current Day

12. CPM stands for?

a. Character per minute b. Component per minute

c. Character cases per minute d. None

SECTION – B

1. How positive thinking helps in achieving self-confidence.
2. What is the usage of typing Ergonomics?
3. Define greenhouse gases?
4. Is it possible to remove the new addition in the document using a single command? If, yes then name that command.
5. Which are the different areas of healthcare in which IT is used?
6. Name various types of Referencing in Excel?
7. How to control the size of the view in the presentation?
8. Why is there a need to add or insert images in the Presentation?

SECTION – C

1. What is a mouse pointer? Name various cursor and mouse pointers.
2. Gives three factors that influence the Indian IT-BPM industry?
3. Write down the steps to create charts using spreadsheets?
4. How to group and ungroup the objects in Slide?
5. What is display under Status Bar of MS Word?
6. What is the purpose of Drag and drop action of Mouse?

SECTION – D

1. Write a short note of speeding up data entry using Fill handle?
2. How to check spelling and grammar mistakes in the MS Word window? Give colors that indicate different mistakes in the document.

Notes